Revolutionary Masculinity and Racial Inequality

Revolutionary Masculinity and Racial Inequality

Gendering War and Politics in Cuba

BONNIE A. LUCERO

University of New Mexico Press ❖ Albuquerque

© 2018 by Bonnie A. Lucero
All rights reserved. Published 2018
Printed in the United States of America

Library of Congress Cataloging-in-Publication Data

First Paperback Edition, 2021
Paperback ISBN: 978-0-8263-6333-6

Names: Lucero, Bonnie A., author.
Title: Revolutionary masculinity and racial inequality:
gendering war and politics in Cuba / Bonnie A. Lucero.
Description: Albuquerque: University of New Mexico Press,
2018. | Includes bibliographical references and index. |
Identifiers: LCCN 2018006293 (print) | LCCN 2018032729 (e-book) |
ISBN 9780826360106 (e-book) ISBN 9780826360090 (printed case: alk. paper)
Subjects: LCSH: Cuba—Race relations—History. |
Masculinity—Political aspects—Cuba.
Classification: LCC F1789.A1 (e-book) | LCC F1789.
A1 L83 2018 (print) | DDC 305.80097291—dc23
LC record available at https://lccn.loc.gov/2018006293

Publication of this book was made possible in part by a generous
contribution from the Newcomb College Institute at Tulane University.

Cover illustration: "Quintín Bandera and his mule,"
in Thomas R. Dawley Jr., "Campaigning with Gómez,"
American Magazine 47 (November 1898–April 1899), 541.
Composed in Minion Pro

In solidarity with Black Lives Matter and other movements for racial justice across the world.

Contents

List of Illustrations
ix

Acknowledgments
xi

INTRODUCTION
Gendered Language amid Racial Silence in Cuba
1

Part I
From Effeminate Colonials to Manly Soldiers: Forging
Revolutionary Masculinity on the Battlefield, 1895–1898

CHAPTER ONE
"To Acquire the Dictate of Free Men": Decolonizing
Masculinity through Military Service
23

CHAPTER TWO
Forging Patriarch-Soldiers: Womanhood and White Patriarchy
in the Construction of Insurgent Manhood
47

CHAPTER THREE
Mambí or *Majá*?: Measures of Merit and Double Standards of Military Authority
75

Part II
From Brave Soldiers to New Men?: Claiming Martial Manhood during the Transition from Intervention to Occupation, 1898–1899

CHAPTER FOUR
"To Manage with Virility Our Own Affairs": Defining the New Man between Military Intervention and Occupation
107

CHAPTER FIVE
Testing the Racial Limits of Martial Manhood: Black Political Exclusion and Patriarchal Claims-Making
135

CHAPTER SIX
Agents of Order or Disorder?: Black Veterans, Urban Law Enforcement, and the Racial Politics of Violence
155

Part III
From Revolutionaries to Neocolonials: The Specter of Black Criminality and the Conditionality of Public Authority, 1900–1902

CHAPTER SEVEN
Not Simply "Because One Happens to Belong to the Male Species": Race, Rural Law Enforcement, and Political Disorder amid Restricted Suffrage
181

CHAPTER EIGHT
"The Colored Patriot and His Box of Matches": Black Criminality, White Radicalism, and the Redefinition of the New Man in an Era of Universal Manhood Suffrage
213

CONCLUSION
The Racial Limits of Revolutionary Masculinity
245

Notes
257

Bibliography
309

Index
329

Illustrations

FIGURES

Figure I.1.	Map of the major cities of Santa Clara Province, 1899	16
Figure 1.1.	José Miguel Gómez	36
Figure 1.2.	Battle of Mal Tiempo	38
Figure 2.1.	The Olayita Massacre	50
Figure 2.2.	Group of children reconcentrated near Sagua	51
Figure 2.3.	Reconcentrated families near Sagua	52
Figure 2.4.	Male survivor of reconcentration	52
Figure 3.1.	Map of the major sugar plantations and military trenches in Santa Clara Province	76
Figure 3.2.	Gerardo Machado y Morales	88
Figure 3.3.	José González Planas	90
Figure 3.4.	Francisco Carrillo	91
Figure 4.1.	Walter B. Barker	121
Figure 4.2.	John C. Bates	122
Figure 5.1.	James H. Wilson	136
Figure 6.1.	Lady Cuba—A Soldier's Obligation	160
Figure 6.2.	"Looking forward"	162
Figure 6.3.	"The Civil Government . . . of Cuba"	163
Figure 7.1.	"Down with the Intrusive Skirts!"	205
Figure 8.1.	Quintín Bandera	218
Figure 8.2.	"Here you are"	225
Figure 8.3.	"Good Government vs. Revolution—An Easy Choice"	226
Figure 8.4.	Higinio Esquerra	238
Figure 8.5.	White rural guardsmen patrol a celebration of the republic in Sagua, May 1902	242

TABLES

Table I.1.	Age distribution in Santa Clara, Puerto Príncipe, and Santiago	15
Table 2.1.	Marriage, partnership, and family, 1899	63
Table 4.1.	Police employed in selected towns in province of Matanzas, by race, 1899	129
Table 4.2.	Pay schedules for rural guard of Santa Clara Province	130
Table 7.1.	Private armed guards in Cienfuegos, 1899–1900	188
Table 7.2.	Prisoners by race, Santa Clara Province, 1899	194
Table 7.3.	White mayors of selected cities in Santa Clara, elected in June 1900	207

Acknowledgments

IN THE ENDLESS SOLITARY HOURS I HAVE SPENT WRITING AND rewriting this book, I have remembered fondly the fleeting moments of human interaction that defined my research and shaped my thinking.

The first person who comes to mind is my fearless mother, Blythe Lucero, who worked tirelessly to raise my brother and me in Richmond, California, and now wages her third battle against cancer. Her example of hard work and perseverance through what seemed like never-ending travails instilled in me the persistence and work ethic necessary to publish this book despite the many obstacles along the way.

My fascination with Cuba began nearly twenty years ago, when I overheard a conversation about the "evils" of communism. I asked my neighbor, Cassandra Spangler, Esq., what communism was, and she replied that it had to do with everyone being equal. Having grown up poor, I was intrigued by this idea. I wondered if it was possible to create a society with less suffering from poverty and inequality, and if it was, what it would look like. In my quest to answer these questions, I came across the Cuban Revolution, a movement that purportedly broke the chains of imperialism and cured the racial, gender, and class inequalities that had historically defined Cuban society. That historical watershed piqued my interest in both Cuba and the idea of social justice. Around that same time, I sat through a ninth-grade US history lesson about the Spanish-American War, which, we were told, was a brilliant example of US benevolence and humanitarianism. I struggled to reconcile what was clearly an invasion with the glowing historical narrative I learned about it. That lesson stayed with me through the years. It laid the foundation for my interest in US empire in Latin America, particularly during the time period I address in this book. But it was also pivotal in shaping my early impression of history as a hopelessly conservative discipline bent on preserving the dominant order.

That skepticism about history as a discipline led me to pursue my fascination with Cuba through interdisciplinary channels. My first attempt to explore Cuba came while studying International Relations at the University of the Pacific's School of International Studies with the support of the Bill Gates Millennium Scholarship. Study abroad was a part of my degree program, but I landed in college right in the middle of the Bush years, when it was difficult for US citizens to travel to Cuba. I searched for a way to get to the island, and ended up enrolling in SUNY Oswego's Cuba program, then one of the only programs to allow direct enrollment at the University of Havana. Over the course of six months, I fell in love with an island, a people, and a historic quest for justice.

Upon my return, I unknowingly started to become a historian of that island's struggle. I wrote my senior thesis on the history of Cuban slavery, with the generous guidance of Dr. Arturo Giraldez at the University of the Pacific. As an MPhil student in Latin American Studies at Cambridge University, I had the good fortune of working with another brilliant historian, Dr. Gabriela Ramos, who further demonstrated the transformative potential of historical work. She guided me to explore the history of race, and offered invaluable support through some challenging personal times toward the end of my MPhil program. These two positive experiences with history led me to pursue my doctoral work in a discipline whose relevance and impact had been lost on me for much of my life. At the University of North Carolina, my adviser, Dr. Louis A. Pérez Jr. was an inspiration even before I met him in 2009. His *Cuba between Empires* was the very first academic book I ever bought for myself. He was and continues to be an exemplary role model. Under his guidance, I undertook the research for my dissertation, part of which informs this book.

During my multiple research trips to Cuba over the years, I have incurred tremendous debts of gratitude and have gained revered friendships. Words cannot express my sincere gratitude to my wonderful *familia cienfueguera*. Orlando García Martínez provided ongoing and invaluable support obtaining visas and getting access to archives, and he generously shared his time, expertise, and work with me over the years. He invited me into his family, whom I love as my own. I have been especially privileged to enjoy the friendship of his daughter, Anabel García García, who spent long, hot hours on the Cienfuegos archives patio with me, as we paged through dusty, oversized notarial protocols and pieced together bug-eaten leaflets. She was also there to confront the ongoing difficulties we experienced in that archive, facing them fiercely and unapologetically.

I have also greatly appreciated the friendship of my colleagues in Santa Clara: Roide Orlando Alfaro Velázquez and Asnety Chinea Franco at the Universidad Central de Las Villas, who accompanied me at the Archivo Municipal de Remedios and waited many hours with me to access the collections at the Museo Municipal de Remedios. I thank Carlos Coll at the Archivo Provincial de Las Villas for his comradery and for embarking on that bumpy *camión* ride to Sancti Spíritus. Thank you as well to the staff at the Archivo Municipal de Trinidad, especially Adita; to the staff at the Archivo Municipal de Remedios, especially Estela Maritza Rodríguez Estupiñán; and thank you to the staff at the Archivo Provincial de Sancti Spíritus, especially Zandra Rodríguez Carvajal, for facilitating access to the rich collections there.

During my research in various parts of the United States, I also benefited from the support of friends, colleagues, and archival staff. I want to acknowledge the generous support of the Cuban Heritage Collection, which sponsored my research through a predissertation fellowship in 2011 and a dissertation research fellowship in 2012. The Massachusetts Historical Society likewise provided invaluable support that enabled me to consult their collections in 2011 and again in 2012. I also want to thank Dr. Sarah Barksdale, Dr. Warren Milteer, and Dr. Valerie Martínez, who kept me company during long stretches at the National Archives in Washington, DC, and College Park.

Thank you as well to my support system, now dispersed throughout the country, but always a text away—Dr. Cassia P. Roth, Dr. Jeanine Navarrete, Dr. Sara Juengst, and Dr. Juan Coronado. I am grateful as well to my friends and colleagues at my previous institution, Dr. Dennis Hart and Dr. Young-Rae Oum, for supporting my work and for offering their solidarity during the most trying times of my academic career, and Dr. Mayra Ávila and Dr. Jamie Starling, who provided much-needed diversion from the writing process and invaluable dog-sitting during my research trips. Thank you as well to Sally Kenney and the Newcomb College Institute for their support during the final leg of this project.

Finally, thank you to Asunción Lavrín, for noticing the manuscript's potential and getting it in front of the right eyes, and to Clark Whitehorn, for seeing the project through to fruition.

INTRODUCTION

Gendered Language amid Racial Silence in Cuba

Decolonization . . . infuses a new rhythm, specific to a new generation of men, with a new language and a new humanity. Decolonization is truly the creation of new men. But such a creation cannot be attributed to a supernatural power: The "thing" colonized becomes a man through the very process of liberation.
— FRANZ FANON, *Wretched of the Earth*, 1961

The privileged act of naming often affords those in power access to modes of communication and enables them to project an interpretation, a definition, a description of their work and actions, that may not be accurate, that may obscure what is really taking place.
— BELL HOOKS, *Teaching to Transgress*, 1994

"A MAN IS MORE THAN WHITE, BLACK OR MULATTO. A CUBAN IS more than mulatto, black or white," proclaimed the revered Cuban patriot José Martí on the eve of Cuba's War of Independence (1895–1898).[1] With his now-famous refrain, this white, Cuban-born son of Spaniards drew upon the island's recent history of cross-racial anticolonial struggle to reconceptualize the parameters of Cuban nationality and manhood. Like his mainland Spanish-American counterparts nearly a century earlier, Martí invoked the fraternal bonds of *cubanidad* to sound a call to arms against Spanish colonial rule and all that it represented.² Cuban independence, the political materialization of nationalism, promised nothing less than social vindication for all men who joined the anticolonial struggle, regardless of birth, race, or status.

Among the first to heed this call were men of African descent. Most of these men left behind humble country abodes, and marched, machetes in hand, toward the battlefield, where they fought alongside their white compatriots in racially integrated infantry units. Many of these black *mambises* were veterans of previous wars, some having earned promotions on the basis of their prior military achievements. A few prominent black officers, like Lugarteniente Antonio Maceo and major generals Quintín Bandera and José González Planas, ascended to the highest officer ranks. If the demographics of the military were any indication, it seemed that Martí's lofty promise might actually come to fruition in the form of a raceless republic.

Between the outbreak of war in 1895 and the end of the US military occupation in 1902, however, colonial racial hierarchies did not recede. Rather, they persisted in Cuban society at large and among the men of the Cuban army, even as they fought under the banner of a supposedly raceless Cuban nationalism. During the war, black men were purged from the revolutionary leadership for infractions that white men committed with impunity. During the subsequent US military intervention in 1898, men of African descent faced extreme privation as they were denied rations, gainful employment, and formal authority on par with their rank. All the while, white insurgent leaders continued to benefit from charitable donations and enjoyed lavish banquets in their honor. Additionally, periodic episodes of anti-black violence punctuated the general exclusion of black men from political power and local authority during the US military occupation (1899–1902). Yet racial brotherhood remained central to Cuban national identity as city councils across the island renamed streets after both black and white independence heroes, teachers clandestinely commemorated black patriots, and white political elites clamored for the codification of universal male suffrage in the Constitution.³ How could such stark racial inequality and racist violence exist in a society known for its progressive racial politics?

At first glance, the coexistence of practical racial exclusion and racially inclusive discourse seems paradoxical. After all, the same white patriots who publically celebrated racial inclusion enacted violence and exclusion upon their African-descended counterparts. However, these two realities were not in fact as contradictory as they appear. While colonial racial hierarchies remained firmly intact, the way Cuban men thought, talked, and wrote about this relation of power evolved. One of the most important catalysts of this change was precisely the ideological consolidation of racelessness as a core component of Cuban nationalism.[4] Within this emerging culture of racial silence, direct references to race became socially unacceptable, because they now constituted unpatriotic violations of Martí's sacred raceless nationalism. Yet disallowing explicit discussion of race did not mean that racial hierarchy no longer existed. Rather, stigmatizing explicit discussion of race actually helped perpetuate the subordination of black Cubans because it abolished the very vocabulary necessary to name racial injustice.[5]

In light of Cuba's turn-of-the-century racial silence, racial inequality and exclusion increasingly found discursive expression in alternative idioms—what I term coded expressions or *metalanguages* for race. With metalanguage, I invoke two interrelated concepts. In its most conventional formulation, a metalanguage is a vocabulary used to describe another *language*, as Roland Barthes initially defined the concept.[6] However, I also refer to the "discursive representation and construction of social relations," as Evelyn B. Higginbotham theorized, in her exploration of the role of race in US women's history.[7]

In turn-of-the-century Cuba, the most crucial of these metalanguages for race was gender. Drawing on the dual concept of metalanguage, I examine the ways gendered language operated as a vocabulary naming relations of power between and among men and women, and at another level, how the same words assumed racial meanings and came to replace the now socially defunct language of race. To be sure, gendered language described a particular set of social relations of power in which men wielded authority over women and subordinate men. This patriarchal arrangement existed alongside, and also constituted, numerous other axes of inequality including class (rich over poor), sexuality (heterosexual over homosexual), nation (citizen over noncitizen), and most importantly for this book, race (white over nonwhite).

Each of these axes of inequality bore a specific vocabulary that named, reproduced, and in some cases allowed for the negotiation of existing relations of power. In the case of gender in Cuba, for instance, the popular refrain that "el hombre está hecho para la calle, y la mujer para la casa" (men are made for the streets and women for the home), captured the patriarchal ideals of male breadwinning and female domesticity.[8] Men invoked the term *padres de familia* to valorize their patriarchal roles as protectors of and providers for women and children. Men who failed to fulfill their patriarchal roles by rejecting formal work were denigrated as unmanly and criminalized as vagrants. Simultaneously, many women assumed the role of *dama de casa*, performing the dominant ideals of female domesticity that rewarded women's subordination to men. At the same time, women who flouted patriarchal control by venturing beyond the home risked accruing the punitive label of *mujer pública*, a euphemism for prostitute.[9]

For much of the colonial period, explicitly racial language existed alongside and intersected this gendered language. Bureaucratic and ecclesiastical records were often racially segregated, with racial labels marking black and brown people, while whites remained unmarked other than by the honorific titles of class privilege, *don* and *doña*. In the realm of culture, Cuban *costumbristas* constructed textual, visual, and embodied gendered racial types that pervaded literature, theater productions, and ubiquitous cigar *marquillas*.[10] Representations of black men shifted in response to changing social and political conditions, but usually vacillated between supposedly deviant "African" figures such as the *negro curro*, *ñáñigo*, and *negro brujo*, and more Hispanicized, free men of color, such as the *mulato fino*, the *calesero*, and the *negro catedrático*. Although these tropes acknowledged different legal and class statuses among the African-descended population, more "positive" representations of black men tended to frame their displays of wealth, intelligence, and authority as comical imitations of whiteness or mocked them as ridiculously farfetched.[11] The explicit nature of this racial vocabulary, though often derogatory toward nonwhites, nonetheless allowed some degree of transparency about the discursive representation of these social relations of power.

However, in late nineteenth-century Cuba, the anticolonial struggle and gradual slave emancipation transformed the discursive landscape by rendering explicitly racial language socially and culturally unacceptable among the men of the Cuban army. Seemingly color-blind titles like *ciudadano*, *soldado*, *compatriota* emerged within the anticolonial movement, as patriots like Martí attempted to forge ties of national belonging and as insurgent leaders sought to unify soldiers across racial and class lines. Although racial labels persisted in certain aspects of colonial and neocolonial life, the revolutionary emphasis on horizontal rather than vertical relationships gave birth to a nationalist ideology of racial brotherhood.[12]

One of the most fascinating and yet understudied aspects of this discursive shift is the profoundly gendered nature of the emerging raceless vocabulary. Discursively, insurgents downplayed racial difference by foregrounding gender sameness. They constructed a shared masculinity by valorizing Cuban men's patriotic military service. Nonetheless, discursive racial silence did not erase persisting racial inequalities. Rather, it catalyzed shifts in the meaning of the gendered vocabulary itself. Cuban insurgents filled the void of racial silence by appropriating existing gendered language to express persisting power inequalities.

Gendered language had long relied on implicit assumptions about race, class, and sexuality, underscoring the intersecting and mutually constitutive nature of these systems of inequality.[13] Honor offers one of the clearest examples of this intersectionality. In Cuba's nineteenth-century slave society, the regulation of women's sexuality served as a critical pillar of racial hierarchy as white men were charged with enforcing racial purity and defending familial status by controlling with whom and under what circumstances white women had sex. Yet, those same white men were not held to the same standard of sexual honor, and they often engaged in extramarital and interracial sex with little or no real impact on their honor. Within Cuba's racialized sexual economy, white men's sexual exploitation of and preference for concubinage rather than marriage with African-descended women contributed not only to stereotypes about black women's sexual dishonor, but also devalued black men's patriarchal roles as guardians of black women.[14]

After two anticolonial struggles between 1868 and 1880 and with the final demise of slavery in 1886, colonial racial and gendered concepts like honor as status persisted, even as new meritocratic notions of honor as virtue emerged. Insurgents reconstituted the racial assumptions inherent in colonial notions of honor as status into a new, seemingly raceless vocabulary. For instance, the unifying masculine labels employed among the men of the Cuban army, though devoid of explicit racial markers, became infused with implicit racial meanings. A good Cuban soldier (mambí) was implicitly coded white, while a bad Cuban soldier (*majá*) was commonly associated with black men. These implicitly racialized masculine types continued to shape power relations after the war, even as new gendered tropes emerged in politics. In fact, under US rule the entire notion of political fitness, though explicitly contingent only on manhood, silently hinged on whiteness and all its presumed cultural accoutrements. The result was the emergence of explicitly and profoundly gendered language as the key vocabulary through which insurgent men engaged racial hierarchy.

Thus, in the context of racial silence, gendered discourse assumed a double function. It not only continued to signify relations of gendered power. It also signaled the *absence* of racial language. By extension it supposedly described the demise of racism within the Cuban army and stood in to reproduce and rationalize persisting racial inequality. It functioned as both language and metalanguage. These implicit racial meanings in gendered language hold the key to understanding how and why nationalist discourses of racial harmony remained so powerful even as racial hierarchy persisted among the men of the Cuban army.

To explain this dynamic, I examine the evolving relationship between racially inclusive discourse and racially exclusive practice by gendering war and postwar politics. Both the anticolonial struggle and the contest for local and national power that emerged in its wake formed part of the intensely gendered public sphere. In turn-of-the-twentieth-century Cuba, only males could operate legitimately outside the patriarchal household.[15] However, being assigned to the male sex was insufficient to qualify a person for inclusion let alone authority in the public sphere. Rather, only males who possessed certain venerated characteristics and behaved in specific ways could hope to obtain the title and privileges of manhood. In the context of the predominantly male domains of war and politics, then, the verb *to gender* means examining soldiers, politicians, and ordinary citizens not as universal, normative actors but rather as uniquely gendered male subjects in their own right.[16] Within Cuba's racially stratified society, gendering war and politics entails paying attention to the specific ways ideas and practices of race on the battlefield and, later at the ballot box, drew upon, reflected, and constituted the kind of man who could participate in these activities.

During the intense political and social tumult of the transition from colony to republic, Cuban men's ideas about manhood underwent dramatic changes. For much of the nineteenth century, being a man in Cuba was synonymous with whiteness and peninsular birth. Public recognition of immutable status markers, like legitimate birth and legal whiteness (honor as status), provided the cultural framework by which white, European-born Spaniards justified the colonial subordination of Cuban-born men of all colors.[17] A man's honor afforded him preferential access to wealth, property ownership, and education, traits that supposedly demonstrated the celebrated manly virtues of rationality, independence, and intelligence. For white Cuban-born men, the denial of some of the privileges of (peninsular) whiteness amounted to a practical feminization as a subject people. Colonial notions of masculinity did not, however, feminize all Cuban men in the same ways. Men of African descent were excluded from manhood not only based on the presumption of their illegitimate creole or African birth, but also on the basis of their race, class, and proximity to the recently defunct institution of slavery.

During the final War of Independence, insurgents challenged their condition as feminized colonial subjects by redefining what it meant to be a Cuban man. Drawing on their experiences in the previous two anticolonial wars, insurgents articulated a new decolonizing gendered discourse that centered patriotic military service in the Cuban army as the cornerstone of an aspirationally independent Cuban manhood. By partaking in anticolonial struggle, insurgents could usher the nation toward independence and in the process, redeem themselves from colonial subjugation. Through those redemptive gendered acts, they could become manly citizens of an independent republic. Revolutionary masculinity was born.

Revolutionary masculinity was *revolutionary* in at least two respects. First, it was, at its core, anticolonial, emerging as a counterpoint to the gendered logic of Spanish colonialism. White insurgents sought to redeem themselves from feminized colonial subordination by emphasizing merit over status. Recasting masculinity as a function of military service rather than birth enabled Cuban-born men to create an alternative to conventional colonial hierarchies that had historically privileged Spanish men for their peninsular origin. White insurgents thus redefined manhood in their own image, building a foundation on which to construct the legitimacy of their claims to self-government.

Revolutionary masculinity was also revolutionary in a second way. When white insurgents envisioned military merit as the basis of manhood, they not only undermined the logic of Cuban-born men's subordination under Spanish colonial rule, they employed a logic that could just as easily undermine colonial racial hierarchies. Revolutionary masculinity theoretically afforded all Cuban men, regardless of race, the chance to prove their manhood by joining the insurrection. Black Cuban men appropriated revolutionary masculinity to challenge, on the basis of individual merit, their historic social subordination to white men.

Black insurgents' racially subversive appropriations of revolutionary masculinity challenged the increasingly precarious white monopoly on military authority and set off an ongoing struggle over the meanings of manhood. According to white insurgents, racially inclusive discourse did not necessarily grant each man an equal role in the emerging nation.[18] Though initially facilitating a degree of inclusion on the basis of shared military service, revolutionary masculinity quickly became a powerful instrument of white privilege in practice. In the Cuban army itself, white soldiers employed stigmatizing, gendered labels to delegitimize their black counterparts, and often refused to respect the authority of black officers. The US military intervention only compounded this struggle, as US officials dismantled white Cubans' racial privilege by dismissing them as uncivilized "Latins" and therefore unfit for self-government. Still publically celebrating the fraternal bonds of military service as the basis of racial brotherhood, white insurgents responded to challenges to their racial privilege by deploying revolutionary masculinity in racially exclusive ways to justify their own claims to political authority. In this way, revolutionary masculinity failed to translate into tangible gains for black men despite the racial inclusivity that it seemed to imply.

I argue that revolutionary masculinity enabled the growing disparity between color-blind discourse and exclusionary practice precisely because it encoded ideas about race in the seemingly color-blind language of gender. This gendered metalanguage allowed white insurgents to reproduce white privilege without overt reference to race while inhibiting nonwhite men from naming the forms of racial discrimination they continued to face in explicitly racial terms. While black men cited their military merit as the foundation for their claims to military and political authority, white insurgents referenced implicitly racialized notions of patriarchy, respect for authority, and sexual morality to exclude black men from positions of power. White insurgents used revolutionary masculinity to explain, naturalize, and justify a new—but no less unequal—social hierarchy in which they were the "natural" bearers of military and, subsequently, of political authority. In this sense, revolutionary masculinity did not erase social difference but rather provided a new ideological basis for racial inequality. It allowed racial harmony to remain a powerful pillar of Cuban nationalism even as the racial silence it imposed perpetuated racial inequality and violence in the lived realities of many black Cubans.

Slavery, Colonialism, and the Birth of Cuba's Racial Silence

Cuba's peculiar variant of raceless nationalism grew out of the historic entanglement of race, slavery, and empire that had defined the island since the late eighteenth century. The English occupation of Havana (1762–1763) liberalized Spanish trade restrictions, inaugurating an unprecedented wave of slave importations in the late eighteenth century. These enslaved men and women formed the essential labor force fueling the rise of sugar in Cuba, especially after the Haitian Revolution (1791-1804) decimated sugar production in neighboring St. Domingue. By the early nineteenth century, Cuba had replaced St. Domingue as the world's largest producer of sugar, and one of the Atlantic's most significant importers of enslaved Africans. Cuba's late turn toward sugar and slavery posed two interrelated challenges. First, the institution expanded in Cuba at the very moment that slavery came under increasing scrutiny across the Atlantic world following Britain's 1807 abolition of the slave trade.[19] Second, as American peoples across the hemisphere threw off the yoke of European colonial rule, Cuban planters increasingly turned to the Spanish military to ward off a Haitian-style slave revolution, thereby strengthening Spanish colonialism.[20]

Not until slavery ceased to be profitable in Cuba's economically depressed east in the mid-nineteenth century did the foundation of Spanish colonialism on the island begin to crumble. Just as slavery had long been the cornerstone of Spanish rule there, Cuba's anticolonial struggle assumed abolitionist, and to a degree, antiracist principles. With the outbreak of the Ten Years' War in 1868, white Cuban planters from Oriente Province, led by Carlos Manuel de Céspedes, freed their slaves under the condition that they join their incipient anticolonial struggle against Spain.[21] Although the first insurrection failed to secure independence, it catalyzed a series of colonial reforms, including the gradual abolition of slavery.

The ensuing process of legal emancipation was protracted, tentative, and conditional, owing more to political rivalry than genuine moral concern over the inhumanities of slavery. In an effort to wrest black loyalty from insurgent hands, the colonial government implemented the Moret Law in 1870, dealing the inaugural legal blow to slavery by freeing the elderly and children born to enslaved mothers. Only after a second failed anticolonial struggle, the Guerra Chiquita (Little War, 1879-1880), did the Spanish government finally spell out the terms for slavery's demise. The 1880 Patronato Law replaced slavery with a system of apprenticeship, even as most *patronos* continued to labor under the same owner and conditions—a continuation of unfreedom in all but name.[22] The Patronato sputtered to a halt in 1886.

The end of slavery destroyed the political and racial foundations of Spanish rule in Cuba. Fittingly, the Fecund Truce (1880-1895), which had brought Cuban insurgents and their Spanish foes to a tenuous peace following the Guerra Chiquita, came to an end not even a decade later. The outbreak of the final anticolonial war in 1895 promised to build upon previous insurgent abolitionism by offering Cubans of African descent inclusion within an independent, democratic, and raceless republic in exchange for their military service.[23] Continuing the legacy of their military achievements in the previous two wars, some black soldiers ascended the military ranks to achieve officer status, while white veterans vocally celebrated the racial unity of cubanidad. Quite simply, racelessness offered black Cubans the "possibility of integration" by providing a vocabulary through which they could claim inclusion, rights, and prestige on the basis of shared military service.[24]

When insurgents stood on the precipice of victory in 1898, the United States intervened to declare its own triumph over Spain. The onset of the US military occupation in 1899 brought new challenges for both Cuban independence and racial unity. Although insurgents no longer had to fight against Spanish rule, national self-determination remained far from reach. In fact, Cuban veterans had to demonstrate to the architects of an expanding US empire that a racially heterogeneous society born of Spanish colonialism was indeed *civilized enough* for self-government.[25] In an era when civilization was synonymous with whiteness (defined in terms of northern and western European/Anglo and Saxon racial stock), the ability of Cuban veterans to consummate their hard-earned independence was contingent upon proving their fitness for self-government. Under US military rule, political fitness was defined by the preservation of racial order, and by extension, the abandonment of the cross-racial implications of revolutionary masculinity.

Incremental advances notwithstanding, many black Cubans must have been disappointed at how little the lofty promises of racelessness materialized in their everyday lives as they returned from the battlefield. With but few exceptions, black men remained excluded from holding formal political office. Even as white candidates fought over black voters, elected politicians rarely addressed the concerns of their African-descended constituents.[26] Moreover, profound racial disparities in literacy, professional employment, and land ownership evinced the persisting poverty and social marginalization of black Cubans.[27]

Racial exclusion persisted well beyond the first US military occupation, carrying over to the early Cuban republic. Black Cubans who protested against racial inequality faced harsh censure. When a group of black political activists sought to address their political exclusion by forming their own political party, the Independent Party of Color in 1908, the state responded first by legally banning it with the 1910 Morúa Law, not coincidentally introduced by one of Cuba's only black senators, Martín Morúa Delgado. Then, in 1912, white Rural Guardsmen and vigilantes brutally slaughtered thousands of black activists for protesting the prohibition of race-based political organizations in a political system that disproportionately favored whites.[28]

The overt anti-black violence characterizing this so-called "Race War," though typically presented as an aberration in Cuba's supposed racial harmony, was in fact no anomaly. The massacre had deep roots in the racial exclusions of the colonial period and in slavery, and it evolved in response to the political exigencies posed by US imperialism. As this book will demonstrate, the particular dynamic of racial exclusion and violence emerged out of gendered relations of power among men in the War of Independence and the island's tumultuous encounters with US military occupation. White insurgents themselves had targeted black officers in a series of courts-martial between 1896 and 1898. Moreover, in 1899, 1902, and again in 1906 when the second US military occupation began, prominent black insurgent generals were slain by their white former compatriots-in-arms. In the context of persisting racial exclusion, each violent incident was doubtlessly punctuated with many more that evaded the documentary record.

These episodes within a broader pattern of racial exclusion and violence have remained relatively marginal to prevailing histories of Cuba. I contend that this silence is rooted in the general absence of gender analysis in scholarship on race during Cuba's transition from colony to republic. Indeed, historical analysis of gender has remained largely separate from scholarship on black men's experiences of racial inequality in turn-of-the-century Cuba. Most work on gender in Cuba's public sphere focuses on elite white women.[29] At the same time, most studies connecting race and gender have foregrounded the longstanding contributions of nonwhite and working women outside the home by exploring the struggles of enslaved mothers and prostitutes.[30]

The historiographical conflation of gender with women has left little conceptual room for examining men as gendered subjects in their own right.[31] As research on masculinity has slowly emerged in the historiography on twentieth-century Cuba, only a few studies have considered the link between blackness and masculinity during Cuba's transition from colony to republic.[32] In her case study of the court-martial of Quintín Bandera, Ada Ferrer alluded to the regional identities and gender expectations that inflected this black officer's experience of war.[33] Other scholars have revealed how gendered, racial stereotypes of black men as witches (*negros brujos*) or hypersexual predators were used to justify racial exclusion and anti-black violence in the early Cuban republic.[34]

Building on this incipient understanding of Cuban men as gendered subjects is crucial for understanding the way racial inequality functioned in Cuba. Race alone fails to explain how white veterans, who publically celebrated the revolutionary legacies of cross-racial anticolonial struggle, could perpetrate such overt acts of racial violence against their former compatriots-in-arms. Soldier and citizen—the very categories being contested in these episodes of racial violence—were not universal, gender-neutral categories, but rather intensely gendered roles through which Cuban males laid claim to manhood and all of its social and political privileges.[35] Drawing on and expanding feminist notions of the relationality of gender, *Revolutionary Masculinity and Racial Inequality* zeroes in on the interaction between black and white men—in the Cuban army and subsequently in the post-war political sphere—and between men and women subsumed within a broader patriarchal society.[36] From those critical gender and racial relations emerged key definitions of manhood that provided the very foundation upon which Cuban men constructed racial hierarchy.

Race and Masculinity in Central Cuba

The intricacies of these relations of power were forged not only, or even primarily at the national level. Rather, they took shape within particular political and social contexts enmeshed in specific localities. In order to examine the relational aspects of race and gender, this book makes a case for a more explicit discussion of the politics of geographical place in historical scholarship on Cuba.

Yet, most historians have examined Cuba's turn-of-the-century racial inequality through the lens of nationalism. The nationalist turn in US scholarship following Benedict Anderson's theory of "imagined communities" prompted several important studies on the ways race fit into the construction of nationalism in turn-of-the-century Cuba.[37] For example, Ferrer posited the coexistence of racism and antiracism within Cuban nationalism during the wars of independence. Subsequently, renditions of Ferrer's dual nationalisms thesis have shaped scholarship on inequality in the early republic.[38] Lillian Guerra's account of competing nationalisms in the twentieth century shows that different sectors in Cuban society envisioned Cuban nationality as having widely diverging implications for social hierarchy.[39]

There is no question that nationalism was a crucial ideological force driving the reproduction of racial hierarchy in Cuba. Nevertheless, narrating

Cuba's racial inequality through the lens of nation tells an incomplete story, one that risks perpetuating the exclusionary precepts inherent in the nation-building process. The predominance of the national perspective in Cuban history presents two main difficulties in navigating Cuba's racial silence. First, some national narratives of Cuban history have suffered from the association of color-blind nationalism with revolutionary solidarity (and the parallel conflation of racial dissent with counterrevolution). Until recently, this tendency has pre-empted critical engagement with race.[40] Second, national studies tend to homogenize Cuba's profoundly regionalized history. Far too many "national" studies claim to encapsulate the "Cuban" experience but only use evidence about Havana or documents drawn from Havana's archives without clearly articulating the limitations inherent in conflating the capital city with "Cuba." The silence of race in discourse means that the greater part of the story of Cuba's racial inequality has been left untold in national narratives.

Revolutionary Masculinity and Racial Inequality employs a microhistorical approach to reveal the particular configurations of race and gender within a small but nationally significant subset of military and political figures: the men of the Fourth Corps of the Cuban army, which operated mainly in the central Cuban province of Santa Clara. By focusing on this group of men, the book illuminates precisely how the structures of racial and gender inequality emerged and evolved in response to broader developments of post-emancipation, anticolonial struggle, empire, and nation-building.[41] To do this, I conducted extensive research in local, provincial, and national archives across Cuba and the United States. In Cuba, I scoured well-known collections in Havana archives as well as underutilized and untapped sources in provincial, municipal, and parochial archives, libraries, and private holdings in Cienfuegos, Remedios, Sancti Spíritus, Santa Clara, and Trinidad. In the United States, I sifted through the massive collections at the National Archives and Library of Congress as well as various smaller archives and libraries from Massachusetts to Mississippi. Relying on the correspondence and memoirs written by insurgent men, I reconstruct—and later deconstruct—the discourse of revolutionary masculinity. Then, I situate the men who crafted and applied that discourse within their daily social and political context by piecing together official reports, letters of protest, manifestos, newspaper clippings, and diaries. In this way, I excavate the concrete ways revolutionary masculinity impacted Santa Clara's black soldiers and veterans.

The book's geographical focus on the central Cuban province of Santa Clara allows me to trace the lives and career trajectories of dozens of black insurgent men in their specific social and political contexts. Where national-level studies have enabled scholars to identify the coexistence of racism and antiracism in Cuban society, my microhistorical methodology allows me to explain how and why they coexisted. To do this, I uncover the gendered mechanisms of racial inequality by analyzing how insurgents applied revolutionary masculinity. I expose the hidden racial meanings and double standards within raceless discourse and discover the tangible ways this rhetoric reproduced racial inequality.

Santa Clara is the ideal case study for examining war and politics during Cuba's transition from colony to republic. At the turn of the twentieth century, Santa Clara was the largest of Cuba's six provinces in terms of land area and it contained 23 percent of the island's total population.[42] The combination of rich agricultural production, foreign capital investment, and commercial development made Santa Clara one of the wealthiest and most politically important regions in Cuba, one deeply integrated into broader international networks and transnational flows. Home to the so-called *llanura roja*, the fertile red plains that nourished some of the world's largest and most profitable sugar plantations as well as smaller tobacco farms, Santa Clara emerged as a key agricultural hub in the nineteenth century. In large part due to this economic prosperity, the population grew faster than that of any other Cuban province between 1861 and 1899, when it doubled from 271,310 to 356,536.

Santa Clara's urban industrial and commercial hubs connected this rich agricultural landscape to the broader Atlantic world. The province's most populous urban centers included eleven cities with populations over ten thousand: Calabazar, Camajuaní, Cienfuegos, Placetas, Remedios, Sagua la Grande, Sancti Spíritus, Santa Clara, Santo Domingo, Trinidad, and Vueltas.[43] By far the most politically and economically important of these cities was Cienfuegos. Founded as a Francophile white colony in 1819, Cienfuegos quickly became home to a thriving, politically active, free black community built by formerly enslaved men and women as well as migrants from as far as Curaçao, Florida, and South Carolina, and as close as Havana, Trinidad, and Cumanayagua. The booming sugar plantations skirting its rural wards attracted significant North American investment and made the port a commercial hub for the entire central region. Known as one of Cuba's most modern cities, Cienfuegos housed one of the island's most important ports and

Table I.I. Age distribution in Santa Clara, Puerto Príncipe, and Santiago

	Santa Clara	Puerto Príncipe	Santiago
Infants (0–4)	7%	11%	10%
Children (5–14)	29%	32%	33%
Soldier-age (15–44)	50%	42%	44%
Elderly (45 and over)	14%	15%	13%
Median age	21	18	18

Note: Figures rounded to nearest whole number.
Source: *Report on the Census of Cuba, 1899*, 90–91.

grew to be the island's third-most-populous urban center by the turn of the twentieth century.[44]

The men of Santa Clara were central to island-wide processes of war and postwar politics. During the War of Independence, insurgents executed some of their most important military operations in Santa Clara. The Cuban victory at the Battle of Mal Tiempo in December 1895, for instance, marked a critical turning point in the war, as insurgent leaders Máximo Gómez and Antonio Maceo invaded the west to spread the revolution to the entire island.[45]

By the end of the war, Santa Clara was the only Cuban province to experience significant population growth since 1887. The province had Cuba's highest infant mortality rate and exhibited significantly higher populations of soldier age (15–44) than the eastern provinces of Santiago or Puerto Príncipe (fig. I.2). Notably, Santa Clara had the largest total excess of males of any Cuban province, a result, in large part, of the wartime redistribution of the male population from eastern Cuba.[46] These dynamics may also help explain why Santa Clara's population became more heavily black between 1887 and 1899. Indeed, a 10-percentage-point increase in Santa Clara's population of African descent alone transformed one of the island's demographically whiter regions into one more representative of the island-wide population. Whereas the African-descended population of Havana registered at 27.4 percent, the larger black and mixed-race populations of Santa Clara (29.9 percent), of Cienfuegos District (32.7 percent), and Cienfuegos City (34.8) more closely approximated the island-wide percentage of 32.1.[47] This confluence of racial and gendered demographic changes made Santa Clara Province a rich site of negotiation in the meanings of manhood and the shape of racial hierarchy. Moreover, although this study does not pretend to offer any "national" narrative, these demographic changes paralleled those occurring in other

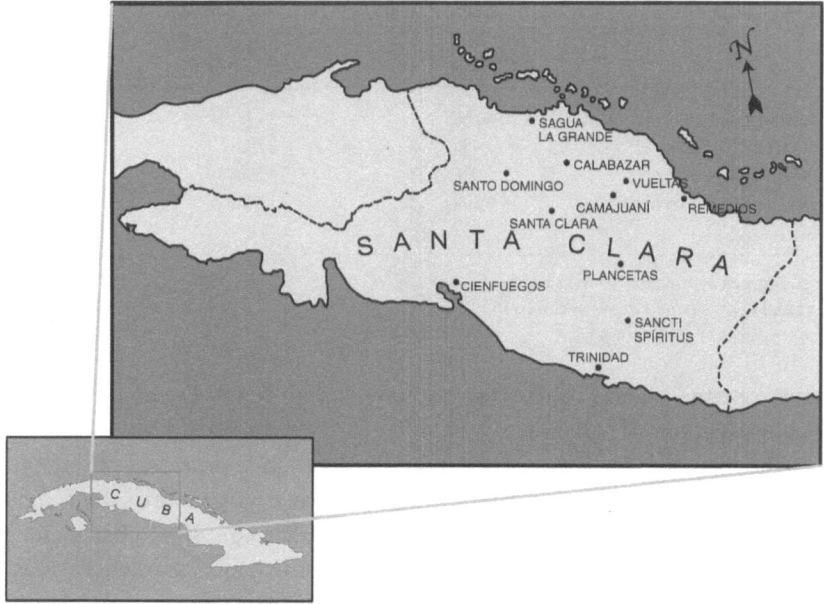

Figure I.1. Map of the major cities of Santa Clara Province, 1899. Credit: Blythe Graphics.

provinces, suggesting that the dynamics shaping Santa Clara likely speak to broader island-wide patterns.

After the war, the men of Santa Clara quickly emerged as dominant figures in national politics. Indeed, the province became known as the "Presidential Cradle," as it was home to a disproportionate number of Cuban presidents over the first half century of the Cuban republic. Perhaps the best example is Cuba's second president, José Miguel Gómez, a native of Sancti Spíritus, who served as one of the highest-ranking officers of the Fourth Corps of the Cuban army, and filled the office of provincial governor during the first military occupation. Havana-native Juan Bruno Zayas, a prominent Cuban officer in Las Villas, had a brother, Alfredo Zayas, who became the fourth Cuban president.[48] Even one of Cuba's most prominent early-twentieth-century black congressmen, Martín Morúa Delgado, though born in Matanzas, held one of his first political positions in the town of Palmira in Santa Clara province. These cases suggest that the social conditions shaping power struggles in Santa Clara cannot simply be dismissed as regional idiosyncrasies but rather they clearly wielded powerful implications for broader island-wide political and military processes during this critical period of transition from colony to republic.

Given the profound entwinement of military service and local political power, this book traces the struggles of the men of the Fourth Corps of the Cuban Army to define and appropriate revolutionary masculinity in three key moments. Part I analyzes the ways insurgent men constructed and deployed revolutionary masculinity to reinforce or contest the racial hierarchy in the Cuban army during the War of Independence. Chapter 1 traces the emergence of revolutionary masculinity as a seemingly color-blind, gendered discourse rejecting colonial power relations which feminized Cuban-born men. Chapter 2 reveals the contested nature of revolutionary masculinity's practical meanings. It posits that the persisting devaluation of black womanhood provided the ideological foundation that would reproduce and justify racial hierarchies among insurgent men, despite the equalizing discourse of revolutionary masculinity. Chapter 3 carries this theme forward by examining the ways ideas and language surrounding "good" and "bad" soldiers tended to reproduce white privilege.

Part II investigates a second moment in this process: the transition from war to peace following the US military intervention in 1898 and the first year of US military occupation. The chapters of this section collectively trace how fierce struggles for political power catalyzed subtle shifts in the way veterans envisioned and applied revolutionary masculinity. Chapter 4 highlights the challenges Cuban veterans of all colors faced in implementing their gendered claims to political power as a natural extension of their military merit. One of the key results of these struggles was a renewed emphasis on whiteness over military service—a tool with which white revolutionaries demonstrated their "political fitness" to US military officials. Chapter 5 charts the ways black veterans challenged this emerging white political order by claiming informal authority on the basis of military service and patriarchal protections of black and working women. Chapter 6 analyzes the process by which white veterans and US military officials dismantled the remaining sources of black veterans' claims to authority by disbanding the Cuban army and "reforming" law enforcement. This major turning point set the scene for state-sponsored anti-black violence against men who refused to observe the racial silence that certain visions of revolutionary masculinity demanded.

Part III examines a third moment: the period following the consolidation of the US military occupation in 1900. This section foregrounds the ways white fears of black men's political authority defined electoral politics and policing. Chapter 7 examines the development of an implicitly racial, criminalizing discourse after the enfranchisement of black veterans in 1900. Allusions to black criminality allowed conservative whites to justify racialized policing, all the while upholding revolutionary masculinity's theoretical promise of racial equality. Chapter 8 assesses the practical outcomes of black men's claims to revolutionary masculinity during the last year of US rule, showing the emergence of a new set of ideas about masculinity and politics.

In telling this story from a microhistorical perspective, this book exposes the previously hidden gendered dimensions of Cuba's color-blind myth. By the inauguration of the Cuban republic in May 1902, there was very little about dominant uses of revolutionary masculinity that was "revolutionary." It had increasingly become a tool with which the politically ambitious presented themselves as raceless while weaving racial exclusion into the very foundation of the emerging Cuban republic. A Cuban may well have been more than black, white, or mulatto, as Martí and others preached; but race circumscribed what his manhood meant in practice.

A Note on Terminology

Throughout this book, I use the labels *people of African descent* and *black Cubans* to refer to all individuals who recognized themselves or were otherwise treated as having African ancestry. These labels are applied to people who would have been classified as *morenos/negros* (black), *mulatos/pardos* (mulatto), any other of the many less common racial denominations used to describe people of varying degrees of "African" or black lineage. By using this terminology, my intention is not to eclipse the complexity of race in Cuba or superimpose a US-style, black-white binary.[49] Rather, I use these labels inclusively to denote the common experiences of racial discrimination individuals of varying degrees of African ancestry faced with regard to their masculine authority in the military and postwar politics. My research suggests that lighter complexion was often insufficient to protect men of mixed racial heritage from racialized gendered assumptions about their alleged intellectual inferiority, incapacity for leadership, hypersexuality, and aversion to work. The fact that white men often assumed black deviance meant that men of African descent were forced to constantly prove their compliance to unspoken codes of racial etiquette and bourgeois notions of manhood. The way a black man navigated this unspoken racial and gendered double standard, I find, was more significant than his degree of blackness in shaping white perceptions of his masculinity.

Although naming nonwhiteness is now a standard practice in academic scholarship, it tends to reinforce the supposedly natural quality of whiteness by allowing the latter to remain unmarked.[50] I seek to destabilize this implicit white-normativity by naming whiteness as well. In this vein, I use the racial label of *white* to identify native- or foreign-born people of all or mostly European ancestry residing in Cuba. Like blackness, though, whiteness was a contested terrain. During Spanish colonial rule, peninsular origin and legitimate birth held implied meanings about racial purity, and a man's class status likewise often spelled the difference between residing in exclusively white social circles and racially integrated plebeian ones. Later, the US presence in Cuba brought two historically distinct systems of racial hierarchy into direct contact, leading to further negotiations of whiteness. Whereas many Cubans of Spanish descent identified themselves as white, US military officials refused them the racial privileges associated with whiteness and stigmatized them as members of the supposedly inferior Latin races. Thus, when distinguishing between white Cuban and white US American, I employ the turn-of-the-century terminology of *Latin* and *Anglo* races, respectively. The ensuing racial negotiations of whiteness gave birth to new ideas and performances of white Cuban manhood, as this book shows.

I employ a chronologically specific set of terms to describe various groups of revolutionary men in the military during wartime and in politics during the postwar period. I use the term *insurgent* to signify a soldier or officer in the Cuban army during the war. Although usually invoked as a synonym for insurgent, the label *mambí* in this book refers to the ideal Cuban soldier, who embodied revolutionary masculine ideals of bravery, self-abnegation, and morality. I distinguish insurgents who served in the Liberating Army from *separatists*, who served in a civil and political capacity in the New York-based Partido Revolucionario Cubano (PRC). The descriptor *revolutionary* refers to both separatists and insurgents. When discussing postwar politics in Parts II and III, I employ the term *veteran* to refer to men who formerly served in the Cuban army, regardless of their race. I refer to *black and working-class veterans*, where applicable, to acknowledge the shared experiences of disenfranchisement among broad swathes of people of African descent and workers during the US military occupation. Conversely, I employ the term *civil authorities* to encompass the men who assumed political power at the municipal and provincial levels under US rule. A significant subgroup of these almost exclusively white public men were veterans, whose military service formed an important foundation for their political careers. I call these white veterans-turned-political-elites *New Men*. Because of their veteran status, these political elites were forced to adhere, at least nominally, to color-blindness, even as their obligation to the military occupation often challenged their ability or willingness to do so.

Two additional groups require explanation. First, I use two main terms to identify individuals and institutions involving the United States of America. I employ *US* rather than *American* as a descriptor to qualify subjects, such as the military intervention, military occupation, military government officials, and military personnel. I use the problematic term *US Americans* to describe US-born residents in Cuba. This is a stylistic choice, not meant to support the imperialist claim of the United States over the hemisphere. Second, I use the broad label, *opponents of separatist rule*, to refer to annexationists, members and sympathizers of the Autonomist Party, former Spanish soldiers, and wealthy planters and merchants (many of whom had US citizenship). These men collectively fought to retain US rule in Cuba by undermining separatists' and especially veterans' claims to political authority.

Finally, out of respect for black men's struggles for basic recognition, I include as many of their names and images as possible. For the reader, coming across so many names may seem daunting at first. However, this choice reflects my vision of this book's relevance to movements for racial justice across the world as we confront a resurgence in white supremacy and an intensification of gendered relations of power. I consciously chose to name those who ordinarily remain nameless in dominant historical narratives. This is my small contribution to recognizing the legitimacy of their lives and political struggles and to calling out the anti-black violence which claimed so many of their lives and continues to claim others today.

Part I

From Effeminate Colonials to Manly Soldiers

Forging Revolutionary Masculinity on the Battlefield, 1895–1898

CHAPTER ONE

"To Acquire the Dictate of Free Men"

Decolonizing Masculinity through Military Service

➤ IN THE NINETEENTH CENTURY, CUBAN-BORN MEN STRUGGLED TO reconcile their status as colonial subjects with their visions of themselves as men. Under Spanish colonial rule, prevailing attitudes about manhood in Cuba centered on two interlocking sets of well-known duties and privileges: patriarchal authority in the private sphere and independence in the public sphere. The essentialist vision of man as protector and provider can be identified as an almost ubiquitous gendered concept in societies across the modern world.[1] However, in late colonial Cuba, men's patriarchal duties were defined by specific social and cultural notions of male honor. At the center of this matrix was men's role as heads of household, a role that informed men's behavior inside and outside the home. In order to maintain their honor, Cuban men were responsible for providing for their dependents. They were also charged with protecting their female kin from the sexual advances of other men.[2]

Cuban men relied on a certain degree of independence in the public sphere in order to carry out their patriarchal responsibilities. To support their families, they needed to earn a living through work outside the home with— and often for—other men. Their responsibility to marry and later defend the sexual honor of their wives and daughters often required them to compete with other men for power and influence. Cuban men needed to negotiate with other men in the public sphere to uphold their private responsibilities toward their dependents as heads of household. Thus, patriarchs expected their private familial duties to entitle them to authority within the family unit, and some degree of economic autonomy and respectability beyond the household. Perhaps most importantly, Cuban men increasingly envisioned their fulfillment of patriarchal duties as contingent on their ability to influence institutions and power structures governing their society. Thus, patriarchal authority in the private sphere was intertwined with manly independence in the public sphere and, by extension, with political influence and the possibility of national self-determination.[3]

Under Spanish rule, even the most privileged Cuban-born men faced material barriers to claiming the masculine privileges of political autonomy and economic independence to the extent their peninsular counterparts did. They were both politically and socially subordinate to Spaniards. Their creole birth, often suspected to imply illegitimacy and possible racial stain, limited their access to certain occupations and largely excluded them from political office. Because these forms of subordination materially affected their livelihoods, challenged their claims to respectability vis-à-vis other men, and limited their ability to influence political and social institutions, it can be said that Cuban-born men experienced Spanish colonial rule as a condition of feminization.[4] The gendered nature of Cuban men's colonial subjugation was captured in vivid detail in a political cartoon depicting them as "a young swarthy woman, languid and beautiful," sprawled lazily in a hammock, smoking a cigar, "while a little black girl, behind her, refreshes her with a great fan of thick feathers."[5] The representation of a lazy, feminine Cuba further reinforced the subordination of Cuban men who already suffered the emasculating effects of political disenfranchisement.

Cuba's historic class stratification and racial hierarchy among native-born men meant that colonial subjugation did not feminize all Cuban men in the same ways, however.[6] While creole birth disadvantaged both white and black men, the high social value placed on legitimate birth and racial purity (*limpieza de sangre*) posed additional challenges to men of African descent as they attempted to enjoy the privileges of manhood. As elite white men demanded political rights within colonial society on the basis of their white maleness, this same argument challenged a black man's place in the political community on the basis that his race was a defect to his manhood. Moreover, peninsular and creole-born white men's collective abuse of black people's labor and sexual exploitation of black women and girls reproduced harmful stereotypes about black women's dishonor and black men's dependence, and by extension, undermined black men's patriarchal authority.[7] The persisting subjugation of African-descended people in prevailing labor regimes, presumptions about social prestige, and the sexual economy served as pillars of a three-tiered hierarchy of men under Spanish rule: Spanish colonizers, white native-born elite, and racially heterogeneous common people, a great many of them black.

As much of mainland Spanish America reacted to these mounting social tensions between Creoles and *peninsulares* by throwing off the yoke of Spanish colonialism in the early nineteenth century, Cuba remained loyal to the Spanish Crown. Cuba's status as the Ever-Faithful Isle hinged on an inherently racial logic. White Cuban Creoles exchanged their loyalty for Spanish military protection from a growing enslaved population in the wake of the Haitian Revolution. As much as white Cuban men may have resented their colonial subjugation, they forewent masculine redemption to protect their racial privilege. Within the guise of loyal subjectivity, Cuban-born men could only hope to gain political voice by imitating Spanishness, an act that reproduced their subordinate position.[8]

The alliance of the white peninsulares and Creoles against the perceived threat of African-descended people was short-lived, however. Elite white Cuban-born men gradually forged a proto-national sensibility over the course of the nineteenth century. At the center of this incipient nationalism was white Cuban-born men's privileged racial status: in a slave society, their whiteness was the foundation for their claims to manhood. As Spain half-heartedly dismantled the slave trade to Cuba through a series of anti-slaving treaties with Great Britain, the white Cuban planter class cultivated a national identity bent on prolonging slavery and protecting white men's racial privilege. This culminated in the annexationism of the 1840s and 1850s, in which white Cubans turned to the US South as a natural ally to their racial goals.[9]

The implicitly racial logic of this incipient Cuban nationalism did not disappear with the demise of slavery in the United States in 1865. On the contrary, by the 1860s Cuban-born men inaugurated their struggle for national self-determination on the grounds that Cuba should be governed by (white) Cuban men. After all, the only "defect" they had to overcome in order to make their claims to self-government legible in prevailing political discourse was their creole birth. If they dismissed birth status as inconsequential, then elite white creole men were at the very apex of the island's social hierarchy. Elite white Cuban-born men thus attempted to challenge their own political subordination to Spaniards by emphasizing merit over immutable birth status.

As these white men began dismantling the logic of their colonial subjugation, they inadvertently compromised the foundation of their own racial privilege. If merit were truly a better indicator of manhood than birth status, then black men too could redeem themselves from colonial subjugation and its intrinsic racial hierarchy. White rebels also relied on black manpower to make their struggle viable on the battlefield. In order to recruit these men, white insurgent leaders constructed overt racial prejudice as an offensive relic of Spanish colonial oppression, one that had to be abandoned in order to build the nation. They rejected explicit racial language entirely, declaring that it had no place in the Cuban army. Instead, they opted for a color-blind vocabulary emphasizing a shared manhood based on military merit. If overtly racist vocabulary disqualified Spaniards as legitimate political leaders, then racial silence qualified Cuban-born whites to lead their compatriots to liberation.

White insurgent leaders filled the linguistic void of racial silence with revolutionary masculinity, a new gendered discourse that described social relations among men without explicit reference to race. Centering the brotherly bonds of patriotic military service in the Cuban army, insurgents envisioned manhood as the common thread uniting black and white men in anticolonial struggle. Insurgents enacted their new vision of martial manhood by representing Cuban soldiers as uniformly brave, selfless men. By re-envisioning masculinity as a function of merit, insurgents discursively destroyed the remaining premise of Spanish colonial rule: social hierarchy based on birth status. However, it also paved the way for even more radical challenge to existing social relations. Within this framework, men of African descent could theoretically prove their manhood through patriotic military service.

I argue that revolutionary masculinity emerged as a compelling decolonizing discourse through which various groups of Cuban men challenged the feminizing power of their colonial subjugation to lay claim to independent manhood. In particular, the meritocratic logic of revolutionary masculinity lent itself to being appropriated by black men to contest their subordination to whites within the colonial racial hierarchy. To a degree, the inclusion of nonwhite men in the struggle showed the racially transformative potential of the discourse. However, the supposedly raceless gendered language of revolutionary masculinity did not necessarily transform the existing relations of power between black and white men in the Cuban army. Elite white men may have resented their social and political subordination to peninsular Spaniards enough to arm men of African descent, but they were loath to relinquish their historic racial privilege. The practical impact revolutionary masculinity had on the racial hierarchy was determined by an ongoing struggle among diverse sectors of Cuban men in response to particular historical moments.

"By Far the Greatest Portion Are Negroes"

Cuba's third anticolonial insurrection arrived at the rural wards of Santa Clara Province in February 1895. Heeding the call to arms, a diverse array of black men flocked to the fledgling regiments of the Fourth Army Corps. Among these early insurgents were decorated veterans of the Ten Years' War (1868–1878), like José González Planas, the educated son of an African-born father, and Benigno Najarro, a rural shopkeeper. Others, like Cruces-native Valentín Sosa and Víctor Acea of Palmira, abandoned back-breaking labor in the region's dense cane fields, employing their machetes instead to carve out a new future free of the colonial racial hierarchy. Some men, like Claudio Sarría and Ciriaco Quesada, rose from their humble births to enslaved parents to lead local insurgent units. José González SOA (*sin otro apellido*, without another last name) and Agustín Najarro left servitude on the region's cattle ranches for the *manigua*. While a few prominent veterans of previous wars assumed leadership roles, rural laborers formed the very nucleus of the region's anticolonial struggle.[10]

Black participation in the Fourth Army Corps only expanded through late 1895. Beginning in October, General Antonio Maceo, identified as mulatto, and white Dominican-born General-in-Chief Máximo Gómez led the thousands of men under their command from eastern Cuba toward Santa Clara in the so-called Invasion Campaign. Thousands of black *orientales* (men from eastern Cuba), including veteran officers like José Camacho Yera and Quintín Bandera, and others hailing from as far as the Dominican Republic like Dionisio Gil, poured into the province.[11] This campaign not only fortified Santa Clara's forces by placing seasoned officers in key leadership roles, but also encouraged local black men to enlist in the Fourth Corps, the vast majority joining in the first year of the war.[12]

In a province where only 30 percent of the population was of African descent, the high rate of black enlistment made the Fourth Corps conspicuous to say the least.[13] Observers from within Cuba and from abroad routinely speculated that black men dominated the insurrection there. One man claimed that "by far the greatest portion of [insurgents] are negroes—I should say at least 80 per cent."[14] A former Cuban insurgent mused hyperbolically that 95 percent of black Cubans joined the insurrection.[15] One black insurgent even described serving in the Cuban army as "the tradition of my race."[16] So pronounced was black participation among central Cuba's anticolonial army that some Spanish soldiers grumbled of their "misfortune" that they could not kill more white insurgents. After a skirmish with insurgent forces, one Spanish soldier remarked with dismay that his unit found "only one insurgent corpse, and this was a negro." This Spanish soldier's disappointment suggests that he considered killing a white insurgent in battle a special prize given his assumption that more insurgents were black than white.[17]

Accurate statistics on the demography of the Cuban army are elusive. The usual appeals of military service—social mobility, greater access to the symbolic and practical implements of masculine authority such as firearms, a path to citizenship—likely contributed to what scholars widely recognize as high indices of black enlistment.[18] The insurrection relied on black enlistment to fill the rank and file and on experienced black veteran officers to carry out important military operations. However, the exaggerated claims about the preponderance of black men in the insurrection were more about harnessing the political significance of blackness in Cuba's late colonial context than they were about actual numbers. Indeed, black participation in the Cuban army stirred up historic racial tensions that had afflicted the previous two anticolonial struggles. The abolitionist character of the insurrection during the Ten Years' War (1868–1878) led Spaniards to conflate independence with looming race war. The centrality of black veterans in the Protest of Baraguá against the unsatisfactory conditions of the Pact of Zanjón in 1878 and the ensuing Guerra Chiquita, from 1879 to 1880, also stoked fears that racial unrest would ensue if Spanish rule ended. These fears had materialized into powerful racist propaganda aimed at delegitimizing the insurrection as a racial uprising.[19]

Although black military service was no longer inflected with debates over slavery and abolition by 1895, race still offered a powerful basis for Spanish counterinsurgency propaganda. Drawing on the longer history of white anxiety over the island's black population, officers of the Spanish army depicted the insurrection as little more than another black rebellion or a bunch of bandits. The impending racial smear campaign hinged on two key ideas linking whiteness to manhood. First, prevailing political discourse framed self-government as the domain of civilized white men. By this logic, insurgents' claims to self-rule may have seemed just if they were white men. However, by depicting the Cuban army as hyperbolically black, Spanish racial propaganda ridiculed the notion of nonwhites laying claim to political rights reserved for white men. Second, Spaniards implied that colonial rule was the only way to guarantee racial order, a notion that had its roots in early nineteenth-century white anxieties about slave uprisings. Although slavery was now defunct, the racially heterogeneous nature of the insurrection and the presence of a few black officers supposedly illustrated the racial dangers of independence. The revival of this negative racialized image of the insurrection also threatened to derail insurgent efforts to secure recruitment from wealthy whites at home and political support from the international community.

As early as February 1895 Spanish officers warned their subordinates to keep a close eye on the "attitude of the negroes in Cienfuegos."[20] Such a direct invocation of race as the basis for political mobilization revealed deep-seated anxieties about the role of black men in the anticolonial struggle following Cuba's recent transition from slavery to free labor. Much of Spanish resentment stemmed from their paternalist assumption that black Cubans owed them gratitude for abolishing slavery in 1886. Former captain-general Camilo García Polavieja lamented that "the majority of the colored race, when we broke their bondage, became separatists."[21] His bitter recollections framed black enlistment in the Cuban army as a sign of ingratitude, a violation of the expected exchange of black loyalism for emancipation from slavery.

As the sparks of insurrection ignited into full-blown war, Spaniards revived old racial stereotypes to discredit independence as a legitimate political cause. In the conservative and loyalist press, the insurrection was represented in terms of racialized gender transgression, often invoking the myth of the black rapist. A political cartoon in the conservative daily Havana newspaper *Diario de la Marina* portrayed the insurrection as a "brutal black man" with "excessive" lips, imposing himself on a "young white woman" representing Cuba. Another cartoon caricatured the insurrection as a knife-wielding black man "assassinating a [white] Cuban woman." Unconfirmed reports of black insurgents raping white women also surfaced.[22]

Spanish officials also disparaged the insurgents' racial and gender transgressions by comparing the anticolonial struggle to the Haitian Revolution. Spanish general Arsenio Martínez Campos reportedly characterized the black soldiers of the Invasion Force as "largely of San Domingan origin."[23] He also invoked the Haitian Revolution to lament the "immense disgrace" of "yet another scandal" in Cuba. Campos was concerned not because of its political significance, but rather because "of the amount that we will spend" and "the men we will lose" quashing the rebellion.[24] Other Spanish officials shared these views, making "much of the conspicuity of the Maceos, in the efforts to persuade people that the insurrection is an affair of black men chiefly, and means the conversion of Cuba into a larger San Domingo."[25]

The conservative press echoed these allusions to Haiti. In April 1895 *Diario de la Marina* published an article depicting the insurrection as a vehicle for transforming black laborers into powerful chiefs. Other articles described the insurgents as black and barbaric, and claimed black insurgent chiefs refused to enlist white soldiers and sought to establish a black dictatorship.[26] In one instance the newspaper depicted the insurrection as a black man "blotting Cuba from the map," likely a reference to the destroyed wealth of St. Domingue or possibly the decades of non-recognition from the international community.[27] These references to the Haitian Revolution harnessed white fears that the insurrection could destabilize white supremacy.[28]

Disparaging references to the role of eastern Cuba in the insurrection proved equally powerful, given its association with blackness and its proximity and ongoing connections to Haiti. When eastern Cuban troops invaded Santa Clara in late 1895, Spanish officers exploited negative racial attitudes about Oriente Province to denigrate the insurrection as an alien black uprising. "Prepare yourselves soldiers, nine thousand oriental negroes are coming," read a sign posted in late 1895 outside a dwelling house on the Central Hormiguero, one of three large sugar mills just outside of Cienfuegos.[29] Drawing on racialized notions of Oriente Province as the blackest and most revolutionary part of Cuba, this propaganda portrayed Santa Clara as a peaceful and white population being "invaded" by black eastern revolutionaries. In this way, the sign marked an effort to galvanize loyalist sentiment among Santa Clara's rural white population.[30]

In other instances, Spanish counterinsurgency propaganda was not as racially explicit, but it still unambiguously invoked racial ideas. Spanish leaders often employed racially charged allegations of criminality to discredit the insurgents, for instance. One of the preferred images deployed in Spanish counterinsurgency propaganda was that of the bandit. The Spanish governor of Santa Clara Province called the insurgents savages, arsonists, and bandits who dishonor the Cuban people.[31] Another high-ranking Spanish official denounced the insurgents as illegitimate criminals, claiming that in central Cuba there was "nobody there but bandits."[32] Another Spaniard condemned a group of Santa Clara insurgents as "evil-hearted men," who perpetrated the "most repugnant acts of vandalism," stealing civilian clothing and leaving "men and women completely naked."³³ Countless other Spanish soldiers across Santa Clara echoed these negative allegations of banditry.³⁴

Spanish authorities were not altogether wrong about the presence of bandits among the rebel troops. Known bandits like José Álvarez Arteaga, Matagás, and Tuerto Matos did join the Cuban army, and participated in operations in Santa Clara Province.³⁵ Nevertheless, Spanish propaganda characterizing *all* insurgents as bandits undermined the political legitimacy of the revolution by dismissing politicized anticolonial violence as mere crime. Moreover, the label of bandit implicated insurgents in the "degraded masculinity," laziness, and dishonesty of criminals.³⁶ Spanish accusations of banditry therefore can be read as an attempt to dismantle insurgent claims to honorable manhood by criminalizing their military service and dismissing its political underpinnings.³⁷

The emasculating implications of this criminalizing discourse came to the fore when prominent Spanish officials disparaged the military skill of their enemies. For instance, one former Spanish governor of Santa Clara Province who later served as captain-general disparaged the insurgents for having "no knowledge of the honor of arms," a natural consequence of recruiting "all the idle and evil men." He rejoiced that "good citizens"—namely white men—did not join the insurrection.³⁸ He further characterized the chiefs of the Invasion Force as "natural leaders of anarchism, with nothing to lose" in large part because of their racial backgrounds. He insultingly labeled the two highest-ranking insurgent officials, Máximo Gómez and Antonio Maceo, as "a soldier of fortune" and "a mulatto with ambition," respectively. Such insults implied these rebellious men flouted "the laws of civilization," a term that invoked whiteness and masculinity.³⁹

Although this criminalizing propaganda often omitted explicitly racial language, the racial undertones were unmistakable. After all, Spanish and Cuban ideas about crime drew on late nineteenth-century scientific racist assumptions emanating from Europe that tied blackness to criminal deviance.⁴⁰ The racial implications of criminality were never so clear as when Spanish soldiers characterized Cuban soldiers as *ñáñigos* (members of the secret Afro-Cuban religious society of Abakúa). A pejorative label employed by criminologists and law enforcement personnel since at least the mid-nineteenth century, the term ñáñigo doubled as a racial insult and a criminal type. Either way, it often served as justification for brutal violence. Spanish soldiers routinely used this racialized criminal label to disparage their enemies. In Rodas, Spanish soldiers detained one *pacífico* (noncombatant), on suspicions of collaborating with the insurgents. Calling him a "shameless traitor and ñáñigo," they slashed him to pieces in the nearby canefield.[41] In another case, Spaniards mowed down one mulatto insurgent on a central Cuban battlefield, continuing their hunt for "another ñáñigo about here."[42] Alongside the racialization of the insurrection, the dehumanizing discourse of criminal savagery implied in the term ñáñigo helped Spanish soldiers rationalize wanton violence against suspected insurgents as a legitimate part of their military duty. In that regard, the Eurocentric notions of civilization sustaining the label of ñáñigo foreshadowed the early republican stereotype of the black sorcerer, a black man depicted as kidnapping white children for sacrifice in African religious ceremonies.[43]

Spanish counterinsurgency propaganda was not about race alone. It hinged on a carefully constructed relationship between blackness and rebellion, which symbolized the unfitness of Cuban men for political independence. After all, the Spanish army did not frown upon all forms of black military service. On the contrary, Spanish officials embraced black enlistment in the Spanish army as a duty of loyal subjects.[44] Informal forces known as guerrillas, in particular, gained a decidedly negative reputation as composed of the "worst elements" of society. One observer claimed that the men in these units were as "villainous a mob of jail sweepings as could be gathered anywhere in the world."[45] However, the disparaging racial attitudes regarding the black and Chinese guerrillas did not seem to impact public perceptions of the Spanish army. Rather, the act of rebellion against Spanish rule was what rendered the racial backgrounds of insurgents significant in Spanish eyes. This negative conflation of blackness and insurrection was precisely what insurgents had to fight against in order to redeem themselves as men capable of self-government in the months and years to come.[46]

"Nobody Worries about the Color of the Man"

Insurgents were keenly aware of the potentially harmful effects of Spanish racializing counterinsurgency propaganda. While black and working-class men provided much of the military manpower, the Cuban army also struggled to secure necessary support from wealthy white men at home and abroad. After all, economic contributions from wealthy donors were key to purchasing the arms and munitions the insurgents needed to wage war. Thousands of miles from the central Cuban battlefield, in New York, the PRC struggled to secure ongoing financial support to help provision the Cuban army, while also gaining international recognition for the cause. Spanish racial propaganda tarnished the reputation of the insurrection and made (white) potential contributors less likely to support the cause.[47]

PRC fears materialized when a flurry of unfavorable racial images of Cuban insurgents appeared in US newspapers in early 1896—precisely as insurgent leaders Máximo Gómez and Antonio Maceo expanded the insurrection westward from the demographically blacker east in the so-called Invasion of the West or Invasion Campaign. Numerous articles echoed Spanish propaganda depicting insurgents as a "mass of blacks and mixed bloods." Some articles simply alleged that the insurrection was fought "mostly by the blacks," and that "few notable whites" supported it.[48] Others decried the alleged cruelties committed by insurgents—"not the white ones, of whom there are comparatively few, but the negroes and mulattoes."[49] Still others reproduced Spanish allusions to the Haitian Revolution, claiming the insurgents were "largely of San Domingan origin," and referencing Antonio Maceo's alleged "amalgamation of the West Indian negroes into what is known as the Antilles League."[50] These references reinforced negative assumptions that the Cuban insurrection was but a racial uprising, unworthy of US support.

Insurgent leaders, for their part, eschewed these negative racial images. One prominent white insurgent leader claimed that colonial authorities attempted to inspire "fear in the revolution" by inciting an "insensitive fear ... of the black race." However, this was "never justified in Cuba," he claimed. "Only those who hate black people see hatred in the black man," he declared.[51] This insurgent chief's radical denunciation of Spanish propaganda as racism undermined Spanish rule in Cuba by depicting the Spanish government as out of touch with the *true* character of the Cuban people. While Spaniards cast black participation in the Cuban army as a marker of illegitimacy and dishonor, prominent insurgent leaders across the island retorted that Spanish appeals to popular racial anxieties constituted shameless racism.

Allusions to Cuban color-blindness provided a powerful antidote against what insurgents increasingly claimed was *Spanish* racism. One prominent white insurgent leader scoffed at Spanish rumors depicting the separatist struggle as a race war. When asked if he feared a race war following Cuban independence, he replied heartily: "No, decidedly no!"[52] Another insurgent officer claimed that meritocracy reigned in the insurgent camps, and that "nobody worries about the color of the man, but rather about his capabilities."⁵³ These insurgent officers suggested that race was inconsequential in the Cuban army.

While white insurgent officers flatly rejected Spanish allegations of racial tensions, it was difficult for them to deny that black men constituted a disproportionate number of their soldiers. Because the specter of blackness seemed to invoke racial anxiety automatically, insurgents faced a critical challenge: they needed to reconcile their claims to independent self-government with the fact that so many insurgents were black. Insurgents resolved this apparent paradox by constructing a new vision of what it meant to be a man. This emergent gendered discourse defined manhood as a function of merit, rather than birth status.

Military service in the Cuban army became the principle mechanism through which Cuban men demonstrated their masculinity. Military service was considered manly not only because insurgents envisioned the associated arms-bearing and "indelible displays of constancy and bravery" as something only a man could do. It was presumed manly as well because of its liberating potential. After all, military service in the Cuban army would, as one white central Cuban chief put it, empower Cuban men "to acquire the dictate of free men through armed Revolution, honoring the graves of their loved ones."⁵⁴ Santa Clara-native and white insurgent official José Braulio Alemán concurred. Only by taking up arms, he argued, could the men of Las Villas be "worthy of our history"—even if it meant building "Cuban Liberty" upon the "smashed skulls of the damned despots!"⁵⁵ Building on the affective power of historic martyrdom and the promise of future freedom, insurgent leaders constructed military service in the Cuban army as a moral duty of the current generation of Cuban men.

The meritocratic undertones of revolutionary masculinity reinvigorated the masculine ideal cultivated during the first two anticolonial wars. Invoking "the manly heritage of their forefathers," insurgent leaders defined the ideal Cuban man in their own image. The mambí was first and foremost a soldier. More than that, he was an honorable and virtuous Cuban soldier, who selflessly devoted himself to the cause of national liberation.⁵⁶ As General-in-Chief Máximo Gómez himself proclaimed, military service in the Cuban army was "bound up with virtue."⁵⁷ By contributing to this struggle, white men proved themselves as the "true sons of Cuba," whose "virile" military service to Cuban freedom transformed them into real men.⁵⁸ In this sense, being a mambí theoretically had no racial qualifications. Insurgents, whether white or black, were *men*, first and foremost, united in a shared struggle against

Spanish oppression. Soldiers of African descent could therefore participate in and even lead the raceless anticolonial struggle, precisely because military service transformed black males into Cuban men.

In their diaries, letters, and memoirs of the war, insurgents employed vividly gendered language to celebrate a shared manliness among the diverse soldiers of the Cuban army. They envisioned this new revolutionary masculinity as a function of honorable military conduct, namely bravery and self-abnegation. First, insurgent men framed their military successes as a product of their masculine prowess, particularly, strength, ingenuity, and courage in the face of danger. Second, insurgents took pride in the considerable sacrifices they made to fulfill their manly duty of military service. By emphasizing these universalizing values, insurgents foregrounded military merit rather than immutable status markers like birth and race as the key to manliness. They employed revolutionary masculinity to dismantle the colonial hierarchy and forge a new social order in which Cuban men could assume their rightful roles of public authority in an independent Cuba.

"A Man with a Machete in his Hand"

Insurgents faced nearly insurmountable challenges at the outset of the war. The numerical advantage of Spanish forces alone was daunting. At the outset of the insurrection, captain-general Emilio Calleja commanded a garrison of seventeen thousand Spanish soldiers in Cuba against a geographically isolated force of a few thousand insurgents in Oriente Province. At the close of 1895, Spanish forces had swelled to over one hundred thousand men, including professional soldiers, and a growing number of volunteers and irregular forces.[59] Key to this increase was Calleja's successor, Arsenio Martínez Campos, whose policy of attraction expanded Spanish forces by enlisting Cubans.[60] At the same time, insurgents, then concentrated in Oriente and Santa Clara Provinces, were scarcely more than one-tenth that number. In Santa Clara, between three thousand and four thousand local insurgents, located mainly in the hills of Siguanea and in the swamps of Ciénaga de Zapata, faced off against more than twenty-five thousand Spanish soldiers.[61]

Amid such unfavorable numerical odds, bravery emerged as one of the most valuable qualities of an insurgent man. Cuban soldiers valorized their men for fearlessly confronting a numerically superior, professionally outfitted Spanish army. José Miguel Gómez, an insurgent officer from Sancti Spíritus,

Figure 1.1. José Miguel Gómez. Source: "José Miguel Gómez," *La Mariposa: Semanario Dedicado a las Bellas,* Trinidad, October 13, 1901.

boasted that his men learned to "fight with valor and enthusiasm against an army very much superior in numbers."[62] Though the recruits arrived to the battlefield untrained, they gained experience and began to see the struggle "as a question of honor" in which they could emerge "victorious."[63]

In this vein, other central Cuban officers celebrated Dominican-born general-in-chief Máximo Gómez as the model of manly bravery. While Spanish officials routinely dismissed him as "too old" for military service, the "venerated" general earned a reputation among his own soldiers as "an extraordinary man" for his "thirty years of tireless battle."[64] Gómez exemplified "a prowess which will be handed down to posterity as a sample of the astuteness and intrepidity."[65] His example of idealized military manhood inspired optimism and excitement as he and Maceo led the Invasion Campaign through central

Cuba in late 1895. As they passed through, thousands of men enlisted to follow his example.[66]

Although enlistment in Santa Clara's rebel army surged by late 1895, insurgent troops still lacked basic provisions, especially firearms and ammunition. One white officer recalled that only 20 or 25 percent of insurgent troops around Cienfuegos were armed. Another white officer recollected that his men were in poor condition, with "no arms, ragged, barefoot," with hundreds "nearly naked" and hungry.[67] Without enough rifles and munitions to supply the entire force, many insurgents relied on machetes, a mundane agricultural instrument widely available to the largely rural recruits. "Among us," explained one veteran of Mal Tiempo, "the machete has many applications. It serves to build a house: it serves very often to get food; and it serves as a weapon in battle."[68] While the machete represented a man's patriarchal role as breadwinner and protector during peacetime, in the context of anticolonial struggle, it came to represent a new masculine role, that of soldier.

The machete quickly became one of the most powerful symbols of insurgent bravery—a core component of revolutionary masculinity. Emphasizing their own bravery in the face of unfavorable circumstances of battle, Cuban insurgents boasted decisive defeats over thousands of rifle-toting Spaniards. The soldiers of Santa Clara "had great confidence in the machete," one white officer claimed. Similarly, Italian-born officer Orestes Ferrara romantically declared that the "victorious machete of the Cuban soldier" sent even veteran Spanish soldiers, whose hands were "blackened with gunpowder" fleeing in all directions.[69]

Nowhere more than at the Battle of Mal Tiempo in December 1895 did insurgents celebrate their heroic use of the machete as proof of their masculinity. There, the poorly provisioned Invasion Force, alongside seven hundred men mainly from Sagua and Remedios under the command of Juan Bruno Zayas, secured a decisive victory over well-armed Spanish columns just outside the loyalist hub of Cruces. Insurgents had discharged the better part of their ammunition on the march toward Cienfuegos. Lacking sufficient rounds to fight the enemy head on, Gómez ordered his troops to hold their fire, even as a Spanish column of over one thousand men fired vigorously upon them. Rebel forces reportedly ambushed the enemy with machetes, slashing so many Spaniards that their "clothing was all dyed with the enemy's blood."[70] Mal Tiempo illustrated the symbolic masculine power of the machete. Though historians have recently challenged this notion that insurgents relied almost exclusively on machetes during the battle, the discursive construction of Mal Tiempo as a triumphant underdog victory reveals how central ideas of bravery and courage were for insurgents' ideas about their manhood.[71]

Indeed, the stories of insurgent heroism and bravery, rather than the acts themselves, quickly transformed the Battle of Mal Tiempo into a vindication of insurgents' military prowess, and by extension a symbol of their masculinity. Like his men, Gómez defied the rain of Spanish bullets, bravely charging forward. He faced a torrent of bullets, two striking his horse, and one penetrating his hat. "Don't you mind that," Gómez reportedly told his men. "There are more Spaniards over there and it is necessary to go there and cut them down with machetes."[72] This story likely inspired a 1899 sketch of the battle, depicting Gómez standing atop his fallen horse with machete triumphantly drawn on a Spaniard (fig. 1.2).

Other insurgents noted that a man's skill with the machete and his strength of will also played an important role in the Cuban victory at Mal Tiempo. One Mal Tiempo veteran professed that a man's success with a machete "depends on the valor of the individual" and his fearlessness in the face of danger. "Perhaps we may be mistaken," he continued, "but we think

Figure 1.2. Battle of Mal Tiempo. Source: "Mal Tiempo," in *Cuba y América, Revista Quincenal*, November 5, 1899, 3:70, p. 3, in USNAII/MGC/RG 140/E 3, File 6462.

that a man with a machete in his hand, provided that he does not feel fear, will be able to accomplish any enterprise with said arm," and even more so if he is "aided by the momentum of the horse."⁷³ By mythologizing the bravery, strength, and ingenuity of the machete-wielding insurgent, Cuban soldiers depicted themselves as the embodiment of manhood.

Part of what made insurgent military service at Mal Tiempo so emblematically masculine was that Cuban soldiers combined military valor with an unfettered willingness to risk their lives for Cuba Libre. One insurgent publication from Santa Clara celebrated the "valiant acts" of the Cuban soldiers whose commitment to the "sacred ideal of Liberty" does not permit them to "run away from dangers."⁷⁴ These laudatory words reveal the expectation that Cuban soldiers would confront the most unfavorable odds without hesitation.

Insurgents underscored their manhood in part by contrasting their own bravery with Spanish cowardice. Cuban insurgents ridiculed the ineffectiveness and cowardice of Spain's numerically superior and better-provisioned force.⁷⁵ Attacking the military prowess of their enemy, insurgents alleged that Spaniards avoided direct combat with insurgent troops. White insurgent leader Enrique Villuendas remarked that the Spanish forces had a large cavalry, but they were known for being "cowardly and fleeing terrified at the first shots."⁷⁶ Other white leaders, like Alemán, disparaged Spanish forces for cowardly exploiting their unfair advantage over insurgents to commit gruesome cruelties. Upon discovering Spanish forces had massacred a small force of insurgents, Alemán angrily called their commanding officer a "coward" who "blush[es] with shame, as if it were the demonstration of your impotence."⁷⁷ This emasculating language condemned Spanish failures on the battlefield as indicators of cowardice, dishonor, and a lack of virility. The allusion to blushing feminized the Spanish general, further stripping him of claims to manhood.

Other insurgents suggested that Spaniards made utterly incompetent soldiers, incapable of defending basic fortifications and easily manipulated by insurgent forces.⁷⁸ White insurgent chief José Miguel Gómez argued that Spaniards squandered their "immense resources in men, in means of communication, and in money and military advantages" because of their lack of bravery and military skill. "With those resources, a little more than six months would have been sufficient to have reduced the insurrection to absolute impotency," Gómez estimated, implicitly comparing the deficiencies of Spanish men to the military prowess of the insurgents, who triumphed despite considerably unfavorable odds.⁷⁹

While insurgents ridiculed their enemies for cowardice, insurgent chiefs encouraged their men to embrace danger and self-sacrifice on the battlefield as the ultimate proof of their masculinity. Some chiefs celebrated death in honor of the patria as a noble achievement. One white officer remembered that "we [insurgents] were all disposed to die to gain the victory or destroy the whole Island of Cuba."[80] In the same vein, Máximo Gómez proclaimed that the death of a man was worth more on the battlefield than in peace.[81] During the Battle of Mal Tiempo, mulatto general Antonio Maceo prophetically vowed to triumph or die wrapped in the Cuban flag.[82] Even if defeat or capture was imminent, an honorable death could vindicate the soldier's claims to moral purity. Insurgent leaders, for example, venerated Juan Bruno Zayas for fighting enemy forces to the death.[83] Suicide offered another honorable alternative to the "dishonor of surrendering to the enemy," because it represented the ultimate sacrifice to the cause of liberation.[84] These allusions to patriotic death underscore how unwavering devotion, whether it resulted in victory or defeat, was central to insurgent visions of their manhood.

Even in the absence of death-defying heroism or martyrdom, sacrifice emerged as a decidedly gendered realm through which insurgent men performed their devotion to Cuban freedom. As the white chief José Rogelio Castillo wrote, on the battlefield, "abnegation is the best norm" for Cuban men.[85] Many insurgents sought to realize this ideal, often emphasizing their willingness to sacrifice material comforts to help secure Cuban freedom. After spending "seven days without eating anything except green mangoes," one white officer in the Brigade of Cienfuegos wrote to a friend asking for rations for sick soldiers, and nothing for himself.[86] He later confessed that he ultimately consumed the provisions his friend sent, illustrating the ways his "exaggerated" concern with upholding a masculine image as self-sufficient and self-abnegating among other men led him to deceitfully hide his own suffering. His unwillingness to ask for help implies that he considered his inability to fend for himself on the battlefield too shameful to warrant aid.

Some insurgent men performed their manly self-abnegation by refusing expensive celebrations in their honor. One anonymous soldier admonished a women's patriotic club for apparently planning a luxurious banquet for the Cuban officers when there were better uses for those resources.[87] Several other soldiers expressed similar concern. The white officer Carlos Trujillo noted that "the desire of the honorable men of the revolution" is that money not be wasted on the banquet, especially when "there are too many children in homes without bread." He assured his female compatriot that "the vanity of a few hours of flattery" was "not necessary to deserve the esteem of honorable patriots and men."[88] Another white insurgent chief in the Brigade of Cienfuegos informed his superior officer that he "did not want to accept" a banquet offered to him in gratitude by country people following a resounding victory over Spanish forces at the small country town of Ojo de Agua. Framing his conduct as manly sacrifice, the white officer explained that he sought only to "comply with my conscience," for "this is what it demands of me and my good decision will not support any act in this life that is not great, noble and decorous."[89] While he declared that his moral conduct stemmed from his noble character, the fact that he reported his actions to his superior officer suggests a degree of performativity in upholding a prevailing masculine role as a morally upright, self-abnegating soldier.

Even as Cuban officers emphasized the sacrifice of all their men, they still viewed those made by wealthy men as particularly meritorious. White insurgent officer José de Jesús Monteagudo, for example, emphasized the disparities between the prewar life of many of his men and the wartime misery and suffering they faced, agreeing that many men who had enjoyed "wealth and luxury" in peace, found themselves nearly naked and barefoot during the war.[90] Such observations tended to slight the sacrifices of poorer men as less valuable and less patriotic, because these men were presumably accustomed to poverty and suffering. In contrast, wealthy men's willingness to give up personal comforts allegedly proved their love of country.

Racial Hierarchy among Equals

At no point in celebrating these manly military achievements did insurgents explicitly mention race. Nor did they overtly limit the honorable label of mambí to white men alone. Rather, they constructed the manly qualities of bravery and self-abnegation as part of an essentialized and idyllic Cuban martial manhood, one that was theoretically raceless. This gendered discourse of revolutionary masculinity enabled insurgent leaders to deflect Spanish racial counterinsurgency propaganda by labeling explicit racial language as a relic of the racist Spanish colonial past. Decentering race and foregrounding a meritocratic notion of manhood legitimized the cross-racial nature of the insurrection. In turn, this racial silence allowed them to dismiss allegations that the insurrection was simply a racial uprising. Most importantly, this universalizing rhetoric of shared manhood empowered insurgents to transform themselves discursively from effeminate colonial subjects into real men unscathed by birth status. Claiming this form of merit-based military manhood was the first step toward securing the political independence they sought and becoming citizens in their own free republic.

If manhood was a function of merit, rather than birth status, then it was theoretically available to all Cuban men who served in the Cuban army. However, in demographically whiter central Cuba, it took some time for the discursive inclusivity of revolutionary masculinity to find expression in practice. There, the racial labor hierarchy of the sugar industry still reigned, in part because the previous wars of independence had not produced the extent of social upheaval evidenced in Cuba's eastern provinces. Thus, the initial organization of the Fourth Corps of the Liberating Army catapulted prominent white men into positions of military leadership, often at the expense of experienced black veteran officers. Arriving in Santa Clara in summer 1895 at the head of an armed expedition, Polish-native Carlos Roloff assumed command of the Fourth Corps. His fellow expeditionary Serafín Sánchez was appointed chief of the First Division, centered in Sancti Spíritus, Trinidad, and Remedios, while Manuel Suárez, one of the first men to rebel in Santa Clara, took command of the Second Division operating in Villa Clara, Cienfuegos, and Sagua. Prior to the Invasion Campaign, all the brigadier generals, the colonels, and lieutenant coronels of the Fourth Corps were white.[91]

Nonetheless, by late 1895, the inclusive thrust of revolutionary masculinity did seem to provoke modest changes in the racial relations of power in the Fourth Corps. As thousands of black soldiers poured into central Cuba with the Invasion Force, their military successes seemed to carve out space for mass enlistment of black men, and the promotion of a small number of black officers under the pretense of merit-based manhood. Military triumphs like the one at Mal Tiempo inspired a wave of local enlistment in the insurrection: over two hundred men, most of them from rural areas, many of them black, entered the Brigade of Cienfuegos in December 1895 alone.[92] Although the leadership remained predominantly white, prominent black officers from eastern Cuba began to enter leadership positions in the Fourth Corps around that time. That December, Quintín Bandera assumed a position as brigadier general in Trinidad; José González Planas, then a lieutenant colonel, assumed command of forces in Remedios; and Juan B. Benítez also earned a promotion to that lieutenant colonel as well.[93] In February 1896, two hundred soldiers from Cienfuegos transferred to the infantry commanded by Bandera, while José Camacho Yera, a black chief from Santiago, occupied another leadership role in the Brigade of Cienfuegos. Moreover, local black officers, like Isidro Acea, were swept westward into the Fifth and Sixth Corps.[94]

Seeming to uphold the racially inclusive vision of insurgent manhood, white insurgent leaders celebrated not only their own honorable military service, but also that of their black compatriots. They frequently invoked the exceptional bravery of black men to "prove" their adherence to color-blind military meritocracy. To that effect, Leopoldo Figueroa, a prominent white officer who would later serve as mayor of Cienfuegos, praised the bravery of José González Planas, a black officer who then served as brigadier general in charge of the Brigade of Remedios. Though crediting ultimate military victory to the white chief of the Fourth Corps Francisco Carrillo, Figueroa noted that the black officer demonstrated his "bravery and superiority over their enemy."[95] Likewise, Salvador Betancourt Cisneros lauded the famed insurgent general Antonio Maceo who "has negro blood in him" but is "the pride of us all." He also cited the "scores of gallant officers who are mulattoes" as further evidence of the racial unity characterizing the Cuban army. So long as "the darker race of Cuba produces such men we have nothing to fear," Cisneros declared triumphantly.[96] Similarly white insurgents also admitted that their black compatriots, too, suffered in the name of Cuba Libre.[97] These examples suggest that revolutionary masculinity offered black soldiers "an arsenal of tools," to use Brodwyn Fischer's words, with which to negotiate their status, access to authority, and claims to resources "on the basis of rights rather than of patronage or charity"—at least sometimes.[98]

Although revolutionary masculinity had provoked modest adjustments in the racial hierarchy of the Fourth Corps, racial inequality remained at the very core of the military structure. Most locally born black men remained at the lowest ranks, mainly as ordinary enlisted soldiers, and a small number held noncommissioned officer positions. This pattern was particularly strikingly in the Brigade of Cienfuegos, where Captain Claudio Sarría was the only locally born black man to reach a position of command by mid-1896.[99] The disproportionate representation of prominent white men in the upper echelons of the military hierarchy suggests that racial and class factors still wielded strong influence over a man's rank in the Fourth Corps.

In addition, inequality was at the very core of the Cuban army's classic division into infantry and cavalry. While the cavalry forces usually enjoyed greater glamor than infantry forces in Western militaries more generally,[100] in the multiracial, socioeconomically diverse Cuban army, infantry was more often composed of poor—and disproportionately black—men. In the words of one white insurgent officer, the man "who went by foot" was "the plebeian soldier."[101] Moreover, it was common for observers to describe black soldiers traveling by foot. One US American noted that the two hundred "orientales" under Quintín Bandera, for example, were "a ragged line of nearly naked blacks *on foot*," who "wore hats of all shapes, with frayed brims, and without brims, while some were all brims and no crown."[102] Deviations from this largely racial division of infantry and cavalry forces seemed to provoke confusion and resentment. One white foot soldier recounted with disdain his tortuous march by foot "until, his body [was] lacerated and his spirit thinned." He was particularly resentful of his black superior officer, Bandera, who rode on horseback "stroked and comfortable."[103] It should come as no surprise that José González Planas, one of the most important black officers after Maceo and Bandera, was relegated to commanding infantry for most of his career until after his promotion to brigadier general.[104]

Cavalrymen, by contrast, were usually wealthy, white men who owned horses. In the context of post-emancipation Santa Clara, access to a horse in itself was as much of a racial signifier as it was a socioeconomic marker, given that just a decade earlier enslaved men were not allowed to own horses.[105] One white insurgent alluded to the racial exclusivity of horse ownership, noting, in condescension, that in the rare instances black men had horses, they were usually of lesser quality, for which they compensated by "maintaining a tight rein" to make it seem like "at least by appearance" that they had quality horses.[106]

As much as horse ownership served as a marker of racial privilege, in the context of war, it became an instrument of manhood. Cavalrymen emphasized their manliness over infantrymen: "The man who rode a horse was a heroic man," explained one white insurgent, who was initially assigned to an infantry force. He claimed that he was "saved" by a "cultured" man from Camagüey, who gave him a horse. Once on the horse, he confessed that he "felt more manly than before" and that he gained greater respectability. Rather than trudging barefoot, "now we felt like better warriors," he proclaimed.[107] The ability to access the material markers of privilege not only impacted a man's physical ability to achieve success in battle, but also distinguished him as symbolically more manly than peers who lacked such possessions.

As long as the Fourth Corps enjoyed military successes, revolutionary masculinity seemed to yield at least some practical benefits for a small number of black soldiers. However, as insurgents entered a prolonged period of military turmoil between 1896 and 1897, the powerful current of racial hierarchy and the demographic changes assumed new meaning. The Invasion Campaign had already destabilized the fragile post-emancipation racial hierarchy in Santa Clara.[108] With the added tension of military setbacks, white central Cuban insurgents evinced growing anxiety regarding the presence of black easterners in positions of military authority. The next two chapters examine the limits of racial inclusivity in insurgents' practical applications of revolutionary masculinity in two pivotal moments: the initial implementation of the reconcentration policy in 1896 and a series of major insurgent losses in late 1896 and early 1897.

CHAPTER TWO

Forging Patriarch-Soldiers

Womanhood and White Patriarchy in the Construction of Insurgent Manhood

THE INSURGENT VICTORIES OF LATE 1895 WERE SHORT-LIVED. AS the Invasion Force marched triumphantly westward through Santa Clara Province, the Spanish government removed Captain-General Arsenio Martínez Campos, who had failed to pacify the island. By January 1896 Valeriano Weyler succeeded the interim captain-general, Sabás Marín y González, inaugurating his term with what he claimed to be an infallible plan to crush the insurrection. His most infamous deed was formalizing and expanding an existing policy that became known as reconcentration. Seeking to isolate insurgents from their presumed rural support bases, Weyler ordered the forced relocation of civilians from their rural homes into concentration camps on the outskirts of urban centers.[1] In February 1896 he imposed the policy on Oriente, Puerto Príncipe, and the eastern portion of Santa Clara Province, gradually expanding it to the rest of the island. By January 1897 the entire province of Santa Clara fell under reconcentration orders. Because the policy exacerbated the alienation of rural dwellers from their means of subsistence, the toll on civilian life was devastating. Of one hundred forty thousand *reconcentrados* in Santa Clara Province, 38 percent died.[2] Contagious disease and malnutrition claimed the lives of three hundred reconcentrados per month in Cienfuegos alone.³

For insurgents, reconcentration was not simply another military policy, or even one that unfairly targeted noncombatants. They perceived that the policy disproportionately impacted women and children. Thus, it constituted a flagrant assault on their gendered sensibilities about war as a fundamentally masculine enterprise. Moreover, insurgents considered reconcentration a crime against women, in particular, because it thrust them into the very center of a war supposedly fought between men.

Reconcentration was not only an assault on Cuban women; it also constituted an offense against insurgent men themselves. The unique vulnerabilities of Cuban women and children under reconcentration exacerbated the existing tensions between insurgent men's military duties and their patriarchal responsibilities. After all, insurgents' visions of themselves as men not only hinged on their military service, but also their roles as heads of household.⁴ Fulfilling their manly obligation to serve in the Cuban army required most insurgents to leave their families behind. From the battlefield, they could not effectively perform their expected roles as husbands and fathers to provide honorable subsistence for their dependents, safeguard the sexual honor of their female kin, and now to protect their families from enemy forces. Insurgents thus faced an inherent contradiction between their roles as soldiers and their identities as husbands and fathers.

The intensification of these gender tensions under reconcentration caused insurgent men to reimagine revolutionary masculinity to encompass not only their military duties, but also their patriarchal responsibilities. In order to construct this emergent subjectivity as soldier-patriarch, insurgents first framed Spaniards' actions as the antithesis of honorable military and patriarchal conduct. Denouncing Spanish military conduct as unmanly enabled insurgents to reimagine their own soldierly duties as a defense of Cuban womanhood, writ large, from Spanish predations. In this way, insurgents compensated for their inability to protect their own families by defending the figurative Cuban woman. This symbolic defense of Cuban womanhood helped insurgent men redeem their patriarchal sensibilities and reconcile the two competing roles constituting their manhood. In this way, insurgents used their relationships with women to negotiate their masculinity vis-à-vis other men.

Insurgents' efforts to reconcile patriarchal and military duties relied on particular tropes about Cuban womanhood. Drawing on colonial notions of honor as a function of female chastity, insurgent men constructed two female archetypes. They portrayed loyalist women as deceitful, impure seductresses, and prostitutes, who allegedly used their transgressive sexuality in the service of Spain. In marked contrast was the inherently honorable Cuban woman, either legitimately married or chastely widowed, who served the insurrection as self-abnegating mothers or subservient patriots.[5] This idyllic image of Cuban women as universally honorable and thus worthy of protection enabled insurgent men to reassert their patriarchal authority from the battlefield by framing their military service as a defense of Cuban womanhood.

I argue that the reincorporation of patriarchal duty into insurgent visions of manhood reinforced racial hierarchy among the men of the Fourth Corps by reactivating colonial notions of honor as status. Despite the universalizing language of national masculine types, insurgents implicitly defined Cuban manhood and womanhood as racialized categories. These gender ideals became mechanisms of racial hierarchy within the rebel army, as insurgents applied them unevenly to white and nonwhite people. In particular, insurgents' renewed subjectivities as soldier-patriarchs implicitly relied on an idealized vision of Cuban womanhood as inherently white. By reproducing colonial notions of honorable womanhood as white, white insurgent leaders implicitly circumscribed access to the soldier-patriarch ideal to white men. In turn, the ongoing devaluation of black womanhood served as a discursive platform for the exclusion of black men from the ideal of soldier-patriarch. In essence, insurgents repackaged the colonial double standard of honor by reproducing the racial and class assumptions in the gendered language of patriarchy.

Reconcentration's Damsels in Distress

Weyler's decree gave rural dwellers only eight days to leave their homes for the nearest city, a window so short that it ensured some degree of noncompliance.[6] In the event that rural families did not comply, Spanish soldiers were permitted to dislodge them by force. Beginning in early 1896, insurgents wrote vivid accounts of the atrocities Spaniards allegedly committed against Cuban noncombatants in what they termed Weyler's "war of extermination."[7] In March that year, one insurgent officer reported that three hundred Spanish soldiers had been dispatched to force families from their homes in one provincial town.[8] Later that year, insurgent chief J. W. Aguirre reported that the "enemy, like usual set fire to several houses of pacific residents" in a small

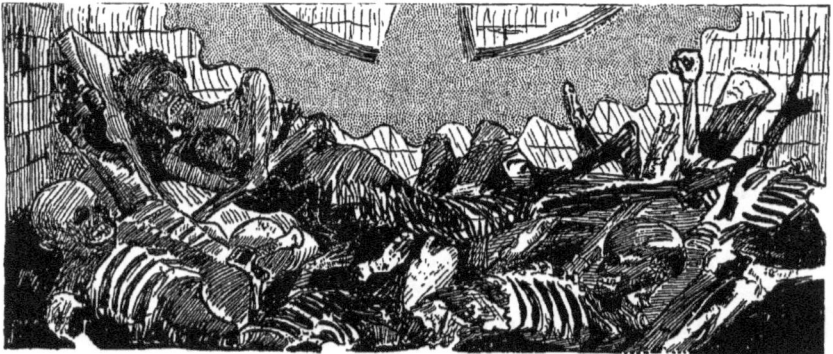

Figure 2.1. The Olayita Massacre. Source: Flint, *Marching with Gómez*, 102.

town west of Sagua la Grande.⁹ Similar accounts of Spaniards who "burned and violated" the homes of civilians appeared in *Las Villas*, a central Cuban insurgent publication, suggesting that such tactics were widespread.¹⁰

Spaniards allegedly burned and pillaged entire country towns. In one case, Spanish forces stormed the town of Olayita after a devastating encounter with the Cuban forces under Quintín Bandera near a plantation outside Sagua la Grande. Setting fire to the houses, they burned to death dozens of local residents, including girls and women.¹¹ One observer sketched the charred remains of the victims, including one woman clasping a baby when she was burned alive (fig. 2.1).

In other cases, Spaniards simply slaughtered noncombatants suspected of collaborating with insurgents. In one famous central Cuban battle, Spanish troops allegedly sacked the house of noncombatants and cut them down with machetes. One young white woman was forced to watch as they slaughtered her sick father. She allegedly "tried to rush in between them [Spanish forces] and the old man," but the Spanish soldiers attacked her, "wounding her with thrusts of bayonets." The sexualized language and allusions to the phallic symbolism of Spanish bayonets invoked metaphors of rape to denounce Spanish cruelties. She allegedly refused treatment from the Spanish surgeon before dying "from shock and pain." Insurgents framed her death as noble sacrifice because of her refusal to submit to the enemy.¹² In another instance, Spanish forces removed from their homes and hacked to death numerous *pacíficos*, including an eighty-year-old man and an eleven-year-old boy. The same Spanish column killed sixteen pacíficos near Cienfuegos and abandoned another four, leaving them to fend for themselves in a nearby town not their own.[13]

Rural dwellers who avoided or survived these attacks were corralled into makeshift camps on the urban outskirts. There, Spaniards left families often completely devoid of provisions causing them to suffer "the most horrible misery." Surviving images of reconcentration in central Cuba often featured starving and malnourished children (fig. 2.2).[14] Indeed, because of the lack of rations, reconcentrados faced "the sad condition of starving to death," according to one insurgent officer.[15] Starvation, disease, and unhygienic conditions all contributed to high morbidity and mortality rates among reconcentrated families. Women, children, and the elderly were reportedly "dying like rats" in one central Cuban camp.[16]

Insurgents decried reconcentration as a flagrant display of Spanish dishonor precisely because these enemy forces targeted women and children rather than fighting honorably against enemy combatants. One insurgent

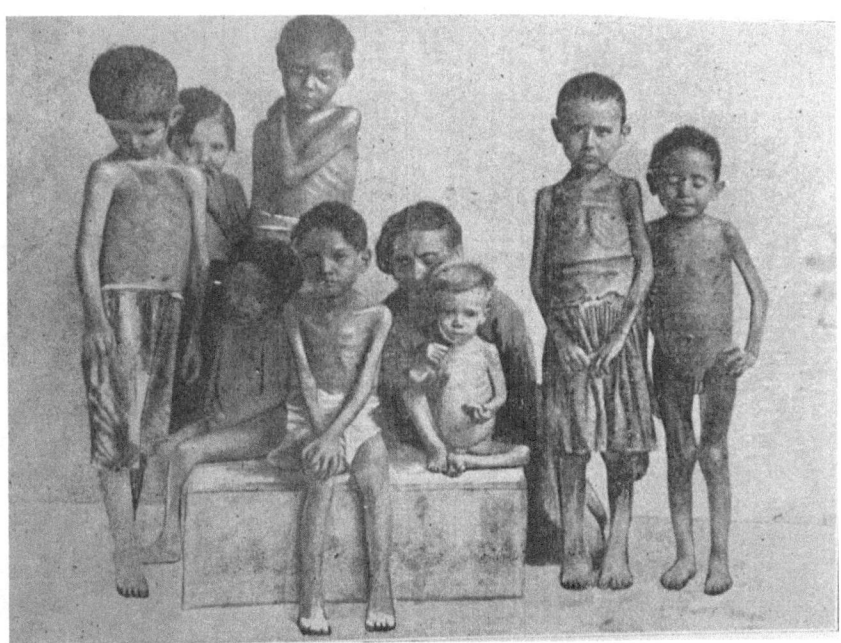

Figure 2.2. Group of children reconcentrated near Sagua. Source: Machado, ¡Piedad! Recuerdos de la Reconcentración, 23.

Figure 2.3. Reconcentrated families near Sagua. Source: Machado, *¡Piedad! Recuerdos de la Reconcentración*, 17.

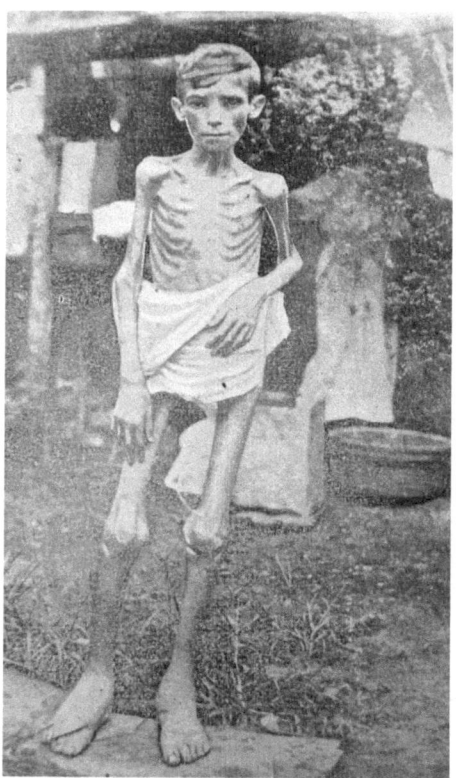

Figure 2.4. Male survivor of reconcentration. Source: Machado, *¡Piedad! Recuerdos de la Reconcentración*, 55.

charged that reconcentration proved that Spaniards were dishonorable and thirsty for the "blood of citizens."[17] Similarly, an article in *Las Villas* sarcastically referring to enemy forces as "braves," denounced these and similar cruelties as evidence of "the cowardice and vile proceedings the soldiers of Weyler."[18] Alemán condemned Spaniards for "killing cockroaches [while] letting the mice live."[19] With this unflattering analogy, Alemán underscored the cowardice of Spaniards for victimizing dependent civilians rather than confronting insurgent men.

Women with ties or perceived affiliations with the insurrection were particularly vulnerable to Spanish attack. White insurgent officer Sixto Roque del Sol, for example, noted that his men washed their own clothing because "if you sent any of your clothes to be washed by some female friend, the [Spanish] soldiers would take vengeance on that friend" instead of confronting the man.[20] Some insurgent officers reported that Spaniards even targeted their wives, families, and mistresses. "How vile and cowardly are our enemies," exclaimed another white officer, Alejandro Rodríguez, whose wife was kidnapped by Spanish forces in early 1897.[21] Other insurgents reviled at the "extreme" Spaniards had reached in "jailing women" and even cutting their hair to mark them with shame. According to one insurgent, Spaniards reached "the culmination of their cowardice," when they allegedly filled the jail at Cienfuegos with women prisoners.[22]

In the eyes of insurgent leaders, such atrocious treatment of women was incompatible with military honor. Although wartime violence against women certainly existed before Weyler, the Spanish captain-general became a symbol of gender transgressive cowardice when he expanded reconcentration. Writing to Weyler in early 1896, mulatto general Antonio Maceo confessed his initial incredulity that "a soldier holding your high rank" could commit "such an accumulation of atrocities, so many crimes repugnant and dishonoring to any man of honor." However, upon reading so many reports of Spanish abuses against women, Maceo confessed that he was forced to "see with alarm [and] with horror, how the wretched reputation you enjoy is confirmed and how the deeds that disclose your barbarous irritation are repeated."[23] Weyler obtained a reputation as unmanly—a "sinvergüenza," "inhuman," "a thief, and shameless, and totally without character" in large part due to the assumption that reconcentration targeted women.[24] This unmanly image of the Spanish general was subsequently immortalized in the revolutionary-era children's cartoon, *Elpidio Valdés*, which caricatured Weyler for his Napoleonesque short stature, brusque demeanor, and unsympathetic authoritarian character.

Insurgent vilification of reconcentration relied on a key assumption: that reconcentration disproportionately victimized women.[25] Yet, the degree to which the policy actually targeted women may have been exaggerated. Surviving evidence from several of Santa Clara's reconcentration camps suggests that men of working age composed a far larger proportion of camp dwellers than previously imagined. Indeed, in one reconcentration camp in Sancti Spíritus, nearly half the reconcentrated families included men of working age.[26] In another camp on Central Limones near Cienfuegos, 85 of the 231 charitable donations went to male reconcentrados. The fact that men at this camp usually received significantly larger quantities of monetary aid suggest that they were, or at least were presumed to be, heads of household with dependents.[27]

Evidence from a neighboring reconcentration camp at Central Parque Alto demonstrates that although more reconcentrados were female, male heads of household were not altogether uncommon, representing fourteen of twenty-nine parties listed. Some of these men were described as elderly, orphaned, or disabled, attributes that distinguished them from able-bodied men and rendered them part of the vulnerable population insurgents were required to protect.[28] This evidence suggests that while women and children certainly figured prominently as victims of reconcentration, male heads of household were more common than insurgent discourse and subsequent scholarship have allowed.

The tendency to conflate reconcentration with abuses against women, though not entirely accurate, proved central to insurgents' visions of themselves as men. Spanish policies targeting noncombatants violated the gendered assumptions that war was to be fought among able-bodied men. While insurgents may have frowned upon Spanish policies targeting elderly, disabled, or underage men and boys, they deemed enemy mistreatment of women to be particularly egregious.

Part of what made reconcentration so offensive to insurgents' gender sensibilities was the fact that it violated the sanctity of the patriarchal household. When Spanish soldiers forced women from their homes, they not only unfairly targeted a supposedly weaker sex that required male protection.[29] After all, insurgents idealized women's natural role as inherently domestic and subservient to the (middle-class) male breadwinner.[30] Cuban women were to remain at home, as virginal daughters resisting the hypothetical advances of unrelated men, chaste wives patiently awaiting their husbands' return from battle, virtuous mothers selflessly caring for their children, or mourning widows whose grief did not permit them to seek pleasure in other men.

Insurgents sought to preserve this domestic femininity during the war with as little alteration as possible. They envisioned Cuban women's role during the war in terms of enduring the absence of their male protector and provider. Women were supposed to "watch with pride" as their husbands, brothers, fathers, and other male kin "left to fulfill their obligation" on the battlefield.[31] A woman's principal patriotic sacrifice was to "remain resigned, prisoner of the fever of nostalgia, in the abandoned and insecure home, where everything speaks to her of the object of her illusions," while husbands and fathers were to "run the risks of battle" to achieve their "political ideals."[32] Within this gender ideal, a woman only contributed to the revolution by selflessly bidding farewell to her male kin and continuing to uphold Cuban honor through their domesticity. She was supposed to embrace the "poverty" and "loneliness" that inevitably awaited her in order to work "in her own sphere to bring glory to the common task."[33] The ideal woman endured moral and material suffering in the confines of her home—a prescription that offered very little in the way of practical strategies for women's subsistence.

If Cuban women were to remain in their homes during the war, then Cuban men were theoretically still obliged to protect them. After all, insurgents envisioned manly soldiers as "gentlemen" who took "care that no drop of blood be shed outside the battlefield" and were "merciful to the many unfortunate peaceful citizens."[34] Yet, these idyllic images of women's patriotic domesticity were largely shattered during reconcentration, forcing insurgent men to admit that their soldierly duties had compromised their ability to fulfill their patriarchal responsibilities.

The real and imagined gender transgressions of reconcentration tore insurgent men between their soldierly and patriarchal duties. To be sure, some insurgents longed to return to their own households to attend to their suffering families. One soldier captured the guilt and internal conflict that likely afflicted "almost all of us who are in the army." During the entire time of my service, "my family has been completely abandoned without anyone even to give them meat" and "today I cannot even give a cup of hot water to my sick children . . . and nevertheless the chief wants me to abandon my family as they are and return to the force."[35] Another soldier wrote from Sagua that the war made him "abandon everything to avoid falling victim to its barbarities." Over a year and a half behind on rent, this man lamented that his soldierly duties impeded him from fulfilling his responsibilities as head of household.[36]

Reconcentration compounded these feelings of patriarchal guilt by posing a direct physical threat to insurgent men's female kin. When Spanish soldiers enacted reconcentration, they not only unfairly targeted a supposedly weaker sex, they also transgressed the tenuous patriarchal authority to which insurgent men clung from afar. The assumption that Spaniards mainly targeted women during reconcentration exposed the dangers of insurgent's absence from the home front, heightening the conflict many men felt between their soldierly and patriarchal roles. The powerful, yet problematic assumption that reconcentration specifically victimized women allowed insurgent men to construct Cuban women as a damsels in distress whom they were charged with protecting. Insurgents thus reimagined themselves not only as patriotic soldiers fighting for national sovereignty, but also patriarchal soldiers protecting and avenging Cuban womanhood from Spanish abuses.

A Soldier's Patriarchal Duty

Recognizing that their soldierly duties would not permit them to protect their own families directly, insurgents recentered their patriarchal duties within their roles as soldiers. Whereas before the war, they had served as heads of household in their own patriarchal family units, under reconcentration, they assumed new roles as patriarchs of a national family. In that capacity, they assumed the duty to protect Cuban womanhood, writ large. In turn, fulfilling this patriarchal role provided a way for insurgents to reconcile their own internal conflicts between their obligation to protect their own families from the ravages of war and their soldierly responsibility to fight bravely and selflessly.

In the context of reconcentration, insurgents enacted their newly reactivated patriarchal roles by protecting noncombatant families, and especially women, from Spanish cruelty. Insurgent chiefs prescribed the "most zealous care over the weak[er] beings: the women, the elderly and the children."[37] Indeed, some insurgents prided themselves on helping women in need. White insurgent officer and commander of the Fourth Corps, Francisco Carrillo, for one, was so concerned with the suffering of women and children reconcentrated at Arroyo Blanco that he threatened to liberate them from Spanish oppression by attacking enemy forces himself.[38] Another white officer, Carlos Trujillo, proudly distributed women's clothing donated by the patriotic women's association Club Cubanita to "people who found themselves almost naked" and in the most "precarious and disconcerting situation," a deed that metaphorically restored these women to decency and modesty.[39]

In some instances, insurgent men interpreted Spanish abuses against Cuban women as an affront to their personal honor as patriarchs. A profanity-laden tirade by white insurgent chief José Braulio Alemán against a Spanish leader for persecuting a Cuban mother illustrates how some insurgent men envisioned the vindication of Spanish gender transgressions as their manly duty.[40] In April 1897 the Spanish officer José García Aldave had refused to engage Alemán's force of two hundred men in direct combat. Instead, he waited until Alemán's forces left the area to massacre a small unit of twenty insurgents who remained. Next, the "miserable gachupín," as Alemán called him, allegedly ordered "six thousand bayonets" to chase a defenseless Cuban mother and her young daughter from their home in the mountains of Villa Clara.

Alemán's indignation about the series of incidents centered the interrelated construction of military honor as a function of direct confrontation of enemy forces, and the assumption that targeting noncombatants, especially women, was dishonorable and unmanly. Like his compatriots, Alemán bristled at Spaniards' flagrant violations of the norms of honorable warfare, which required soldiers to engage in direct military confrontation with enemy troops. Aldave did the exact opposite. Upon hearing "our bullets," Alemán snarled at Aldave, "you cower and flee," even when Spanish forces drastically outnumbered insurgents.[41] Such conduct evinced a lack of bravery, and constituted what Alemán called the "deed of a bitch [*mujerzuela*]." While Alemán employed allegations of cowardice to challenge the military bravery of the Spanish chief, he also feminized his opponent by comparing him unfavorably to a dishonorable woman.

Worse than his cowardice in the face of insurgent forces was Aldave's gender transgressions against a Cuban woman. He ordered "hundreds of your drunken soldiers" to target "a defenseless woman."[42] Alemán charged that such unmanly actions constituted a personal affront to his honor as a soldier and (figurative) patriarch. "It is you who have offended me," he declared, self-assuredly in a letter to the Spanish chief. Insulting the manliness and virility of the Spanish general, Alemán challenged Aldave to a duel to correct the disrespect he had allegedly suffered. By challenging Aldave to a duel, Alemán flouted colonial social hierarchies privileging peninsular birth over creole birth by asserting social parity with his enemy. After all, only men of equal social standing could engage legitimately in a duel. If a social equal refused to engage in a duel, he was exposed as a coward, however, if a man viewed his challenger as socially inferior, it was dishonorable for him to accept the contest.[43] Thus, in order for Alemán to make his claim to social equality credible, he had to induce Aldave to accept the duel.

Alemán employed threats and insults against the Spanish chief's manhood to ensure that his opponent acknowledged his status claim by accepting the duel. "For once, be a man," he demanded haughtily. "Show me that Spaniards know how to be men of honor. Show the nobility that Spanish chiefs praise. For once, be honorable."[44] Alemán's provocations aimed to convince the Spanish chief that he had to demonstrate his own bravery by accepting the duel, which in turn would afford Alemán the opportunity to vindicate his own honor and status claim. After all, "it would be a dishonor for me to beat a coward," wrote Alemán.[45] If García Aldave did not accept the duel, Alemán threatened to figuratively "slap and spit [on]" his opponent by publishing his letter.[46] Aldave ignored the challenge.

Part of Alemán's indignation stemmed from his assumption that the Cuban woman who Aldave targeted was honorable. Alemán depicted the mother as the idealized self-abnegating, sexually virtuous woman, "whose only shame was being Cuban." His notion of women's honor fused the conventional emphasis on female domesticity and especially patriotic motherhood with more masculine qualities like bravery in the face of danger and even citizenship. Comparing the woman to her aggressor, Alemán concluded that she was "more dignified" and had "greater patriotic heart and more civic virtue than" Aldave.[47] By comparing the Spanish officer with the Cuban mother, Alemán essentially undercut the Spanish officer's manhood and implied that even Cuban women were more honorable than Spanish men.

In order to construct the Cuban woman as honorable, Alemán relied not only on the vilification of Spanish cowardice, but also on the presumed sexual transgressions of enemy women. He implicitly compared the sexual virtue of the Cuban mother to the alleged sexual deviance of both Aldave and his female kin. Drawing on the prevailing heteronormative assumptions of patriarchy, Alemán alleged that Aldave was impotent and even homosexual. "You shall see, fagot," Alemán hissed, "that Cubans know how to punish the valiant Spaniards who burn the homes of Cuban families and chase women and children to slay them." This, he claimed could only be "the work of the noble children of the Spanish excrement."[48] As the normative polarization between heterosexual normalcy and homosexual deviance began to take greater shape in the nineteenth century, sexuality became a powerful tool for disciplining men perceived to deviate from their prescribed patriarchal roles.[49] In this case, Alemán's sexualized insults against the Spanish chief constituted a symbolic inversion of the typical dichotomy of masculine colonizer and effeminate colonized.[50] By casting Aldave as sexually deviant, Alemán feminized the colonizer and masculinized the colonized.

Alemán's final series of insults against Aldave targeted the sexual morality of his mother and wife. He announced: "I infer you on the honor of your mother, [and] on that of your wife the offense of calling them prostitutes, being yourself beyond cowardly, you ruffian and ungentlemanly swine!"[51] Whereas Alemán had celebrated the Cuban woman's assumption of positively valued masculine attributes like bravery and civic virtue, he vilified enemy women for their transgression of the domestic ideal. Calling these women prostitutes foregrounded their illegitimate presence in the public sphere, which in turn highlighted their alleged physical corruption and moral perversion. Yet this insult was about more than policing femininity. It also indicated the Spanish chief's failure to protect, provide for, and perhaps most importantly, to control his female relatives. If Aldave's mother were a prostitute, then he was a bastard son, lacking the honorable birth that presumably afforded him privilege over native-born men. Moreover, the implication that his wife was a prostitute implied that Aldave had failed to provide for her (materially and sexually), was unable control her sexuality, and that he was a disgraced cuckold.

Alemán was not the only insurgent to invoke sexual dishonor to disparage enemy women. Indeed, Máximo Gómez himself used similar allegations of prostitution when dealing with two women suspected of being traitors in Puerto Príncipe. Cuban soldiers detained two women leaving town late at night. Summoned by General Gómez, one of the women explained that she had a sick child in town. Gómez did not believe her, likely assuming the women were enemy couriers or informants.[52] Interrogating the alleged mother, he asked: "How can a woman, weak as she is, go at night, knowing she is violating an order talking [to] or dealing with the enemy? Is this the deed of an honorable Cuban woman or is it the proceeding of a prostitute?"[53] Suggesting that honorable women should remain in their homes at night, Gómez cast Cuban womanhood as inherently honorable, and constructed women's sexual deviance and transgression of domesticity as conduct indicating betrayal of the Cuban cause.

In a similar case, insurgents encountered a "young and well-dressed" woman, accompanied by two men who claimed to be her brother and brother-in-law. They detained her because of her allegedly immoral appearance. The woman told white rebel chief Enrique Loynaz del Castillo that she had a sick child at home and "had gone out in search of tubers or plantains so as not to die of starvation." Loynaz was skeptical, pointing out that "the makeup on her cheeks contrasted with the affliction that the illness of her child should have caused her."[54] His comment about the woman's makeup, though not an explicit reference to prostitution, hinted at her supposed sexual promiscuity. He implied that her concern for her own appearance was inconsistent with the values and norms of modesty and self-sacrifice associated with proper Cuban motherhood.

Despite his doubts about the woman's character, Loynaz commended himself for not asking the lady to disrobe, "for the sake of respect." Instead, he searched the saddle of the group's horse, immediately finding a Spanish pass (*salvaconducto*), awarded "for their valuable service." Loynaz ordered the men hung, but he vacillated on how to deal with the female enemy. "The woman well deserved the same punishment; but it was so hard to order it," he recollected in his diary.[55] One of his officers also expressed hesitation, begging his superior officer not to put him "in the position of hanging a woman." Loynaz conceded, ordering his men to keep the woman prisoner until they saw a place to leave her. In so doing, he proved his commitment to the revolution by remaining firm in punishing the spies, while proving his gentility by sparing the woman's life, a representation of events that likely bolstered his own claims to honor as a courageous soldier and gentlemanly patriarch.

Although the epithet of prostitution implied the immorality of enemy women, it also invoked their figurative infidelity and transgression of the prevailing norms of femininity and sexual honor. Because insurgents defined both masculinity and femininity in terms of contribution to the insurrection, all those who did not actively commit to the cause were perceived to fail in their gender-specific duties. For men, failing to contribute meant being an effeminate coward, while for a woman, refusal to support Cuba Libre was equated with the worst moral transgression possible: prostitution. By labeling enemy women prostitutes, Cuban insurgents contrasted their dishonor and moral and sexual licentiousness with the propriety and virtue of honorable Cuban women. Insurgent denigrations against enemy women's sexual immorality constituted an indirect but powerful attack on Spanish men's claims to masculinity, because male honor was derived from the control of female sexuality.[56]

Sexual Honor and Its Racial Discontents

Even as white Cuban insurgents conflated honor with a broadly defined Cuban femininity, their ideas about womanhood did not necessarily include all Cuban women. Their visions of female honor, so intimately intertwined with sexual propriety and domesticity, retained many of the class and racial connotations they had during the late colonial period. Prevailing conceptions of honor, as translated into sexual morality and marriage, remained implicitly coded as middle-class.[57] After all, only women whose families could afford a single breadwinner could conform to the standard of domesticity. Because race was so deeply intertwined with class standing, the inherently middle-class standard of domesticity was generally limited symbolically if not practically to white women. Insurgent ideas of Cuban womanhood as inherently honorable therefore cast women who warranted protection as implicitly white. In turn, only white men could lay claim to patriarchal honor by saving white women. By extension, the devaluation of black womanhood as supposedly transgressive and dishonorable practically excluded black men from claiming honor on the basis of patriarchal authority.

The racial implications of honor were never more apparent than in insurgent references to women's sexual morality. White women were presumed to be honorable and sexually moral. This racialized gender assumption proved remarkably resilient, even when it clearly conflicted with Cuban women's lived realities. Máximo Gómez, for instance, expressed utter shock at the prospect of an unmarried, but sexually active white woman. Stumbling across "a pretty young woman with a babe in her arms, and a fair-looking man with a rifle," Gómez scolded and disarmed the man for "enjoy[ing] yourself while we are wearing out our skins." Then, he interrogated him about the marital status of his female companion: He exclaimed: "What? This woman has no husband and is not your wife!" Then, he began scolding the woman: "It is the fault of you, such women as you, willing to amuse yourselves when the country is in danger; making *majases* [cowards] of weak men when the Fatherland lacks defenders." He blamed her sexual licentiousness, immodesty, and her unwillingness to sacrifice personal pleasures for seducing men out of their patriotic duty.⁵⁸ Gómez's shock and horror at the specter of a white woman who failed to uphold domestic ideals evinced just how deeply entrenched whiteness was in insurgent conceptions of honorable womanhood. White deviations from the ideal, like the woman referenced above, however, did not seem to destabilize these racialized gender assumptions about sexual honor.

Whereas white women were assumed to be honorable, black women suffered from preconceived notions about their inherent dishonor and immorality. For instance, assumptions of black women's sexual licentiousness largely excluded them from prevailing ideas of female honor. This view is captured perfectly in the condescending idea that "keeping up appearances [of marriage]," was "*the most that we can demand with respect to morality from certain elements.*"⁵⁹ This implicit reference to black women's sexual dishonor hinged on perceptions that formal marriage was largely limited to whites in the late nineteenth century. By extension, poor imitation of gendered conventions, like formal marriage, rather than actual sexual morality became the condescending expectation some whites held of their black compatriots.

Contrary to this stigmatizing perception, black families did engage in formal marriage. The costs associated with formal marriage meant that upwardly mobile people of African descent typically enjoyed greater access to marriage than poor black families. Social pressures among middle-class black communities framed marriage as a key to respectability. To claim the hallmarks of "true manhood," this view implied, black men had to enter into a formal marriage, providing for their wife's domesticity, and ensuring their children's legitimate birth. Others avoided marriage but attempted to legitimize their natural-born children by documenting their official recognition of paternity.⁶⁰

Nonetheless, rates of marriage among people of African descent tended to be lower than those among whites. By the end of the century, whites were nearly four times more likely to marry formally than people of African descent in Santa Clara Province, statistics that reflected broader island-wide patterns (fig. 2.4).⁶¹ However, the racial discrepancy in marriage rates was not rooted in any inherent difference in morality among whites and blacks, as the above observer might have argued. Rather, racial disparities in marriage rates were more about post-emancipation racialized class stratification and labor hierarchies. A myriad of systemic factors, including poverty, legal barriers to socially unequal marriages, the historic devaluation of black womanhood, and women's desire for economic autonomy also contributed to lower marriage rates among black Cubans.⁶²

Following the abolition of slavery in 1886, many recently liberated women

Table 2.1. Marriage, partnership, and family, 1899

	Widows per 100 wives	Percent married		Concubinage per 100 marriages, white/black		Percent female breadwinners	
		white	black	white	black	white	black
Havana City	57	34.5	8	20	273	—	—
Santa Clara Province	50	32.3	9.8	19	234	—	—
Cuba	51	32.4	9.6	23	257	3.6	18.2

Source: US War Department, *Report on the Census of Cuba, 1899*, 81–83, 119–120.

of color left behind their male family members and husbands in the sugar districts and sought employment in cities, resulting in a disproportionate number of female-headed households in urban areas.[63] In fact, the proportion of black female breadwinners was nearly six times higher than among whites at the end of the century. Rates of concubinage were consequently much higher among Cubans of African descent—17 percent, as opposed to nearly 4 percent for whites, numbers which were slightly higher in urban areas.[64] Lower formal marriage rates among people of African descent translated into higher rates of illegitimacy, another key component of honor.

Irrespective of the actual reasons for the racial disparity in marriage rates and the presence of diverse family structures among black Cubans, low rates of formal marriage among people of African descent fueled racial stereotypes about the alleged sexual immorality of black women, and by extension the illegitimacy of their sexual unions and offspring. Indeed, few black women were able to escape assumptions about their inherent sexual immorality, which transcended class difference and likely inspired the popular Cuban refrain still in use today: "Just as there is no sweet tamarind, there is no *mulata* virgin."[65] Late nineteenth-century government and ecclesiastical officials reproduced these negative assumptions in the way they recorded the vital information of people of African descent. For example, it was common practice for parish priests baptizing black children to omit the paternal lineage from the records, even when it is evident from the family's other ecclesiastical and government records that the mother knew the father's name and the two were formally married.⁶⁶ Whether intentional or merely careless, these omissions marked the child as illegitimate, the father as failing in his patriarchal duty, and the mother as sexually transgressive, which circularly re-inscribed the exclusion of black women from honor.⁶⁷

On the battlefield, this devaluation of black womanhood through derogatory assumptions about black women's sexual licentiousness and immorality systematically translated most tangibly into two key racial double standards for women: white insurgent men's greater willingness to defend white women's sexuality from predatory men, and the more stringent enforcement of the domestic ideal upon black women. Insurgent men seemed more willing to recognize sexual assault committed against white women than against black women. Black and white insurgents suspected of violating racially unmarked women and girls were periodically sentenced to death as a public spectacle upholding insurgent men's performance of sexual restraint and patriarchal protection. One white soldier accused of raping a woman and molesting an eleven-year-old girl, both presumably white, was executed the morning after his summary trial in September 1895.⁶⁸ In another instance, an insurgent soldier accused of raping a racially unmarked woman was sentenced to be hanged.⁶⁹ By swiftly and publically punishing sexual predators among their own men, insurgent men publically performed their roles as defenders of honorable womanhood.

The vast majority of sexual assault cases tried by insurgents involved white women victims or women who can be presumed to be white because of the absence of racial markers. I could find only one case involving a woman of color—an anonymous "black girl" assaulted by a black officer in a town his unit passed. He was sentenced to death and "hung under the porch of a deserted cottage."⁷⁰ While the prosecution of a black man for sexual assault was not itself surprising, it likely played an important role in validating the black female victim's claims. Would she have been taken seriously if the perpetrator were white? Other insurgents mentioned a trial of "a black rapist" in 1896, but did not mention the race of the alleged victim.⁷¹ The dearth of documentation concerning the sexual coercion of black women, especially when committed by white men cannot be interpreted as evidence that such crimes never occurred. Rather it likely alludes to white insurgents' inability to conceive of black women's sexual honor in a society that defined it as white. The persisting stereotype of black female sexual deviance was likely taken to justify white men's presumption that these women were sexually available to them and also perhaps un-rapeable.[72]

A second hypocrisy in insurgent visions of honorable womanhood was the way they applied the domestic ideal unevenly to black and white women. One of the key examples of this racial double standard of female domesticity emerges in insurgent ideas about patriotic motherhood. Of all the gender-appropriate ways a Cuban woman could demonstrate her patriotism, insurgents envisioned motherhood as the ultimate patriotic contribution women could hope to make to the revolution. As mothers, Cuban women could literally reproduce the emerging nation by giving birth to (male) children. Moreover, they could strengthen the insurrection by teaching their boys to assume their roles as manly patriots.

The honor of motherhood seemed to extend to all Cuban women, regardless of color. Insurgents created an entire mythology surrounding idyllic motherhood in the Maceo family, a union formed by a white father and a mulata mother. Mariana Grajales contributed all her adult sons to the insurrection. Most of the Maceo brothers, including Antonio and José, died serving the Cuban cause. Grajales' patriotism stemmed from her role as caretaker and mother of male heroes.[73] This vision of women's honor as a function of their motherly reproduction of Cuban manhood implied that women who fulfilled these gender-appropriate patriotic functions merited patriarchal protection from Cuban men.

As much as the example of the Maceo family suggests insurgents' embrace of a color-blind motherhood, the quintessential archetype of Cuban women's patriotism implicitly foregrounded whiteness. Insurgent visions of racialized Cuban femininity found expression in a popular familial trope of the brave (white) Creole mother and the menacing Spanish father.[74] A revolutionary newspaper celebrated this implicitly white Cuban motherhood, running the story of one Cuban mother, who encouraged her children to join the insurrection. The story was made that much more harrowing because the woman's Spanish husband, chief of a guerrilla force, attempted to entice their children to serve Spain with promises of officer rank under his command. Overhearing "with shame" this unsavory proposition, the "very dignified Cuban" mother allegedly defied her husband "to instill in her children love for the patria." Invoking her motherly duty as a Cuban woman, she told her sons "with tears in her eyes that she would prefer to see them dead before dressed in the guerrilla uniform." All three of her children ultimately joined the insurrection. Their "firm resolution to fight without compromise nor trepidation until achieving our freedom" was not only a testament to the bravery and honor of these boys, who the paper implied possessed greater manliness than their Spanish father. The story also venerated the civic virtue of their white Cuban-born mother, who fulfilled her womanly duty through patriotic motherhood.[75]

More severe than the double standard of women's conformity to the domestic ideal was insurgents' hypocritical attitudes toward black and white women's gender transgressions. White women who transgressed the domestic ideal, whether by extending their conventionally feminine caretaking roles to the public sphere or assuming more masculine roles in combat, were largely still seen as honorable by white men. In contrast, nonwhite women were expected to prove constantly their conformity to the domestic ideal. When they moved beyond the home in the same ways white women did, white men condemned their transgressions as reflections not only of their individual dishonor, but also of nonwhite men's failure as patriarchs.

Middle-class and elite white women routinely stretched the limits of domesticity through their activism in patriotic clubs, only to receive the applause of insurgent men. These patriotic clubswomen, though largely drawing on their accepted gender roles as wives and mothers, assumed active roles in the public sphere, a place normally reserved for men. The wealthy white matron from Santa Clara, Marta Abreu, earned the praise of insurgent men when she assumed a public political stance by funneling ten thousand pesos to the insurgent cause. In Cienfuegos, Rita Suárez del Villar formed the patriotic women's society Club Cubanita, through which she and other local white women sent care packages to prominent Cuban officers. Grateful insurgent men greeted these charitable acts with gratitude. One man proclaimed that Rita had demonstrated that "Cuban women do know how to rise to the height of their brothers and if their sex does not allow them to match them in the magnitude of the sacrifice, their heart places them even higher."[76] Other elite women across the province including Cármen Gutierrez (Yara) through her club, "Hermanitas de Juan Bruno Zayas" in Santa Clara, María Escobar Laredo (known as Esmeralda and later Vencedor) with her Club Cubano in the port city of Caibarién, Antonia Romero Loyola (alias La Torcaza) in Remedios, and the Association of Women Protectors of the Revolution undertook similar patriotic activities, often delighting their male counterparts.[77]

Even as white insurgents materially benefited from white women's patriotic activities, some officers did express a desire for women to return to their more "natural" domestic roles. They framed their hesitations in terms of the protection of white womanhood. In a lengthy letter, one white Cuban soldier praised Rita and her associates for their "bravery," but expressed his desire to restore white women to the protected cloister of their homes. The soldier lamented that the demands of war had forced members of Club Cubanita in their patriotic zeal to abandon "so many feminine delicatenesses in order only to live in the eternal preoccupation of the servant of Cuban liberty." Playing the part of a protective father or older brother, he warned Rita to exercise caution, and to use "much discretion while Spanish soldiers remain in our cities."[78] By imposing male authority even over the glorified patriotism of Club Cubanita, this Cuban soldier revealed how white men's valorization of their own masculinity hinged upon the protection and control over honorable white women.

If white clubswomen pushed the boundaries of domesticity, white mambisas transgressed it completely by living and working within the supposedly masculine space of the battlefield. In fact, insurgents had attempted to preserve the masculine purity of the public sphere by creating a policy that explicitly excluded women from the rebel camps.[79] This policy invoked dominant notions of civilization premised on presumably natural sex differences that in turn justified women's confinement to the domestic sphere.[80] Yet, insurgents could never fully enforce this rule, nor was the total exclusion of women feasible. Women of all backgrounds routinely violated this policy when they came to the camps as washer women, cooks, nurses, prostitutes, camp followers, and even warriors. Máximo Gómez called the presence of women on the battlefield an "escándalo" (scandal) because it seemingly challenged insurgents' conflation of military service and manliness.[81]

As much as the general-in-chief criticized women's presence in the rebel camps, other insurgent leaders praised the self-sacrifice of white women who served as nurses on the battlefield, extending their roles as caretakers beyond the "natural" space of the home. These "heroic Cuban women" transformed themselves into "improvised medical professionals," as one white officer patronizingly wrote. In this capacity, the "affectionate and intelligent nurse" offered "sustenance and hope to the weak-bodied and weak-spirited" patriots and at times even defended her patients "as a soldier" from the enemy forces that dishonorably attacked hospitals.[82]

Young white women earned insurgent men's praise for straddling these contradictory expectations of feminine caregiving and masculine bravery. Rosa de Hernández, the "pretty young wife" of an insurgent officer, "sacrificed every comfort in life, except that of being with her husband, for the

Cuban cause." Even in the "hottest fire" she stood ready to "gallop to the side of a wounded officer or enlisted man," whether black or white.[83] Though "diffident and little inclined to talk about herself," like any decent middle-class woman, she claimed not to feel fear during battle, believing that "one only falls when the time comes." Insurgents celebrated her bravery and patriotic sacrifice after Spanish forces attacked a house where she tended to her sick husband. Even though she hoisted a white flag with a red cross on it, Spanish troops still stormed the makeshift hospital, "sent a bullet through the sick man's brain" while he lay immobilized in bed, killed one of the black assistants, and wounded another. Tearing her away from her husband's corpse, the Spaniards forced Hernández to march all day with them, only to imprison her in a facility for male detainees. Valeriano Weyler later condemned her to eternal detention in a penal settlement.[84] While one Spanish man remarked unfavorably on her presence on the battlefield, calling her "a mad woman [*histérica*]," and alleging that her husband "must be whipped [*bonachón*]" to allow her to become involved in the war, most insurgents eulogized her patriotism.[85] White men likely viewed nursing as a benign extension of women's "natural" caretaking roles, figuratively reframing the relationship between nurse and patient as that of mother and son, or wife and husband.

Nonetheless, such an analogy would fail to explain white men's acceptance of even more severe gender transgressions by white women. The decidedly masculine act of bearing arms, for instance, did not seem to prevent white insurgents from celebrating the femininity of white mambisas or lavishing them with complements about their physical beauty. Insurgents described Luz Cardona, the young white wife of white insurgent general José Miró Argenter, who lived on the battlefield during the war, as "very pretty," even though her presence lent an "irregular" appearance to the troop.[86] Likewise, insurgents did not seem to object when the white mambisa Paulina Ruíz, who accompanied her husband in battle, rode "very gallantly under a hot shower of Mauser bullets." She wore trousers, allegedly killed two guerrillas with the swing of her machete on the front lines of one skirmish, and participated in at least ten other battles without sustaining injuries.[87] Yet insurgents described her as "pretty," "slim," "gentle," and "graceful"—adjectives closely associated with properly secluded, middle-class young white women. Although one observer described her pejoratively as "too plucky and too proud," other officers generally praised her and she was even awarded officer rank. Máximo Gómez was allegedly scandalized by the story of Ruíz, but he neglected to punish the white insurgent leader who allowed it. Rather he urged his soldiers to keep her and other women away from combat zones.[88]

White mambisas were not immune from criticism, but generally enjoyed a favorable reputation among white insurgents. Luz Noriega Teresa, the wife of an insurgent doctor, for example, did draw some criticism for her gender transgressions. Nonetheless, the critiques of her actually elucidate white insurgents' paternalist desire to protect white womanhood.[89] One prominent white officer praised her for her "feminine beauty," but criticized her "masculine valor." Still, his objection implied a desire to return her to the sanctity of domesticity rather than a condemnation of her dishonor. After all, insurgents celebrated valor as a positive attribute in both Cuban men and women. This officer pitched his objection to her presence not in terms of any negative qualities she possessed, but rather in terms of his desire to protect her from aspects of war that "a lady should not see and hear."[90] Another insurgent man wrote that he did not know "if he liked her," though he certainly did not object to her beauty, which he mentioned more than once. Other men described her in a more sympathetic light, emphasizing her dedication to her husband and her fierce patriotism when confronted with the enemy.[91] The patriarchal nature of these comments suggests that white men's rare objections to women's presence on the battlefield reflected their desire to preserve the domesticity of women of their race and class.

For all the praise and protection these white rebel women received, it seemed that their presence on the battlefield did not necessarily reflect negatively on their husbands for failing to maintain the patriarchal household. Instead, these women earned praise from insurgent men of similar racial and class backgrounds for representing a new ideal of revolutionary womanhood. The presence of white women outside the home was not "ideal" according to many insurgent men. However, the valorization of patriotic self-abnegation allowed white women to extend their domestic role into the public sphere, and in some cases transgress these gendered expectations completely without suffering much negative consequence. In turn, white women's willingness to sacrifice their domestic comfort supposedly demonstrated their dual devotion to the revolution and to their husbands, qualities insurgent men accepted as part of honorable womanhood.

While white women's gender transgressions were legitimized under the banner of revolutionary femininity, black women were not afforded similar privileges. Insurgent visions of Cuban womanhood were based on a circular logic that made the presumption of honor a precondition of a woman's ability to claim honor. Because white women were presumed to be honorable, insurgents justified their gender transgressions as temporary adaptations to the conditions of war and as symbols of patriotism. Yet, because black women were presumed to be dishonorable, any transgression of gender ideals became evidence of the immorality of which they were already suspected.

On the battlefield, black women performed many of the same functions white women did, from accompanying their husbands as camp followers to taking up the machete for the Cuban cause. The black woman Faustina Heredia accompanied her partner, Mateo de Jesús Hernández, to the insurrection, where she performed unspecified duties and later married.[92] Another black woman, Bárbara Pérez, who worked as a washerwoman for Spanish troops, reportedly took bullets from the uniform pockets and gave them to insurgent men. Although most women in the battlefields were black women "who have followed their husbands, sharing the hardship of the always moving camp and the chances of a stray bullet," many also fought alongside insurgent men, just like their white counterparts.[93]

Seldom did these black women enjoy the same veneration from male insurgents as did white mambisas. The emphasis on the bravery and self-sacrifice of the white women contrasted with the usual depiction of black women in subordinated roles, serving white families. In one insurgent narrative, a presumably black wet nurse held a white child, "begging for mercy," until "a soldier, standing outside, put his rifle to the infant's head and shot the poor thing dead." The tragic death of the white child hinted at the supposed inadequacy of the black woman's patriotic sacrifice.[94]

When black women indisputably demonstrated bravery on the battlefield, insurgents disparaged their activities as evidence of masculinization or hypersexuality. Attention to the clothing and language used by black women on the battlefield occasionally served as a source of condemnation of their supposed gender transgressions. Two black women (*morenitas*) in the Brigade of Colón endured sharp censure from white insurgents for dressing as men and having "bad tongues." One of them, María H. Santana accompanied her partner José Matilde Ortega (alias Sanguily) into battle, drawing criticism for being too loud (*bullisosa*), too much of a problem (*jolongo*), and far too outspoken for "giving her opinion and criticizing everything."[95] One insurgent described a young black woman whom he found wounded as boyish in appearance, her tender age rendering her feminine form not yet pronounced. He also noticed the woman's masculine attire, which he claimed, made her appear even more masculine, even though white women who wore pants, like Paulina, were still praised for their feminine beauty.[96]

While the active presence of white women on the battlefield did not seem to reflect poorly on white men, insurgents sometimes interpreted the presence of black women in the rebel camps as an indication of black men's patriarchal failures. White officer Eduardo Rosell y Malpica criticized a black officer for including black women in his camp, claiming that it was "inconvenient" to travel with them. He reported witnessing an uproar over men being taken from the frontlines of battle to protect and attend to one of the women, María. Despite these complaints about her, "he does not know how to break away from her," Rosell lamented, disparaging the black officer's lack of authority over his lover.[97] In other cases the supposed gender transgressions of black women who wore men's clothing and toted machetes was used to censure black men. One critic noted that "these women are fiercer than the men." Connecting the reversal of proper gender roles to their racial background, he added, "many of them are mulattoes." The discursive masculinization of black women implied the emasculation of (black) insurgent men.[98] The double standard for black and white women's presence on the battlefield evinced the persisting judgment of black women based on gendered assumptions about their race, rather than their actual merits.[99]

In the rare instances that black insurgents came to the defense of black women, they became the object of ridicule by their white compatriots. To be sure, white insurgents fumed at one prominent black officer's "clumsy and punishable declaration" that his black concubine had actually defended herself alongside male soldiers. Giving "prestige to a concubine" insulted men who were "worthy of more."[100] Other insurgents disparaged the military participation of black women on similar grounds. One man claimed that these black women "carry machetes, as tools rather than as weapons," seeming to belittle their military value. They "wear bloomers, even trousers, and sleep in hammocks or on bits of rubber cloth on the hard ground, but they do not fight in the skirmish line with rifle or shotgun, like the men, for they form part of the impedimenta," he explained, depicting these women as camp followers rather than brave patriots.[101]

There is no question that the context of revolution destabilized gender ideologies, empowering some women to transcend the "traditional" female roles of wife and mother.[102] Nevertheless, the above examples suggest that racial privilege circumscribed what groups of women could commit these socially "acceptable" gender transgressions. Whereas any woman's transgression of the domestic sphere theoretically subjected her to dishonor, in practice, these actions only became problematic when committed by women historically excluded from honor. White women, particularly the wives of important white officers, were exempted from prescriptions of domesticity and excused for their incursions into the supposedly male realm of battle because of their presumed status as honorable.

In turn, women whose racial background rendered their claims to domesticity and sexual honor dubious could seldom escape assumptions of their dishonor in the public sphere. Consequently, the same actions that earned white women praise for self-abnegation and patriotic bravery were deemed dishonorable and transgressive when committed by black women. This racial double standard of revolutionary femininity relied on the persistence of colonial ideas about black women's supposed inconformity to bourgeois gender ideals, which in turn allegedly reflected ongoing immoralities. The continued stigmatization of black women served to highlight the virtue of white women, whose gender transgressions were framed as temporary or exceptional anomalies in service of the patria and the patriarchy. White women were thus implicitly the only women worthy of patriarchal protection.

Patriarchy as a Mechanism of Racial Hierarchy among Cuban Soldiers

The racial double standard of womanhood had direct implications for insurgent men's claims to revolutionary masculinity. If not all Cuban women were worthy of protection, then not all men could draw masculine honor from protecting women. The racially inflected assumptions about black women's inherent dishonor translated to suspicion about black men's claims to manhood as husbands and fathers. Black women's supposed dishonor and immorality presumably emanated from the failure of black men to perform adequately the values of the heteronormative, patriarchal, bourgeois family.[103] In essence, the racial double standard of Cuban womanhood served as the foundation for excluding black men from patriarchal honor.

White insurgents scrutinized the sexual unions and family practices of black men, often framing perceived deviations from the white bourgeois norm as proof of black men's patriarchal failings. This repackaging of colonial notions of white patriarchy enabled white insurgents to refuse to recognize their black counterparts as honorable patriarchs. Men who had not fulfilled their patriarchal responsibilities, in turn, could not hope to claim patriarchal authority over their own families, let alone over the Cuban national family. The exclusion of black men from patriarchal honor allowed white insurgents to declare themselves as the lone honorable defenders of white womanhood. They continued to claim patriarchal honor, even as they often failed to live up to these ideals in practice, mirroring what Susan Fraiman calls the "white male chivalric fallacy."[104]

White insurgents rejected black men's attempts to gain social recognition as patriarchs, even when their actions disproved assumptions of gender transgression. There is perhaps no clearer example of insurgent refusal to recognize black patriarchal authority than the treatment of Benigno Ortiz, a black soldier and father camped at the Ciénaga de Zapata, a remote region of Santa Clara. Ortiz recounted a dispute with one of the white families over roosters, whose crowing threatened to expose the settlement to discovery by enemy forces. Ortiz presented himself as "a devoted father" who despite his natural inclination for bravery had lofty aspirations for the future of his family. "I am naturally valiant," Ortiz declared, referencing the insurgent expectation for bravery on the battlefield, "especially if I forget myself," he continued, nodding toward the expectation of manly self-abnegation. "But when I think of these children, I feel fear of bullets," he confessed reflectively, tempering the virile bravery he first mentioned with a softer side as a breadwinner and provider, compliant with proper middle-class gender roles.[105] Using fatherhood as the basis of his argument, he asked the white family to dispose of the roosters for the safety of his children.

The white family rejected Ortiz's claim to patriarchal authority. The wife of one of the white men living in the settlement justified her desire to keep the roosters by claiming that "one is a very fine game-cock that was loaned to us to keep." This woman's dismissal of Ortiz as a legitimate patriarch cannot be separated from the disparaging perceptions of his and other black families at the same camp. Indeed, the black children were alternately described as "black, wriggling broods," and "a swarm of naked pickaninnies tugging at their mammy's skirts." These terms pathologized the number of children, implying the hypersexuality of the mother and likely illegitimate birth of the children. Other descriptors emphasized the animalistic, unrefined character of the children, who could be found "burrowing in the red soil" and wearing "glass beads around their necks like little savages." Although white residents "instinctively" kept apart from these black families, Ortiz vowed to fulfill his patriarchal duty to kill the roosters in order to protect his family.[106]

The double standard of patriarchal authority for black and white insurgents revealed the racial inequalities bubbling underneath the idyllic surface of revolutionary masculinity (and femininity). While insurgent criticisms of reconcentration as an attack on women recentered insurgents' patriarchal roles, the string of military setbacks that followed placed additional pressure on insurgents as soldiers—and as men. The next chapter charts how white insurgent leaders responded to these challenges by identifying an implicitly racialized enemy within, eventually giving birth to a parallel racial double standard for military service.

CHAPTER THREE

Mambí or *Majá*?

Measures of Merit and Double Standards of Military Authority

AT THE SAME TIME CAPTAIN-GENERAL VALERIANO WEYLER IMPLE-mented reconcentration, he also launched a series of military offensives to drive the insurgents back eastward.[1] Spanish forces reinforced their positions at key strategic points across the island, stationing thousands of fresh soldiers in central Cuba. They also mobilized over one thousand local men into informal forces called guerrillas around the area's three largest sugar mills (Constancia, Hormiguero, and Soledad) among three hundred forty others in the so-called zone of cultivation near Cienfuegos (fig. 3.1).

As Spaniards ramped up their operations, severe shortages in arms, ammunition, and basic supplies left many insurgent chiefs unable to continue fighting.[2] Spanish forces had discovered and destroyed the insurgent stronghold at Siguanea, where insurgents and sympathizers manufactured shoes and clothing for the troops.[3] Moreover, donations of critical supplies from sympathizers slowed to a trickle as the Spanish presence in Santa Clara swelled.[4] Although they had usually resorted to raiding and foraging to supply these unmet needs, the PRC began to crack down on these activities to avoid the negative publicity insurgent attacks on private property might draw.[5] Consequently, insurgents were in a "lamentable state," almost completely "barefoot with their feet destroyed," while the cavalry was lacking a single "horse

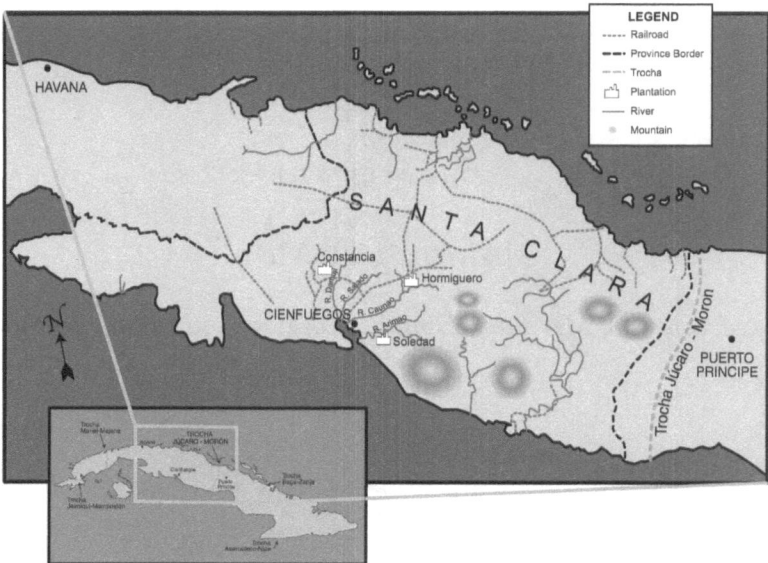

Figure 3.1. Map of the major sugar plantations and military trenches in Santa Clara Province. Credit: Blythe Graphics.

capable of trotting."[6] Shipments of ammunitions had also declined in late 1895 and early 1896 as the PRC under Tomás Estrada Palma shifted its focus from supplying arms to securing diplomatic recognition from Washington.[7]

While insurgents suffered these material obstacles to their military operations, Weyler's offensives reversed many of the decisive victories insurgents had secured over the previous year. By March 1896 Spanish forces had driven Máximo Gómez's force from Matanzas all the way east of Santa Clara to Puerto Príncipe, and they had isolated Antonio Maceo west of the Trocha Mariel-Majana. Over the next year, the Fourth Corps recorded an unprecedented number of casualties, among whom were some of central Cuba's most prominent leaders. Even as central Cuban forces demonstrated their strength in a powerful attack on the provincial capital of Santa Clara, the heavily mourned loss of Leoncio Vidal marked the start of a string of major casualties in the province. Beloved Santa Claran chief Juan Bruno Zayas was slain by Spanish forces outside Havana in July 1896.

At the same time, the Cuban army as a whole mourned the loss of several high-ranking chiefs. The mulatto officer José Maceo (brother of Antonio Maceo) succumbed to Spanish bullets in the Battle of Loma del Gato in eastern Cuba in July 1896. Spanish forces claimed the life of Serafín Sánchez, inspector general of the Cuban army and former interim chief of the Fourth Corps, in November 1896. Both mulatto general Antonio Maceo and white chief Panchito Gómez (Máximo Gómez's son), were slain in December 1896. These setbacks exacerbated the low morale among insurgent chiefs, who alternately described these "dark month[s]" in terms of a "spiritual crisis."[8] These conditions also contributed to high rates of defection from the Cuban army between February and May 1897. Desertions reached "alarming" proportions in the Brigade of Cienfuegos as well as the Invasion Force.[9]

The so-called spiritual crisis led some insurgent leaders to question an assumption that had, up until that point, served the central tenet of revolutionary masculinity: that military service necessarily demonstrated manhood. If bravery and self-sacrifice had been central to the early insurgent victories, then the series of defeats implied a dearth of those manly characteristics among the men of the Cuban army. Insurgent leaders identified a disquieting pattern of cowardice, selfishness, and immorality, which they called, disparagingly, *majasería*. Men who engaged in this unmanly conduct were not the honorable mambises insurgent leaders had celebrated for their bravery, self-abnegation, and patriarchal honor at the start of the war. Rather, they were majases.

In late nineteenth-century Cuba, the word majá generally referred to two things—a menacing-looking but non-venomous snake and an idle person (*holgazán*) or vagrant. In the context of the insurrection, the label majá fused both original meanings—the negative class assumptions implied with ideas of vagrancy, and the connotations of deceit and trickery often symbolized by snakes—to condemn unmanly conduct in Cuban soldiers. It emerged as the absolute counterpoint of the honorable mambí, or brave Cuban soldier. The term encapsulated three key characteristics: cowardice on the battlefield, disregard for the laws of the Cuban army, and an unwillingness to sacrifice sexual pleasures for the revolutionary cause. In this sense it embodied both the undersexed and oversexed variants of deviance from the nationalist struggle.[10]

High-ranking insurgent leaders pointed squarely at the Fourth Corps as one of the epicenters of majasería. General-in-Chief Máximo Gómez and other white leaders alleged that the widespread inactivity, laziness, and immorality in central Cuba had not only caused insurgent defeats. It had also tarnished the purity of the insurrection's manly character. While insurgents reacted to reconcentration by reasserting themselves as patriarchs, they responded to the military setbacks of 1896 and 1897 by denouncing these allegations as insults to their own military authority.

To redeem their soldierly honor in the face of these allegations, white central Cuban chiefs launched their own internal campaign against majasería. At precisely the time insurgents faced the most devastating moments of the war in late 1896 and 1897, white insurgent officers in Santa Clara court-martialed dozens of soldiers and officers on allegations of majasería. The stated objective of the "honor trials" that followed was to "sustain the prestige and the honor of the men of our Army."[11] By presenting themselves as agents of order, disposed to punish others for unmanly conduct, white central Cuban chiefs defended their own reputations as mambises essentially by blaming military setbacks on other soldiers and officers. Not all insurgents were equally susceptible to allegations of majasería, however. In this localized campaign, majasería assumed powerful racial undertones as white insurgent leaders disproportionately denounced alleged immoralities committed by black men, while often condoning similar behavior from their white compatriots.

I argue that white insurgent chiefs across Santa Clara deployed majasería to dismantle black insurgents' claims to masculinity on the basis of their military service. The courts-martial disproportionately targeted black officers, resulting in their censure and demotion for three types of implicitly racialized gender transgressions of military service: unsoldierly conduct, criminality, and sexual immorality. White officers often committed the same infractions with impunity. Thus the unspoken racial dynamics defining these trials exposed the racial limitations of revolutionary masculinity for black soldiers. The racial double standard inherent in white insurgents' application of majasería ultimately reversed the modest adjustments that revolutionary masculinity had prompted in the racial hierarchy of the Fourth Corps. In turn, the trials would have long-lasting impacts on the racial hierarchy among the men of the Fourth Corps.

"We Call These Cowardly Men *Majases*"

Beginning in spring 1896 high-ranking insurgent leaders identified a range of unmanly behaviors among the soldiers of the Cuban army, whom they deemed responsible for the recent military setbacks. General-in-Chief Máximo Gómez cited three main types of gender transgressions that constituted majasería. First, there were cowardly soldiers, who "flee the danger" in an effort "to escape as best they can without exposing their hides to bullets," rather than fighting bravely. This type of man "fail[ed] in his duty" of military service.[12] A second type of majasería involved soldiers who violated the laws of the revolution. So widespread was this type of criminality among Cuban soldiers that Gómez disparagingly labeled them "a bunch of bandits with military rank."[13] A third type of majasería involved soldiers' sexual transgressions. Gómez expected soldiers to conform to the soldierly ideal of self-abnegation, focusing on military obligations instead of sexual needs. The proper place for Cubans who "felt themselves man enough," was "in the camp and on the battlefield," he declared. And on the battlefield, "I do not accept private lives," he announced. Men who distracted themselves with their wives, lovers, or other women allegedly compromised their competencies as soldiers, and were thus guilty of majasería.[14] A man who committed one or more of these transgressions could no longer be considered a mambí. Rather, as Gómez declared, "we call these cowardly men majases."[15]

In central Cuba, where the insurrection had faced some of the more significant setbacks, the problem of majasería was apparently most pronounced. Gómez ordered the military inspectors and other high-ranking officials of the Fourth Corps to deliver an "immediate corrective" to "cure the moral and physical leprosies" afflicting insurrection there. They needed to perform "moralizing work" to rid the insurrection of this "plague" of "parasites."[16] This included rounding up "any vagabond chief or officer or soldier found outside their lines" and punishing men who offend "our dignity and self-love."[17] In essence Gómez ordered local insurgent leaders to extirpate majasería to prove their own military honor and to preserve the pristine masculine image of the revolution.[18]

As Gómez and other high-ranking army officials branded Santa Clara as a dangerous hub of majasería, local white chiefs responded defensively. The notion that dishonorable men lurked within the Cuban army challenged insurgents' earlier construction of all Cuban soldiers as good men. As one disappointed white chief noted, this unmanly conduct "says very little in honor of the Liberating Army."[19] Moreover, it suggested that local insurgent officers, predominantly prominent white men, had failed to provide strong manly leadership, impose sufficient discipline, and command the respect of their men. Thus, white officers of the Fourth Corps interpreted their superior officers' allegations of majasería as a challenge to their own personal military prestige.

In response to Gómez's call to moralize the Fourth Corps, white insurgent leaders in central Cuba launched an internal campaign to extirpate unmanly conduct, especially cowardice, criminality, and sexual immorality. This campaign catalyzed a transformation in white insurgent chiefs' visions of revolutionary masculinity. During the first year of the war, they had celebrated military service in the Cuban army as the basis of a shared manhood among all Cuban soldiers. Yet, majasería implied that serving in the Cuban army was no longer sufficient to prove one's manhood. Rather, the campaign against majasería distinguished honorable from dishonorable military service. Only a man whose military service met certain criteria could be considered a mambí.

Theoretically, the parameters of honorable military service were objective and straightforward. Insurgent men were expected to bravely follow orders to confront enemy forces, follow the revolutionary laws, and prioritize soldierly duties over sexual desires. None of these allegations explicitly referenced race. Rather, they formed part of the gendered expectations of soldierly conduct. Violating any of these soldierly duties suggested serious transgressions against revolutionary masculinity. Unsoldierly behavior revealed a man's failure to fulfill his patriotic duty of military service. Violating the laws of the revolution implied a man's dishonor and criminality, as well as his inability to sustain himself through honorable means. Sexual misconduct underscored a man's transgression against his patriarchal duties to protect and provide for an honorable familial unit.

Yet, in practice, white insurgent chiefs applied these metrics unevenly and situationally, often with their own interests at heart. After all, these men sought to redeem their own reputations as honorable soldiers. To do this, they sought to deflect blame for the military failures away from themselves. Consequently, they were quick to point out the personal shortcomings of other soldiers and officers. Although both white and black men faced allegations of majasería, black officers faced official censure more frequently and were subjected to harsher sanctions than most others. One of the key groups targeted during the Fourth Corps' campaign against majasería were officers from eastern Cuba who had taken command of central Cuban forces during the Invasion Campaign. Local white chiefs perceived these adjustments to local leadership as an affront to their local authority and racial privilege, particularly because many of the eastern Cuban officers were black men. White chiefs also targeted local black officers who they perceived to have trespassed against the racial etiquette by asserting authority on par with their military rank. The result of this majasería campaign was the emergence of a second set of qualifications for black soldiers to be recognized as men. Not only did they have to serve honorably in the military as white men did. They also had to conform to the unspoken racial implications implied with respect for authority, orderliness, and morality.

"Not a Very Soldierly Character"

In April 1896 white officer José Braulio Alemán, then sub-inspector of the Liberating Army, complained of widespread majasería within the Fourth Corps, which he oversaw. In the Brigade of Cienfuegos, there were "so many ignorant men, so many useless chiefs, breastfeeders [*amamatadores*] of bad soldiers, who do not help in my work and will never know how to conduct themselves correctly."[20] Alemán feminized these officers by likening them to unfit mothers, spreading their bad habits of majasería to their discursively infantilized subordinates. Later that year, another white officer complained that the same problems persisted in Cienfuegos, where "majases abound" and local officers refused to help "moralize and punish" the "lazy" and incompetent men there.[21] In early 1897 a third white officer claimed with incredulity that all the chiefs and officers of the Brigade of Cienfuegos "maraud about on their own volition without noticing the obligations they have to their Fatherland."[22] Other units in the Fourth Corps faced similar censure from central Cuban insurgent leaders. One central Cuban chief lamented the utter "disorganization" in the neighboring Martí regiment. There, the soldiers evinced "little or no manliness," allowing themselves "to be discovered by the enemy, [and] losing weapons and horses."[23] In levying these complaints, central Cuban insurgent leaders suggested that the lack of bravery, discipline, and leadership had harmed their reputations and military outcomes in Santa Clara.

In theory any soldier who evinced a lack of soldierly conduct would be subject to charges of majasería. However, in practice, white central Cuban chiefs defined proper soldierly conduct largely as a function of a man's respect for military authority. Respect for authority included a soldier's obligation to comply with orders regardless of the danger involved—that is, to demonstrate bravery. But it also included more subjective qualities like attitude, demeanor, and etiquette, all of which hinged on a man's recognition of his place within the military and social hierarchy. Consequently, most of the charges for unsoldierly conduct centered on perceptions of insubordination.

The exceedingly situational and subjective nature of respect for authority offered fertile terrain for implicit, gender-coded racial discrimination. The case of black lieutenant colonel Isidro Acea illustrates exactly this. In November 1896 the Cienfuegos native received word that a black soldier formerly under his command, Porfirio Sánchez, had faced unfair treatment at the hands of several white officers. During meal time, Sánchez asked for a piece of meat. A white second lieutenant refused, telling him to take the leftover rib bones. He then gave a piece of meat to a (white) woman, likely a camp follower or concubine of a white officer. Sánchez protested, declaring that "those lending services" should receive priority in the distribution of rations. For this, their white commanding officer, Commandant Alfredo Ramírez, punished the black soldier.

Acea intervened on behalf of Sánchez. Acea had been promoted to lieutenant colonel in August 1896, technically affording him seniority over the white commandant, even though the two had formerly held the same rank and served together in the Calixto García Regiment. From this position of military authority, he demanded an explanation for the unjust punishment of Sánchez and requested that the white commandant transfer the black soldier to his command. The response Acea received, however, revealed that Ramírez did not respect the authority of his black superior. "I don't believe it to be my duty to explain to you the reasons for punishing said individual, nor do I believe you authorized to request that I transfer him [to your service] in such a rude manner as you do," Ramírez swiftly retorted. He finished the letter by noting that his superior officer was the only person "authorized to issue orders of such authoritative character."[24] This truculent response may have reflected his resentment that a black man had risen to a rank above his own and that he attempted to enact the authority associated with that rank over him, a white man.

Ramírez elevated the dispute to superior authorities, complaining that Acea had failed to recognize his place within the military hierarchy. The result was a military tribunal that ruled not against the white officer for abuse of power or maintaining a concubine in his camp, but against Acea for allegedly overstepping his authority. Court-martial authorities claimed that Sánchez had directed his complaint to the wrong authority. Because Acea served in a different unit, the tribunal judged that the white officer "acted perfectly within his rights to not accede to the demands placed upon him."[25] While the tribunal ignored the white officer's other offenses, they condemned Acea for attempting to use the authority of his superior rank. Even though there is no evidence that the tribunal punished Acea, it did reinforce ideas that were clearly already at play in the insurgent camps: that white officers could violate the expectations of soldierly conduct with impunity and that they did not necessarily have any obligation to respect the authority of black officers. Moreover, by ignoring the initial injustice that provoked the incident, which had been motivated by similar double standards of privilege and access, the tribunal effectively prioritized white egos over black grievances.

These same double standards of military authority also seem to have informed another incident in April 1897, when the mulatto colonel José González Calunga suffered allegations of disrespecting authority. A veteran of the Ten Years' War (1868–1878), Calunga entered the War of Independence in his home province of Oriente at the rank of captain. He secured promotions based on his strong military record in the Invasion Campaign alongside Máximo Gómez, even as he faced scrutiny from white officers who did not consider him worthy of his rank.[26]

His accuser was none other than José Braulio Alemán, the young white officer from Santa Clara who, in his capacity as sub-inspector general of the Cuban army, had launched a campaign to eliminate majasería in central Cuba. The trouble began when a white lieutenant colonel under Alemán's orders, arrived in Morón, on the eastern boundary of Santa Clara Province, where Calunga already operated. Alemán had essentially attempted to replace Calunga with a white officer of inferior rank. Calunga sent the white lieutenant colonel away. Thereafter, the black colonel sent one of his black lieutenant colonels to inform Alemán that he received orders of this nature only from General Máximo Gómez. Calunga seemingly resented what appeared to be a relatively common tendency of white officers to discount and circumvent the authority of black chiefs.

Alemán responded with a tirade against the black officers that, although initially framed in gendered language, ultimately revealed his implicit disapproval of black men's military authority. Denouncing Calunga as a "simpleton," and a "rude, ignorant, and incorrect man," Alemán claimed that the black colonel had no concept of "what Patria is, nor what shame or honor are."[27] Referring to the race of the two black officers, he lamented that "those brutish coronels who are not decent people, nor do they know how to read or write, and [are] stupid, racist, and animals."[28] Alemán's references to the low education levels of the black officers suggests he resented Calunga's transgression of class hierarchy. However, when coupled with the insults about their stupidity and comparison to animals, Alemán hinted at racial views that linked intelligence with notions of biological race.[29] Moreover, his allusion to Calunga's alleged "racism" betrayed Alemán's anxiety over what he saw as the deterioration of white privilege by black military authority. By framing black authority as racism, Alemán's rant revealed his assumption that a man's honor hinged on his recognition of and conformity with his place within the class and racial hierarchy, an idea that diverged substantially from the unifying ideal of revolutionary masculinity.

Máximo Gómez's response to Alemán's complaint further underscored presumptions of incompetence and unworthiness of black men, regardless of their rank. Gómez was sympathetic to the unfavorable descriptions of the black colonel, who had served in his *escolta* during the Invasion Campaign. He only defended Calunga on the basis of his ignorance, reinforcing assumptions of black incapacity for leadership. Although Calunga was "a courageous and honorable man," Gómez wrote, "he is not a man of clear intelligence and never owing to evil but rather to excess zeal would he commit an inconvenience like what he has obliged you to present in your very just claim." Gómez reassured Alemán that he agreed with his complaints and encouraged him to "forgive your comrade for his indiscretion."[30] Although Gómez reminded Alemán that patriotism entailed collaborating across racial lines, he implicitly upheld white privilege urging his white comrade to look past the supposed innate inferiorities of the black soldiers in support of the revolution.[31]

It should come as no surprise that Acea and Calunga faced such vehement rejections of their military authority. After all, officers of Santa Clara Province held implicit assumptions linking officer rank with whiteness. White insurgents frequently benefited from policies rewarding social prestige with military rank, often without regard for actual military merit. José Miguel Gómez himself admitted that promotions "were sometimes made on account of the political influence and social standing of the individuals," criteria which he implied had also benefited him.[32] Gómez justified his own rank based not only on his military service but on his reputation as an *hombre de bien*, a man of social prestige and wealth.

The Fourth Corps was riddled with similar cases of intellectuals and professionals obtaining high military rank without significant military achievements. The young white medical doctor Juan Bruno Zayas, for instance, joined the insurrection in April 1895 and in less than a month he was promoted to the high rank of lieutenant colonel, handed command of an infantry unit, and later transferred to lead a more prestigious cavalry unit. By August that year, he was a colonel.[33] In another notorious case, the white officer Alfredo Rego promoted a white corporal to the rank of captain without military achievement at all, leading critics to denounce the practice of promotion by "dedazo" (a euphemism for personal favoritism). Some officers allegedly assigned promotions to family members, friends, and patrons "without recognizing the meaning of the rank they award."[34] White officer Bernabé Boza noted that the numerous "'captains' and 'commandants'" joining the insurrection only achieved such ranks because of their education or social prestige, not for their military capabilities. "Many of these 'cavalry captains' don't even know how to ride a horse," while some of the infantry officers cannot even march on foot without "sticking out their tongue and giving up."[35] These men all underscored the ways social prestige (a quality implicitly defined by whiteness) often afforded white men unearned military rank.

In contrast, black men's attainment of officer rank seemed almost inconceivable, or at least counterintuitive to some white insurgents. Even high-ranking black officers, including Antonio Maceo himself, were acutely aware of the uneven distribution of promotions across racial groups and explicitly recognized white suspicions about the supposed racial motivations informing their promotions of other men of African descent.[36] Even though the primary beneficiaries of unfair promotions without military merit were in fact well-connected white men, black officers, above all, faced greater obstacles in gaining acceptance of their officer rank.

The Quijotesque story of an encounter between a white soldier and a black officer highlights just how powerful racial assumptions were in evaluating a man's military authority. Seemingly envious of the comparative luxuries enjoyed by some officers and himself feeling the pangs of hunger, white insurgent Israel Consuegra y Guzmán confessed his desire to become a "jefecito" one day. "I wanted to demonstrate it practically, getting into it with an old black man" who sat chewing a piece of cane stalk. "I turned toward him, employing the most authoritarian form and giving my voice the tone of a 'big man,' I told him: 'Hey citizen! What are you doing sitting there? Fall into line immediately or I will beat you with the flat of my machete!'" Consuegra soon discovered that he was speaking to a colonel when he saw the three stars in the form of a triangle on his uniform. Rather than adjusting his understanding of military rank, Consuegra concluded that he should avoid other "hard-headed negroes with stars."[37] Another equally revealing episode about assumptions surrounding race and rank involved José Matilde Ortega (alias Sanguily), a young mulatto, who left behind his life as a servant to earn officer rank in the Cuban army in Matanzas. A white insurgent noted that if his former master had joined "he would have only been an assistant," rather than lieutenant colonel.[38] The implication was that black men became officers not because they deserved the rank, but because of the supposed dearth of white men to promote. These cases suggest that the subjective idea of respect for authority, which subsumed prescriptive racial etiquette, disproportionately disadvantaged black officers. Black officers who attempted to assert the authority of their rank often confronted resistance from white men who did not recognize or respect their officer status, and who perceived their authority as a violation of unwritten racial etiquette.

"A Bunch of Bandits with Military Rank"

Soldiers who violated the laws of the revolution could also be denounced as majases. One of the most serious crimes a soldier could commit against the revolution was the violation of a series of laws inaugurated in July 1895 prohibiting commercial activity and paralyzing the sugar and cattle industries.[39] Many central Cuban officers expressed outrage that their compatriots embezzled supplies sent by PRC-sponsored expeditions and smuggled commodities prohibited by the revolution such as tobacco.[40] The white central Cuban chief Alejandro Rodríguez denounced the "acts of banditry" committed with impunity "by other chiefs in the west of this division."[41] Alemán lamented the "immorality" of all the "vagrants" under the protection of their chiefs.[42] Others similarly bemoaned the abundance of "bad patriots and egotistical men" who sought to profit from the needs of the Liberating Army.[43]

Much like soldierly conduct, the perception of criminal acts like stealing, vagrancy, and assault took on different meanings depending on who performed them. Some apologists exculpated (white) soldiers involved in these crimes, claiming that the abysmal material conditions of the Cuban army drove otherwise honorable insurgents to commit bandit-like crimes just to survive. One starving soldier noted that "the man who does not have money, does not eat well [come sin sal]" and soldiers who "who only bear arms" did not have money.[44] Some soldiers responded to this harsh reality by violating insurgent laws to make money to buy food and other necessities. In many instances, local chiefs overlooked petty crime, understanding that it stemmed from material need. "To be too severe with our soldiers is almost impossible," noted the white officer Eduardo Rosell y Malpica: "They are not paid, they are not clothed, they lack shoes, they are not fed, and it is necessary to let them maraud and recur to their families [and] to their friends to cover their needs."[45] Other central Cuban officers seemed to take a similar approach, leading some chiefs to conclude that the men of the Fourth Corps were "not yet an army, but rather bands, that are only different from bandits in the number of men and the sanctity of the cause that unites them."[46] The boundaries between legitimate and illegitimate violence, between necessity and immorality were blurry and unstable. These inconsistencies meant that men's actions gained legitimacy or illegitimacy based on their context and who performed the deeds.

White officers often evaded sanction for their crimes due in part to the presumption of their innocence, and also because they often benefited from higher-ranking whites defending them. In mid-1896 José Braulio Alemán initiated a series of courts-martial, which he claimed would be "applauded by honorable men."[47] Yet, he faced stiff resistance against his attempts to punish several white officers under the command of Gerardo Machado (first elected mayor of Santa Clara in 1900 and later fifth president of the republic, 1925–1933) for illegally engaging in commerce in July 1896. Machado accused Alemán of overstepping his authority and interfering in his military operations, a response that echoed Calunga's. Yet, rather than elevate the dispute to Gómez, as he had with the black colonel, Alemán simply communicated his disappointment and directed his energies elsewhere. He dismissively replied to Machado: "I believed that you would help me in my patriotic work. I was mistaken. I recognize the error."[48] Although he noted that he did not need Machado's permission to exercise his patriotic duty, he also did not seem to have pursued the case.

Alemán may not have had much luck prosecuting prominent white officers, but he fared much better in his attacks on black officers. Among his early targets was a black colonel, Juan B. Benítez, whom he charged with "very grave misdemeanors of insubordination, negligence, abandonment of military service, and falsifying public documentation."[49] He claimed that Benítez allowed the extraction of tobacco and other commercial items, allegations strikingly similar to those Alemán had levied against Machado's men. Unlike Machado's men, however, Benítez did not benefit from the protection of white patrons.

Alemán immediately elevated the dispute to Máximo Gómez, complaining about the black officer's "attitude." By invoking such a subjective quality, Alemán emphasized some of the same implicitly classed and racialized qualities he had levied against Calunga. Drawing on assumptions that officers should be formally educated, the white inspector disparaged the black officer as "the negation of human intellect" for his illiteracy.[50] He further

Figure 3.2. Gerardo Machado y Morales. Source: "Gerardo Machado y Morales," *El Demócrata: Periódco Polítco y de Información*, Santa Clara, Número Extraordinario [n.d., 1902].

characterized him as "dispossessed of honor" for his alleged involvement in criminal activities.[51]

Before even convening a court-martial, Alemán denounced the black colonel's alleged unsoldierly conduct and criminal acts to depict him as unfit for military leadership. "The continuation of Colonel Benítez as chief would be dangerous because of his negligence, his lack of will, his refusal to concentrate the forces, and the bad example his conduct gives the others," accused Alemán in a letter to Gómez.[52] Insubordination allegedly "stained his name." In addition, Benítez's alleged reputation as a "horse thief and kidnapper" and fugitive from the law was "inappropriate for military honor and for honorable patriots" and took "away prestige" from the revolution.[53] Because he was "known for his evil deeds and unknown as a soldier," his leadership impeded insurgents' ability "to earn sympathy among the good elements who aided the Revolution in the villages."[54] By labeling him a criminal, illiterate, and incompetent, Alemán attacked Benítez's claims manhood and undermined his military authority.

In the same period, black captain Claudio Sarría faced court-martial for demanding money from Damián Machado, a Chinese contractor for Central Soledad.[55] Describing him and his men as "imps" who "hang people up to the branches by the roadside at their will and pleasure," the North American owner of Soledad, Edwin F. Atkins vowed to arm a force of guerrillas, at the head of which he appointed a man with personal interests in killing Sarría.[56] Before Atkins's guerrilla force could get their hands on Sarría, insurgents court-martialed him. Sarría denied the charges, arguing that he was a "brave soldier," and had "always served the fatherland with the due honor of a true son of Cuba." Despite his pleas, the military tribunal convicted him and, in his words, "unjustly demoted" him to the rank of private.[57] In another case, a "burly black corporal, of vast breadth of shoulder and a gorilla-like cast of features" was tried and found guilty of insubordination for allegedly pointing his rifle at a (white) officer on two occasions. He was executed.[58]

Among the more high-profile disciplinary measures taken during this period involved José González Planas, who finished the war as major general with an impeccable record of military service. Born in 1850 to an African-born father and Cuban-born mother in Santa Clara, González Planas learned to read and write at an early age. His bravery and military skill earned him the rank of corporal in the Ten Years' War, and commandant by the end of the Guerra Chiquita (1879–1880). With the outbreak of the War of Independence in 1895, he left his new home in the central Cuban town of Lajas where he led the society of color La Fraternidad, to join the insurrection, then as a lieutenant colonel. He was among the first to organize the Brigade of Cienfuegos in August, taking charge of the infantry while Alfredo Rego, one of his early detractors, headed the cavalry. Indeed, the personal differences between González Planas and Rego caused him to leave the area that he had called home prior to the war. He served under Quintín Bandera, alongside eastern chiefs including Colonel José Camacho Yera in December, and finally served under the orders of his old chief, Serafín Sánchez, in January 1896, being named chief of the Brigade of Remedios by April that year.[59]

Shortly after being promoted to brigadier general, González Planas came under scrutiny for some military setbacks. In July 1896 Francisco Carrillo, Serafín Sánchez's successor as chief of the Fourth Corps, wrote to González Planas, scolding him for the numerous strategic positions occupied by the Spaniards, which "reflects negatively on your military prestige."[60] In May 1897 Máximo Gómez, who just months earlier had congratulated the brigadier on his military accomplishments, began to doubt González's honor. Referring to a report by Francisco Carrillo, Gómez described González Planas as "a valiant man, but not very energetic," evidenced by a recent surprise attack by Spanish troops on his

Figure 3.3. José González Planas. Courtesy of Archivo Histórico Municipal de Remedios.

Figure 3.4. Francisco Carrillo. Courtesy of Archivo Histórico Municipal de Remedios.

camp. "And I believe it," Gómez wrote, "as it explains the surprise the Spanish have given him." Although Gómez recognized the contrast in the report Carrillo gave and the previously untarnished record of service of the black chief, he lamented the lack of recent triumphs.[61] The two white chiefs seemed to single out González Planas for military difficulties caused not by his inactivity, but rather by circumstances largely beyond his control, such as the lack of provisions and the reinforcement of Spanish forces across central Cuba.

González Planas again came under fire for allegations of banditry, insubordination, majasería, and "vandalistic deeds," including robbing families, impersonating Spaniards, and shooting up ranches. These allegations emerged after the defection of numerous high-ranking insurgent officials and doctors to the Spanish army following the announcement of autonomy in late 1897.[62] One of these men, González Planas's former aide-de-camp, José Nodarse, allegedly sent a series of defamatory letters to the few white soldiers under González Planas's command, likely seeking to inspire further desertions. Writing under his pen-name Vulcano, González Planas reassured one of his confidants, María Laredo Escobar (under the masculinized alias Vencedor) that the defections were of "no importance." The guilty parties were "men of passions, racists and bitter enemies" of the revolution.[63]

Despite their dubious origins, Máximo Gómez took the allegations very seriously, again doubting the general's good reputation. "The lion is not as brave as they have made him out to be," a disappointed Gómez wrote.[64] Gómez even speculated that the black officer caused more trouble for the insurgents than he did for the Spaniards.[65] The men of González Planas's force found the allegations insulting, claiming that they were not only false, but aimed to "discredit" the black chief. One black insurgent, Manuel José Delgado, mused in a subsequent letter to prominent black patriot Juan Gualberto Gómez about how someone "who has not engaged in a single battle in the entire war" could accuse valiant soldiers of majasería.[66]

In April 1898 González Planas recorded in his diary that he was ordered to turn over his brigade and submit himself to a court-martial.[67] "Fortunately the truth shone through," as one of the brigadier's black compatriots noted, forcing his acquittal.[68] The persistent scrutiny of one of the highest-ranking black officers in the Fourth Army Corps suggests that military rank, far from shielding black men from racially motivated accusations, actually subjected them to greater scrutiny.

The prevailing presumption of black criminality seemed to afford greater credence to allegations of crime attributed to black men. The black soldier Ricardo Batrell Oviedo noted, for example, that whites received more leniency in the military courts-martial than blacks, even in cases in which the alleged crimes of white suspects were more egregious than those of their black counterparts, and even when there was a notable lack of evidence against black suspects. In this light, Batrell recounted the story of black commandant Severino Ricardo, in his unit in Matanzas. A year after the execution of his cousin, José Matagás, on charges of banditry, Severino faced charges of theft. The principal witness did not testify and no clear evidence connected him with the alleged crime, yet the court-martial found him guilty and sentenced him to execution, despite the protests of his compatriots. Meanwhile, two white officers who were "more implicated" in the crime were absolved. Batrell painfully described the antecedents to the execution, whereby his compatriot was symbolically emasculated when he was stripped of his rank, then robbed of his life.[69] Many other black men shared Severino's fate, among whom Batrell listed the bandit-turned-revolutionary Desiderio "Tuerto" (one-eyed) Matos, Simeón Sánchez, and a man nicknamed Cajizote as victims of "false accusation."[70]

Other cases across Santa Clara seemed to conform to this double standard of legality for white and black men. Brigadier Alfredo Rego, for example, proved "to be drastic with some chiefs of the black race who committed indiscipline."[71] In 1897 the white officer demoted at least two officers and ordered the execution of "Tuerto" Matos.[72] Boasting of his success in moralizing his forces, Rego wrote to Máximo Gómez declaring, "You will like my Infantry. They are well-disciplined; contentment and much union reigns among them." He admitted that he had been "at the beginning somewhat severe to the extreme," but he suggested that his disciplinary measures had helped produce a better force.[73] These cases suggest that allegations of crime had emerged as a powerful affront to the honor of black men, regardless of their social standing, military status, or performance on the battlefield. Racially specific ideas about criminality resulted in unequal access to justice for black and white insurgents.

"A Bunch of Negroes . . . Taking Care of Negresses"

In addition to transgressions against military hierarchy and revolutionary laws, majasería also encompassed more private matters, like insurgent men's intimate lives. In their zeal to construct an honorable image of the revolution, insurgent leaders also subjected soldiers' sexual activities to public scrutiny, a type of social policing usually reserved for women and nonwhites. Insurgents' obligation to fulfill their masculine duty of military service theoretically required them to abstain from the moral, physical, and material comforts offered by women. Men who flouted their soldierly duty to seek pleasure in women violated the ideals of masculine self-abnegation, exposing their incomplete commitment to the revolution. These men risked being labeled majases.

In practice, however, access to women and, by extension, to their domestic, sexual, and reproductive labor, constituted one of the principal privileges of officer rank. So long as officer rank coincided with whiteness, the widespread practice of sex on the battlefield attracted little scrutiny from military leaders. However, the modest adjustments in the racial hierarchy of the Fourth Corps resulted in a small number of black men assuming command over various military units in central Cuba. The erosion of white control over officer rank produced tensions among the officers of the Fourth Corps, who disagreed over the racial parameters of masculine authority. Sexual immorality emerged as a convenient mechanism to denounce black officers' unfitness for authority in a gendered lexicon without explicitly voicing opposition in racial terms.

Even though prescriptions about sexual morality concerned soldiers across race, class, and rank, the only men to face prosecution for these gender transgressions were black men with officer rank. Several court-martial cases featured intensely gendered allegations about the sexual conduct of black men, including maintaining a concubine and claims of sexual misconduct with noncombatants. At the same time, white officers committed even more egregious sexual transgressions with impunity.

The uneven prosecution of sexual immorality among black and white officers underscores white anxiety about the perceived erosion of white control over military authority. White officers exploited the implicit racial connotations of sexual morality to justify their attacks on black officers as gendered defenses of insurgent honor, rather than explicitly voicing their racial assumptions and resentments. Máximo Gómez argued that the immorality "of men without virtues" tarnished the moral purity and honor of the Cuban army and contributed to its military failures.[74] He urged his subordinates to protect "the purity of the Revolution," from further stain and to prevent "its glorious flag from being dragged through the mud."[75] The gendered nature of these charges enabled insurgent leaders to frame their case as a defense of insurgent honor, without explicit reference to race. The racial silence inherent in these gendered ideas thereby helped uphold the raceless ideal that a Cuban man gained honor based on his merits rather than his race. The resulting demotions of black officers based on gendered charges helped preserve white control over the highest ranks in the military, which later legitimized their monopoly on political power.

The well-documented court-martial of Quintín Bandera is one of the clearest examples of the insurgent double standard on sexual morality. Born in 1834 to formerly enslaved parents in Santiago, Bandera lent distinguished service to the Cuban army in all three wars of independence. He assumed an important leadership role in the Invasion Campaign, commanding the predominantly black volunteer infantry force from eastern Cuba twice through the Spanish Trocha Júcaro-Moron into Santa Clara. Earning praise for his bravery and military acumen, Bandera replaced Juan Bravo as the commander of the Brigade of Trinidad following the invasion of central Cuba.[76] After the death of Antonio Maceo in December 1896, Bandera was one of the highest-ranking men of African descent in the Cuban army.

In May 1897, mere months after Bandera's ascension to the rank of division general, several of his compatriots levied serious charges against him for disobedience, sedition, insubordination, and immorality. Like the allegations against other black officers, the ones levied against Bandera were decidedly gendered, drawing on established ideas that insurgent manhood hinged on bravery, self-abnegation, and patriotic devotion. The first three charges had appeared in other majasería-related cases, and the trial featured some of the same racially charged gendered language regarding respect, attitude, and military authority. Testimony by Juan Massó Parra, a white chief of the Brigade of Trinidad who famously later led his entire troop to defect to the Spanish army, attacked Bandera for his alleged presumptuousness regarding his own status and importance to the revolution. He noted that Bandera assumed "an intransigent and rude attitude," even refusing to obey orders to turn over his men because he had promised to take them back home to Oriente. Intangible evidence like Bandera's "attitude" and his alleged lack of humility suggested that the white officer expected Bandera to comply with the platitudes of racial etiquette. White officers' concern with Bandera's demeanor suggests that his most egregious crime was attempting to exercise his rank.

While the first three offenses largely reflected broader patterns, the fourth accusation—that of immorality—rarely appeared in other cases. Much of the ensuing court-martial trial focused on Bandera's alleged "majasería with a concubine," prompting public investigation into Bandera's intimate life. Accusers claimed that Bandera's active sex life had derailed his military efforts. Linking his sexual conduct directly to his military outcomes, Máximo Gómez wrote of Bandera's "apparently very incorrect conduct as a soldier," arguing that "said chief was not inspired by patriotic ideas and honorable and glorious aspirations as an honorable man and upright soldier."[77] After hearing testimony from mainly white officers and a handful of Bandera's subordinates, the tribunal eventually found him guilty and stripped him of his rank and command.[78]

Bandera himself understood the trial as a rejection of his authority as a black man. He confessed that he foresaw such persecution because the white chiefs of central Cuba "did not want to be led by officers of color."[79] Nevertheless, previous interpretations of this case have emphasized the limits of race in explaining Bandera's fall from power. Ferrer, for example, has argued that Bandera violated the gendered ideal of sexual abnegation, rendering his conduct particularly offensive to bourgeois visions of manhood and undermining his claims to military authority. She suggests that Bandera's supposed gender transgressions formed part of a broader classist objection to his leadership: white officers rejected the possibility that "rustic men" of humble, rural origins, and hailing from outside the locality, asserted authority over local men who occupied more privileged social and racial positions in colonial society.[80]

Class and regionalism certainly played a role in the social tensions defining Bandera's court-martial. White and black officers alike routinely complained that central Cuban men privileged local allegiances over national ones, often to the detriment of the revolution. One white chief noted that central Cubans were "so localist" that they label a man from another locality "as an intruder and usurper of their rights," and then attempt to derail their operations with "calumnies and false information" to make it seem "that they are the only ones apt" to lead.[81] Moreover, the PRC imposed obviously classist qualifications for military promotion, including literacy and education.[82]

Nonetheless, framing Bandera's court-martial and demotion in terms of class or regional tensions neglects the powerful racial double standard defining insurgent visions of men's sexual conduct and self-abnegation. By situating this case within the broader pattern of gendered prosecutions of black officers, this chapter shows that classed notions of masculinity served as a metalanguage for implicitly racialized objections to Bandera's authority. In turn, this argument largely validates the black general's own understanding that the case was fundamentally about the racial limits of military authority.

White officers expressed their anxieties about black authority in numerous objections to Bandera's masculine conduct, including in critiques of the clothing he and his female partner wore. Massó Parra pointed to his lavish dress as proof that Bandera was living "the good life," implicitly invoking prevailing ideas about racial etiquette that associated respectable clothing with whiteness. It might be tempting to read Bandera's clothing as a form of racial resistance or a performative self-representation.[83] However, the fact that Massó Parra and other white officers took issue with the "suit of new cloth" worn by Bandera more likely revealed white resentment over a black man unapologetically embracing an officer status most white men more comfortably equated with whiteness. Nobody objected when white officers wore new clothing to mark their social status and rank. However, Massó Parra seemed to assume that Bandera, as a black man, could not afford such fancy clothing, or at very least should not wear it out of respect for racial etiquette.

This implicit racial assumption led him to imply that Bandera had failed to sacrifice sufficient material comforts to demonstrate his devotion to the cause or had otherwise acquired the clothing through dishonorable means. The clothes allegedly symbolized Bandera's preference to live the "good life" rather than fulfill his military duties. In this vein, Massó Parra criticized Bandera and his concubine's lavish dress as "the greatest insult" to the poverty faced by many (white) families. While the black general and his mistresses ate well and rode horses, innocent white families "with much, much hunger" marched in "caravans by foot" from the villages and mourned crops Bandera had allegedly destroyed.[84] Others alleged that Bandera had removed a widow from her home in order to install his concubine therein. These allegations, which Bandera swore "on his honor as a Cuban" were not true proved incendiary not because they were unprecedented or particularly egregious.[85] Many white insurgents engaged in similar activities. Rather, they were powerful because they hinged on racial assumptions. They juxtaposed impoverished (white) women with black women and men enjoying higher standards of living, ideas which chafed against presumptions that conflated whiteness and high status.

Indeed, white insurgent chiefs from central Cuba offered ample evidence that the distaste for Bandera's conduct was rooted in a rejection of black men exercising authority. Objections to his military leadership were rooted in implicitly racialized notions of place. After all, Bandera, a native of the demographically blacker eastern provinces, commanded a racially integrated force in the wealthier, traditionally loyalist, and whiter central provinces.[86] Before he died, white inspector general Serafín Sánchez overturned Antonio Maceo's order to place Bandera in charge of the Fourth Corps' Second Division, judging the military leadership of "*the* BLACK GENERAL" to be "*inconvenient for the cause of command in this territory.*"[87] Similarly, when Bandera assumed command of the Brigade of Trinidad, another white chief commented that "undoubtedly, given the *conditions* of Quintín, he will not be very convenient in Las Villas."[88] Alfredo Rego, a white chief in the Brigade of Cienfuegos who had previously snubbed the black officer González Planas, similarly confided in a private document to another white officer that Bandera's leadership was not welcome in the central provinces: we must "convince Quintín Bandera that he is not a General nor is he the chief of this brigade, until they make him understand."[89] Another white officer warned of certain "frictions [*rozamientos*]" caused by Bandera's command of the Brigade of Trinidad.[90] Although most of these men did not explicitly refer to Bandera's race, notions of his "inconvenience" and "condition" suggested that racial considerations informed white officers' rejection of his leadership.

Among Bandera's most vocal detractors was the white central Cuban officer José María "Mayía" Rodríguez, who refused to provide Bandera's men with the necessary provisions and neglected to give the black general orders to fight. Bandera repeatedly complained of Mayía's unfair treatment, which prevented Bandera from fighting and subjected him to allegations of unsoldierly conduct. He even requested to transfer out of his command: "It is impossible for me to continue under the orders of this chief," who "orders me [to do] nothing and so insults my prestige," Bandera wrote in May 1897.[91]

At the same time as he effectively sabotaged Bandera's military operations, Mayía wrote multiple letters complaining of the black general's sexual immorality, despite Mayía being known to maintain concubines of his own. In a rare direct articulation of racial tensions, Mayía called Bandera and his men "a bunch of Negroes and bandits taking care of Negresses" (*negros y bandidos cuidadores de negras*).[92] He said nothing about a white doctor's female partner (*mujer*) who rode alongside Bandera's "concubine" along with two other women who were "not señoritas" accompanying their men.[93] The difference in labels attached to the various women conveyed specifically racialized assumptions about black and white men's intimate acts. Whereas Mayía disparagingly labeled black men's female partners as mistresses or concubines to imply dishonorable, out-of-wedlock sex, he presumed honor and legitimacy of white men's partners by calling them wives.

Most correspondence and testimony about Bandera's sexual conduct lacked the kind of explicit racial language that appeared in Mayía's allegations. The racial silence defining this case emerges with greatest clarity in the selection of men for court-martial duty. José González Planas (the same black officer who survived allegations of criminality just months earlier) served as the head of the court-martial, despite having a lower rank than Bandera at the time.[94] Appointing a black officer to condemn another black officer seemingly mitigated the clear racial undertones of the trial and offered a counterpoint to Bandera's supposed transgressions of racial etiquette. González Planas had supposedly achieved the ideal. He reportedly retained unparalleled humility despite his rank, rarely challenging the authority of white officers. Moreover, he earned praise for respecting racial hierarchy in his intimate life by declining the company of white women.[95] He was perceived to conform to bourgeois ideals of manhood by "keeping up appearances" of marriage. His adherence to the sexual values of middle-class white society led some white men to accept González Planas as "gentlemanly and good," and dub him "that great Cuban with a dark complexion but a white soul."[96]

The appointment of González Planas to head the tribunal essentially juxtaposed two opposing ways of embodying black masculinity: the supposedly transgressive hypersexuality of Bandera and the masculine sexual ideal of respectable, restrained and (quasi-)legitimate intimacy that González Planas presumably upheld. These masculine types clearly invoked class differences, with the idealization of self-restraint an obvious tenet of bourgeois gender sensibilities. As Ferrer argues, Bandera symbolized a distinct version of black masculinity, one defined by his "rustic" character as a "son of the people," in contrast to more refined middle-class notions of manliness.[97] However, these types also invoked race. González Planas earned praise not because of his class status, but rather because his conformity to bourgeois notions of manhood communicated his respect for, valorization, and emulation of whiteness.

This trial highlights a broader pattern of prominent black officers' involvement in the policing of black male sexuality. Other prominent black officers, including Dimas Zamora, Antonio and José Maceo, and Guillermo Moncada, had previously reprimanded Bandera at one point or another during his long military career.[98] High-ranking black officers had vested interests in publically castigating Bandera. The sexual immoralities and insubordination allegedly perpetrated by Bandera seemingly reinforced prevailing racial stereotypes labeling black men as vagrants and hypersexualized beings. Allowing this version of black masculinity threatened the whitened respectable image other black leaders sought to construct in order to win the acceptance of white officers like Máximo Gómez and Calixto García.[99] Successful black officers may have policed other black men's sexuality to reinforce their own reputations as morally upright. On at least two occasions Antonio Maceo lifted the penalties imposed on Bandera. This fact, combined with Maceo's own insecurity about white perceptions of his relationships to other black officers, suggests that Bandera's alleged record of deviance may not have resulted from his transgressions alone. It likely also reflected black officers' performative rejection of loyalties that whites may have interpreted as racially inspired.

Another case in which the sexuality of black men came under close scrutiny was that of José Matilde Ortega (alias Sanguily). He was accompanied by his partner, María H. Santana, a woman known for being too loud (*bullisosa*), and "giving her opinion and criticizing everything." Sanguily drew criticism not only for failing to control his woman, but also for allegedly diverting resources away from military operations to protect her. One white insurgent complained that Sanguily had "distracted" five or six armed men from their military duties and occupied three or four weapons to ensure her care, when such men and resources were in desperate need on the frontlines. He claimed that the presence of a woman contributed to the disorganization of an already rowdy and undisciplined group of men, almost all of whom were "of color." These men were already morally suspect, he implied, and did not need "such incentive to decompose themselves" further. He further noted that despite his complaints about her, "he does not know how to break away from her." The white insurgent reported these accusations to the commanding officer, urging prosecution.[100]

Even men as illustrious as José Maceo could not escape rumors of racialized sexual transgression. Before his death in July 1896, Maceo reportedly maintained two or three "mulaticas" in the rebel camps. One of these, Agripina Barroso Lazo, known as "La Negra," accompanied him long enough to have his child.[101] Despite his lengthy service record and venerated patriotic family, José Maceo faced demotion from his position as commander of the province of Santiago to a narrower responsibility over the city of Santiago.[102] Maceo's sexual conduct never received the degree of scrutiny evident in Bandera's trial, and it is unclear the extent to which the allegations influenced his demotion. However, the confluence of concerns about his perceived sexual transgressions and public challenges to black men's military authority were nonetheless striking.[103]

White officers frequently engaged in sexual relations with women on and off the battlefield, but rarely faced the kinds of consequences that black men did. In fact, other white men often made excuses for the sexual transgressions of their racial peers. One insurgent officer remarked apologetically that in rare instances, an otherwise honorable patriarch exercised the "bad judgment" of privileging his own family over his duty to serve his country.[104] Others admitted that the sexual improprieties were more widespread among white insurgents. Numerous (white) soldiers allegedly enlisted in the Cuban army not out of patriotic devotion, but rather to obtain an "easy life [*vida holgada*], better and more abundant food; sometimes the envied love and affection of a woman."[105] One white insurgent noted that some officers preferred to "eat well and have women," rather than lead their soldiers honorably into battle.[106] Another white chief lamented the high number of officers who maintained concubines on the battlefield, noting that "there is not one of them who is content with one lover, all of them have various [concubines]."[107]

Some of these men even allowed their sexual escapades to derail their military ventures. José Rafael Legón, for example, had to alter his military plans on account of "a feminine scandal" mounted by his lover—a half cousin of his, no less—cementing his reputation as an "*enamorado*."[108] Other officers in Santa Clara even left their positions in the battlefield to spend the "boring hours" with their mistresses in neighboring villages.[109] One man known as "El Mejicano" nearly started a fight with the manager of a local sugar estate to see a mulatto woman living there.[110]

Yet, white officers rarely faced official sanction for their sexual transgressions. Máximo Gómez himself knew of numerous white chiefs who maintained concubines at the same time as Bandera. Mayía, who Gómez privately described as "another bandit, murderer, [and] thief" allegedly "tucked himself away in the hills with women," having sequestered one of his concubines from a rural village. He even disobeyed orders, refusing to confront the enemy under "futile pretexts incapable of justifying [the disobedience]," and he failed to take any measures "to make the Spaniards respect him." Other white officers, like Enrique Loynaz del Castillo, allegedly abducted a girl to be his concubine, stealing milk from peasants to feed her.[111] Similarly, Brigadier José Luis Robau López, the son of a plantation owner in Puerto Príncipe, who emerged as an insurgent chief in Santa Clara, was known to maintain a lover, a country girl who ran away from her family to be with him on the battlefield.[112] Likewise, the escapades of a white insurgent, Pepe Aguilar, who reportedly enjoyed "making love to peasant girls," apparently went without comment from Cuban officers.[113] With direct knowledge of many of these cases, Máximo Gómez lamented "the crimes of so many bad Cubans who have forgotten their duties," but ultimately failed to hold the white men accountable. After all, he and several key central Cuban officers discussed how even Francisco Carrillo, the chief of the Fourth Corps, sought the "easy pleasures on a ranch with a concubine."[114] Although Gómez and others openly discussed the immorality of these men, they never brought charges against them. In fact, these white officers avoided even the slightest reprimand allegedly because "nobody has given me a formal complaint to catch him and subject him to the rigor of justice."[115] White men were largely spared from the humiliation of having their private lives aired in public. These examples suggest that gallivanting around with various women out of wedlock was a rather mundane part of white officer life.

Some white officers did face court-martial, but the charges never reflected their sexual transgressions, sparing the public shaming of overt discussion of their intimate lives. The case of Roberto Bermúdez, a white farmer from Las Villas who observed "Don Juan-esque" conduct and maintained relations with a young white woman who later bore his child, illustrates this point. In

1898, days before the Treaty of Paris officially ended the war with Spain, a court-martial sentenced Bermúdez to death by firing squad for murder and abuses of power, though it made no mention of his intimate affairs.[116]

The uneven application of insurgent ideals of sexual morality unveiled a hidden double standard operating within the discourse of revolutionary masculinity: not only were black men held to a higher standard of sexual morality than white men; that standard was so high, that it was nearly impossible to achieve it. Black officers were constantly forced to prove their compliance with a standard implicitly modeled on white, middle-class sexual values, while white men transgressed the same standards without consequences. White officers enjoyed the privilege of being presumed honorable, despite their conduct. Rather than suggesting that whites avoided sanction altogether, these cases suggest that the sexual conduct of black officers drew closer scrutiny *because* of the racial anxieties that surrounded their military positions in a time when insurgents struggled to define the parameters of future political power. Allegations of sexual immorality became a tool to undercut the honor of prominent military men of color.

The Racial Meanings of Military Rank on the Eve of Independence

The series of trials by court-martial of black officers revealed a clear racial double standard of military honor. This double standard shattered the key assumption undergirding revolutionary masculinity—that men, regardless of race, could demonstrate their manhood through military service. Instead, the campaign against majasería revealed that black manhood was always provisional, contingent on the constant demonstration of compliance to evolving masculine ideals, and subject to the approval of white men. Importantly, white men were largely exempt from the same standards, routinely flouting their soldierly duties, committing crimes against the revolution, and engaging in extramarital sex without facing meaningful consequences.[117]

The timing of these trials by court-martial was unmistakable. Allegations of majasería initially emerged as a response to military setbacks accompanying Weyler's military offensives, but the courts-martial continued through a period of important political developments within the revolution. By summer 1897 insurgent leaders prepared to elect delegates to the constitutional assembly mandated by the 1895 Constitución de Jimaguayú. The Yaya Assembly, as the meeting was called, catalyzed a frenzied struggle among insurgent officers over political authority. Revolutionary masculinity theoretically afforded all officers, regardless of race or class, a chance to wield political authority on par with their military merit. Ultimately, however, the campaign against majasería had tarnished the reputations of the highest-ranking black officers in the Fourth Corps. White insurgents evinced their discomfort with extending the meritocratic principle to the political realm, and all of the Fourth Corps' delegates to the Yaya Assembly were prominent white officers.[118]

Two key developments outside of Cuba exacerbated this retrenchment of racial hierarchy within the insurrection. First, at precisely the same time as insurgents prepared to revise their constitution, the assassination of Spanish prime minister Antonio Cánovas del Castillo in August 1897 set in motion a political transition in Spain. Spanish voters ushered out the conservative government of Cánovas's successor Marcelo de Azcárraga Ugarte, and reelected Liberals under Práxedes Mateo Sagasta. Assuming power in October 1897, Liberals promptly dismissed Weyler as captain-general. His replacement, Manuel Blanco, vowed to bring peace to the island. He ended reconcentration and downgraded Spanish military operations. Responding in part to US pressure to end the war, the Spanish government granted Cuba autonomy under a new constitution in November. The island's first autonomous government took power in January 1898 with elections scheduled for May.[119] Insurgents responded to Spain's softening posture by declaring that no half measures would sway them from securing absolute and immediate independence.

Second, as insurgents stood on the precipice of victory, the explosion of the battleship Maine in February 1898 gave new direction to US foreign policy toward Cuba, which had previously centered on the non-recognition of insurgent belligerency. The explosion gave the United States a pretext to help "liberate" Cubans from Spanish rule, as expansionists had sought since the late eighteenth century, and as many sympathetic US Americans had demanded since the beginning of reconcentration.[120] Likely recognizing the dangers to Cuban sovereignty posed by the long history of US designs on the island, Republican Senator Henry M. Teller composed an amendment to the Joint Resolution. The Teller Amendment, as it came to be known, placed conditions on US military intervention in Cuba, forcing the expansionist nation to renounce any claim over the island's sovereignty. US president McKinley signed the legislation on April 20, 1898.[121] The war commenced the following day with a US naval blockade of Cuba's major harbors. At the same time, US forces also arrived in the Philippines, Guam, and Puerto Rico. By early June US troops, including all four of the US army's black regiments—the 24th and 25th Infantry as well as the 9th and 10th Cavalry—landed in eastern Cuba.

While many insurgents viewed the US intervention as an unjust intrusion in their anticolonial struggle, men less committed to the ideal of absolute and immediate independence welcomed it with open arms. Over the last months of the war, almost ten thousand new recruits poured into the Cuban army—nearly two hundred in the Brigade of Cienfuegos alone.[122] These Cuban deserters, former Spanish soldiers, Autonomists, and noncombatants (pacíficos), many of whom were educated, white urban professionals, likely sought to take advantage of the impending defeat of Spain by joining the winning side. Insurgent leaders, for their part, welcomed them "with the utmost benevolence," granting amnesty to all except violent criminals.[123] This onslaught of last-minute enlistments underscored a general consensus that military service was essential, or at the very least highly desirable, for future claims to political power.

The decision by the PRC to reward formal education with officer rank disproportionately gave official impetus to longstanding preferences for elite social standing and formal education. After all, white officers had celebrated "illustrious and educated young men" and "enlightened" chiefs as some of the revolution's finest representatives.[124] However, the official order further blurred the meanings of military rank by rewarding predominantly wealthy, educated, white new recruits simply by virtue of their social status and education, and not their actual military service.[125] At least five men who joined the Brigade of Cienfuegos in 1898 reached the rank of first or second sergeant, and one reached the rank of sub-lieutenant, promotions which many darker, poorer, and less educated enlistees did not reach after three years of battle.[126] In addition to provoking considerable anger among insurgent men with longer records of service, this readjustment reinforced social status over merit in the final round of promotions.[127]

Most importantly of all, these racial adjustments in the Fourth Corps offered a convenient gendered justification for racial exclusion in postwar politics. By culling black men from officer ranks and denying them access to the accoutrements of respectability, white officers forged an important military foundation for black political exclusion. If military rank measured military merit, then the overwhelming whiteness of the officers of the Fourth Corps surely indicated that white men were most deserving of political power. The contentious struggles to define the racial parameters of political authority are the subject of the next section.

Part II

From Brave Soldiers to New Men?

Claiming Martial Manhood during the Transition from Intervention to Occupation, 1898–1899

CHAPTER FOUR

"To Manage with Virility Our Own Affairs"

Defining the New Man between Military Intervention and Occupation

THE END OF THE SPANISH-CUBAN-AMERICAN WAR IN AUGUST 1898 brought four centuries of Spanish colonial rule to an end. Cuban insurgents, now veterans, celebrated the defeat of Spain as the culmination of thirty years of armed anticolonial struggle and, most importantly, as the redemption of Cuban manhood from feminized colonial subjugation. These men now faced new challenges, however. They had to transform their war-torn island into an independent republic, and convert masses of colonial subjects into citizens. They also had to negotiate a new imperial presence: that of the United States.

The grandiose feat of building the Cuban republic required a new kind of manly leadership, one with unwavering commitment to the values of the revolution. In the words of one patriot, this new masculine figure would consolidate Cuba's hard-earned independence, allowing Cuban men to "manage with virility our own affairs." Once in power, his task would be to preserve Cuban freedom and guarantee "the happiness and aggrandizement of the nascent democratic Republic."[1] Nobody was better suited to carry out these lofty goals than the very men who had risked their lives to secure Cuban independence in the first place.

From the ashes of the Liberating Army, the New Man was born. Veterans envisioned their military service as proof of their manly virtue. They presumed that veteran status would translate to some form of public authority after the war—at very least respectable, gainful employment, but preferably political enfranchisement. Yet, for high-stakes positions of political leadership, veteran status alone proved insufficient. One prominent white veteran who served in Santa Clara Province described some of the additional qualities a veteran needed in order to be considered fit for political power: "It is indispensable that the men who direct the Government have three things: honor, honor and honor."[2] The entire premise of revolutionary masculinity involved the redefinition of honor as a function of merit, specifically military service. Many veterans continued to privilege military merit, measured most tangibly by rank, as the best indicator of manhood. Veteran officers believed that they had proved their honor through their leadership roles and manly military authority during the war, which in turn had vested them with the executive skills and revolutionary credentials necessary to take the reins of government. They invoked the concept of martial manhood to frame their military leadership as the strongest credential for political power after the war.[3] Officers thus defined the New Man in their image, as a veteran officer-turned-political elite.

Rank proved to be a problematic indicator of military merit. Although it theoretically reflected a meritocratic measure of a man's military service, in practice, the Cuban army's military hierarchy reproduced white privilege. Racialized assumptions about military authority and patriarchy had enabled white officers to prosecute key black officers during the campaign against majasería and to reward formally educated (white) professionals with officer rank despite their military inexperience. These racial double standards not only demonstrated that colonial notions of honor as status still carried significant weight among veterans. They contributed to a disproportionately white military leadership. A small number of black men successfully infiltrated the upper echelons of military leadership, and some of them had managed to dodge the campaign against majasería. However, in effect, the persistence of this implicitly racialized notion of masculine authority largely circumscribed the privileged title of New Man to white veteran officers.

White officers' claims to martial manhood failed to gain traction among more privileged groups of men in postwar Cuba. Within the revolution itself, the men of the Cuban Revolutionary Party (PRC) considered their civil service to Cuba Libre a stronger foundation for postwar political power than veterans' military service. Because separatists generally came from more privileged racial and socioeconomic backgrounds and, particularly after the 1895 death of José Martí, embodied more conservative social and political values, their vision of political fitness would produce an even more racially exclusive and elite leadership than white veterans imagined. For them, a white man's wealth, education, social standing, and political experience trumped armed combat as a qualifier for postwar political power.[4]

Beyond veterans and separatists, several powerful groups dismissed the value of revolutionary credentials entirely as a foundation for political power. Santa Clara's wealthy sugar elite, pacíficos, Autonomists, and former Loyalists—including Spanish army regulars, Spanish volunteers, and guerrillas—formed part of a broad coalition of men, who vehemently rejected revolutionary political power in favor of a prolonged or indefinite US presence in Cuba. More conservative members of this group advocated US annexation of Cuba as the only way to guarantee order and stability. More moderate sectors sought to retain recently elected Autonomists in political power. These men, whom I call opponents of separatist rule, grew to be an increasingly vocal and powerful influence on US military personnel. Their opposition to veterans helped crystallize the racial and cultural preconceptions white US military officials already held about the men of the Cuban army.

In Santa Clara Province, US officials initially resisted turning over political power to men with any level of involvement in the insurrection, but they were particularly suspicious of veterans of the multiracial Cuban army. The few black veterans who had reached and maintained officer status largely faced exclusion from regional politics. Some scholars have argued that white veterans transitioned more easily from military rank to civilian authority.[5] However, this chapter shows that white veterans, too, struggled to access postwar political power.

At the core of veterans' initial marginalization from postwar political power were competing conceptions of whiteness. White veterans occupied a privileged racial position within Cuban society, however many US officials did not consider them white by virtue of their Spanish heritage and Catholic faith.[6] For US officials, whiteness presumed Anglo-Saxon lineage and Protestant faith, both considered critical tenets of civilization. In turn only civilized societies could produce real men, with this true manhood understood to be a precondition of citizenship.[7] US officials cited the supposed excitability, tendency toward revolution, and personal irresponsibility of so-called Latin races to disparage even the highest-ranking, most prominent white veterans as unfit for political power. US officials alleged that these qualities rendered white veterans too unstable and politically radical to safeguard peace and order. These negative attitudes informed policies by which US military officials excluded Cuban veterans from entering the cities and assuming political power immediately after the war.[8] The reproduction of the old political order during the early period of US rule effectively re-inscribed veterans' political subordination under a new regime and thwarted their claims to New Man status.

I argue that white veterans confronted this new challenge to their manhood by attempting to prove their capacity for self-government, a process they enacted through the performance of whiteness. They recognized whiteness as an implicit precondition of manhood and national self-determination under US rule, but they overwhelmingly rejected the notion of civilization as an exclusively Anglo-Protestant domain. Rather, white veterans cultivated a white masculine identity grounded in their honorable military service, which they envisioned as proof of both their executive abilities and their elite social status. They protested their political exclusion as an unjust denial of their rights as (white) men and honorable veterans of the war.

Performing whiteness under US rule caught white veterans between their ties of cross-racial military solidarity and their supposed responsibility to preserve racial order. Some New Men embraced the latter duty, representing themselves as guarantors of the racial order by appointing white men to fill administrative vacancies and demanding that black veterans return to work in the cane fields. Nevertheless, at least some white veterans distinguished between racial hierarchy and total exclusion of black men. Drawing on the racially universalizing rationale of revolutionary masculinity, these newly appointed New Men funneled the soldiers formerly under their command into local jobs under their authority. By concentrating a small number of black veterans in the lowest-ranking and most poorly paid positions, New Men created a local administrative hierarchy that mirrored and intensified the racial power structures that had defined the revolution. However, this example of New Men's military patronage represented a small nod toward revolutionary masculinity's theoretical racial inclusivity, one that put them at odds with US military officials.

"He Who Does Not Work, Does Not Deserve Compassion"

In the weeks and months after the cessation of hostilities, the veterans of the Fourth Corps confronted what must have been a disappointing first glimpse at peace. Three years of war had laid waste to the central Cuban countryside.

Reconcentration had all but eliminated subsistence agriculture. Veterans, poor and working-class in their majority, lacked access to basic rations and clothing. The Cuban army's inability to pay soldiers for their services and the lack of formal gainful employment left thousands of veterans in the most profound destitution.[9] One white central Cuban chief noted that the ordinary soldier was "hungry and covering his flesh with rags."[10] This bleak postwar economic situation forced many veterans to accept aid during this transitionary period.

The dynamics of postwar relief evinced key tensions between revolutionary support for white veteran officers as New Men and US suspicions about their political fitness. Initially, numerous patriotic societies across central Cuba directed much of the postwar relief effort in Santa Clara Province. As they had during the war, these benevolent acts exacerbated existing racial and class privileges within the Fourth Corps. The limited provisions patriotic societies sent consistently benefited the army's white officer elite to the detriment of black officers and soldiers, who were disproportionately marginalized from vital channels of assistance. The charitable activities of the elite white woman patriot "La Cubanita" in Cienfuegos, for instance, materially benefited the prestigious white officers with whom the women maintained correspondence. These men benefited tangibly from their relationships with Rita, often receiving packages containing luxury goods like chocolate for individual consumption alongside items for collective benefit such as clothes and medicine. Moreover, even items that conceivably could have been deemed necessities like hammocks, boots, and clothing, were often requested by the club's elite male beneficiaries in terms of their own individual need, rather than for collective use. One white officer, for example, requested a wallet, a fresh set of clothes, shoes, and a holster, items that would allow him to maintain a clean and respectable appearance, and contributed to his reestablishment as a respectable middle-class man in postwar life.[11]

Moreover, many patriotic clubs preferred to throw lavish parties and banquets to honor prominent white officers, rather than sending aid to the thousands of destitute men mobilized in the countryside. One veteran of elite pedigree condemned "superficial" patriots for wasting "money on parties and foolishness." He opined that it was their moral obligation as elites to feed and clothe those who are "dying of hunger" and "have suffered privation and calamities."[12] Similarly, another patriot argued that devoting resources to anything other than helping impoverished soldiers, widows, and families would be akin to "dancing on the blood of our brothers." Several patriotic societies passed resolutions to limit these frivolous expenditures and focus on sending aid.[13]

Few people of African descent benefited directly from these elite women's patriotic clubs. In early 1898 another white officer wrote to La Cubanita, requesting aid for a "young man of color called Joaquín, of your same last name," who had likely been the family's servant before the war. "This comrade," the officer wrote, "finds himself in a very bad state" and is in desperate need of "a change of clothes to fight against the weather." He suggested Rita send the clothes to him, with a note "for Joaquín." The white officer invoked Joaquín's manly bravery and self-sacrifice in his appeal, observing that Joaquín had "lost everything" and "still suffers somewhat from the wound" he had sustained earlier in the war.[14] When no clothing had arrived by April, the white officer reiterated his request. His rationale was revealing: "I want him to see that we do not have privileges."[15] This very logic betrays that privilege did define the experience of men on the battlefield, as he attempted to conceal his own racial privilege by constructing a counter-example. There is little evidence that the club honored the exceedingly rare request on behalf of this black soldier, or any others.[16]

Even officer rank failed to save black veterans from the uneven distribution of aid. One of the Fourth Corps' highest-ranking black officers, Major General José González Planas complained that he had been excluded from vital networks of patriotic assistance after the war, even though he was stationed near his benefactor and maintained correspondence with her.[17] He noted that his men were denied much-needed rations while having their promotions delayed, despite having "been perhaps the one [unit] which has worked the hardest on the battlefield," and whose "abnegation and discipline, few had matched." He lamented that "in Las Villas, there has not been another [brigade] that has registered more suffering nor more military deeds."[18] In light of these "cruel arbitrarities," the sharp pangs of hunger threatened to disband the force.[19] Simultaneously, the white chief of the Fourth Corps, Francisco Carrillo, allegedly hoarded resources for himself and his white subordinate, major general José Miguel Gómez.[20]

The uneven distribution of patriotic charity suggested that racial background likely informed insurgent leaderships' perceptions of which men needed and deserved assistance. After all, access to clean clothing, shoes, and other personal necessities helped legitimize the status, rank, and authority of the beneficiaries. These items were not only tangible symbols of these men's patriarchal authority over elite women. They also buttressed veterans' claims to public authority by making it possible to visibly distinguish men of elite status from ordinary soldiers. These were powerful arguments as white veterans struggled to convince US military officials that they were the rightful bearers of postwar authority.[21] Black men's exclusion from these benefits, by contrast, only exacerbated already prevalent ideas that "half naked," "barefoot," and "ragged" black soldiers were unworthy of political power.[22]

In the months after the war, the United States contributed to these existing relief efforts, joining Cuban organizations and dozens of US-based charities and religious missionaries. Between the end of the war and June 1899, the US military distributed over two hundred thousand rations in the jurisdiction of Cienfuegos alone.[23] However, US officials quickly abandoned support for these humanitarian activities. Rather than acknowledging the need for temporary assistance in the wake of a destructive war, US authorities claimed that veterans' destitution stemmed from their unmanly aversion to work. This assumption allowed them to denigrate veterans' acceptance of aid as evidence of their faltering masculinity.

US planters and military officials alike criticized veterans for accepting aid, claiming this action evinced their lack of manly qualities and their unfitness for political power. One wealthy estate owner synthesized the "prevailing" view that accepting alms "reduces the *condition of man*."[24] James H. Wilson, who later became US military governor of Matanzas and Santa Clara wrote that in offering rations the United States was "fostering a habit of dependence upon paternal government by actual charity or by employment in public works."[25] Dismissing the existence of any real destitution, another military official proclaimed that the people of Santa Clara had resorted to "professional begging" to take advantage of US generosity.[26]

Critics also claimed that Cuban men's alleged reliance on charity prevented them from assuming their masculine responsibility to work. Wilson claimed that doling out aid had the effect of "weaning the laborer from his habits of toil in the fields; taking from him the independence whose benefits we are constantly preaching."[27] An article in the *New York Times* claimed that government rations "demoralize" the poor and "prevent them from seeking employment."[28] One US philanthropist in Santa Clara went to the extreme of equating Cuban men's reliance on charity with social death.[29] He declared that "a man who is capable should work to live; he who does not work, does not deserve compassion: he should die."[30] At the root of this disdain for charity was the assumption that a man's duty was to earn his own subsistence. A man who did not work failed to fulfill his responsibilities to his family and to society at large. If veterans could not prove their economic self-sufficiency, they had failed as men, and certainly were unprepared for political power.[31]

Some military officials and property owners sought to ameliorate the "harmful" effects of charity by obliging indigent veterans to work for aid that had been donated to them. In postwar Trinidad, where ten people died each day from starvation, the US military commander boasted: "I have had the people earn their rations by working, street cleaning, etc., deeming this better than merely giving away food. In this way I have been able to secure a great deal of valuable work." Laborers employed by the Sanitary Department in Trinidad were "paid nothing but a day's rations for a day's work." Even officers and soldiers of the Cuban army who "walk the beat during the hot hours of the day" and during the night received as their only pay the "surplus rations" of nearby US troops.[32] Similarly, the managers at Constancia estate claimed to "help" the poor by allowing them to work in the fields to keep up the "appearance" that the aid was in "recompense for work."[33] While Cuban philanthropists envisioned charity as a mechanism to support white veterans' claims to political power, US authorities judged Cuban veterans' acceptance of aid as evidence that even white officers lacked the masculine self-reliance necessary for self-government.

These unfavorable attitudes toward Cuban acceptance of aid formed one of the pillars of an emerging US contempt for their Cuban allies. US military officials seemed to treat Spaniards with greater respect and consideration than they did Cubans.[34] Cuban veterans across Santa Clara Province complained of insults, racial epithets, and violent attacks perpetrated against them by US soldiers, some of whom even destroyed and desecrated Cuban flags.[35] US officials prohibited Cuban soldiers from entering the cities, judging "that the relations were too strained between Cubans and Spaniards to render such a course either desirable or safe."[36] Yet, they allowed Spanish soldiers to march into cities they had "so honorably defended" to "save the honor of Spanish arms" rather than being "humiliated and [having] their bravery depreciated."[37] Even though the entire premise of the Spanish-American War had been to avenge Spanish cruelties, after the war, US military officials rapidly shifted their perception of Spaniards from murderous enemies to an "unconquered and unvanquished" army of equals. They seemed to befriend Spaniards, sometimes accepting gifts such as the "handsome Spanish flag" given to one US officer in Cienfuegos.[38] The discursive emasculation of Cuban veterans and redemption of Spanish military honor helped justify a stronger US role in what proved to be an arduous, protracted transition from Spanish to Cuban sovereignty.

"Our Negroes Will Work as Before in the Cane-Fields"

US officials' gendered disdain for charity was directly tied to their notion that an ordinary man's social value was rooted in his productive labor. In this regard, few Cubans could disagree that some form of work was central to being a good man. However, ideas about what form that productive labor would take varied widely according to the racial and social status of the man. For the vast, racially heterogeneous masses of the Fourth Corps, most of whom came from rural, agricultural backgrounds, the most practical aspiration for postwar life lay in independent farming. After all, like their counterparts across Latin America and the Caribbean, men envisioned their military service as the foundation for claiming the manly rights and privileges previously denied to them, such as carrying a firearm and some degree of upward social mobility that would carry them beyond the cane fields.[39]

Some veterans argued that this form of productive labor offered an honorable future for Cuban men. Indeed, one white separatist suggested that the redemption of Cuban men from their feminized colonial status lay in the virtue of independent farming. He envisioned the ideal Cuban man as "a robust and agile young man," his "forehead wrapped with the revolutionary hat," standing "erect over an immense cultivated field, stepping on a broken chain," symbolizing Spanish rule. He straddled revolutionary tradition symbolized by the "redemptive machete, hanging at his side," and productive agricultural labor, represented by his grip on "the helm of a plow, driven deep into the generous soil."[40] Implicitly tied to the possibility of rural land ownership, independent farming (likely an allusion as well to male fecundity) would help reconstruct the prosperity of the country and transform peasants into economically self-reliant citizens.

Although independent agriculture promised to transform impoverished veterans into productive citizens, most Cuban veterans lacked the capital necessary to establish their own farms. One US official remarked that the ordinary veteran or countryperson had "never been educated to anything but plantation work, and has not at present the means with which to work small farms independently."⁴¹ Recognizing these facts, men from across the socioeconomic and political spectrums noted the need for some form of assistance to help reintegrate veterans into postwar life. One prominent white veteran officer called for full payment of Cuban veterans to facilitate their return to agriculture. He recommended that the program give priority to the veteran-patriarchs "who have served the longest," because these men had "suffered the most" and are in more dire need of "gaining their sustenance and that of those dependent upon them."⁴² He argued that facilitating veterans' return to productive labor was crucial for economic recovery and the democratic government.

Other veterans advocated for an agricultural bank to lend money, tools, and other farming implements to encourage political stability and economic prosperity. One white veteran officer claimed that such aid would help rebuild the country and reincorporate veterans under the "shelter of formal work, which is worth infinitely more than the indefinite alms, creator of the disaffection to work." More than the practical benefits of putting men to work, an agricultural center would promote "the responsibility of citizenship, extinguishing in the free man the feeling" of enslavement, while also favoring "individual independence" and the stability of the republic.⁴³

These men reframed the debate on the gendered implications of assistance. Early on, wealthy white patriots feared that accepting charity from the US would discredit Cuban men, transforming them into puppets in exchange for "a stomach full of cornmeal," or worse, that it would come at the expense of "the respect and affection of the [US American] ally."⁴⁴ However, veterans retorted that payment for military service and agricultural loans could not be confused with dependency, nor an aversion to work. These exchanges, which veterans had *earned*, actually facilitated their transition to productive labor. As one patriot explained, while accepting aid would "surely not be dignified when we can usufruct the goods of our very fertile soil," temporary assistance in the form of loans should be "permitted and tolerated" to facilitate poor men's return to work. After all, their obligation as men was "to think of the lives of our children, of the dignity of the Cuban name," which required returning to work.⁴⁵ By naming the distribution of money and resources as payment or loans, white veterans attempted to remove the emasculating stigma of dependency from these exchanges.

US military officials refused to accept these arguments in favor of gainful employment in independent agriculture, just as they had dismissed white officers' claims to political authority on the basis of their alleged unmanly dependence on charity. Rather, the military government implemented policies that favored the economic recovery of plantation owners, whose enormous profits relied on the exploitation of a large, pliable, unorganized rural work force. The US government heaped hundreds of millions of dollars upon Cuba's wealthiest residents in the form of "indemnity" for property destroyed during the insurrection through the Spanish Claims Commission. Some of the biggest beneficiaries of this policy were the wealthiest members of Cuban society: native and naturalized US citizens who owned sugar plantations.[46]

At the same time, US military officials reduced the distribution of rations and refused to establish an agricultural bank in Santa Clara, ensuring that veterans lacked access to lines of credit necessary to buy land and become economically independent.[47] Against the historical backdrop of recent slave emancipation, these policies disproportionately impacted people of African descent, who had constituted the main labor force on central Cuba's sprawling sugar plantations and usually lacked the resources necessary to establish their own farms. Denying assistance to rural families placed material limits on what one US official disparagingly called the black Cuban's supposed "instinct of land ownership."[48] This policy reinforced the pre-abolition racial hierarchy by precluding rural families from gaining economic independence through independent farming.

It is perhaps unsurprising that US officials attempted to thwart black veterans' aspirations for gainful employment in favor of securing a labor force for (US-owned) plantations. However, white separatists threw their support behind these policies to prove their political fitness by performing whiteness through their support for the racial hierarchy. Most famously, Bartolomé Masó, a white patriot who had been elected president of the provisional government of Cuba in 1897, called for black veterans to return to their inferior prewar social positions. He assured US military officials that "our negroes will work as before [the war] in the cane-fields, and I see no reason to anticipate trouble from them."[49] While Cuban men of all colors had the masculine obligation to work, Masó articulated a clear hierarchy in the kinds of jobs blacks and whites should perform, which mirrored and reinforced existing patterns of racial inequality.

Masó's promise that black men would resume their prewar social subordination seemed more than likely considering the abysmal employment prospects in postwar central Cuba. One US military official observed that "able-bodied men" near the cities, sugar plantations, and public works projects could have found limited work in manual labor, however the wages were "too small to enable the laborer to save money enough to become independent."[50] After all the large *ingenio* owners tended to pay "the ordinary laborer not more than sufficient to supply his daily needs."[51] General distaste for plantation work was reflected in a rural unemployment rate of around 57 percent.[52] Nevertheless, the lack of alternatives as well as US officials' refusal to establish an agricultural bank forced many rural dwellers to be "swallowed up in the big plantations."[53] Men who resumed their prewar occupations in the sugar industry once again subjected themselves to the perpetual indebtedness, humiliation, and dependence inevitably accompanying the poorly paid, back-breaking, and seasonal labor. Men who rejected plantation work often remained unemployed and destitute.

Black veterans were among the hardest hit by elite insistence on plantation work. While some veterans returned to the plantations, others—among whom were hundreds of formerly enslaved people—flatly refused to accept a figurative return to prewar racial subordination. After all, they knew that black men were usually relegated to the most menial and poorly remunerated work.[54] Some black veterans may have demonstrated their rejection by simply refusing to take jobs on plantations. Greater than half the workforce of Central Soledad had been black in the 1880s, but it had dwindled to only 39 percent by 1899.[55] Instead, some black veterans held out for gainful employment on par with their military rank.

Law enforcement offered one of the most realistic of black veterans' postwar employment prospects. Between the end of the war and the first months of the occupation, "armed insurgents, principally blacks," simply appointed themselves as local law enforcement officials in 350 interior towns across the province as a temporary extension of their military service.[56] One US official, who disparagingly called veterans' police work "voluntary guard duty," bragged that he "at all times declined to recognize the Cuban army." Consequently, these men remained without remuneration "except voluntary contributions from the communities."[57] The ongoing destitution of these veterans forced them to resort to their own devices to secure payment for their services by "taxing" local residents.[58]

Opponents of separatist rule quickly expressed their horror that veterans, particularly black ones, had assumed local authority of their own volition.[59] The manager of one US-owned estate complained of a "small detachment of Cuban troops" stationed near his estate who were "more detrimental than useful," claiming that "we are compelled against our will to furnish them quarters, clothing and food, not daring to refuse their demands for fear of their deviltry."[60] One wealthy North American planter remarked that the veterans were "collecting taxes and managing affairs quite independent of other authority."[61] These actions evoked fears that black veterans might be unwilling to return to their prewar social places.

What most preoccupied opponents of separatist rule was the fact that black veterans remained armed and mobilized in their military units. Veterans' self-declared authority heightened fears about postwar political violence. Cuban veterans initially "showed a disposition to wreak vengeance" on Spaniards and especially guerrillas—Cuban-born Loyalists who served in Spain's informal militias and performed "any sort of 'dirty' work not relished by regular troops."[62] Violent revenge attacks against Spaniards and Loyalists apparently persisted well after the evacuation of Spanish forces.[63] One Spanish commander at Cienfuegos informed US military officials that former guerrillas had suffered various "acts of violence" at the hands of Cuban veterans.[64] One Cuban shot a guerrilla accused of selling an insurgent's flesh as meat during the war. Spaniards and Loyalists were hacked to death or shot.[65] Stories of corpses "terribly mutilated with machetes" and other stories of violent harassment of Spaniards continued to surface for months to come.[66] Consequently, Spaniards and Loyalists also wrote to John C. Bates, US commander of the Department of Santa Clara, requesting that "American soldiers preserve better order," and "guarantee the lives and interests of the Spaniards."[67] To make matters worse, in early 1899, Bates ordered planters to disband their private guard forces.[68]

With no armed protection in the face of such alleged racial disorder and political tumult, opponents of separatist rule demanded US military protection. In March 1899 Bates ordered an investigation of conditions in rural Santa Clara.[69] The lengthy report barely mentioned disorder between Soledad estate and Hormiguero (both owned by US citizens).[70] The central Cuban countryside was defined not by crime but rather by the sheer destitution of rural dwellers. Black veterans, including "a Cuban negro lieutenant, with 15 men of similar color" and a one-eyed officer of "villainous countenance," attempted to scrape together a living through police duty. Four hundred other Cuban soldiers struggled to feed themselves by cultivating abandoned fields. The investigator urged insurgents to find work at the local sugar plantations, rather than awaiting a "payout" from the United States.[71] He also recommended a small detachment of US troops be dispatched to the area to show that the US has "assumed control of Cuba and that depredations such as cane burning and cattle stealing will not be tolerated."[72] Bates heeded the advice, dispatching US troops to sugar mills in early 1899.[73]

US officials' disparaging opinions about veterans' faltering manhood materialized into policies that revitalized social hierarchy along racial, national, and political lines. At the very apex of the hierarchy were wealthy North American planters, who collectively benefited from hundreds of millions of dollars in indemnification through the Spanish Claims Commission. At the very bottom of society were black veterans, whom US officials, planters, and even white separatists corralled back into exploitative plantation work. White veterans hovered somewhere between these two groups, too unmanly in their acceptance of charity to qualify for political power.

"Thief of Its Own Gift"

By the inauguration of the US military occupation in January 1899, US officials' negative views of white veterans' alleged dependence on charity and aversion to work began to crystalize into a decidedly racial narrative. Drawing on their service in the US Civil War (1861–1865), and subsequent Indian Wars, US officials—irrespective of their prior Union or Confederate affiliation—perceived Cubans as yet another feminized nonwhite population in need of civilizing.[74] They employed a wide range of insulting metaphors, equating black and white Cubans indiscriminately with African Americans, Native Americans, children, women, savages, and criminals.[75]

One of the most vocal critics of Cuban men was Mississippi-native and Confederate veteran, Walter B. Barker, a former US Consul at Sagua la Grande, and subsequently captain of the port in Cienfuegos.[76] Though initially venerated for his charitable treatment of reconcentrados during the war, Barker became known for his abusive treatment of Cuban veterans under US rule.[77] His virulent anti-black sentiment proved central to his views of Cuban men. At the outset of the occupation, he erroneously claimed that "the colored element is largely in excess of the whites," because "the sole survivors" of reconcentration "proved to be negro[e]s."[78] Barker argued that even Cubans who claimed to be white were not "equal to self-government." In a single letter, he labeled them "dishonest," "weak-minded," "indolent," and "improvident," among other emasculating insults. The Cuban man, he claimed in the same letter, was "as tractable as a child," "wholly lacking in executive

Figure 4.1. Walter B. Barker. Source: Machado, *¡Piedad! Recuerdos de la Reconcentración*, 32.

ability," and manifested "no further interest than to secure a lucrative position with little or no work."⁷⁹ Like the Native Americans who were always "crying for a new Agent and more beef," the Cubans "are ever clamoring for a new Governor-General, less work and more 'dinero,'" Barker wrote patronizingly.⁸⁰ His depiction of Cuban veterans as uniformly racially degenerate, intellectually inferior, and selfish provided a powerful counterpoint to their visions of themselves as honorable war heroes.

Amid these unflattering racial analogies, US military officials refused to recognize service in the Cuban army as legitimate evidence of martial manhood. One US official even doubted the military merit of the largely white Cuban troops under José Miguel Gómez, one of the Fourth Corps' most prestigious white veterans. He diminished their military service as mainly involving skills of farmers and ranchers and certainly "not as difficult to them as might appear." The US official even asked Gómez himself if his rank was "in

Figure 4.2. John C. Bates. Source: McIntosh, *The Little I Saw of Cuba*, 46.

recognition of active service," a question that betrayed certain doubts regarding the meaning of insurgent rank.[81]

Negating veterans' military service provided a rationale for excluding them from political office during the occupation. Bates purportedly took "fitness into consideration first" when filling vacant positions of local authority.[82] He judged Spaniards and especially Autonomists to be "generally worthy and capable men, sincerely interested in the maintenance of order, in the reconstruction of civil government and in the re-establishment of industry and commerce." These political moderates "performed their duties loyally and faithfully, maintaining perfect order, as far as was within their power, relieving suffering and want in their respective jurisdictions."⁸³ Consequently, veterans remained marginalized from local political power.

The persistence of Spanish and Autonomist power was nowhere more egregious than among the "disgraceful" appointment of judges. Cuban veterans "felt a great deal disappointed in seeing so many of the judges of the old gang of 'Weyler and Blanco' reappointed." They "expected new men of better history" in these positions, preferably ones with revolutionary credentials.⁸⁴ One of most controversial appointments was that of Juan Venancio Schwiep, whom US authorities retained as district judge of Remedios and later promoted. Veterans were so adamant in their opposition to Schwiep that even US authorities found it difficult (though not impossible) to justify the retention of such a "discredited fucker [*cogedor*]."⁸⁵ Likewise, the continuation of Spaniards in local policing resulted in grave injustices for Cuban veterans and seemingly limitless impunity for Spanish offenders.⁸⁶

US military officials also overlooked white veterans for vacancies on city councils, leaving the Autonomist majority firmly intact.⁸⁷ Two of Santa Clara's most politically important cities—Cienfuegos and Trinidad—in large measure lacked revolutionary representation. In one acerbic newspaper article, a veteran dismissed the new city council of Trinidad as a bunch of annexationists, Autonomists, pacíficos, and conservatives, including one of "Weyler's administrators," and an officer of the Spanish volunteers. "At the rate we are going, not a single good, dignified man remains in Cuba!" the author quipped satirically.⁸⁸ Veterans in Cienfuegos fared even worse than in Trinidad. Not a single veteran secured a position in the city council of Cienfuegos.⁸⁹

US officials' refusal to appoint veterans to positions of local authority inspired profound dissatisfaction among Santa Clara's New Men, many of whom envisioned political power as a natural extension of their racial privilege and military service. One Santa Clara newspaper published a searing indictment of US favoritism toward "the leeches of the old regime" for important local positions: "even though the flag of freedom and order waves, the administrative positions generally are still not occupied by their legitimate servants."⁹⁰ In a similar article, titled "Nuestros hombres" ("Our Men"), a critic demanded that "the men of the revolution" be allowed to assume their rightful positions at the helm of government. Although the article offered an inclusive definition of revolutionary men, which included both separatists and veterans, it urged US officials to give priority to soldiers "who, gun on shoulder, shredded their skins [*ripiaron la piel*] on the battlefield."⁹¹ Military service in the Cuban army, these men insisted, was not only a cornerstone of manhood, but also of veterans' legitimate claims to political power.

High-ranking white officers in particular voiced their disapproval of what they saw as the military government's unjust denigration of their political aspirations as New Men. White major general José de Jesús Monteagudo lamented that "in Las Villas, in essence, the politics of caste and the zealous domination that the Spanish governors practiced have not changed; what has changed is the person doing it." He claimed that Bates exhibited "blatant hostility toward us Cubans," and favored Spaniards and guerrillas, "whose hands were not at all clean of Cuban blood" for important positions of power. "Disgracefully, I did not find in General Bates the resolved, intelligent, and thoughtful man who should represent the Government of Washington," wrote a disappointed Monteagudo. "I only found the orderly military man, the irresolute and untrusting politician, the man dominated by prejudices and impediments against everything Cuban." Interestingly, Monteagudo did not disparage the US presence, but rather criticized what he viewed as Bates's failure to enforce white veterans' claims to political power. To him, Bates's refusal to acknowledge officer rank as a legitimate foundation for political power insulted white officers.[92]

Similar objections to Bates's alleged anti-veteran attitudes surfaced in other parts of Santa Clara. In Cienfuegos veterans complained that Bates held an unjustly "terrible impression" of the men who took "an active part in the war." One white veteran complained that the US military commander "feels disdain for us," considering veterans to be "incapable" and "difficult to subjugate."[93] Responding to similar challenges, another white veteran in Trinidad declared that although he was "indeed grateful to the Americans," they needed to understand that Cubans were "much easier to lead than to drive."[94] The disappointment and frustration expressed by these white veterans revealed both high expectations of the US military government as well as a strong desire for control over civil affairs—a right they argued that they had earned based on their military service.

For some disillusioned veterans, the slow political transition was evidence of the military government's bad faith regarding Cubans' political future. One critic claimed that the United States was a "thief of its own gift." They had forced Spain to relinquish sovereignty first to give "the gift of independence" to Cubans, "only later to have the pleasure of stealing it from us" by "wrongfully" assuming sovereignty over Cuba. Some prominent separatists dismissed this pessimistic view as those of a disgruntled minority, but as US rule persisted with no end date in sight, it gained more credence.[95]

US officials continued to dismiss veterans' martial manhood, but they could not exclude the men of the revolution entirely. Bates appointed a small number of white separatists and a few of the most prestigious white veterans. In Trinidad one separatist who "did not fight [*no fue al verde*]," and one veteran who could be counted among the "worthy men of real merits" obtained appointments in the city council.[96] In Cienfuegos the only representative of the revolution was Mayor José Antonio Frías. A former separatist who worked in the PRC alongside future president Tomás Estrada Palma, Frías represented the most prestigious elements of the revolution. Upon assuming the mayoral office in January 1899, Frías quickly reminded the city council of their patriotic obligation to "demonstrate that we are apt for the administration of public interests and dignified, for that matter, to build a free and independent fatherland, the supreme aspiration of the Cuban people."[97] His speech reveals just how painfully aware he and other separatists must have been about US officials' reluctance to cede local authority to them.

Race and Veterans' Public Authority

Once white separatists assumed local authority, they began to distribute secondary positions of local leadership to other revolutionaries, including some prominent veteran officers. Veterans' access to lower-ranking public office and administrative appointments hinged on their position within patron-client networks forged during the revolution, as other scholars have suggested.[98] If the Cuban veterans who acquired political appointments in the first months of US rule had one trait in common, it was that the vast majority of them were white men of prestige in their local communities.

Most black veterans of the Fourth Corps remained marginal to these crucial patronage ties. The case of Martín Reinoso suggests that racial considerations, though seldom mentioned explicitly, factored heavily into whom white separatists named to important secondary posts. A distinguished personality among the black elite of Cienfuegos, Reinoso had served as the veterinarian in the Brigade of Cienfuegos.[99] On the premise of this honorable military service, he petitioned to the city council in April of 1899 for the related position of meat inspector. One Autonomist city councilman opposed his petition, arguing that his lack of a professional title rendered him ineligible for the position: "However meritorious the services he rendered to the Patria were, as they undoubtedly are according to the recommendations he presents from various Generals," he concluded that it was "not possible legally to accede to [Reinoso's] desires."[100] Quite simply, Reinoso's military service earned him public recognition as an honorable Cuban man, but it proved insufficient to secure public office.[101] The city council voted to deny Reinoso the position, an outcome not suffered by any other candidate that year. Reinoso's unsuccessful petition reveals that the city council of Cienfuegos proved unwilling to consider apparently well-qualified black veterans even for relatively unimportant positions in municipal administration. The absence of other black applicants suggests that most black men tacitly understood the hidden racial constraints on public employment.

In order to understand why Reinoso and other veterans accepted a decision so blatantly informed by racial prejudice, it is necessary to examine the arguments for denying his application. City councilmen framed their rejection of Reinoso not in terms of his race, but rather in terms of the implicitly racialized qualities of middle-class manhood that he lacked. The emphasis on formal education over military service as the most important qualification for this job paralleled the earlier perpetuation of white privilege in the Cuban army by emphasizing attributes to which whites enjoyed greater access than men of African descent. By May only two candidates came before the city council—both were white men, neither was a veteran.[102] The selection of a white non-veteran over a black veteran suggests that black military service was less valuable than white social prestige in determining fitness for public employment—a general pattern that seemed to define postwar politics across the province.[103]

A lack of formal credentials, though cited as the main reason for rejecting Reinoso, did not seem to be an issue for white veterans. For example, Higinio Esquerra lacked formal education, yet he was still deemed capable of exercising supreme authority over the Cienfuegos Rural Guard, and later became mayor—positions with much more at stake than that of meat inspector.[104] In fact, the city council voted to fund housing for the leadership of the Brigade of Cienfuegos, including Esquerra in March 1899, while neglecting the needs of the impoverished and multiracial rank and file, who remained in squalor outside the city.[105]

Even white men with poor or no military records obtained office. The white veteran Abelardo Rodríguez, who Máximo Gómez outed as a "cowardly man," a parasite, and a majá for stealing aid sent by a patriotic women's club, had no problem securing a position in the special police.[106] Whereas the political fitness of white men, regardless of their political affiliation, could be taken for granted as a fact, men of African descent had to continuously prove their masculinity by adhering to a constantly evolving set of criteria, which in this case included formal education. The selective application of the standards of masculinity disproportionately barred black veterans from gainful government employment.

For black veterans in particular, the lack of parity between their own military achievements and their postwar economic, social, and political status constituted one of greatest failures of the revolution. Black veterans expressed their disenchantment with their postwar political exclusion in no uncertain terms.[107] One black officer who served in central Cuba recounted the injustice of his postwar unemployment and poverty: "Today after thirty years of war, of the thirteen wounds received in the camp of honor, I find myself, it is sad to confess, without resources of any kind." Worst of all, he claimed that no one could help him, because "those who were and are my compatriots . . . are as poor as I am." This black veteran's "precarious situation" obliged him to beg for charity.[108]

The exclusion of black veterans from local political power reproduced a twofold barrier to their postwar authority among the men of Santa Clara Province. First, it communicated that their military service was insufficient to qualify them for political power. They were thus barred from directing the republic they helped forge. Second, the exclusion of black men from political authority on par with their military rank closed off one of the only avenues of gainful employment potentially available to non-elite men. White men's preferential access to political power (and to formal employment more generally) enabled them not only to validate their military service and social prestige, but also to fulfill their financial obligations to their families, making it possible to keep their wives and other female kin at home. Their ability to uphold female domesticity helped these white veterans consolidate their private authority over the domestic realm. By contrast, the uneven access to formal authority and the material benefits it afforded disproportionately undermined the ability of black veterans to fulfill their duties of patriarchal manhood—protecting and providing for their families.

Amid the general racial exclusivity of local politics, the formalization of law enforcement bodies in early 1899 created new opportunities for veterans to acquire formal public authority. Bates recognized that the continued mobilization of Cuban soldiers constituted the single most significant threat to the occupying government. He suspected that these men were "very liable to give us serious trouble unless we take care of them."[109] In an effort to mitigate this supposed threat, he supported local veteran officers' demands to employ Cuban veterans in two local bodies of law enforcement: urban law enforcement bodies called municipal police under the authority of the mayor in each of Santa Clara's municipalities and a paramilitary force called the Rural Guard, which operated in the countryside under the authority of US officials and the civil governor of Santa Clara Province.[110] The reorganization of these law enforcement bodies provided a relatively cheap and effective way to incorporate these men into the state under the supervision of the military government.

During the first months of 1899, Bates convened committees in cities across Santa Clara to staff municipal police forces. These boards, composed of white US officials and members of the largely Autonomist city councils, were charged with hiring men of the "better classes," to staff urban law enforcement bodies. Committees appointed prominent white veterans as the chiefs of municipal police forces. From these positions of authority, these white veteran officers ushered their loyal subordinates into formal employment under their direction, consolidating their networks of military patronage. Due to the racially integrated nature of the Fourth Corps' rank and file, some black veterans entered these jobs—a small triumph for black men's claims to revolutionary masculinity.

The inclusion of black men in the municipal police forces apparently took US military officials by surprise.[111] The US police inspector commented directly on this point, declaring that the force in Cienfuegos contained "quite a number of negroes." Another military official described the patrolmen as "mostly negroes."[112] Although the exact number of black veterans employed cannot be determined from the available sources, police of varying degrees of African ancestry employed in Cienfuegos included Roberto Galarraga, Rogelio Celada Zayas, and Epifanio Ordoñez.[113] The police force was one of the only municipal or provincial institutions to employ significant numbers of black veterans.[114]

Data from neighboring Matanzas Province suggests that other municipal police forces similarly employed black veterans in significant numbers. Single men and veterans composed the majority of the forces in all the province's cities and towns: in a force of 473 men, 318 were veterans. The racial

Table 4.1. Police employed in selected towns in province of Matanzas, by race, 1899

	White	Black	Mulatto	Percentage of African descent
Alacranes	10	0	0	0
Bolondrón	18	5	3	30
Cabezas	10	0	1	9
Canasí	7	0	2	22
Cárdenas	46	3	2	10
Carlos Rojas	2	2	0	50
Colón	21	0	5	19
Cuevitas	9	1	2	25
Guamacaro	9	0	1	10
Jagüey Grande	12	0	1	8
Jovellanos	10	0	5	33
Macagua	4	2	3	56
Macuriges	16	2	7	36
Matanzas City	165	0	5	3
Martí	5	0	2	29
Máximo Gómez	7	0	2	22
Méndez Capote	5	1	2	38
Palmillas	9	1	3	31
Perico	5	0	1	17
Roque	10	1	0	9
Sabanilla	6	1	0	14
San José de los Ramos	6	2	2	40
Santa Ana	4	1	1	33
Unión de Reyes	5	0	0	0

Source: "Summary of Relevant Facts of the Matanzas Municipal Police," September 30, 1899, Box 19, no file, RUSA/RG 395/E 1331.

statistics varied widely across the different towns, but overall, 72 policemen or 15 percent of the men employed in municipal police forces across Matanzas were of African descent (see table 4.1). The employment of black veterans distinguished municipal police forces in Santa Clara and Matanzas from their counterparts in Havana, where policemen were generally white.[115]

US officials exerted more direct control over the Rural Guard. They sought to hire only the "fittest" applicants. Recruits had to be single, between twenty-five and thirty-five years old, literate, and "physically sound." They also had to be "temperate," and possess "good moral character," as "certified by three citizens of good standing"—criteria that required them to maintain social networks with prominent (white) citizens. In the handwritten copy of the employment criteria, appeared another qualification crossed out with a thick black line: honorable discharge from the Cuban army.[116]

US officials struggled to attract the white men they desired. Most prominent white officers refused to accept the exploitative terms of employment in the Rural Guard, expressing particular disappointment in the low pay and conditional authority Bates offered them. Rural Guardsmen were expected to provision themselves, adding additional expenses to an already poorly remunerated position.[117] The prospect of being forced to take an oath of loyalty to the military government also offended many veterans.[118] In fact, many white officers initially declined to accept permanent positions in the guard at all, a decision that largely derailed recruitment efforts. Bates explained that the men "I wanted for the chief officers of police declined to take the office at the rate of pay named in the scheme approved, and the men generally refused to take office unless their officers approved."[119] Some officers even preferred rations and clothing as payment for their temporary services, rather than such a small amount of money.

Bates attempted to make the Rural Guard more attractive to white veteran officers by expanding the number of officer positions and increasing salaries for the highest ranks (table 4.2).[120] The salary increases at the upper

Table 4.2. Pay schedules for rural guard of Santa Clara Province

Position	Monthly salary (number of positions at this rank in parentheses)	
	March 1899	April 1899
Chief	200	300
Assistant chief	125 (2)	—
Secretary	100	125
Assistant secretary	—	40 (4)
Chief of judicial district	75 (6)	200 (4)
Captains	—	100 (10)
Lieutenants	—	60 (25)
Sergeants	30 (150)	34 (50)
Policemen (guards)	25 (625)	29.50 (500)
Traveling expenses	—	665
Monthly total	21,000	21,000

Source: "General Wilson, Telegram in Regard to Organization of Rural Police in Santa Clara Province," May 8, 1899, Box 11, File 2601, USNAII/MGC/RG 140/E 3.

levels of the guard enabled US authorities to recruit white major general José de Jesús Monteagudo as chief of Santa Clara's Rural Guard. Monteagudo drew upon the multiracial Fourth Corps to staff the rest of the force. In April 1899 over 130 veterans found employment in the force "at a time when employment was difficult to obtain."[121] The number surged to six hundred by June that year, even as the salaries of ordinary guards remained inordinately low.[122]

The majority of Rural Guardsmen were white veterans. However, men of African descent composed approximately 20 percent of the force. The Rural Guard's rank structure reproduced longstanding associations between whiteness and officer rank. White veterans typically occupied well-paid leadership positions, while most black Rural Guardsmen "never held any rank."[123] There were, nonetheless, two important exceptions to the rule of white leadership in the Rural Guard. Black major general José González Planas initially served as a district chief. His son, Captain Eloy González (who would later emerge as a black activist during the early republic), commanded a post in that district. The Rural Guard, alongside the municipal police and the firemen's corps, thus formed an important early exception to the broader pattern of racial exclusion in government employment under US rule.

Opponents of separatist rule vehemently rejected the newly organized Rural Guard force, citing political and racial inadequacies. They protested that black veterans, even at the lowest levels of the Rural Guard, could never defend propertied interests. The force's few black officers, especially González Planas, became the target of considerable race prejudice.[124] Opponents of separatist rule advocated placing the Rural Guard under the command of US officers to help planters "feel more secure in their work." At the very least, they sought to rid the force of men "unfit" for authority, retaining only men of the "respectable classes," who they assumed would "maintain order" by being "constantly on the lookout for law-breakers."[125] In light of these attitudes, opponents of separatist rule sought to exclude veterans, and especially black men, from rural law enforcement.

To argue against employing veterans in rural law enforcement, opponents of separatist rule relied on two key assumptions. First, drawing on the racialized and criminalized tropes Spaniards deployed against insurgents during the war, opponents of separatist rule blamed black veterans for the destruction of private property during the war and claimed they would continue to wreak havoc on sugar estates if allowed to retain their arms. This belief was rooted less in actual occurrences than in flawed and decontextualized interpretations of insurgent military operations as wanton destruction of private property. Planters used these interpretations to portray black veterans' participation in the war as evidence of their propensity toward violence, an indication of a "barbaric" inability to control emotional impulses, a failure to observe social boundaries, and atavistic tendencies.[126] They extended these racialized claims to incriminate the revolution more generally by exaggerating the role of black men within the Cuban army, claiming central Cuban insurgent forces were "frequently, if not generally officered by blacks" and that black men were a majority in the army.[127]

Second, opponents of separatist rule assumed that ties of racial and military solidarity would lead veterans to protect other veterans, and black men to favor other black men in the enforcement of laws. The multiracial nature of the Rural Guard became increasingly problematic when the withdrawal of US volunteers in April 1899 all but eliminated the military government's direct protection of private property. If black veterans were the main criminals, then surely veterans, especially black ones, could not be trusted to enforce the laws, opponents of separatist rule deduced using racist logic.

Opponents of separatist rule fabricated the evidence they needed to support these claims of black veterans' criminality. They embellished and even invented wholesale dramatic stories of violent crimes and unrelenting attacks on private property perpetrated by unnamed black veterans. In March, Edwin F. Atkins, North American owner of Central Soledad and one of the most vocal opponents of separatist rule, voiced his unease that thousands of veterans remained armed and mobilized throughout the central Cuban countryside, in spite of the impending withdrawal of US volunteers: "Insurgents are still under arms and it looks as if they intend to remain so. If troops are withdrawn there is sure to be trouble."[128] Country towns near his estate were already "full of insurgents and idlers who go about every night followed by a mob crying 'down' with everything that doesn't please them."[129] By April he again warned of imminent trouble: "The insurgents are still armed and prepared for a row and I cannot see that any progress is being made in disarming them."[130] Wealthy planters across Santa Clara, he decried, had lost their ability to enforce their privilege by force. US newspapers echoed Atkins's alarmism, alleging that "Brigandism" was "on the increase in the country, and a reign of terror prevails in towns where no United States soldiers are quartered."[131] By casting petty crime rooted in postwar poverty as an extension of the (criminal) destruction by (black) insurgents during the war, wealthy property owners effectively conflated crime with blackness and particularly with black veterans status.[132]

US planters in central Cuba served as the primary informants for a growing number of hyperbolic stories of black criminality peppering US newspapers. One US newspaper ran a story identifying the "so-called bandits" terrorizing the countryside as "mostly negroes" who came from the East with the Invasion Force. These black veterans reportedly took "full possession of the towns outside of the railroads, and are living there during the day and robbing at night."[133] This presumptive framing of banditry as black implicitly informed countless other alarming headlines. Another newspaper article published in the United States claimed that some Cubans may say they want work, "but to loot is their delight."[134] Alarming headlines such as "Terrorized by Bandits," "Upland Country is Held by Brigands and Outlaws," and "Towns Held by Cuban Brigands" stoked fears over the allegedly rampant physical violence, threats, and murder.[135] Collectively, these stories depicted black veterans as the cause of central Cuba's postwar disorder, and Cuba as a lawless, chaotic, and savage land in dire need of US supervision.

These allusions to racialized crime gave birth to a new criminal type: the criminalized black veteran. Like ideas of majasería, the specter of the black veteran criminal depended on a racial double standard of masculine conduct. Certain actions usually associated with masculine honor, such as gun ownership, military service, public displays of authority, or even attempts to mobilize politically, were often perceived to be less legitimate and more transgressive when performed by black men. Without the perception of legitimacy, black men's everyday enactments of manhood became markers of dishonor and social deviance. Allusions to black criminality not only delegitimized the black veterans who remained mobilized in the countryside, they also undermined black Rural Guardsmen's appropriations of revolutionary masculinity to make limited claims on New Man status. By invoking black veterans' alleged racial loyalties, opponents of separatist rule essentially delegitimized black Rural Guardsmen's legitimacy as agents of law enforcement. Rather, their claims to authority served as evidence of hypermasculinity—the excesses of manly physical strength, virility, and authority, channeled toward securing personal gain rather than presumably more noble qualities of self-abnegation and self-control. In that way, these criminalizing discourses offered a powerful counterweight to black veterans' claims even to the minutest forms of public authority.[136]

This link between race and crime, which historians have posited became salient in Cuba's early republican period, actually circulated much earlier. By the US military occupation, it served as a powerful pretext to extend and expand the US presence on the island.[137] The controversy surrounding the organization of the Rural Guard foreshadowed major limits on martial manhood as veterans attempted to translate their military authority into equivalent forms of political power. The Rural Guard experiment taught US military authorities that revolutionary masculinity, though limited, remained an influential discourse even among otherwise respectable white veterans. The next chapter examines how black veterans at various degrees of integration within networks of military patronage laid claim to public authority on the basis of their military service and patriarchal roles.

CHAPTER FIVE

Testing the Racial Limits of Martial Manhood

Black Political Exclusion and Patriarchal Claims-Making

IN MAY 1899 CUBAN VETERANS IN SANTA CLARA PROVINCE WELcomed a transition in US military leadership, one they hoped would help them realize their claims on local authority. The military commander of the newly consolidated Department of Matanzas and Santa Clara, James H. Wilson, seemed quite sympathetic to veterans. He believed that his main duty was to administer the transition to Cuban self-government, a responsibility outlined in the Teller Amendment, which required the United States to relinquish claims to sovereignty over Cuba before entering the Spanish-American War in 1898.[1] Wilson criticized his predecessor, John C. Bates, for retaining local power for himself, his men, and the Autonomists and Spaniards already in office, rather than distributing it to the men of the revolution. Referring to the overzealous US officers under Bates's command, Wilson complained that "each little jackass seemed to feel he was called upon to command the people, manage their public business, and supervise their daily duties."[2] Wilson lamented that this "niggardly and improper" behavior had tainted the "high benevolence" of the United States, causing Cuban veterans to question US motives during the occupation.[3]

Whereas Bates had generally assumed that Cuban veterans were unfit for office due to their inferior racial character and political radicalism, Wilson

Figure 5.1. James H. Wilson. Courtesy of the Delaware Historical Society.

developed more nuanced racial attitudes. He rejected the popular belief that the entire Cuban population was "mongrel and constitutes a part of 'Niggerdom.'" He did hold decidedly negative views toward the island's "African" population, which he claimed was caught "in a partially developed stage of political and moral evolution."[4] Yet, Wilson seemed to hold more favorable views of Cuba's white population. Although he still held prevailing assumptions about the alleged inferiority, laziness, "bad habits," and inefficiency of the "Latin races," Wilson was skeptical of some of the more overtly anti-Latin racial views to which many of his compatriots subscribed.[5] For instance, he rejected the popular assumption that Cubans were "tropical and barbaric," inherently "revolutionary," and possessed a "temperament" that was incompatible with "Saxons."[6]

Rather, Wilson found many prominent white veterans "entirely unobjectionable" for local authority.[7] Most of the veterans he met were high-ranking white officers, often from prominent local families. These men struck Wilson as "manly, independent, patriotic fellow[s]."[8] In contrast to Bates, Wilson was open to allowing veterans into positions of civil authority, believing that "kind and generous treatment will beget kind and generous counter-treatment; open and manly friendship will beget open and manly confidence and respect."[9] Under his governorship, white veterans assumed unprecedented degrees of formal authority in local government and administration across Santa Clara Province.

Amid the seeming détente between US officials and New Men under Wilson's leadership, black veterans largely remained excluded from formal political power. In response, these men sought public authority beyond the political realm, as agents of order, labor leaders, and patriarchs. Black veterans' claims to alternate forms of political authority exacerbated local US military officials' racially driven opposition to veterans' authority. A new set of struggles emerged among various groups of Cuban veterans and US military officials at the local level. The result was a series of violent conflicts between black veterans, (white) New Men, and white US authorities, which erupted across Santa Clara Province, and also across the island more generally.[10] In this chapter, I interrogate the parameters of black men's claims to postwar public authority through a close analysis of two riots that erupted in Cienfuegos in mid-1899: a dispute in May between predominantly black workers and white US civilian employees[11] over wages owed, and a riot that erupted after black Cuban veterans confronted drunken white US soldiers over their abuses against local women in June. Both these riots involved a third group of black veterans, who rejected US men's claims to supreme authority through their roles as municipal police.

I argue that black veterans of varying degrees of incorporation in networks of military patronage deployed an expanded notion of revolutionary masculinity to lay claim to public authority. Black veterans who remained excluded from the formal structures of public employment foregrounded not only their histories of military service but also their patriarchal roles as heads of household and protectors of women to claim informal public authority. Members of the multiracial police force drew on their military service and their formal authority as law enforcement officers to position themselves as defenders of Cuban freedom in the face of the US occupation. Although these gendered claims initially resonated with some white local political elites, US authorities responded to black veterans' demands with violence against demonstrators and police. These violent encounters underscored an ongoing negotiation over black veterans' claims to manhood and, by extension, to authority in the public sphere.

Patriarchs in Protest during the May Riot

In central Cuba's major cities, gainful employment was scarce. More than half of the urban population was out of work. In the city of Cienfuegos, a full two-thirds of residents remained "without gainful occupation" in 1899.[12] Although the majority of urban dwellers struggled in central Cuba's war-torn economy, black families especially suffered as the few well-paid employment opportunities available were largely closed off to black men. The scarcity of formal gainful employment for black men trapped black families between two competing sets of social expectations. Middle-class gender ideals demanded that men provide for women and children as patriarchal heads of household, ensuring the honor and domesticity of women. Yet, with most opportunities for gainful employment closed off to black men, the burden of the family economy often fell on black women. One black activist in Cienfuegos noted that black men's inability to find gainful employment pushed black women into exploitative labor relations. Many black women secured informal work as seamstresses, for instance, where they "die at the foot of a sewing machine to earn one or two *reales* a day."[13] Lack of employment opportunities for (black) men translated into the exploitation of women, nullifying the role of Cuban men as their protectors. The obstacles black working-class men faced in securing gainful employment undercut their ability to assert authority over their female kin and communities, thereby impeding their access to the patriarchal power and male privilege enjoyed by many white men.[14] The centrality of formal employment to a man's private and familial success underscored the inseparability of the two terrains in which men enacted their postwar citizenship: the patriarchal household and the workplace.[15]

One of the few avenues of formal employment available to black men after the war was dock work. Across Cuba, dock work had long been an occupation performed mainly by men of African descent, and beginning in the mid-nineteenth century black dockworkers had begun to organize, negotiating better pay and working conditions through collective action. In the port city of Cienfuegos, black stevedores had begun mobilizing at least as early as the 1870s. By the end of the war, Cienfuegos dockworkers had a thriving union with hundreds of members, strong enough to negotiate wages and working conditions with some of the most powerful white men of the city.[16]

Under US rule, the captain of the port, under the auspices of the US quartermaster, was a significant employer of stevedores. Over the first several months of the military occupation, stevedores engaged in a series of disputes with Captain of the Port Walter B. Barker, over delayed or withheld pay—a problem generally afflicting many public employees, including teachers and police.[17] For dockworkers whose wages were already meager and sporadic, late pay posed extreme difficulties for their family economies and inhibited their fulfillment of their patriarchal duties. Stevedores responded by organizing protests to demand their wages. For example, in February 1899 the quartermaster allegedly did not have sufficient funds to pay them, causing "a mob of several hundred" to besiege his office "for days and nights justly clamoring for their pay." Barker initially sympathized with the laborers: "I can no longer face a starving people who have done work for the government and I need not say to you *should be paid*," he fumed indignantly to his boss.[18]

Despite Barker's initial sympathy, US responses to workers' demands were much less compassionate later that year. By May stevedores employed by the military government were still suffering from irregular, delayed, and withheld pay. US civilian employees at the Office of the Captain of the Port in Cienfuegos refused to pay the stevedores their wages, citing a lack of available funds.[19] On one such occasion on May 16, 1899, a large group of workers—many black, some veterans—assembled in front of the office, awaiting their pay. Lacking the funds to compensate the workers, they assured the workers that they would be paid the following day and instructed them to disperse.[20]

The promise of future payment proved unsatisfactory to these workers. According to one witness, the workers "refused to go off, saying that they wanted their money." Another witness claimed that the workers "became angry, and they said they must have their money."[21] Fearing their employer was trying to cheat them out of their money, workers insisted that they be paid that day. They declared that they "needed" the money to subsist in a war-torn economy in which the high prices of food, medicines, and other necessities made maintaining a family exceedingly difficult. This was a matter of their personal dignity. Their wages, however meager, were the fruit of their labor, and collecting the money due them was about enforcing their honor and respectability as men in the public sphere. Within the pattern of late and irregular payment, these men's access to their wages also impacted their patriarchal responsibilities, placing pressure on their family economies. Without their wages, the workers lacked the means to support themselves and their families, which materially impacted their ability to fulfill their duties as breadwinners. If wages were essential to men's status as breadwinners, then a lack of wages threatened to undermine their authority as patriarchs in the private sphere.

US employees in the Office of the Captain of the Port responded to the workers' pleas not with sympathy, but rather with violence. Barker came out of his office, "beating everyone he found" with the butt of his revolver.[22] Apparently, this propensity toward violence was not atypical for Barker, who apparently earned the name "the fighting Consul" during his time at Sagua for his habit of threatening to use his gun to get his way.[23] Barker's subordinates joined in the attacks on workers, subsequently justifying their violence as self-defense. Some of them cited the workers' alleged *threats* of violence if "not paid at once" as a justification to attack them.[24] Barker's head stevedore, Luis Lewis, testified that he saw several members of the crowd assaulting a quartermaster employee. After he told them to disperse, "several of them attacked him with knives and machetes."[25] One of the laborers even drew his dagger, another quartermaster employee claimed.

While framing workers' alleged or threatened violence as an egregious transgression against US authority, the same US officers and employees valorized their own violence against workers as a vindication of the proper social order. Captain F. N. Thevenet, Barkers's chief clerk, brandished "a stick or piece of iron of some description," with which he repelled the crowd to retire to the next block.[26] The fact that these men, as civilian employees of the military government, were not initially subject to military court-martial only incentivized the violence.

One of the most contentious exchanges involved the black veteran noncommissioned officer José Brunet, who several US employees identified as one of the leaders of the mob. US accounts described Brunet as "most violent" and emphasized his aggression and undue violence, suggesting that US officers and employees may have taken offense at his lack of deference and perceived violation of racial etiquette. Barker reported that Brunet left as ordered only to return "with his gun to enforce his demand for pay."[27] Alleging Brunet was threatening an unarmed US employee, Barker's warden, Ben Bane, fired three shots, two wounding Brunet severely.[28]

Nineteen-year-old Brunet told quite a different story of how he sustained the injuries. Testifying from his hospital bed, he swore that he left as ordered. As he walked away, a quartermaster employee bludgeoned him with a dull object, causing severe wounds on the top of his head and over his right eye. Brunet then drew his machete to defend himself from Bane, who was pointing a gun at him. He struck the warden on the arm, "with the intention of diverting the weapon," but he was unsuccessful. Bane fired twice, one bullet striking him in the left leg. Brunet fled as far as San Fernando Street, where he encountered a police officer who helped him to the hospital. Brunet identified an eyewitness to corroborate his testimony: the black second sergeant Antonio Sarría. Although US military authorities never pursued this lead, at least one white informant confirmed the brutal flogging of Brunet.[29] Hearing the shots fired, members of the multiracial municipal police force quickly rushed to the scene, only to face the same violence workers did.

This violence against Brunet and his fellow veteran-workers evinced fierce disagreement about who could legitimately exercise local authority. Black veterans like Brunet laid claim to public authority beyond the realm of formal politics on the basis of their role as patriarchal heads of household and agents of the state, respectively. Yet, to US quartermaster employees, even the simplest claims to authority, such as the workers' demands for their hard-earned wages, were unacceptable. Bolder claims to authority, like refusing to obey white men, then, warranted violence. Certainly, the white quartermaster employees seemed to conform to this logic as they enforced Brunet's racial and class subordination by force.

The May riot assumed different, seemingly irreconcilable meanings among veterans and agents of the US military government. Veterans interpreted the riot as further evidence that their US American "allies" did not respect them as the true liberators of Cuba and rejected what little authority they had been able to attain under US rule. By contrast, US employees and military officials interpreted the May riot as the embodiment of the insurrection's most troubling consequences: white and black veterans' presumption of martial manhood. Black veteran-workers' bold challenges to US personnel showed a shocking disregard for formerly accepted codes of racial etiquette. The fact that white civil authorities had employed a police force that came to the defense of the workers, not US Americans, further symbolized a revolting lack of gratitude toward the "high benevolence" of the United States.[30]

Guardians of Cuban Womanhood: Black Veterans and Patriarchal Authority

Another riot erupted on the streets of Cienfuegos on June 24, just days before payment of veterans was scheduled to commence there. Black veterans and white US employees violently clashed during San Juan Day festivities. Although none of the parties in the conflict ever explicitly invoked the terms of payment as a cause of the incident, the riot clearly erupted in response to ongoing disputes over the national, political, and most importantly racial parameters of masculine authority, which underlay much of the discontent over disbandment. In essence, the conflict foregrounded competing understandings of black veterans' manhood in postwar society and under US rule.

On the afternoon of the riot, the town streets were bustling, as people of diverse racial and national backgrounds watched the parade, sipped beverages at the saloons, and enjoyed a variety of adult entertainment. Three white US quartermaster employees, Campbell McDowell, Andrew E. Fuller, and Julian C. Baker, joined the celebration after eating in a local café and sipping bitters at a nearby saloon. "We were not drunk, but we were feeling pretty good, and we were making quite a lot of noise," remembered one of the men. As they strolled through the red light district in the southwestern portion of the city, they were captivated by the ladies in the window of one of the many brothels lining Santa Clara Street. They decided to enter. When a prostitute denied the men entry into her house, they became enraged. They began banging on the door and forming a commotion outside the brothel. One of the men admitted that they had kicked the door a few times and pushed it, in addition to knocking at the window and telling the prostitute to let them in while harassing a Chinese Cuban man outside the brothel.[31]

Among the first Cubans to react to the offense were two black veterans of the Brigade of Cienfuegos: veteran officer Claudio Sarría and Esteban Montejo, a former runaway slave-turned-soldier. Although Sarría left but few written records, Montejo recorded his memories of this and other experiences through an anthropologist intermediary, who eventually published them in *Biografía de un cimarrón* (Biography of a Runaway Slave) in 1966. The publication date coincided with the height of Cuba's post-revolutionary anti-imperialist fervor, likely amplifying Montejo's critical tone toward US officials. However, his testimony fits with the existing archival record, from which the voices of black veterans were largely excluded. *Biografía de un cimarrón* may well be guilty of collapsing past and present, as many critics have alleged, but Montejo's testimony still offers one of many perspectives on how black Cuban veterans—a group to which he undeniably belonged—experienced this moment of US rule.[32]

Sarría, Montejo, and other black veterans had noticed US soldiers' and employees' conduct with local women. Montejo remembered that US soldiers and employees, who were "almost always drunk," frequented the red light district, and usually solicited sex by exclaiming "Foky, foky, Margarita" to any woman they encountered.³³ Montejo's testimony suggests that these men not only solicited sex from known prostitutes, but also from women who simply resided in the predominantly black neighborhood containing the "public woman's ward."³⁴ Those men, "rotten as they were, wanted to *take* (*cogerse*) all the creole women as if they were meat at the market."³⁵ When Sarría and his men found out about "that business," they started to watch the US soldiers and civilians. These gender transgressions offered a striking postwar parallel with the Spanish abuses of Cuban women during reconcentration—an analogy likely not lost on Montejo, Sarría, and other black veterans.

Invoking the same ideas of patriarchal duty that had become so salient during insurgents' response to reconcentration, black veterans identified a new perpetrator of gender transgressions: US soldiers and employees. On San Juan Day in 1899 they decided to put an end to those US gender transgressions. "With the story of the foky, foky, they screwed themselves," Montejo recalled.³⁶ He remembered the interaction that compelled him and his compatriots into action: "We watched and, sure enough, a small group began to mess around.... They got into it with the women, they touched their butts and they laughed. I believe that [even] during the war I did not feel such a fire inside [me] as [I did] that day."³⁷ Black veterans decided to "take up the machete" to end US men's abuses once and for all that day. In an assertion of their patriarchal obligation to protect Cuban women, Sarría "gave the order to charge with machetes," and swiftly revoked the US employees' presumed right to the bodies of Cuban women.

A crowd quickly formed in support of Sarría and his men. US officials described the crowd as a "mob" which was "very much against" the US Americans. Local men demanded that the US employees be arrested. In response, the US employees hurled gendered insults in broken Spanish at the crowd. One US witness testified that the US employees "said they were 'caibrones' [*cabrones*/bastards] and were swearing at them." When asked what "caibrones" meant, Thevenet explained: "I understand it is the fix a man is in when somebody else is with his wife." Although the label of *cabrón* was a relatively common insult, particularly among working-class Cubans, it is revealing in this case because these US employees framed their sexual relations with local Cuban prostitutes as evidence of Cuban men's patriarchal failures. In turn, this insult essentially challenged Cuban men to defend their honor by defending Cuban women.³⁸ Black veterans did exactly this.

Sarría and Montejo's confrontation with US Americans fit within broader negotiations of racial and sexual relations of power under US rule. Over the first six months of the military occupation, rape and the specter of sexual abuse became a powerful rhetorical device in publically expressing contempt for the US presence in Cuba. To be sure, local newspapers and correspondence featured countless reports of US soldiers and officers raping and attempting to rape the wives and daughters of white Cuban men.[39] White veterans and separatists in particular resented these violent gendered abuses not only because they regarded US soldiers' and employees' presumptions of unbridled access to Cuban women as disrespectful of Cuban men's patriarchal roles. As well, sexual violence became a metaphor for the excesses of the US military occupation, which figuratively transformed honorable freedom fighters into imperial subjects once again. Sexual misconduct was a symptom of US savagery. As such, they served as the foundation of a powerful argument against US claims to civilization—the principal rational for the military occupation.[40]

As much as black veterans' actions drew on established canons of revolutionary masculinity, they also challenged the racial and sexual assumptions defining patriarchal authority. Although one island newspaper declared outright that the "race feeling" had caused the San Juan Day riot, the conflict just as clearly evinced a broader negotiation of black veterans' manhood, one enacted on the bodies of racially othered and sexually transgressive women.[41] After all, the actions of Sarría and his men differed from those of their more privileged counterparts in several important respects. The most salient charges of US sexual misconduct centered on the threat to respectable (white) women, especially the corruption of young virgins, as an offense against white men's patriarchal honor. By contrast, Sarría and his men challenged white US Americans' racialized sexual violence against local public women. This represented a rarely documented claim to patriarchal honor on the basis of protecting black and working-class women. By challenging the implicit whiteness of patriarchal authority, these black veterans articulated a powerful claim to masculine honor in the public sphere.

"We Have Got the Wrong Sort of Policemen Here"

In both riots, municipal police intervened on behalf of black Cuban veterans to quell the disturbances. They promptly identified the white US employees and soldiers as the culprits of the disorder. During the May riot, white police officer Gonzalo Acosta arrived on the scene after hearing shots fired. He reported seeing two white US civilians with "drawn revolvers aiming at the crowd."[42] Concluding rightly that these men had fired the shots, Acosta drew his machete on the two men, forcing them to holster their weapons. Protesting against the arrest, one of the US employees claimed "in bad Spanish," that he and others worked for the captain of the port's office. By invoking the authority of the US military government, this civilian employee exposed his belief that US Americans were not subject to the authority of the local police.

Just as Acosta sheathed his machete, other US employees quickly intervened in the arrest of their two comrades. Lewis grabbed Acosta by the arms, while two others disarmed him—a practical as well as symbolic gesture that stripped him of the symbols of his military service and his position of authority.[43] Striking Acosta repeatedly with their revolvers, the US employees "hoisted him up" and with "great hollering" carried him to the captain of the port. A subdued and disarmed Acosta became the symbol of a violent reappropriation of claims to local authority by white agents of the occupying government. The violent spectacle of disarming and beating a municipal authority figure offered a prompt corrective to what these men saw as a transgression against US control over the city.

In a futile attempt to free their unlucky comrade, white municipal police officers Federico Martí and Pablo Castellón drew their machetes. Martí and Castellón faced brutal treatment and humiliating disrespect for their authority at the hands of quartermaster employees.[44] In their subsequent testimony, US quartermaster employees unrepentantly narrated their violent confrontation with the police, emphasizing their own bravery and the legitimacy of their violence in service of US dignity, while portraying themselves as the natural authorities.[45] One of those employees, E. H. Harrison, recounted his reaction when "a Cuban soldier" allegedly charged at Barker with a machete. "We will take care of him," he remembered saying. With the help of Sergeant Franklin of the Signal Corps, several of Barker's men disarmed that policeman. Charles H. Evans testified that he "immediately jumped behind" the other officer, grabbing him with both arms as Barker seized his machete. Both municipal police officers ended up disarmed and arrested by US civilian employees.

Such violence and disrespect against the municipal police amounted to nothing less than a figurative emasculation, communicating that US citizens refused to recognize, let alone respect, the formal public authority of Cuban men. Acosta was so outraged by the treatment he suffered that he attempted to secure revenge after the riot. Rather than targeting the US employees who had humiliated him, Acosta confronted a fellow white Cuban, Luis Lewis, who was in charge of paying workers employed by the captain of the port. A veteran himself, Acosta was likely aware of Lewis's dubious record of military service and his defection from the Cuban army. After the riot, Acosta found out that Lewis was also one of the men who had disarmed him. In Acosta's eyes, Lewis was a two-time traitor, who had not only failed in his soldierly duties, but also colluded with the occupying government that stood in the way of Cuban independence. Lewis testified that Acosta "walked straight up to me, drew his pistol, and fired at me three times." Avoiding the shots, Lewis fled as his assailant pursued him and continued firing.[46] Barker later declared that Acosta "did shoot and attempt to kill one of my head stevedores who was unarmed."[47] His actions would come to haunt Acosta and his local compatriots.

US officials cited Acosta's so-called revenge attack as evidence of Cuban veterans' unfitness for public authority. They accused the police of being too "promiscuous" with firearms—a belief they repeated often to disparage the force. Military officials had ordered the police only to use their firearms in case of emergency, but instead they occasionally became "excited and used their revolvers unnecessarily."[48] Considering the liberal use of firearms by US officials and employees, this statement suggests that US officials did not respect municipal authority and especially resented any attempt to levy it against US citizens. Some US officials proposed limiting municipal policemen's ability to use their weapons "except in extreme cases in personal defense" or even stripping them of their weapons entirely.[49] However, US officials were equally fearful that "nearly every male citizen goes armed with a machete," and judged that "it would not be wise to take the revolver from the police at the present time." However, there was growing support for stripping policemen of their machetes, likely an effort to decenter veteran status within the force.[50]

Nor was the May riot the first episode of US violence against the racially heterogeneous municipal police. US soldiers and employees in Cienfuegos had enacted their disrespect for police in disruptive, uncooperative, and often violent encounters with the racially heterogeneous municipal police for months following the official organization of the force. In April white veteran and police chief Joaquín Oropesa complained to municipal mayor José Antonio Frías that a particular US soldier consistently displayed "disorderly conduct" and "is always intoxicated." The soldier had been arrested numerous times, but these sanctions failed to change his behavior, causing Oropesa to declare him a "public nuisance."⁵¹ The same month, soldiers of the provost general stole a policeman's rifle, and in May a similar incident occurred.⁵² The belligerence of these soldiers and civilian employees exemplified a growing conflict between US military officials and municipal authorities over the parameters of civil authority, especially the kinds of men who might enjoy access to these privileged roles. US officials had continued in their established trajectory of disrespect against municipal police.

Even with an unmistakable history of US soldiers' belligerence toward municipal police, US military officials maintained the same narrative of police culpability in their explanations of the San Juan Day riot. They claimed that the police were incapable of preserving order because of the poor quality (racial heterogeneity) of men employed therein. They also alleged that racially suspect municipal police officers used excessive force against white US employees, and were the first to fire their weapons during the San Juan Day riot. Certainly the drunken white suspects themselves told harrowing tales of being beaten by the police, who, they said: "Pulled machetes and they hit us with the sides of the machetes. They beat all three of us with the flat of the machetes."⁵³ Police abuses against these men were so flagrant that several US officers driving by the scene in a carriage stopped so they could "rescue them," as one man put it.⁵⁴ Although one of the drunken employees passed out from inebriation, his two fellow rabble-rousers managed to break free of the police and enter the carriage.⁵⁵ The carriage driver "whipped up the horses," who charged forward through the crowd, "knocking down some of the people, as they tried to stop it."⁵⁶ US officials testified that police fired upon the carriage. One US official claimed that "I do not exaggerate when I say more than fifty shots were fired and twenty of them at me," in the moments after the carriage sped away with the US Americans inside. "That the police tried to kill me is beyond a doubt," he concluded.⁵⁷

Yet, numerous witnesses disputed this testimony, claiming that US officials actually used force first, fired the first shots, and further escalated the situation by calling in troops. To be sure, it was difficult to deny that the drunken US employees resisted arrest from the very beginning, using force against the crowd and abusing the police. Once the men broke free of police custody and entered the carriage, they allegedly fired several rounds as they sped off. One of the rounds wounded Officer Epifanio Ordoñez, who had been patrolling the district that day.⁵⁸ In response, Officer Garrido shot twice in the air in a futile attempt to deter the carriage. US forces then called in troops stationed at the nearby railroad station to "restore order." These soldiers formed a picket behind the wall of the railroad station, firing on the crowd. Their bullets wounded several people and killed one "honorable head of household" before municipal authorities were able to convince them to stand down.[59]

US officials' obviously hyperbolic claims about municipal police officers' promiscuity with firearms boiled down to one conclusion: the men employed in the police force were "unfit to discharge the responsible duties of their office."[60] One US official captured this idea perfectly when he testified that "my idea is that we have got the wrong sort of policemen here, policemen who on any pretext draw revolver or machete, when, as an American understands it, when somebody draws a revolver, somebody is to be killed."[61] Testimony from numerous military officials and employees in the wake of the San Juan Day riot reveals more precisely what this US official meant by "the wrong sort of policemen." It meant the employment of men whom US officials presumed to be their racial inferiors.

One of the assumptions underlying these claims was that men of the so-called Latin races were naturally "excitable" in temperament, and therefore prone to "promiscuity" with firearms and were otherwise unfit for police duty. One US officer declared that the police "should not be allowed to fire in the streets of the city," as "they are too nervous and excitable to be entrusted with such power."[62] The reference to the "excitability" of the Cubans drew on prevailing racial ideas about Latin people as more emotional and unstable than their Anglo-Saxon counterparts, a generalization employed to bolster his claim that men of questionable racial makeup were unfit for police work.

Some US officials claimed that Cuban men's physical inferiority exacerbated their already unstable temperament. James H. Wilson noted that "the Cubans, as a rule, have not sufficient size, strength and self-reliance to make first class policemen."[63] Another US official suggested that because a Cuban police officer was "physically weaker than the American," he "has felt himself at a disadvantage and in consequence has been too prone to use his revolver."[64] These racialized assertions about the physical and racial inadequacies of the police helped bolster the claims of certain US officials that Cuban separatists and veterans were not fit for self-government, even at the municipal level. This claim, in turn, justified their own intervention into civil affairs.

Beyond the broad assumption of Latin racial inferiority, US officials particularly resented the employment of black men in the municipal police force. US military personnel characterized the police alternately as "colored" or "dark," and "yellow," likely a term in this context indicating mixed racial ancestry, among other terms indicating some degree of African ancestry.⁶⁵ Others argued that the men employed in the police force did not meet the standards of "good character" outlined in the guidelines for hiring, in particular securing the recommendations of at least two prominent (white) men.⁶⁶

US Americans from both Confederate and Union states commented disparagingly on the racial composition of the police, often conflating the blackness of the force with violent transgressions against whites. One of the drunken US employees, whose family hailed from the Midwest, noted that "most" of the police he encountered "were black." He testified that the police "sailed into us" as he attempted to force his way into the brothel. A Wisconsin-native testified that he saw a police officer "who was pretty brown" fire "point blank" at a US officer. Another US employee from Mississippi testified that he saw "a policeman, a negro, not the blackest I have noticed on the police force, but he was of the color that I would call a negro, raised [his gun] to shoot the carriage [full of Americans]. I knocked his hand down."⁶⁷ He claimed that two of the three policemen he saw firing shots "were what, in the Southern states, we would call negroes" and that the very first man to fire was a "negro policeman."⁶⁸ The fact that the multiracial municipal police identified US citizens rather than black veterans as the perpetrators of disorder violated US officials' expectations that the police force would be white and would defend whites. It also contradicted their assumption that black men would lack access to firearms and behave deferentially toward whites.⁶⁹

"For the Good Name of Your City, and Cuba"

As much as US military officials complained about the racial composition of the municipal police, civil authorities defended the force by identifying the true culprits of the riots as US soldiers and employees. Based on their decidedly local experiences of US rule, civil authorities in Cienfuegos articulated a grievance common to revolutionary political elites across the island: US officials routinely disrespected and abused Cuban men's civil authority. Chief of Police Joaquín Oropesa charged angrily that the actions of US officials during the May riot constituted "a true abuse of the police whose prestige is under the safeguard of this Chief."⁷⁰ The interim mayor similarly described the events as a *"verdadero atropello"* (a true insult/abuse) of the police, and complained that US authorities refused to return the police officers' weapons, thereby extending the symbolic emasculation they had already suffered.[71] When these same patterns of disrespect continued during the San Juan Day riot, Mayor José Antonio Frías explicitly connected the disrespectful conduct of US employees and soldiers to a broader failure of US officials to recognize and respect Cuban men's civil authority. Confronting one US official who seemingly flaunted his defiance of the police after the San Juan Day riot, Frías interjected: "So the police have no authority and you do not intend to comply with their orders?" The US official did not reply.[72]

US abuses of the police formed part of broader patterns of disrespect against municipal authorities, who struggled with the partial and conditional nature of their authority under US rule. They resented the "attitude of domination or superiority," which "too frequently characterized" the US officials' behavior toward them. Envisioning their roles as independent of and separate from US military authority, municipal authorities initially did not hesitate to disagree with US officials. Mayor Frías, for one, denounced the decision to call in two companies of US soldiers to "clear the street" of an unarmed crowd as not only excessive, but also a violation of civil authority. Chief Oropesa criticized the US soldiers for their own "promiscuity" with weapons during the San Juan Day riot, as they fired not only on a defenseless crowd but also directly at him. One white Cuban officer declared that such violence "was something that should not happen in a civilized country."[73] Another policeman lambasted US soldiers for behaving "so savagely against a defenseless people."[74] These comments underscored the hypocrisy of the supposed US civilizing mission in Cuba when compared with the actual behavior of US citizens on the island. The implications of these critiques were profound from the perspective of the Cuban veterans: if the US Americans, who upheld themselves as the model of civilization, were savages, then the United States had no business occupying Cuba with the goal of civilizing Cubans.

For the most part, civil and even US military authorities at the provincial level were sympathetic to the complaints of municipal authorities. The interim civil governor of Santa Clara, Orestes Ferrara, asked Wilson to "pay particular attention to the matter," noting that Cienfuegos had the embarrassing record of "being the only [city] where such scandals daily take place."[75] Wilson briefly came to the defense of civil authorities, whom he claimed were generally "well-chosen and are fairly representative of not only the intelligence but the property of the country." He described Cienfuegos mayor Frías favorably as "a man of ability and culture," adding that he had "no doubt that [he and] his family have been large property holders."[76] Wilson even acknowledged that the "principal cause" of the San Juan Day riot had been the "provocations and outrages against the police, committed by employees of the intervention." He also issued orders to preempt further misdeeds.[77]

Even as high-ranking US military authorities at the provincial level acknowledged civil authority over local affairs, lower-ranking US officers and civilians at the local level often refused to implement this official policy. Wilson's subordinates in Cienfuegos, particularly Barker and his employees at the port captain's office, simply expected the mayor and police chief to obey them. Barker lamented that municipal authorities "persistently refuse to cooperate" with US officials and he declared that these men "must be given to understand that we are supreme in power and superior in management."[78] This attitude translated into hostility and antagonism against civil authorities following the May riot. Barker complained erroneously that the police chief had incited the police to violence against US officials, rather than ordering them to apprehend the *real* criminals, a claim that failed to recognize US culpability in the disorder. He also alleged that Oropesa had instigated the crowd gathered outside the Office of the Captain of the Port, causing "the mob [to] cheer him." Barker snarled, "There can be no mistake as to the character of this supposed conservator of the peace!"[79]

To be sure, Barker and other US officials in Cienfuegos demanded changes in municipal governance. One US official urged the mayor to dismiss the Cuban police officers involved in the San Juan Day riot "for the good name of your city, and Cuba."[80] Others went even further, attacking the police chief and the mayor. One US official complained that their responses to the riots revealed that neither of these men possessed "a single attribute to qualify them for the position" and he recommended their dismissal from office. Barker sought to replace them with men in the city "who, if not thoroughly competent, would certainly administer municipal affairs with less friction and more progress."[81] The ongoing tensions between white civil authorities and local US military officials in the wake of the riots hinted at the very real possibility that white revolutionaries might lose their positions of local authority.

US military officials in Cienfuegos even sought to remove the exclusively white municipal leadership, whom they viewed as having failed the test of political fitness by allowing black veterans to assume formal authority as agents of municipal law enforcement. Albeit limited, black veterans' access to employment in law enforcement symbolized a frightening decay in the white monopoly on public authority, not to mention a startling perversion of the very premise of law and order. The resurrection of old tropes of black criminality invoked by opponents of separatist rule after the war suggested that only white men could adequately uphold the law. Moreover, the series of conflicts between the municipal police and US soldiers underscored what some US military authorities saw as a dangerous racial and political link between law enforcement and criminals themselves. In particular, the employment of black veterans in law enforcement rendered visible the real and imagined ties of solidarity binding black and working-class men to the highest echelons of municipal and provincial government. The alleged reason for both rural crime and urban disorder was that the veterans employed in law enforcement refused to arrest law breakers with whom they shared a history of military service and racial ties.

White US employees working under Barker similarly criticized Cuban civil authorities for "disrespecting" Barker after the May riot, a claim that implicitly invoked assumptions about racial and social etiquette. One white US employee criticized Oropesa as "very loud and insulting to Captain Barker" and reprimanded him to "stop the rough manner of talking and listen to Captain Barker."[82] Another of Barker's employees noted that Oropesa "was extremely defiant" to Barker.[83]

US officers denounced the mayor for much the same reason following the San Juan Day riot. One white US officer dismissively described Mayor Frías as "very much excited, shaking his finger" in the face of US military officials, and telling them that the San Juan Day riot "was a matter for the municipal authorities, and that [US authorities] had no right to take any part in it." Another US officer suggested that municipal authorities lacked the jurisdiction to limit the actions of US forces. Thus when the mayor attempted to intervene to stop US troops from shooting civilians, the US officer informed him that he needed to "let [them] fire this shot and investigate after."[84] US disdain for the supposedly "excitable" manner of the municipal authorities revealed racialized and gendered assumptions about public authority. Political fitness required a manly "temperate" character and proper control over emotions, qualities white Cubans supposedly lacked because of their Latin blood.[85]

Indeed, among the most significant consequences of the San Juan Day riot was that it led US military officials to conflate their perceptions of racially heterogeneous veterans with their judgments of the exclusively white municipal and provincial leadership. Because the mayor and the chief of police—both prominent white men—had failed to quash veterans' demonstrations, and defended the multiracial police force, they demonstrated their own solidarity with these men, and their allegiance to the socially radical mission of the Liberating Army. US authorities interpreted these actions as evidence of supposed cross-racial solidarity. They assumed that the same cross-racial ties of military patronage and supposed racial loyalties that linked black workers, multiracial police, and white civil authorities during the riots would produce broader solidarities with still-mobilized veterans. If they chose to protest the growing mistreatment of veterans, these revolutionary networks could lead to armed resistance to US rule.

Within this context, even the minutest displays of public authority by black men, if not swiftly suppressed, became evidence of white veterans' and separatists' lack of civilization, inability to preserve order, and unfitness for political authority. By extension, anything that US officials could interpret as insufficient zeal in preserving order could derail white separatists' already tenuous hold on local political power. As a result of these confrontations with US military officials during and after the riots, municipal authorities began to reevaluate their allegiances toward their compatriots-in-arms, and adjust their posture toward the military government. These processes are traced in the next chapter.

CHAPTER SIX

Agents of Order or Disorder?

Black Veterans, Urban Law Enforcement, and the Racial Politics of Violence

⇁ AS MUCH AS THE RIOTS IN MAY AND JUNE 1899 ILLUSTRATED BROADER negotiations about black veterans' place in postwar society, they also exposed competing ideas about fitness for civil authority. The heavy backlash white civil authorities felt from US military officials in the aftermath of the May and June riots underscored just how dangerous real or perceived solidarities with black veterans could be for their political careers. If New Men wanted to sustain their political careers under US rule, they had to disprove these misperceptions about their cross-racial allegiances.

One of the main ways civil authorities made themselves more palatable to US military officials was by distancing themselves from these supposedly revolutionary attributes. Civil authorities attempted to prove their fitness for political power by visibly abandoning public support for black veterans' claims to New Man status. In this regard, they gradually began to embrace the criminalizing discourse invoked by opponents of separatist rule to suppress black men's displays of public authority. In contrast to revolutionary masculinity, which valorized black veterans' masculinity on the basis of their military service, this criminalizing discourse undermined black men's claims to masculinity by implicating them in dishonorable conduct and hypermasculine violence.

The specter of criminalized black veterans offered a powerful rationale for two key policies aimed at redefining the racial parameters of the use of force. First, military and civil authorities collaborated to disarm and demobilize Cuban veterans through the disbandment of the Liberating Army—the very institution that had invested black veterans with their sense of authority. However, this measure failed to address the small number of black veterans who had obtained formal authority in law enforcement bodies during the first months of the occupation. Consequently, military officials demanded a second set of reforms: a total overhaul of the municipal police force to bring the employees in line with propertied interests.

Progressively whitened law enforcement bodies specifically tailored to the defense of propertied interests targeted black men, increasingly perceived to be the principal agents of disorder and crime and the most visible threats to (white) separatist political power. Displays of authority by black veterans, which formerly seemed to garner the acceptance or support of law enforcement, were cast as violations of order, unpatriotic displays that jeopardized the future of the emerging republic. Just as white officers had used the guise of majasería to challenge black officers' military authority, white civil authorities increasingly criminalized displays of public authority or protest by black veterans. Criminalization, in turn, allowed white veterans to punish black men in the name of their manly obligation to preserve order without explicitly invoking race. These institutional changes helped white civil authorities redefine themselves as agents of racial order rather than the racial radicals some US officials had initially suspected them to be.

"To Enter into Negotiations with Their Dignity": New Men's Complicity in the Disbandment of the Liberating Army

During the early months of the US military occupation, high-ranking Cuban veterans entered negotiations with the US government to secure the funds necessary to pay Cuban veterans. The deal they reached involved a loan from the US government for $3 million, a sum significantly less than veteran leaders needed to pay their men. The US government did not miss the opportunity to leverage the loan to secure several of its key interests in Cuba. The terms of the loan subjected Cuban veterans to the humiliation of embarrassingly low payouts of seventy-five dollars, official disarmament, and formal disbandment.[1] These conditions would substantially reduce the power of Cuban veterans to negotiate their postwar status, particularly for men who found themselves outside the conventional boundaries of political power. Most significantly of all, disbandment was made possible by the complicity of mainly white high-ranking Cuban officers, and administered by local white veteran leaders.[2]

US authorities ordered the payment of the Liberating Army's Fourth Corps in central Cuba's major cities in summer 1899, causing hundreds of still-armed, racially heterogeneous veterans to leave the countryside for the cities. Between the May riot and the inauguration of payment in June, rumors circulated that veterans had organized a plan to remain mobilized in protest of the low pay and requirement to surrender their weapons.[3] Signs discouraging the soldiers from accepting the money allegedly appeared throughout Cienfuegos.[4] Local newspapers propagated this fear, citing discontent among veterans regarding the terms of disbandment.[5] What had been the greatest source of planters' anxiety in the countryside became the terror of US military officials in central Cuban cities.

Veterans disapproved of the terms of disbandment for three key reasons. First, most veterans agreed that such an insultingly small sum as seventy-five dollars did not come close to compensating for their military service. While some veterans sought to avoid "conflicts in the [emerging] Republic over money,"[6] others argued that veterans should not cede "even a cent" of what they deserved. But it was not only the amount of money that disturbed veterans, but also the assumptions underlying it. In particular, veterans rejected US officials' insinuation that the payment was a form of charity, rather than legitimate (albeit fractional) compensation for actual services. One critic expressed this sentiment in an article titled "Ni Limosna, Ni Propina," (Neither Alms, Nor Tip) appearing in the Santa Clara newspaper, *El Pueblo*. "The honorable conscience of the entire people," the article read, "does not want to enter in negotiations with their dignity" by accepting a "donation that has a depressing character of alms or the servile condition of a tip."[7] The same author also refuted US officials' assumption that veterans had only fought for the selfish reason of collecting pay. He retorted that veterans had enlisted "without expectations of salary, without arms and without provisions." He continued: "we will return to our homes without resources but with the faith that with hard work . . . we will be free."[8] As US military rule stood in the way of the consummation of this freedom, many veterans believed that accepting the meager monetary payout would only consolidate US presence and further delay independence.

A second objection veterans articulated concerned the requirement that they hand over their weapons in order to collect the money. One veteran noted that the money was "not in reality a disinterested donation if it comes in exchange for the turning over of the weapon and ammunition." For many veterans, their weapon was the most tangible symbol of their military service and the very basis of their manhood. Veterans cited the affective value of their weapons, emphasizing "the personal value it carries, its patriotic abnegation, its liberating sentiments."[9] The Cienfuegos-based newspaper *La Tribuna* further critiqued US policy that "insisted" veterans turn over their weapons to US troops, rather than to civil authorities—an imposition that constituted "another provocation to the already more than afflicted armed element of Cuba."[10] These critiques reveal veterans' widespread suspicion that accepting the tiny payment would essentially eliminate the source of their martial manhood and further reduce the leverage they had to negotiate their postwar status.

Indeed, some veterans argued that they still needed their weapons, because they had not yet secured their goal of freedom. One leaflet warned the men of the "Valiant Army of Las Villas" to prepare once more for the "glorious path of war," this time against US military rule. "Be ready to answer the call," it advised, "with your thoughts fixed upon the great Martí and your hand upon the weapon which will give us peace with victory or death under the shadow of our redeeming flag!"[11] The struggle for full independence, this leaflet implied, was not yet complete, and therefore, veterans could not lay down their weapons—much less turn them over to the new enemy. In the same vein, another critic, writing in the Cienfuegos weekly, *El Siglo*, reminded veterans that they were "free men" who with "honor and dignity" will "willingly die before being sold like miserable slaves to a foreign people."[12] The reference to slavery, however ironic given the persisting racial hierarchy in the Cuban army, served as a powerful rejection of the subjugation and feminization implied in the new neocolonial relationship to the United States.

Certainly, the injustice of forcibly disarming Cuban veterans was not lost on some US military officials, many of whom themselves were veterans of the US Civil War. Wilson, a former union officer and military commander of the Department of Georgia during Reconstruction, argued that Cuban veterans should be allowed to retain their weapons. "I do not believe that if you had fought for four or five years, as these people have fought for the independence of their country against the brutal domination of Spain, you would be willing to give up your gun to anybody, no matter what might be the argument or the inducement offered," he wrote to a military colleague.[13] Cuban veterans could use their "old Remingtons and Mausers" for self-defense "or the ornamentation of their palm-thatched huts, and hand them down undisturbed to their descendants as a loved and honored memento of their service on behalf of Cuban freedom."[14] Wilson articulated with startling clarity the dilemma many Cuban veterans faced: they either had to surrender the symbols of their military honor or submit to the possible consequences of defying US authority. Either option required Cuban veterans to undergo a discursive emasculation.

A third reason some veterans opposed the terms of payment was that it was conditioned on the disbandment of the Liberating Army. One critic lamented the "inconsideration and lack of respect to the Cuban people" in the US military government's "insistence on hurting the [Cuban] military." Requiring disbandment, he argued, aimed to "humiliate" and "discredit" the war heroes before the very country for which it had fought, with the ultimate goal of "usurping from us our liberty."[15] Other veterans argued that disbandment highlighted US deceit and betrayal of the Teller Amendment. One article reproduced in *La Correspondencia* of Cienfuegos called the United States a "wolf in sheep's clothing," and depicted Cuba as "betrayed and chained" under "savage Yankee rage."[16] Another critic similarly viewed disbandment as an ominous sign of the "bad faith" of the United States.[17] Taken together, these objections provided ample rationale for broad discontent among Cuban veterans regarding the terms of disbandment.

Veterans who lacked access to public employment or political power particularly resented what they perceived to be the collusion of their more privileged compatriots in the humiliation of the Liberating Army. In one cartoon published in the Havana-based newspaper *La Protesta*, a large disembodied hand pushes a vulnerable, blindfolded white Lady Cuba toward a stage marked annexation. "M. Gómez, La Discusión, De Pons" are scribbled on the cuff of the hand, naming the complicity of two patriots. Máximo Gómez, who supposedly embodied the elite betrayal of veterans, was perceived as taking a conciliatory posture toward the United States for his part in negotiating the $3 million loan, and thereby destroying the possibility of future armed resistance to US rule.[18] He also urged veterans to eliminate the "causes" for the US occupation by surrendering their weapons.[19] A second scapegoat was white

Figure 6.1. Lady Cuba—A Soldier's Obligation. Source: Untitled political cartoon, *La Protesta*, Havana, September 5, 1899. Instituto de Historia de Cuba, Hemeroteca.

veteran José Pons y Naranjo, a native of Santa Clara who wrote for *La Discusión*, a conservative Havana-based newspaper heavily criticized by the central Cuba's radical press. The cartoon featured a resolute (still white) Cuban veteran, valiantly raising a machete to Uncle Sam to protect Lady Cuba, cast figuratively as national honor. Such imagery suggested that it was the duty of the Cuban soldier, even while lacking the support of their leaders, to defend Cuban liberty by standing up to US military rule.

In Santa Clara Province, veterans expressed similar disdain at the complicity of separatists turned political elites in the disbandment of the army. At the local level, prominent white veteran chiefs like Francisco Carrillo and José de Jesús Monteagudo encouraged and even helped administer demobilization as a step toward eventual independence.[20] In an article titled "Fuera Carretas!" published in the Cienfuegos weekly, *El Siglo*, one critic chastised white civil authorities for being "the first to sing victory when they saw the Cubans turn over their triumphant arms." The irony of disbandment was the fact that "scoundrel[s]" who "never heard the whistle of a bullet" were able to retain their weapons, while freedom fighters were forced to relinquish theirs. The juxtaposition of the veterans' "triumphant arms" and separatists' weapons that were "virgin of struggle" helped cast complicit politicians as devoid of the military honor, and thus in breach of revolutionary visions of masculinity.[21]

Veterans' discontent with the humiliating terms of disbandment was palpable and it translated into clear anxieties among US military officials stationed in central Cuban cities. One white resident claimed nervously that veterans maraud about "the towns, armed, as if they were in battle."[22] In Cienfuegos one US officer claimed hysterically that (black) veterans would erupt into violence "swearing vengeance on all Americans" for attempting to deprive them of their weapons. "The situation is serious," he declared, even requesting a private guard to protect himself and government property.[23] US officials attempted to preempt disorder by prohibiting the assembly of large groups of Cuban veterans in one place, distributing rations, and racially segregating celebrations and festivities.[24]

Nevertheless, in the days and weeks following the San Juan Day riot, veterans across Santa Clara Province reluctantly turned over their firearms, accepted the measly sum of seventy-five dollars, and mustered out. US rule had been reaffirmed. Through their complicity in this process, civil authorities had disarmed a population that US military authorities deemed problematic. In the process, they clung to their positions of civil authority, performing their conformity to US visions of political fitness.

New Men must have been disappointed when, despite their complicity in disbanding the Liberating Army, US officials consolidated a seemingly indefinite US presence on the island. In November 1899 a bill calling for the formation of a civil government under the auspices of the US military occupation came before the US Congress—in apparent violation of the Teller Amendment and without the consent of the Cuban people. The publication of a supremely annexationist political cartoon titled "Looking Forward" in the US magazine *Puck* that same month illustrated the imperialist machinations underlying the policy. On her knees, a white Lady Cuba clutches Uncle Sam's arm, begging him to deliver her from a war-torn countryside laid waste by the insurgents. A prosperous future awaited Cuba under US rule, embodied in a sunny plantation economy with laborers hard at work in the cane fields, sugar mills churning away, and heaping amounts of tropical product ready for export.

Though US audiences may not have flinched at the unrepentant feminization of Cuban men implied in the above political cartoon, the men of the revolution certainly resented such presumptions. Veterans across Santa

Figure 6.2. "Looking forward." Source: J. S. Pughe, "Looking forward," *Puck*, November 1, 1899, Library of Congress, Prints and Photographs Division.

Clara Province, and across the island, protested what they saw as a usurpation of the freedom for which they had fought so long to consolidate and as an affront to their martial manhood.[25] In one of the manifestations erupting across central Cuba, over five thousand Cuban civilians from the country towns of Rodas, Abreus, and Cartagena marched upon the governor's office in Santa Clara to protest the news.

Some veterans resented the US military government's deceit in promising civil government, only to entice Cuban men into accepting prolonged US rule. One political cartoon gracing the folds of the Havana newspaper, *La Discusión*, expressed this sentiment exactly. US president William McKinley towers over two white Cuban veterans in tattered uniforms, luring them ever closer to the United States with a scroll representing civil government. The insurgents, portrayed as aloof and power-hungry, are small and hunched over, suggesting their subordination to McKinley. A sheath binding the scroll obscures an ample space between the words "civil government" at the top and "of Cuba" at the bottom, suggesting a set of hidden conditions underlying the promise. A sinister-looking rodent lurking on the other side of the fence alludes to the bad intentions of the United States, reinforcing the message that the civil government was but a decoy aimed at tricking separatists to accept US rule. The caption cautions separatists not to take their future political independence for granted simply because Spanish rule ended; a new form of subjugation was emerging (see fig. 6.3).

Strikingly absent from the chorus of discontent over the terms of civil government were the mayors of Santa Clara's most important cities. They likely understood better than anyone else the critical importance of remaining silent to preserve their image as agents of order and to maintain harmony with military officials. Yet, with the impending consolidation of civil government under US rule, white civil authorities recognized that their complicity in the disbandment of the Liberating Army and now their silence about the clearly imperialistic character of US rule was insufficient to convince US military officials of their future cooperation. As local leaders, these men were responsible for preserving order, a broad concept that relied on implicit racial and class assumptions. Part of preserving order entailed establishing and maintaining clear parameters on the kind of men who could claim authority.

Figure 6.3. "The Civil Government . . . of Cuba." Source: "El Gobierno Civil . . . de Cuba," *La Discusión*, November 17, 1899, Box 35, File 6462, USNAII/MGC/RG 140/E 3. Caption: "Don't count your chickens before they hatch; those who do feel the shortcoming" (figurative translation).

In essence, this project meant upholding a racial labor hierarchy in which black men formed part of a docile workforce that served the city's wealthy commercial elite, and remained marginal from local authority.

In particular, US officials pointed to white civil authorities' failure to address the problematic racial heterogeneity of the municipal police force, perceived to be a remnant of their cross-racial solidarity and political radicalism. In an effort to salvage their reputations with local US officials, white civil authorities undertook certain reforms of municipal law enforcement. One of the earliest changes manifested in a shift in the overall objectives of the municipal police force. Initially, the organization of the force aimed to promote the employment of veterans, who in turn envisioned their roles in law enforcement as extensions of their military service in defense of Cuban freedom. However, by late 1899, the force assumed a more cooperative posture toward US military authorities. The practical implications of this shift were profound. Between July and November 1899 civil authorities avoided major confrontations with US occupying forces in Cienfuegos. Simultaneously though not coincidentally, the force also assumed a more repressive posture against poor and working-class black men, who were defined as the principal agents of disorder.

"There Was No Other Boss But Him": Black Authority, State Violence, and Narratives of Murder

On the evening of December 29, 1899, a white veteran employed in the Cienfuegos municipal police shot and killed General Dionisio Gil, the black, Dominican-born veteran of the Cuban army. His limp body lay across the railroad tracks in the working-class neighborhood of Pueblo Nuevo, his face splattered with blood from a bullet hole under his eye. A pistol was strewn carelessly near his hand.

An official version of the events leading up to the murder emerged almost immediately. White municipal police chief Joaquín Oropesa claimed that one of his officers had shot Gil after the black general had attempted to kill a city sanitary inspector. Gil injured police and armed guards to evade apprehension. In an effort to restore peace and apprehend the criminal, Oropesa ordered his men to find and detain the general. White police officer Agustín Rabasa, who pursued Gil on horseback, then fired in self-defense. One of the shots penetrated Gil's skull, killing him instantly.

US military authorities readily accepted the police's official version of events. One US official noted that "the killing is justifiable" and no indictments were warranted.[26] Others justified the narrative in part by depicting Gil as a common criminal. Alpheus Henry Bowman of the 2nd US Infantry described Gil as "a disreputable character," a thief, who would appropriate "property without reference to whom it belonged," a man "without occupation, of questionable reputation, and one liable to be engaged in disorder." Bowman framed the general's death as a natural result of his own "disorderly conduct."[27] He further disparaged the general's military record, claiming that he had "acquired a reputation as an expert forager rather than a fighter." By downplaying Gil's history of military honor and constructing a fictitious criminal past, Bowman forced the incident into his own pre-established conceptions of criminality. In this rendition, the police had finally done what was necessary to prevent further "crimes against the peace of the community": they had killed a black "criminal."[28] Characterizing Gil as a criminal seemingly offered a convenient justification for the killing. It legitimized police violence as an instrument of order and part of the consolidation of a modern (white) local state. US authorities finally seemed to approve of the police force's activities.

Nevertheless, these unfavorable impressions of Gil did not resonate with those who knew the general personally. Gil was known in his home country and among many veterans in Cuba as a military hero. Born in 1852 in the city of Concepción de la Vega, Dominican Republic, he served in the military under the rule of Dominican president Ulises Heureaux (1882–1884, 1887–1889, 1889–1899) following the island's second independence from Spain, before joining the Cuban War of Independence on August 6, 1895. Invoking this illustrious military service, Gil's son, Perfecto Gil rejected military officials' characterization of his father as a common criminal and dishonorable soldier. Rather, he asserted that the only criminals were the police, who he called a "bunch of bandits."[29] General-in-Chief of the Liberating Army Máximo Gómez portrayed Gil as a brave soldier, who "honorably defended the liberty of this land." He noted that Gil "was a man of color who was able to make many friends."[30] To these men and many others, Gil was a hero, not a natural criminal.

Among those dissatisfied with the official narrative of the murder were the city's black and working-class veterans. The morning after the incident, veterans and workers, who US military officials described as the "worst classes [of] colored people," gathered outside the Veterans' Center to protest the apparently racial motives of the murder. The protesters demanded access to the general's body to ensure he received an honorable burial.[31] When the courts refused to turn over the body, "the same colored classes made cries in the streets," according to one US official who likened the protesters to howling animals.[32] By December 31 municipal authorities had interred Gil without ceremony.

The unceremonious burial only exacerbated public outcry over what increasingly appeared to be a racially motivated murder. Perfecto Gil decried the poor treatment Cubans had given his father "only because he was black." He commented directly on the lackluster burial: "Not only did they kill him," Perfecto wrote, "but also they treated him like a dog in that [he did] not even [receive] a burial as a Liberating General that he was."[33] Black activists in Cienfuegos and elsewhere struggled for over a decade to honor the remains of the murdered general properly. Successive municipal administrations rejected these efforts and refused to provide even the most basic support. Nonetheless, activists eventually managed to raise the funds to build a modest mausoleum to house his remains in the cemetery and create a small park roughly on the site of his death in the working-class neighborhood of Pueblo Nuevo.[34]

US authorities generally dismissed the popular outrage over Gil's murder. One US official noted that "there has been a good deal of inflammatory talk among the negroes growing out of Gil's killing." Although he dismissed the protests as "without significance, political or otherwise," the anxious letters and telegrams sent by white civil authorities suggest they were seriously pondering the implications that racial mobilizations like this one might have for their political futures.[35]

The unrest in the wake of Gil's murder tested municipal authorities, who actively attempted to prove themselves as agents of order to US authorities. Mayor Frías quickly reassured military officials that civil authorities could handle the unrest without military intervention. He acknowledged military officials' anxieties about the considerable agitation among the "negroes" of the city. However, Frías assured them that "police with modification will preserve order, avoiding alteration of [the] public order." Seeking to ward off military action, he "recommended people to disperse immediately." Frías also enlisted the support of other prominent white revolutionaries visiting the city.[36] Prominent white separatist Bartolomé Masó gave a speech promising to take the greatest care in the situation.[37] White veteran chiefs, including Jesús Rabí and José Miró Argenter cursorily demanded justice then told the protesters to disperse. Even the white general José Braulio Alemán, who supposedly represented the protesters in his capacity as president of the Cienfuegos Veterans' Center, ordered the people to return to their homes.[38]

Although the protesters eventually dispersed, veterans continued to voice their skepticism at the official narrative of Gil's death. Their ongoing discontent likely compelled Alemán to demand further investigation of the murder. In an open letter to the judicial authorities published in *La Tribuna*, Alemán exposed a number of inconsistencies in the official version of events, all of which suggested that the police had not acted in self-defense.[39] Among the most damning evidence was eyewitness testimony confirming that Gil had actually turned himself over to the police and relinquished his weapon peacefully, before Rabasa had shot him. Alemán named a half-dozen witnesses, including police officers José Morales, José Fernández, and Policarpo Lafont, to verify these claims.[40] Although Alemán rectified the official version of events by calling out the police-perpetrated murder, the silences in his statement were equally revealing. Nowhere in his letter did he mention race, which the protesters so vehemently claimed was at the core of the assassination. This racial silence suggested a broader unwillingness to identify, name, and condemn acts of racial oppression and violence.

Eventually investigators confirmed popular suspicions that Rabasa had murdered Gil in cold blood.[41] The true nature of events began on the afternoon of December 29, 1899, with a conflict over local authority and masculine honor between Gil and a white city sanitary inspector, Enrique Quintana. Gil confronted Quintana for his disrespectful treatment of Antonio Achón, the Chinese Cuban manager of the Fonda Mariposa, a local café. Gil admonished Quintana for his abusive behavior, allegedly declaring that with him, Quintana "could not behave as he had with the Chinese man."[42] Some witnesses testified that Gil assumed "an aggressive insolent attitude in words and manner towards Quintana," comments reminiscent of majasería trials about black officers' supposed demeanor toward whites.[43] Quintana assured Gil that he respected him as a patriot, but that he did not recognize him as his boss, demarcating a clear separation between New Men and black veterans, who presumably could never occupy such formal authority. Gil reportedly proclaimed that "there was no other boss but him."[44] At its core, this initial confrontation was not only a disagreement over claims to public authority; it reveals competing visions of the meaning of military service following the war. Whereas Gil attempted to extend his military authority into postwar local affairs, Quintana seemed to privilege social status over military rank as a basis for authority.

The men eventually parted ways, only to settle their dispute violently later that evening. Around nine o'clock, Gil and Quintana encountered each other again at the café. Quintana testified that he suddenly felt a hand around his neck, as Gil pulled him into the Fonda. Gil allegedly beat him over the head with the butt of his revolver, "making him fall to the ground."[45] Several bystanders intervened on behalf of Quintana, who escaped to the street where he blew his whistle for help. A sworn guard from the nearby Dos Hermanos plantation, attempted to stop Gil from fleeing, but the general broke free, reportedly shooting the guard in the gut.[46] According to one report, policeman Antonio Hernández also attempted to detain Gil, only to be shot in the leg.[47] Although Gil successfully evaded apprehension, the multiple attempts by bystanders and residents to detain him suggest that these armed white men judged Gil as a danger without necessarily knowing the details of the dispute. He later surrendered to police, turned over his weapon "because they were Cubans," and proceeded back to town in police custody.[48]

As the detained general and his police escorts crossed the city, they encountered police sergeant Agustín Rabasa on horseback. He "rode forward to the prisoner, inquired who it was, and on receiving from Gil a reply that it was he, Gil, [Rabasa] thrust a revolver in the latter's face and firing killed the prisoner instantly."[49] Witnesses noted that Gil had placed his hand "in a deprecating manner resting on his chest" right before Rabasa shot him. The bullet fractured his cranium, killing him "like a lightning bolt."[50] The horizontal angle of the entry wound confirmed that Rabasa shot Gil point-blank and not from his horse as he had claimed originally.[51]

Rabasa had subsequently fabricated a story to exculpate himself from the charge of murder. He ordered mulatto police officer Rogelio Celada, his subordinate, to fire several shots from Gil's already-confiscated revolver. Another police officer testified that "Celada refused and threw the pistol from him, whereupon someone picked it up fired several shots and subsequently placed it in or near the dead man's hand."[52] Rabasa, assured that the rounds fired from Gil's gun would exonerate him, later confessed: "I was the one who killed him."[53] Policemen were instructed to confirm Rabasa's fictitious testimony. Celada allegedly declared that Gil "was firing at us and we had to kill him," but later recanted, claiming that he had been forced to sign the statement without knowing what was contained therein.[54] Other policemen also reported being pressured by their superior officers to make statements to exonerate Rabasa.

The police conspiracy to hide the murder underscored the practical consequences of New Men's efforts to prove their political fitness. In particular, police chief Oropesa faced increasing pressure to prove himself to US military authorities, who had concluded that he was unfit for public authority because of his antagonistic attitude during the May and June riots. His reputation as the intellectual author of Gil's murder suggests that he performed his political fitness through the violent repression of black men. Indeed, following the investigation, it became increasingly difficult—even for US military officials—to deny the blatantly racial motives for the killing. US Second Infantry Captain F. J. Kernan reported outright that "considerable race prejudice is involved in this affair."[55] The attempts to cover up the murder suggests that white police recognized the inherent contradiction between their status as New Men, premised on martial manhood, and the racialized performance of political fitness by violently suppressing black men. When the conspiracy was revealed, Oropesa, Rabasa, and other New Men were exposed as traitors of revolutionary masculinity.

Black veterans in and beyond Cienfuegos recognized the murder as part of a broader process of postwar racial exclusion, one that stripped black veterans of their military honor and transformed them into second-class citizens. In line with the decidedly racial motives suspected by many poor and working-class *cienfuegueros* and recognized in official reports, one of the most vocal public protests surrounding Gil's assassination was framed boldly and explicitly in racial terms. In a leaflet titled "To the Colored Race, Glory to General Gil," black veterans Captain Pedro P. Mutos and Commandant Juan Sardiñas y Villa (Molina) of Puerto Príncipe claimed that the departure of local ruling elites from the true ideals of patriotism jeopardized the emerging republic. Cuba was becoming the domain of "a certain class, for an oligarchy without conscience, that gives people more rights for being white than to us for being black." Mutos and Sardiñas chastised Cienfuegos political elites for their complicity in the murder and for their collaboration with US military authorities against black and working-class veterans. "The great Dominican soldier," they wrote, "was our pride as he was a humiliation for some Cubans who were before with the Spaniards more Spanish than Santiago, and who are today with the Americans more American than Washington himself."[56] By juxtaposing pro-Spanish and later pro-US sentiment with racism, Mutos and Sardiñas argued that current leaders were unpatriotic because of their race prejudice.

They further chastised white veterans for betraying the Cuban cause and turning their backs on their black compatriots. After all, black men had been the very core of the Liberating Army, Mutos and Sardiñas claimed. They had stood "alone in defending independence while the revolutionary rank was dwindling down by the surrender of the timid ones [whites]." This argument became emblematic of the black struggle for inclusion in the new republic throughout the twentieth century: the centrality of their role in the struggle for independence entitled black men to an equal share of rights and benefits in the emerging republic.[57] Interestingly, this manifesto represented a marked departure for Mutos, who in his earlier writings had emphasized the ability and the obligation of Cubans, white and black, to overcome the racial tensions that certain intellectuals claimed doomed Cuba to perpetual revolution.[58] Now, however, both Mutos and Sardiñas had become bolder in their declarations about race. In one part of the leaflet, the veterans referenced one of the greatest fears among property owners: that black veterans would rise up to take control of the island. "As General Gil rests in eternal glory," it read, "we in this valley of bastardized and adulterated ambitions, will always be disposed to die before consenting to be pariahs in our own land."[59] This closing statement reaffirmed the centrality of military service as a cornerstone of black veterans' claims to authority and honor not only by paying homage to the military merits of General Gil, but also by reminding white veterans and others that this military service entitled them to a certain degree of influence over the political sphere. The emphasis on *consent* figures as both a reference to the social contract implied in governance in *their land* as well as a powerful claim to equal political standing with their white compatriots.

"That Agent of Authority Who Abused Him So Villainously"

Civil authorities' tepid response to the ongoing public outcry over Gil's death only confirmed black veterans' general feelings of alienation from the structures of postwar power. By late January civil authorities apprehended the most immediate perpetrator, Rabasa, who was later tried and found guilty of murder.[60] The court sentenced him to fourteen years in jail and ordered him to pay restitution to Gil's family in the amount of five thousand pesos.[61]

However, the sentencing of Rabasa marked the judicial limits civil authorities were willing to reach. The other police officers implicated in the killing did not face punishment, which incensed both local protesters and the family members of the late general. Perfecto denounced the impunity with which the perpetrators were treated: "the murderers are walking the streets of Cienfuegos so satisfied, not knowing the crime they have committed."[62] The impunity afforded to Rabasa's co-conspirators would loom in the public memory, causing one black activist to contemplate years later the possibility of retroactively jailing them, though civil authorities never acted on these demands.[63] Oropesa also avoided charges despite reportedly being the mastermind of the murder. Gil's murder and the general impunity enjoyed by police marked only the beginning of a much more significant shift in local and provincial law enforcement that followed the inauguration of civil government in January 1900. While US authorities could not directly control how local law enforcement operated, they sought to influence the municipal police through their relationships with the civil authorities to whom the police reported.

Among their most immediate goals was to remove men who had refused to cooperate with US officials in the past. In Cienfuegos US military authorities immediately zeroed in on two prominent white men who had been outspoken critics and antagonists of the local military government over the first half of 1899: Frías and Oropesa. Even though US officials initially accepted the actions of the police in Gil's murder, the discovery of police wrong-doing offered them a convenient excuse to dismiss their longtime nemeses. They cited the murder and failure to quell subsequent protests as grounds for dismissing Oropesa from his post as police chief. Civil authorities complied. Though clearly driven by US military officials, the order came through civil channels: provincial governor José Miguel Gómez directed Mayor Frías to remove Oropesa—a tacit admission of his culpability in the matter. However, Frías refused to abandon his white compatriot. He appointed Oropesa to the city council, a position even more prestigious than his last. The retention of Oropesa in a high-ranking government position revealed an unwavering commitment to wartime patronage alliances among the small circle of local white ruling elites—a well-documented pattern of local politics in Cienfuegos.[64]

Next, military officials targeted Mayor Frías. Although he initially enjoyed a reputation as a "gentleman of education and social distinction," Frías had come under the fire of local military officials like Walter B. Barker for his refusal to submit to US military authority.[65] He had also lost the support of certain planters after taxing them for sanitary work done on their properties. Additionally, he had offended members of the local conservative elite by refusing to grant them and their non-veteran relatives political positions in municipal government. So profound was the personal hatred these men felt for Frías that the editor of the conservative newspaper *La República*, which allegedly represented propertied interests, ran stories insulting him and undermining his honor. On one occasion a rival reportedly insulted the mayor in city hall, calling him "indecent" (*grosero*) and a "scoundrel" (*canalla*), and threatened to draw his pistol. The conflicts over access to public employment and political power that undergirded these exchanges became so extreme that several of the men involved challenged Frías and his allies to fight duels, which never materialized.[66]

By February 1900 just one month after Oropesa was deposed, military officials removed Frías, claiming that his position as mayor was "incompatible" with his tenure as professor at the University of Havana. They presented him with an ultimatum: either remain mayor or keep his professorship. The ultimatum came on the heels of direct confrontations between Frías and US military officials during a recent labor strike. Military officials charged that Frías had failed to suppress a labor strike with sufficient force. Frías chose his professorship and vacated the office of mayor just months before local elections.[67] It was perhaps no coincidence that military authorities waited until after the election to remove Frías from his professorship as well. The removal clearly was not about any conflict of interest, but rather about eliminating obstacles in the way of US military influence over local politics.[68]

The removal of Frías and Oropesa marked the elimination of the two most significant antagonists of US authorities in Cienfuegos. When these revolutionary men initially assumed power in early 1899, they resisted what they viewed to be US abuses of authority or transgressions against Cuban citizens. Yet, when they recognized their resistance posed dangers to their political futures, they attempted to shift away from radical demands for absolute and immediate independence and eliminate the limited cross-racial power sharing they had initially allowed. This betrayal of revolutionary values rendered their platforms less appealing to the masses, even as their revolutionary credentials still afforded them a degree of credibility. For US military authorities, though, Frías and Oropesa had failed to shift quickly enough and thus fell from political grace.

The replacement mayor and police chief, though both decorated white Cuban veterans, did not make the same mistakes. The new mayor was Leopoldo Figueroa, a prominent veteran from the rural town of Santa Isabel de las Lajas who joined the insurrection in 1896, fought under the command of José Miguel Gómez, reached the rank of lieutenant colonel, and finished the war in the Sanitary Corps.[69] He did not live for any prolonged period of time in the United States, but rather studied in Spain and was trained as a pharmacist. Juan José López de Campillo y D'Wolf, a member of the Cienfuegos elite, assumed the position of chief of police in January 1900.[70] Born in Cienfuegos in 1872, Campillo had joined the insurrection in 1895, finishing the war as colonel. Both these men perfectly combined revolutionary credentials that would command the respect of the popular classes and fellow veterans with elite racial and class status, which military authorities assumed would translate into social conservatism and preservation of order.

Campillo did not disappoint US military authorities. He quickly moved to reform what they saw as the most racially degenerate, disorderly, and dangerous body in municipal government: the police. Under his leadership, the personnel of the municipal police force underwent substantial change. There is some evidence that reform efforts included the whitening of the force, although no explicit orders mentioning racial preferences in employment emerged. One black activist suggested that Campillo pushed black men out of the force indirectly, for example, by implementing policies that disproportionately harmed poorer (black) policemen. One such policy imposed a fine equal to two days salary if a police officer fulfilled "an indispensable need" like taking a lunch break.[71] The racial silence of this policy fit within broader patterns of indirect and situational racial exclusion.

Although the exact number of black veterans dismissed from the police is lost with the records of that institution, the mounting complaints against the police by local black residents indicates that a certain shift in the personnel was certainly occurring.[72] Black veterans commented directly on the scarcity of black men in the force. By early 1900 two black veterans publically criticized local political elites for removing black veterans from public positions "for the sole reason of being black."[73] Another black veteran recollected that "in the police force, there was not even one percent blacks, because the Americans got the word out that when the black man had power [*cogiera fuerza*], when he became educated, he was harmful to the white race. In that way the black man was completely separated." Nor were the US officials the only ones responsible for this shift in employment. Rather, white Cubans were complicit and usually enacted the exclusionary practices. According to the same black veteran, "the Cubans of the other race kept quiet, did not do anything, and that is how the situation stayed."[74] With these changes, US perceptions of the police also became more favorable. While they had complained of the preponderance of black policemen in early 1899, by the following year they began describing the whiteness of the force and their greater ability to preserve order.[75]

The apparent whitening of the Cienfuegos police force seemed to bring that city into line with other major urban centers across the island. Military officials in other Cuban cities had implemented policies to limit or eliminate black employment in the police force. Of the 165 police employed in Matanzas city, only five were of African descent.[76] In Havana General William Ludlow who cited the "excitable temperament" of Cubans as a cause of their lack of "calmness and effectiveness," was also known to prohibit the employment of black men in the municipal police force.[77] In that city the initial organization of the police was modeled on parallel institutions in the northeastern US cities, where the overwhelming majority of urban policemen were white.[78] In Havana former New York City police chief John McCullough transformed the "exceedingly raw material" in a "chaotic and thoroughly Spanish" force into a body of "fine specimens of manhood in blue uniform, patrolling the streets of Havana in accordance with a comprehensive and perfectly working system."[79] Of three thousand applicants, only eight hundred "survived" the rigorous testing and "personal scrutiny" of McCullough. Many planters and US military officials believed that the police force, being one of the most important institutions of order, had to be composed of whites, who were believed to be the most orderly elements in society.

Although the premise of police "reform" was to preserve order, some black Cubans challenged the presumed link between order and whiteness. One black writer criticized what he saw as an excessive "preoccupation of races and of colors," which led white Cubans to mistake civilization with racial exclusion. This critic claimed that black men were in fact more suited for important public jobs, like policing, in part because "the colored race is the part of the population that possesses the best elements of information by being intimately mixed with all of the private acts of families."[80] By hiring only whites as police "they have excluded from its midst the class [of people] best informed of all the individual particularities of our population. It is known that there is not a single family that does not have as *confidants* people of the colored race."[81] This critic argued that black men were better suited to police work than whites because they and their families had infiltrated all layers of society through their roles as midwives, domestic servants, cooks, coach drivers, seamstresses, and laundresses, not to mention most occupations of manual labor.

Other black Cubans posed questions about whom precisely this "order" benefited. As the police force increasingly morphed into an instrument of propertied interests, poor and working-class people fell under greater scrutiny, but also grew more suspicious of the police. Before Gil's murder, many humble urban dwellers saw the employment of veterans in the police force as reason to trust the police to protect the people, defend Cuban freedom, and serve justice. However, recent changes had stripped the force of those vital functions. One black Cuban declared that a white police force served no other purpose than decoration: "In its actual composition, the Police [Force] seems more destined to be a public ornament than to the exact discharge of its functions."[82] Clearly, a police force composed mainly of white men could not be trusted to defend the interests of the racially heterogeneous working classes.

Indeed, within months of Campillo assuming command of the Cienfuegos police force, complaints began to surface of corruption and police brutality against poor and working-class residents. Local black activist Nicolás Valverde wrote of some of the outrages in his weekly publication, *Ecos Populares*. His first charge was that the recent transformation of the police force placed the wrong kind of men in positions of power. Hiring white men and even men from outside the locality presumed that "there is not a humble townsman [*hijo del pueblo*] capable of wearing the police uniform with dignity; on the other hand, there is room for cowards, who raise their hand to slap a handcuffed man in the middle of the police station," he charged. Valverde wrote that police abused their authority with impunity: "for that cowardly official, who abuses his authority, there is no law," he protested.[83]

Campillo enacted policies designed to stifle complaints against these police abuses of poor and working-class residents. It became exceedingly difficult to file a complaint in the first place. In order to file charges, a complainant needed a witness, "which seems to us like a way to discourage him from following through, because none of the people in that station would lend himself to the case, fearing to lose their job." Even if a person managed to get a witness and file a complaint, the demands of following through with the procedure were onerous, humiliating, and potentially life-threatening. "The victim is made to appear every fifteen days in the station, to mortify him and make him desist in his right as a citizen, to make claims before the tribunals, against that agent of authority who abused him so villainously."[84] Valverde recognized that part of the persecution of the popular classes stemmed from the intimidation of the lowest-ranking members of the police force, many of whom desperately needed their income. Keeping their jobs and collecting the pay they earned depended on maintaining absolute loyalty to their chief, even when he and other superior officers abused authority or themselves committed crimes.

In some cases, police brutalized residents who levied critiques against the force. The case of Emilio Vega and his wife Juana exemplified police abuses of authority and intimidation of civilians in Cienfuegos. In a café in the working-class neighborhood of Reina in Cienfuegos, Emilio recounted to his friends an earlier encounter he had with police. One policeman entered the café and, overhearing "insubordinate and possibly insulting language toward and about the police," began beating Emilio. Another policeman joined in the assault moments later. Hearing her husband's cries, Juana ran from her home across the street and attempted to free Emilio from the grips of the police. Then, the police turned on her, striking her numerous times, and inflicting severe bruises. Emilio was tried and sentenced to pay a twenty-five-dollar fine and spend three days in jail, after the judge refused to hear testimony on his behalf.

Emilio persisted in his complaints against the police, citing the brutal beating of his wife as evidence of the dishonorable and abusive conduct of the police. Eventually, the complaints came to the attention of military authorities—most likely because Emilio worked for an US-owned company. Although they dismissed his complaints about the beating he suffered, military authorities noted that actions of the police were "inexcusable, particularly in the clubbing of the woman," and suggested the dismissal of the perpetrators.[85] Campillo retorted that he had already removed them for "other reasons," which he did not specify, arguing that it would be unfair to criticize the policemen without hearing their side of the story.[86]

The escalating police brutality against poor and working-class residents evinced a potent failure to address what many Cienfuegos residents saw as an increasing rift between the people and their public servants. This was not simply a matter of the emergence of racial order as one of the essential requirements of holding political power; the contradictory perspectives concerning police employment practices revealed profound disagreement about what kind of man could claim public authority and how they should use it. Black veterans rejected their exclusion from New Man status, claiming informal public authority on the basis of military service. Yet political power and public employment remained out of reach of most black men, and even seemed to be slipping through the fingers of prominent white veterans. The conditionality of New Men's political power simultaneously afforded the most conservative white veterans unprecedented access to local authority while weakening their administrative autonomy. Military officials effectively replaced key local leaders with men more sympathetic to their agenda. The ensuing "reforms" to the municipal police forces evinced New Men's growing collaboration with US military officials as a condition of their political power. As they transformed police into defenders of propertied interests, civil authorities betrayed the politically and socially radical dimensions of revolutionary masculinity, shifting away from defending fellow veterans and separatists and toward cooperating with US military officials. Essentially, harassing and detaining black, poor, and working-class populations had the same repressive and disenfranchising effect on those populations without risking the scandal of public protest.

Amid a rising tide of state violence against poor, working-class, and especially black men, black activists tempered their claims. Valverde insisted that New Men at least recognize and respect the humanity of non-elite residents. New Men largely ignored Valverde's protests, something they simply could not have done a year earlier before the public protests surrounding Gil's assassination. The next chapter explores how civil authorities reconciled their increasing collaboration with the military government with their revolutionary credentials as they approached the first local elections in June 1900.

Part III

From Revolutionaries to Neocolonials

*The Specter of Black Criminality and the
Conditionality of Public Authority, 1900–1902*

CHAPTER SEVEN

Not Simply "Because One Happens to Belong to the Male Species"

Race, Rural Law Enforcement, and Political Disorder amid Restricted Suffrage

◈ THE INAUGURATION OF CIVIL GOVERNMENT IN JANUARY 1900 INTEN- sified New Men's ongoing struggle to reconcile their obligations toward the US military government and their revolutionary commitments. On the one hand, it forced New Men ever closer to US military officials, who wielded immense though often unseen power over their political futures. To secure US support, political elites had to prove their deference and allegiance to the military government. This often required them to temper their demands for absolute and immediate independence and enact policies that alienated them from their networks of military patronage, especially from veterans of poor and working-class backgrounds. On the other hand, civil government also brought the announcement of local elections, scheduled for June 1900. Just as New Men had adjusted their political authority to suit the whims of local US military officials, they were again subjected to the countervailing force of public opinion.

Because whiteness remained an unspoken precondition of political fitness, the yet undetermined electorate would decide between two main types of candidates: New Men, who at least nominally supported absolute and immediate independence, and a more politically and socially conservative group of Autonomists, Spaniards, and pacíficos, who generally supported close ties with the United States. Despite their recent acquiescence to the demands of US military officials, New Men's military service remained a powerful foundation for their claims to political power. Thus veterans of the Liberating Army, regardless of their race, were likely to throw their support behind these white veteran political candidates. In this context, deciding exactly who could vote proved crucial to determining electoral outcomes: restricted suffrage would likely result in the election of Autonomists and conservative separatists, whereas expansive suffrage was expected to favor New Men. Understanding that the electoral outcomes would have a profound impact on the political future of the island, eligibility for suffrage became the source of vociferous disagreement across nearly every sector of the Cuban population and the military government in early 1900.

The debate over the precise parameters of suffrage hinged on the delicate, yet fiercely contested distinction between maleness and manliness. In general, US military officials dismissed the idea of "unlimited manhood suffrage." James H. Wilson, commander of Matanzas and Santa Clara, for one, declared that the vote, "like any other privilege of citizenship, should be based on qualifications," and certainly "not permitted merely because one happens to belong to the male species."[1] Because maleness and manliness were *not* one and the same, as Wilson suggested, defining masculinity was central to determining the parameters of suffrage.

Drawing on their experiences in the US Civil War and Reconstruction, US military officials distinguished between maleness and manhood along the lines of wealth, education, and property—a view that reflected recent limitations on the Fifteenth Amendment to the US Constitution.[2] While former Confederates like Walter B. Barker were inclined to welcome the racially exclusive effects of these restrictions and generally opposed the enfranchisement of black men, former Union officers like Wilson were more reluctant to restrict suffrage explicitly along racial lines. For instance, Wilson wrote that the "race question should not be complicated by the question of suffrage, which should be settled not upon race lines, but upon the lines of intelligence, property interest, and qualification in the affairs of state."[3] He considered it dangerous to invest "the ignorant man with suffrage." Rather he advocated the gradual extension of the franchise "based on an educational test, as it is found desirable and safe to do so."[4] Wilson eschewed the facile conflation of manliness and whiteness. Yet, imposing literacy, education, and wealth qualifications on suffrage essentially guaranteed a wealthy, white electorate, one that excluded most people of African descent and many poor whites. As it had in the post-Reconstruction United States, a literacy requirement alone would have excluded over half of all white Cuban men from the vote and more than three-quarters of black men.[5] Moreover, the racialized assumptions conflating manhood with whiteness ensured that even black men who met the lofty requirements would face greater scrutiny than less qualified white men.

Men who favored close ties with the United States generally supported the US military government's efforts to impose restricted suffrage. In particular, opponents of separatist rule, many of whom viewed indefinite US rule in Cuba as the best way to ensure their own material interests, were among the most vocal supporters of restricted suffrage. The presumed link between race and political radicalism was at the very center of their demands for limiting the electorate. One annexationist advocated for the exclusion of "vagrants, thieves, ñáñigos, bootblacks, newspaper vendors, pimps, and other men of bad character" from suffrage, implying an inherent connection between criminality, blackness, and immorality. Yet it was not only the race or "character" of these men that made them suspect, but also their alleged propensity toward violent rebellion and resistance to US rule. He claimed that Cubans who refused to embrace the military government were "less civilized than the Tagalogs," a reference to the fierce insurrection against US rule in the Philippines.[6] Opponents of separatist rule like this man envisioned the disenfranchisement of these nonwhite radicals as crucial for the preservation of the proper social and political order (under US rule).

Although many opponents of separatist rule were themselves ineligible for political power because of their foreign citizenship, conservative Cubans generally concurred in their preference for restricted suffrage. Former Autonomists and the more conservative sectors of the PRC envisioned the disenfranchisement of the revolutionary popular sectors as the best way to ensure their own electoral victories. Consequently, many of them also supported restricting the vote through property, literacy, and wealth qualifications for suffrage.

Between the announcement of civil government in late 1899 and the formalization of the electoral law in April 1900, the men of the revolution struggled against these efforts to restrict suffrage. Black veterans were among the first men to protest what they suspected to be the US military government's attempt to disenfranchise them. They argued that their military service entitled them to voting rights—an earned right of their martial manhood. In February 1900 a manifesto addressing the "colored liberators in Santa Clara Province" circulated around central Cuba. Its anonymous authors argued that it was "unfair" to deprive "the large majority of colored and working people of their electoral vote." They claimed that it was hypocritical to welcome black men into the army "when good hands were needed to manage the Cuban machete" only to deny them political representation in the society they had helped liberate.[7]

The same manifesto harnessed a common history of revolutionary sacrifice to unite black veterans and workers against their impending political disenfranchisement. "The working man, just the same as the colored man, was an important factor of a triumph whose benefits neither are enjoying," the manifesto declared. Even "if the Cuban workman did not give his blood," or "leave behind his wife and children" or "face enemy fire," he contributed to independence in other manly ways. He gave "his money to aid in the purchase of war material." He provided medicine for "his sick and wounded brethren" at the expense of his own family. He faced imprisonment and torture by the enemy.[8] All these claims relied on the assumption that working men, by virtue of their class status, supported the revolution. By employing an expansive definition of service to the patria, the manifesto made a cross-racial appeal for the enfranchisement of black veterans and workers.

White veterans and separatists also advocated the enfranchisement of men of humbler origins. City councils throughout Santa Clara Province petitioned the civil government to allow universal manhood suffrage in the 1900 local elections.[9] In a telegram, one group of councilmen protested restricted suffrage requirements because they violated "the platform and constitution of the revolutionary party," which centered the "democratic" premise of "Cuba for the Cubans without distinctions nor irritating privileges."[10] Another city council claimed that the restriction violated the "principle of equality," and the elections should be conducted in the most "just and equitable" fashion possible.[11] While city councilmen framed their appeals to inclusion gingerly, activists and writers were not nearly as restrained. One group of protesters chastised the United States for attempting to restrict suffrage, and equated these actions to violating the sovereignty of "a country it did not conquer."[12]

While a significant contingent of veterans supported universal manhood suffrage, the most vocal demands centered on securing the right to vote for veterans in particular. White revolutionaries couched their support of veterans' right to vote within appeals to the revolution's democratic principles, celebrating a supposedly raceless martial manhood. They claimed that all veterans, regardless of race or class, had earned the right to vote through their contributions to the revolution. Similar arguments claiming that "all men who have been born free and who have conquered the right to absolute independence" deserved the right to vote, a qualification that still would have disenfranchised the many formerly enslaved veterans. On the surface these impassioned appeals to liberty, equality, and brotherhood might give the impression that these municipal political elites actually cared about the rights of black veterans. Some of them may have internalized the racial inclusivity originally implied in revolutionary masculinity. However, these white political elites also had vested interests in expansive suffrage, recognizing that they would benefit from popular support for their revolutionary credentials.

The resulting electoral law codified restricted suffrage, but offered certain concessions to advocates of expansive suffrage. US Military Order 164, issued in April 1900, enfranchised male citizens, twenty-one years or older, who were either literate or owned property valued at $250 or more. However, the law waived these property and literacy requirements for veterans of the War of Independence who served honorably in the Cuban army before July 18, 1898.[13] The resulting electorate would include wealthy, educated men and veterans.

Although the suffrage law appeared to be racially neutral, historians have rightly noted that the restrictions effectively excluded the majority of Cuban men and disproportionately disenfranchised men of color.[14] Analyzing the practical impact of this law on men in Santa Clara Province, this chapter suggests that racialized political exclusion extended well beyond what historians have been able to document thus far. I show that the enfranchisement of black veterans coincided with a parallel wave of criminalization and state violence against these newly enfranchised voters during the first two major electoral events under US rule: the municipal elections of June 1900 and the August 1900 elections of delegates for the Cuban Constitutional Convention.

I argue that criminalization emerged as a powerful gendered rational for the repression, incarceration, and disenfranchisement of black men otherwise entitled to the vote, in the name of "order." Opponents of separatist rule drove this development by invoking the invented trope of the black veteran criminal. They knew—perhaps from their experience during Reconstruction in the post–Civil War US South—that incarceration could achieve largely the same disenfranchising affect as racially restrictive laws, all while avoiding the scandal of public protest.[15] They deployed criminalizing discourses to label virtually any display of black authority or demand for rights as a criminal threat to propertied interests. They framed the elections as an inevitable precursor to "Negro Rule," and even alleged that black veterans were planning a criminal insurrection against the US military authority.

These demonstrably false claims captured the attention of US military officials and New Men, particularly in the tense months surrounding the elections. Facing increasing pressure from US military officials to address these racialized allegations, New Men enacted their political fitness by repudiating these fictitious black uprisings and repressing their would-be perpetrators. New Men running for local office drew on recent "reforms" to law enforcement to ramp up racialized policing against black men. The criminalization and incarceration of black men became a strategy by which New Men sought to secure US support for their political aspirations. Even though New Men publically demanded the enfranchisement of all veterans based on their honorable military service, their responses to false claims of black insurrection prevented some black veterans from enjoying these legal rights in practice.

The paradox of New Men's demands for expansive suffrage and their practical implementation of racialized criminalization was palpable. The common denominator of these contradictory discourses and practices was white men's desire for political power. They adeptly performed their revolutionary credentials to garner popular support for their political candidacy by declaring their commitments to universal manhood suffrage and absolute independence. Yet, white civil authorities just as quickly betrayed their public commitment to revolutionary masculinity in order to secure the blessing of US military officials. Even as the racial allegations of crime reported by opponents of separatist rule were broadly recognized as fictitious and politically motivated, New Men's willingness to use their positions of authority to target black veterans as alleged criminals illustrated just how tenuous their commitment to revolutionary masculinity had become.

Rural Law Enforcement "Reform" on the Road to Municipal Elections

Precisely as the men of the revolution secured enfranchisement for all veterans, US military officials enacted a series of major reforms involving rural law enforcement. Amid vocal complaints from opponents of separatist rule regarding widespread rural crime, US military officials transformed rural order in two critical ways. First, Wilson allowed certain approved individuals to bear arms through the concession of permits as early as mid-1899. This policy constituted a marked reversal of his early position on arms-bearing. Initially, Wilson had favored disarming the general population, who he described as a bunch of "people carrying arms and running around and shooting promiscuously."[16] For the first months of his tenure as military governor, he had upheld Bates's orders forcing planters to disband their private guard forces. Yet, planters vocally and continuously complained of the alleged state of disorder in the countryside and the supposed inadequacies of the Rural Guard. They used these alleged grievances to demand US approval for rearming their private guard forces.

Likely an effort to assuage the anxieties planters expressed, Wilson eventually resolved to allow private citizens to hold arms with a special permit.[17] To secure a permit, the applicant had to present the recommendation of several prominent citizens to verify the applicant's good character.[18] This requirement alone practically guaranteed that the vast majority of permits would be conceded to white men. Essentially, this order enabled planters to re-establish private guard forces by writing each of their members a simple recommendation letter. Later, Wilson clarified that the hired guards must be "of the character satisfactory to the civil authorities," an addition that evinced a delicate balancing act between appeasing wealthy planters and recognizing civil authorities. Nonetheless, the fact that he had to stipulate this last point directly suggests an erosion of the state monopoly on the use of force.[19]

Although the concession of arms permits to private guards began in mid-1899, it accelerated following the inauguration of the civil government and the announcement of elections. The number of private guards employed in the Cienfuegos countryside rose from 172 in 1899 to 233 in 1900. By June 1900 the number and placement of private guards had expanded to include posts throughout the countryside and in every municipal district in the Cienfuegos jurisdiction. This marked a powerful return to the racialized access to the use of force that had reigned before the war.[20]

Wilson's concession of arms permits not only catalyzed the privatization of the use of force, it vested important decisions over what constituted crime and how to treat offenders in the most privileged sector of society: wealthy, white property owners. Bostonian planter Edwin F. Atkins alluded to the ways he sought to use this newly reacquired power. Disgruntled over being "expected to do the work of local protection," Atkins suggested that he might be inclined simply to kill perceived offenders, rather than engaging in the

Table 7.1. Private armed guards in Cienfuegos, 1899–1900

Municipality	Number of armed guards, June 1899	Number of armed guards, June 1900
Abreus	81	50
Cartagena	0	8
Cienfuegos	0	85
Cruces	0	13
Hormiguero	49	0
Lajas	22	39
Rodas	10	21
San Fernando de Camarones	0	17
Total	162	233

Source: Mayor José Antonio Frías to Dorst, June 13, 1899, Box 11, File 5354, USNAI/RUSA/RG 395/E 1331; Antonio R. Mora to General James H. Wilson, June 14, 1899, File 5584, USNAI/RUSA/RG 395/E 1331; José del Castillo (Abreus) to General James H. Wilson, June 17, 1899, File 5418; USNAI/RUSA/RG 395/E 1331; Antonio Gallart (Rodas) to General James H. Wilson, June 17, 1899, File 5478, USNAI/RUSA/RG 395/E 1331; R. Pérez (Cruces) to General James H. Wilson, June 15, 1899, File 5420, USNAI/RUSA/RG 395/E 1331; "Statement of the Estates . . . Granted Authority to Maintain Private Guards, under Decree 83," June 2, 1900, Box 36, File 3238, USNAI/RUSA/RG 395/E 1331.

burdensome acts of investigation and humane detention. When confronted with crime, a planter would be forced to take "the law in[to] his own hands," he mused. In these instances, "we might find ourselves in an embarrassing position, should we, in protecting our property, shoot one of them without arrest."[21] By his own admission, Atkins envisioned his preferential access to legal arms-bearing as a tool through which to enforce racial order through lethal force. The same men who had criminalized black veterans to demand racial policing were now granted the ability to use violence for their own purposes. Perhaps most ominously, this violence gained legitimacy under the law.

Building on this expansion of private security, Wilson implemented a second set of reforms, altering and reducing the provincial government's investment in public law enforcement, particularly the Rural Guard. In the months leading up to the municipal elections, Wilson ramped up his ongoing efforts to fix what he saw as a broken system of rural law enforcement. Initially, he zeroed in on the Rural Guard, which at its peak employed over six hundred men, mainly veterans, across Santa Clara Province. He judged such an extensive Rural Guard force as excessive, even "un-American and un-Republican." He claimed that the force was merely a "relic of Spanish tyranny and misgovernment," and prone to become "an instrument of oppression and outrage" in a province that largely lacked rural crime.²² Wilson speculated cynically that "if they do not give more trouble to the province than all the rest of the people in it, I shall miss my guess very badly."²³ Concluding that retaining such a force was "not honorable," Wilson proposed abolishing the Rural Guard altogether and incorporating its men into municipal police forces.²⁴

Wilson's proposal to eliminate the Rural Guard in Santa Clara Province outraged nearly all sectors of the population, albeit for fundamentally different reasons. Veterans and separatists pointed out the hypocrisy of Wilson's proposal. One Cuban claimed that Wilson was merely attempting to aggrandize his own reputation by portraying the area under his command as the "best ruled and administered," all the while neglecting the poverty afflicting veterans and the rural population more broadly.²⁵ Could it be that Wilson, as he claimed, was genuinely interested in "democracy"? asked another critic sharply. No, he concluded. Rather, Wilson attempted to discredit the Rural Guard by invoking the liberal tradition of the United States, "where there is so much democracy, liberty and civilization, [and] they lynch those who steal."²⁶ If the only rationale for dismantling the Rural Guard was to conform to US values, then this critic invoked the US reputation for anti-black racial violence to pinpoint the hypocrisy of such a claim.

Other veterans voiced their opposition to Wilson's plan in terms of their desire to keep veterans employed in the desperate postwar economy. One veteran claimed that disbanding the force would "despoil the Cuban of everything," while undemocratically giving the jobs to US Americans, as Bates had done previously.²⁷ Without these important jobs, hundreds more veterans would struggle to subsist in Santa Clara's broken postwar economy. Did Wilson think that farming implements, oxen, and rations for the hungry would simply "fall from the sky?" asked one critic sarcastically.²⁸ Many veterans countered Wilson's proposal, urging him to expand the Rural Guard to employ more men. Some veterans even encouraged Wilson to reform the Rural Guard by offering higher pay and better equipment to attract higher-quality men.²⁹

Wealthy planters opposed Wilson's proposal for an entirely different set of reasons. They contested his assertion that rural crime barely existed in Santa Clara, claiming instead that it was rampant. They demanded that Wilson expand, not reduce, the Rural Guard, and that he order the force to ensure their personal security and protect private property.³⁰ Wilson largely dismissed planters' claims about crime, which he knew from experience to be hyperbolic and politically motivated, rather than rooted in fact. Although violence and crime had been a problem during the early months of the military occupation, by the time he assumed command in mid-1899, the level of crime in Santa Clara Province was "no greater than might occur in any well-governed country."[31] Major cities were "orderly, and free from violence, rowdyism, and licentiousness."[32] Indeed, many of the alleged crimes that planters reported, on investigation turned out to be completely fabricated, or at best exaggerated.[33] The constant patrolling of the countryside by the Rural Guard "hardly seems necessary now, the country being at peace and no bandits to cope with," Wilson concluded.[34]

In the face of such stringent opposition, Wilson resolved to reduce and reform the Rural Guard, rather than abolishing it. For both these goals, the problem of personnel was key. An inspection of the Rural Guard in June 1899 revealed troubling inadequacies in the quality of men employed in the Rural Guard, particularly at the lower ranks. Notwithstanding the new higher pay scale instituted earlier that year, one US police inspector noted that the force still employed black men. Commenting on black Rural Guardsmen's fitness for the job, he remarked patronizingly that "physically they are superior to the others, and mentally they will average *nearly* as well."[35] References to prevailing racial stereotypes of both the physical prowess and intellectual inferiority of the black male likely helped justify an existing preference for white men in officer positions.

US officials also commented disparagingly on the general unfitness of the men employed in the Rural Guard, commentary that often hinged on disparaging assumptions about their masculinity. The police inspector remarked that the guardsmen at the lower ranks were in "a very dirty, ragged condition."[36] He further observed that "not enough care [has been] taken in picking men of good physique—many boys were also noticed." Age or perceived age based on a cursory judgment of physical and bodily development served to dismiss the fitness of these veterans for duty in the Rural Guard. The inspector claimed that many men were selected for the Rural Guard not because of "fitness" for the job, but "apparently because they had some sort of pony and arms and had served in the Cuban army."[37] Of course, this was a direct result of policies US military officials had imposed on the institution. Specifically, they ordered veterans to use their own horses and weapons from the war, as well as their old Cuban uniforms on the job.

In late 1899 military officials enacted a series of sweeping reforms. The Rural Guard's new charter set strict guidelines about the quality of men employed in the force.[38] Recruits had to conform to a dizzying list of physical specifications, education standards, and temperament requirements. Presumably seeking to rid the force of the many "boys" previously employed therein, the new rules imposed height, weight, and chest breadth requirements on recruits.[39] Among the other requirements were literacy, no criminal antecedents, good health, and "good moral character," a dubious and subjective quality measured by a man's ability to secure recommendations from respectable citizens (i.e., prominent white men). This qualification alone rendered it nearly impossible for black veterans to secure a position in the Rural Guard, effectively eliminating their access to formal authority.[40]

Although none of the criteria for employment explicitly mentioned race, the new more stringent standards seem to have been applied unevenly to black and white men. There was no shortage of cases in which white officers did not meet the requirements but kept their jobs. One white man, who enlisted in the Cuban army in mid-May 1898, could not even sign his own name, yet he retained his position in the rural police until he was convicted of murdering a plantation worker in late 1900.[41]

In contrast, there was no evidence of the employment of a black veteran who did not meet the explicit requirements of the job. On the contrary, even black men who did fulfill all the requisites had short-lived careers. José González Planas, a distinguished veteran who served as chief of the Rural Guard's Fourth District, and one of the only visible exceptions to the rule of white leadership, faced vocal opposition to his appointment. US military authorities judged González Planas "a shrewd man" with "a good record as a leader in the war," and they reluctantly accepted his employment in the force for his "considerable influence among the colored people." However, even they noted that "there appears to be some prejudice against him because of his color."[42] González Planas only served in the force for two years.[43]

In addition to reinforcing the existing preference for whiteness in the force, the new regulations on personnel also betrayed some powerful assumptions US military officials made about white veterans' manhood. They suggested that white Cuban veterans had to be guided away from their supposedly "excitable" racial nature. General rules dictated that rural police be "civil and respectful in demeanor" and maintain "a perfect command of temper." The same document advised rural policemen that "a man must not allow himself to be moved nor excited by any language or threats, however violent. The cooler he keeps himself, the more power he will have over his assailants." Rural policemen were also ordered to "speak the truth at all times and under all circumstances." When asked about a case he must "state all he knows . . .

without any desire to influence the result either for or against the prisoner," a rule that likely sought to mitigate the favoritism Cuban veterans purportedly showed their former compatriots-in-arms.[44]

These more stringent personnel requirements were crucial in reducing the Rural Guard.[45] Between September 1899 and June 1900, Wilson ordered reductions in the Rural Guard, while expanding private arms permits. In March 1900 he reorganized the Rural Guard into four companies, eliminating some of the officer positions associated with the former territorial designations and marginally increasing pay for all positions. By April that year, he reduced the number of privates in each company from 105 to only 89. By June, only 57 privates were employed with each company, decreasing the total number of Rural Guard positions to little more than 300.[46]

Although US military officials judged that further reforms were certainly necessary, they nonetheless celebrated the results of their efforts. Halfway through 1900, Wilson boasted that the men of the Rural Guard were "an intelligent, well-mounted body of men."[47] Rural Guard chief José de Jesús Monteagudo agreed, adding that the "men are becoming more and more suited to their office," successfully "guaranteeing order throughout the province and safeguarding the interests of the planters."[48] Military officials continued to revamp the Rural Guard along these lines over the next years of the military occupation.

The transformation of the personnel accompanied an even more significant shift in the force's character and function. Although the Rural Guard's official charter made occasional nods toward the egalitarian values of the revolution, it also evinced a striking concern over political and national allegiances as well as the presumed criminality of men of African descent and poor backgrounds. For instance, rural policemen were required to treat the "poorest with the same consideration as the richest," but they were also forced to swear their "true faith and allegiance to the Military Government of the United States."[49] Because the US military officials responded first and foremost to the interests of US citizens in Cuba, the Rural Guard, too, shifted toward protecting planters above all.[50] Thus, when planters claimed, as they had grown accustomed to do, that black criminals threatened their security, the Rural Guard had to respond to those denunciations. Among the tangible results of this shift was what one historian called the "repressive and markedly racist character" of law enforcement in US-occupied central Cuba.[51]

To be sure, the Rural Guard frequently pursued black "bandits" and other criminals, simultaneously drawing on and reinforcing the longstanding racial assumptions about criminality. Rural Guardsmen in Cienfuegos and the vicinity frequently pursued so-called bandits explicitly labeled as black for crimes such as petty theft and robbery.[52] In some cases, seemingly innocent black men were jailed due to suspicions of banditry. Manuel Fernández Labrada, a black veteran from Santa Clara Province, wrote a devastating letter from prison detailing the false charges leading to his incarceration. "I am an honorable and hard-working man," he began his letter, "and I launched myself onto the battlefield, and because of my good conduct and good service I obtained the rank of captain in the Liberating Army." After the war, a former Spanish guerrilla lured him into a trap by promising a "venture that would make us lots of money." Manuel seemed to be under the impression that the venture would involve joining a work gang on one of the nearby plantations. Instead, he proposed that they form a gang of bandits, and promised to supply Manuel with arms and munitions. When Manuel threatened to tell the authorities, the guerrilla became enraged. He demanded money, accusing him of never having been part of the Cuban army, and even telling him that "the black man is not worth anything to the white native of Cuba." Escalating to violence, the guerrilla allegedly beat Manuel, causing him two wounds, and later denounced him to authorities for banditry. He admitted that he fought back, landing him in jail.[53]

The Rural Guard was not merely a repressive force anymore. The renewed emphasis on racialized and classed policing also emerged in the shift toward crime "prevention" rather than the mere repression of actual crime. According to its charter, the rural police was a "preventive as well as a repressive force," but "the prevention of crime is of even greater importance than punishment of criminals."[54] Among the most important mechanisms of preventive policing was the concept of vagrancy—a broad umbrella term that encompassed idleness, lack of formal employment, and refusal to conform to the established racial labor hierarchy.[55] Planters and civil authorities both decried the "dangerous character" of "vagrants," who one municipal mayor hyperbolically called "the reserve army of crime."[56] Rural policemen were ordered to "watch narrowly all persons having no visible means of subsistence, and obtain knowledge of reputed thieves, and idle and disorderly characters" to stop disorder before it occurred.[57]

Given the ingrained racial assumptions about criminality, the Rural Guard's shift toward preventive policing likely contributed to the upsurge in the prosecution and incarceration of black men between 1899 and 1900. Men of African descent faced stiff penalties even when their involvement or guilt

Table 7.2. Prisoners by race, Santa Clara Province, 1899

	Black	Mulatto/ Mestizo	White	Chinese	% of African descent
Santa Clara	29*	22	52	4	48
Remedios	29	11	21*	0	66
Sancti Spíritus	5	6	11	0	50
Sagua	13	11*	18	1	56
Trinidad	3	8	12	1	46
Cienfuegos	57*	35*	82	4	51

Note: An *asterisk signifies the inclusion of a female prisoner in the count.
Source: "Statement of Prisoners in Confinement in the Jail at Cienfuegos," "Statement of Prisoners in Confinement in the Jail at Santa Clara," "Statement of Prisoners in Confinement in the Jail at Sancti Spíritus," "Statement of Prisoners in Confinement in the Jail at Trinidad," "Statement of Prisoners in Confinement in the Jail at Trinidad," "Statement of Prisoners in Confinement in the Jail at Remedios," December 31, 1899, Box 61, No File, USNAII/MGC/RG 140/E 3.

in crimes remained unsubstantiated or hypothetical. Evidence from the criminal courts of Cienfuegos and Trinidad suggests that men considered "suspicious" sometimes faced "preventive imprisonment," though the fragmentary nature of the records do not permit definitive comparisons to be made with prior periods.[58] By the end of 1899 black men were disproportionately overrepresented in the jails throughout central Cuba. The percentage of incarcerated men of color in every municipal jail in the province of Santa Clara surpassed the proportion of African-descended individuals in the free population. The difference was particularly notable in Remedios, where two-thirds of the incarcerated population, but not even 29 percent of the free population, was black or mulatto.[59]

The disproportionate incarceration of black men reproduced and exacerbated their political and social marginalization in significant ways. Once in the penal system, prisoners were subjected to forced labor regimes that not only mirrored the coercive relations of slavery, but also reinforced the postemancipation racial labor hierarchy. As early as May 1899 provincial governor José Miguel Gómez ordered that prisoners serving more than ten days in jail could be put to work on public works projects. This order violated the Penal Code, which stipulated that only men sentenced to life in prison or long prison terms could be exploited to benefit the state. Despite its dubious legality, Governor Gómez justified the policy, arguing that "the State is not rich enough to maintain men in idleness."[60] Since men of African descent were overrepresented in the prisons, the state's exploitation of prison labor likely disproportionately impacted black men.

Prisoners also faced humiliation and physical violence, which likely assumed racial undertones given the general whiteness of prison guards. One black prisoner, sentenced to 160 days on unproven allegations of petty larceny, complained of frequent corporal punishment by prison guards. He claimed that one white prison guard handcuffed him, slapped him until he spit blood, and brutalized him with a machete. He was thrown into a cell, still handcuffed, until the following afternoon, when guards removed him to perform hard labor.[61] Prisoners also faced the symbolic violence of humiliating emasculation when the military government issued what one critic called a "draconian order" to "totally shave" all prisoners serving more than a month "including their mustaches." With facial hair closely linked to notions of masculinity, this policy stripped prisoners of their dignity and the symbols of their manhood.[62]

Perhaps the most tangible and egregious way racialized policing and incarceration reinforced black men's second-class citizenship was by limiting their right to vote following the enfranchisement of all veterans in April 1900. The legal woes of black captain Claudio Sarría illustrate what may have been a subtle strategy among wealthy planters with foreign citizenship to assert their own political influence over elections by curtailing black suffrage. Born of enslaved parents on Edwin F. Atkins's Soledad estate, Sarría joined the Liberating Army in 1895 and quickly earned the enmity of wealthy property owners in that vicinity, where he fulfilled orders to destroy property and burn cane. Although Sarría's veteran status made him eligible to vote under the April 1900 electoral law, he faced legal prosecution multiple times in Cienfuegos and Trinidad for theft, just prior to major electoral events in 1900 and 1901. Even though he had registered to vote, these encounters with the law likely impeded him from exercising his right.[63] Racialized discourses of crime, it seems, provided a powerful counterpoint to black men's claims to political inclusion based on revolutionary masculinity. Criminalizing men like Sarría essentially dismantled his honorable military service and replaced it with the dishonorable, decidedly unmanly label of criminal.

Racial Order and Political Fitness amid Restricted Suffrage

Although opponents of separatist rule welcomed the return of their right to arm private militias, they were less convinced about the reforms in state-controlled rural law enforcement, especially in the months leading up to the election. They suspected that veterans employed in the Rural Guard would use their positions of power to influence the election in favor of other veterans. Veterans in Santa Clara Province rallied around the Republican Party (Partido Repúblicano Federal), one of two pro-independence parties vying for political power in the local elections across the island. The party's vehemently nationalist platform foregrounded the desire for absolute and immediate independence, which appealed broadly to veterans of all racial and class backgrounds—including the hundreds of men staffing the Rural Guard. The party's preference for a decentralized federal government and provincial autonomy made it particularly attractive to veterans outside Havana, where the Nationalist Party (Partido Nacional Cubano) dominated the political scene. But it was the party's intimate ties to central Cuban veterans and patronage of local veteran leaders that made it particularly powerful in Santa Clara Province. After all, two of Santa Clara's the most prestigious white veterans founded the party in 1899: provincial governor José Miguel Gómez and mayoral candidate Carlos Mendieta y Montefur, both of whom later served as presidents of the Cuban republic.[64] Gómez and Mendieta turned to their extensive military networks to recruit the province's top-ranking white veterans, including José Braulio Alemán, José de Jesús Monteagudo, José Luis Robau, Orestes Ferrara, and Enrique Villuendas, for the party's leadership. These men, like the Republican Party founders, would continue to influence local and national politics for decades to come.[65] The centrality of veteran status to the Republican Party proved critical in securing the support of the multiracial masses of newly enfranchised veterans for white Republican Party candidates for local office.

Opponents of separatist rule fought desperately to derail Republicans' electoral prospects by restricting suffrage. Restricted suffrage was expected to favor more conservative candidates, including Autonomists and some separatists, who had organized into the Democratic Union Party (Partido Unión Democrática). Members of this party generally supported ongoing collaboration with the United States, a platform that appealed to wealthy, white, propertied men (the only non-veteran individuals who could vote under restricted suffrage). However, opponents of separatist rule feared that the enfranchisement of veterans had destroyed this fragile political advantage. The narrow political base of the opposition party was simply no match for the broad cross-racial support enjoyed by the Republican Party.

Recognizing that their preferred conservative candidates had little chance of winning, opponents of separatist rule attempted to undermine Republicans by attacking candidates based on their veteran status. First, they criticized what they viewed as major conflicts of interest that challenged the ability of civil authorities to guarantee fair elections. In his capacity as civil governor, Gómez was in charge of addressing electoral irregularities across the province. As a veteran and founder of the Republican Party, however, he clearly had a vested interest in the success of his party's predominantly veteran candidates. In a similar vein, as chief of the Rural Guard, Monteagudo was responsible for suppressing rural crime and keeping order during the elections. He supervised the province's only official rural law enforcement body, which was staffed almost exclusively by veterans who had served under his command or alongside him in the Fourth Corps. Like Gómez, Monteagudo formed part of the Republican Party leadership, and even later ran as a Republican candidate for office. Because Monteagudo answered directly to Gómez, some critics feared that electoral tampering in favor of the Republic Party would enjoy impunity, and Democratic Union candidates would stand no chance of being elected. Opponents of separatist rule thus saw the Rural Guard, irrespective of any reforms, as an institution dominated by radicals, who they feared would use their positions in the force to influence the upcoming elections in favor of the Republican Party's pro-independence veteran candidates.

More than anything else, opponents of separatist rule zeroed in on the cross-racial dimensions of military solidarity to undermine the Republican Party. After all, it was well known that Republican candidates drew their support primarily from veterans, among whom were a substantial number of black men. This fact alone would have been subversive enough, but some critics alleged that Republicans were not content to merely receive the support of black men. Opponents of separatist rule claimed that these men (and also Nationalist Party members in other parts of the island) were unrepentantly pro-black. Not only did they actively seek black veterans' votes, they allegedly promised to pursue policies that might benefit black men, and even help put black men in office. Given these supposedly problematic ties to black veterans, Republicans threatened to inaugurate an era of "Negro rule."

With these fictionalized impressions of Republicans, opponents of separatist rule deployed the specter of the black veteran criminal in an effort to provoke US intervention in the elections. However, US officials at the provincial level generally resisted these machinations. One US official celebrated the positive influence of these white veterans on the Cuban populace, claiming that with certain guidance they would be able to defuse existing tensions among various political factions. He claimed that the military government could appeal to "Cuban manhood" to encourage political moderation. "And it is my impression that a strong pressure should be brought to bear on Cuban leaders to exercise a positive influence on Cubans in this direction," he continued. He cautioned: "But unnecessary meddling in the personal quarrels of these people ought to be avoided, until it is very evident that they are unwilling or incompetent to be just even to their late enemies."[66] While leaving open the possibility for future intervention, this military official suggested that they would allow New Men to campaign in peace. With US officials resisting their calls for direct intervention, opponents of separatist rule attempted to derail Republican candidates' reputation among white voters, by characterizing their black veteran constituents as criminals and rebels against US rule. In turn, this strategy would give pro-US Democratic Union candidates a better chance, while also making a case for a stronger US presence during the campaigns for municipal office.

These racialized allusions to crime influenced nearly all the major mayoral races in the province. In the predominantly black town of Palmira, the mayoral candidacy of white veteran incumbent Jacinto Portela provoked outcry over his presumed connections to black veterans. After all, a man who became one of the most prominent black politicians in Cuba, Martín Morúa Delgado, served as secretary of his city council. When Portela entered the mayoral race, Morúa became interim mayor of Palmira, prompting outrage among the town's conservative white residents.[67] One self-described "foreigner addicted to the American Government," decried an impending political crisis, claiming that Morúa was plotting a black takeover of the island. According to this annexationist, Morúa was "an enemy of the Americans [and] of the Intervening Government," and "a furious racist," whose position in the municipal leadership "has alarmed the white people." Moreover, Morúa's ascendancy was part of a broader pattern of black political influence in Palmira: "all the police are blacks, and the school teachers do not know anything, black *regidores*," the annexationist complained. All this amounted to a dangerous future in which "the Negros will govern" following the withdrawal of US forces.[68]

What this man considered so troubling about the political situation in Palmira was not only that Portela had enabled black men to secure positions in municipal government, but also that his impending popular election would almost invariably perpetuate this state of affairs. After all, he had appointed as inspector of the elections his brother, Manuel Portela, who allegedly designated his home as the official polling office to ensure that everyone voted for them, "the veterans, and the blacks." The writer begged the occupying government to send a contingent of US troops to Palmira to keep order and enforce "free" voting, by which he likely meant the disenfranchisement of black men and veterans. If not, then the veterans and the Negros would continue to control the elections.[69]

This notion that a politician's obligation to preserve order required the suppression of black suffrage and political participation also permeated other electoral races across the province. In the vicinity of Remedios, reports of an armed uprising of veterans targeted a prominent veteran officer from eastern Cuba, Lieutenant Colonel Juan Carreras, who had settled in the central Cuban countryside after the war. According to reports, Carreras led a contingent of forty armed men in an uprising on a rural estate. Monteagudo and González Planas responded to the call, detaining two horse thieves, but found no evidence of the so-called armed uprising. Prominent veteran leaders protested the allegations as false and defamatory. One prominent white general reported "protests from various people against the attempt to injure the reputation" of Carreras.[70] The president of the Veterans' Center of Baracoa expressed his "energetic protest against the inexcusable incitement to revolution" and demanded "a stop to the infamous plot."[71] In response, they demanded a thorough investigation of what they claimed to be calumnies and urged military officials to punish the responsible parties, "who intend to throw obstacles in the election" of his compatriots.[72] Upon subsequent investigation, the Rural Guard confirmed that the allegations were in fact false, likely having been an attempt to influence the election in favor of non-veteran candidates.[73]

Opponents of separatist rule were not the only ones to invoke the specter of black veteran criminality to influence the elections. In fact, conservative-leaning white veterans increasingly drew upon this very discourse to perform political fitness and posture themselves as the true agents of (racial) order against more liberal nationalist white veteran candidates. In many of these contests, candidates staked their political fitness on personal honor as measured alternately by revolutionary credentials or their ability to control alleged black criminal activity and electoral tampering.[74]

The mayoral race in the town of Camajuaní was essentially a competition over which white veteran candidate was best suited to preserve order. The two major candidates for mayor were white Cuban veterans of prestigious social backgrounds. However, they envisioned postwar order in fundamentally different ways. Having been appointed by military authorities in 1899, the incumbent, José C. Vidal, brother of the fallen mambí Leoncio Vidal, favored direct collaboration with US military authorities. In contrast, Casimiro Naya y Serrano, a general in the Cuban army, favored greater autonomy from US rule and drew his support from veterans of all colors.

The controversy began with claims that rural law enforcement was inappropriately partisan in the campaign. As election day approached, Vidal complained that Naya and Carlos Mendieta, Republican Party co-founder and pro-independence candidate in the mayoral race in the neighboring town Santo Domingo, exploited their connections to the Rural Guard to pressure voters to support them. Vidal alleged that he had overheard "menacing utterances" at the Veterans' Center, and specifically accused the chief of the Santa Clara Rural Guard, José de Jesús Monteagudo, of threatening him if the election did not come out in Naya's favor. Naya even allegedly attempted to silence claims of electoral tampering that appeared in the local press, which only earned him further condemnation from opponents of separatist rule.[75] These allegations undermined the legitimacy of Naya's bid for political power by depicting him (and other pro-independence candidates) as cheaters and bullies—unfit for political power.

Most revealing of all, Vidal accused his pro-independence opponent of attempting to extend the franchise. He alleged that Naya threatened an electoral official, stating that he would turn in his uniform as captain of the Rural Guard to force them to register to vote any man he presented.[76] Because Vidal drew his support mainly from wealthy white elites, his electoral success depended upon restricting the electorate as much as possible. Moreover, as the incumbent, Vidal also controlled the appointment of electoral officials. Vidal's simultaneous allegations about the illicit mobilization of black men suggest that his efforts to restrict suffrage likely centered on excluding black veterans. Thus, it is probable that at least part of Naya's demands to register voters represented an effort to rectify the illegal disenfranchisement of eligible veterans.

Perhaps unsurprisingly, Vidal made use of his favorable relationship with US authorities to demand US troops be dispatched to "preserve order" until after the elections.[77] In addition to counteracting Naya's efforts to extend suffrage, Vidal sought US troops to suppress the so-called "bandit uprisings" of black men who supposedly sought to influence the election. He cited rumors of "an uprising on the part of the negroes," who reportedly took to the fields because they "did not believe the elections would bring them or their country any good."[78] Linking Naya's candidacy directly to black unrest, Vidal claimed that his opponent had presided over a political rally in early May, at which "many negroes were present." They pledged to "elect the candidate of veterans," even if they had to use force. Subsequently, the black *Nayístas* allegedly descended upon a "meeting of pacíficos" and Canary Islanders who pledged their support for Vidal in drunken songs mocking Naya.[79]

Vidal's invocation of racial unrest to delegitimize his opponent seemed hyperbolic at best. After all, each candidate included three men of African descent on his ticket, though Naya's running mates were of darker complexion and more working-class backgrounds.[80] Even if the disagreement had little to do with Naya's candidacy, the allegations fueled speculation that the contest for mayor was mired in racial conflict. In this sense, it became a potent symbol of the potential racial consequences of the *independentista* platform. Yet, provincial authorities—most of whom were Naya's political allies—did not seem to be swayed by Vidal's allegations. José González Planas, the black major general and Rural Guard officer, doubted any such racial rebellion, while also downplaying the severity of the acts allegedly committed by black bandits.

Other provincial authorities also dismissed the claims of racial unrest as unrealistic. In fact, José Miguel Gómez took offense at Vidal's appeals to US officials, which he viewed as an insulting disregard for his own authority as provincial governor. He reprimanded Vidal for failing to observe the proper chain of command, asserting that the mayors of towns in Santa Clara Province would have to submit to his authority rather than attempting to override him by appealing to US military officials. To address Vidal's concern, Gómez ordered another regiment of Rural Guardsmen, without political interests in Camajuaní, to replace Monteagudo and his men. He also subtly implied the need for harmony among "the Cuban element," lamenting that such "strife" divided them "in such solemn moments for our country."[81] Gómez's call for unity among the men of the revolution must have seemed suspect coming from the founder of the Republican Party. But it also revealed his awareness of the fragility of veterans' access to political power. He knew that US officials were watching veterans for any sign of political unfitness.

After the initial exchange, the dispute between Vidal and Gómez escalated into a contest over personal honor, as each man attempted to posture himself as the ultimate authority on the preservation of order. Vidal insisted that given his "intimate knowledge" of the Rural Guard's "personnel and proceedings" replacing Monteagudo would be "insufficient" to ensure fair elections. Only the presence of US troops, he argued, could "ease the minds and return normalcy." Invoking the US military government's recognition of civil authority, Gómez cited Military Order 124, which required municipal authorities to appeal first to provincial authorities if they needed assistance preserving order.[82] Condescendingly Gómez assured Vidal that he would submit the request for US troops "after you tell me that *you cannot sustain order with your prestige.*"⁸³ By connecting Vidal's inability to preserve order as a function of his inadequate personal prestige, Gómez framed the incumbent's appeals for US troops as a demonstration of his unmanliness, and by extension, his unfitness for political power.

Vidal answered Gómez's assault on his masculinity with a quick defense of his own public reputation and a barrage of gendered insults against the provincial governor. "The duration and extension of self prestige," he wrote to Gómez, "cannot be measured when there are conspiracies on foot to undermine it," essentially blaming the governor's attacks against him for the disorder. Disparaging Gómez's own ability to preserve order, Vidal claimed that removing the Rural Guard failed to resolve the problem, that law enforcement was incapable of suppressing crime, and any assistance from the civil government was of "unknown importance." Consequently, he needed US forces "to guaranty [sic] public tranquility and to prevent disturbances." Ultimately, Gómez submitted the request, but not before denouncing Vidal in a scathing note to military authorities. He declared that in his judgment, US troops were unnecessary and that a mayor "lacking in the necessary prestige to sustain public order should resign his office."⁸⁴ Wilson responded to Vidal's petition by ordering two practice marches of US troops in Camajuaní and Santo Domingo as well as several undercover officers to "prevent undue interference on the part of any body with the freedom of election and especially to prevent any outbreak." He also ordered all Rural Guards withdrawn from Camajuaní and Santo Domingo until after elections, and even summoned Monteagudo to a "meeting."⁸⁵ Naya—the pro-veteran candidate and more open supporter of black voting rights—won the election, but ultimately failed to secure reelection in 1901.

Nor was Gómez the only high-profile provincial authority to be swept up in allegations of disorder during the elections. In neighboring Matanzas, opponents of separatist rule alleged that both the provincial authorities as well as local and provincial law enforcement were inappropriately partisan in the elections there. One letter, written anonymously by four merchants, two property owners, and apparently two Cuban army officers, disparaged the governor's office as "a political Club" dominated by the so-called "Cuban Army Party." These men alleged that the police were "running here and there threatening the ignorant people about their votes." The authors framed these allegations as a "betrayal" of the US military government and begged US military officials to intervene.⁸⁶

The mayoral race in neighboring Trinidad was also marred by allegations of racial disorder. The incumbent, Carlos Yznaga, had resided and attended school in the United States before serving as US Consul in Trinidad (1897–1898). Local veterans, however, were suspicious of Yznaga, considering him dishonorable and a poor representative of revolutionary principles. After all, he had opportunistically enlisted in the Cuban army after the US intervention, and subsequently cooperated closely with US military authorities who were widely despised by Trinidad's popular classes. Just days before the elections, *La Tribuna* published a scathing tirade against Yznaga written by a group of prominent veterans from the city. They characterized him as "an enemy hiding behind the mask of a Cuban man"—a candidate who was "detrimental to our history and our sentiments." Invoking revolutionary masculinity, veterans claimed that Yznaga had no legitimate claim to political power because he was "without [military] history and without merits."[87] Moreover, they censured Yznaga for declaring that he could buy the loyalty of the entire town for only five hundred pesos. Certainly, his lack of revolutionary credentials and his close relationship to US military officials rendered his candidacy unpalatable to the majority of veterans in that locality. Even more telling was Yznaga's alleged exploitation of his elite status to garner political support, rather than earning it through manly actions.

In response to such vocal protest against him, Yznaga invoked the specter of black criminality to discredit his opponent, Republican candidate Charles Lynn, a descendant of North Americans resident in Trinidad, who served in the Ten Years' War and the War of Independence. Yznaga alleged that a "colored party" had emerged in the weeks leading up to the election, and had attempted to swing the election in Lynn's favor. Given Trinidad's significant population of African descent, many of whom enjoyed relative economic privilege as merchants, artisans, and tradesmen, the prospect of a black political party may have seemed plausible to some white men.[88] However, Yznaga claimed that black veterans, including Ricardo Muñoz and Lino Zerquera, had approached him, pledging support for his mayoral candidacy if he would "promise them some of the offices." When Yznaga flatly refused, Muñoz and Zerquera approached Lynn, who allegedly accepted the proposal, and later misappropriated public funds to bribe voters.[89] Despite Yznaga's attempts to derail his campaign, Lynn won the election.

In Cienfuegos the heavy influence of US military officials in local politics distinguished municipal elections there from many of the other cities in Santa Clara Province. Earlier that year, military officials had forced separatist mayor

José Antonio Frías to resign, appointing the conservative white veteran Leopoldo Figueroa to replace him. After his removal from office, Frías left Cienfuegos altogether, briefly resuming his teaching position at the University of Havana. Frías's absence essentially decapitated the opposition in Cienfuegos. Moreover, incumbent mayor Leopoldo Figueroa boasted the unwavering support of US military officials. He also enjoyed broad support among prominent white veterans because of his military service. Nevertheless, Figueroa faced criticism from more radical groups of veterans, who claimed that his wartime position in the Army Sanitary Corps did not qualify as real military service. Figueroa's supporters disparaged these attacks on his personal reputation, claiming they originated with "critical elements" (*elementos advenedizos*) of the radical press, who had allegedly grown accustomed to "perturbing the moral peace." Seeking to redeem Figueroa's public reputation on the eve of election day, his supporters hired a drama company to parade around the streets "paying homage to his public esteem."[90] Figueroa won in what one US official called "the most quiet and orderly" election he had ever witnessed.[91]

Although Figueroa's mayoral bid was essentially uncontested, other contests for local power in Cienfuegos evinced some of the same tensions that had defined mayoral races across the province. In a dispute over the directorship of the civil hospital, veterans rallied around a popular veteran chief, Gonzalo García Vieta, who was later elected mayor. His opponent, "self-proclaimed annexationist" Julio Oritz y Coffigny, held the position for twelve years before being replaced by a veteran during the early days of the occupation. He had been attempting to reclaim his position since then. However, he faced opposition from local veterans, who not only resented his lack of military service, but also found his outspoken support for annexation quite offensive to their pro-independence sensibilities. Upon his removal from the position, Coffigny's wife wrote to a personal friend, the famous female patriot and philanthropist Marta Abreu, asking her to appeal to provincial governor José Miguel Gómez on her husband's behalf.[92] She complied, but Gómez lamented that he could not accede to Abreu's request because Coffigny had "alienated popular sympathies and the revolutionary elements are against him" for "trampling the rites of justice and the dignity of the Cuban people."[93] Even Coffigny's connections to some of the most influential families of the province were insufficient to sever the ties of military and political patronage binding the Republican Party.

During election season, opposition against Coffigny's ongoing efforts to reclaim the directorship peaked. One inflammatory political leaflet labeled

"Because One Happens to Belong to the Male Species"   205

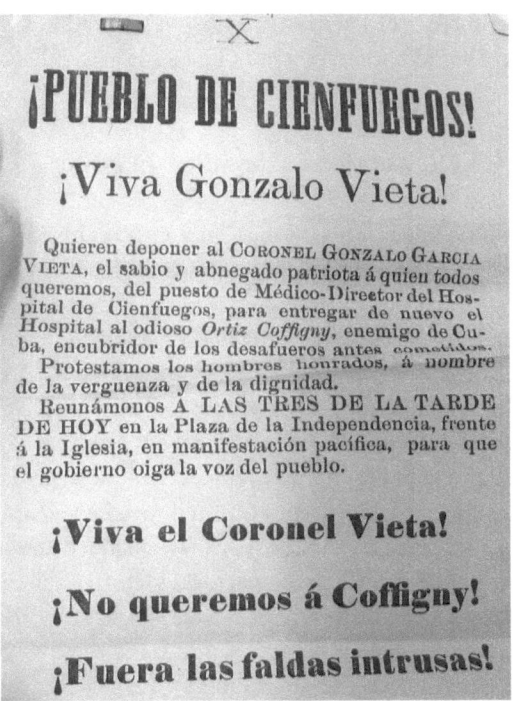

Figure 7.1. "Down with the Intrusive Skirts!" Source: "¡Pueblo de Cienfuegos!" January 11, 1900, Box 49, File 220, USNAII/MGC/RG140/E 3. Translation: Town of Cienfuegos! Long Live Gonzalo [García] Vieta! They want to depose Colonel Gonzalo García Vieta, the wise and self-sacrificing patriot whom we all love, from the post of Medical Director of the Cienfuegos Hospital, to turn over the hospital to the hated [Octavio] Ortiz Coffigny, enemy of Cuba, accomplice to the outrages previously committed. We, the honorable men, protest in the name of shame and dignity. Let's gather AT THREE THIS AFTERNOON in the Plaza of Independence, in front of the church, in peaceful demonstration, so the government hears the voice of the people. Long live Colonel Vieta! We don't want Coffigny! Down with the Intrusive Skirts!

men like him "intrusive skirts."[94] By associating Coffigny with women's clothing, this insult suggested the effeminacy of individuals suspected of betraying the values of the revolution by supporting US rule. The fact that the skirt was short (*intrusa*) also invoked the dishonor of female sexual licentiousness to condemn the allegations of embezzlement and corruption that defined Coffigny's directorship. The skirt offered both easy access and cover for his figurative raping of public resources. Like the mayoral races across the province, this contest over the directorship of the hospital played out in conflicts over the gendered and racial parameters of public authority.

"Revolutionary Bandits" in Power

Neither a restrictive electoral law that only enfranchised about 5 percent of the Cuban population,[95] nor opposition candidates' frequent allegations of racial disorder and gender transgression could deter Republicans at the polls.[96] Extending the vote to veterans had enabled the Republican Party's New Men to activate their powerful networks of military patronage to secure authority over local affairs. In spite of widespread attempts to derail their candidacies, the Republican Party's New Men swept the municipal elections in every major race across Santa Clara Province. General James H. Wilson noted that "in every instance the Mayor and Councilmen elected are Revolutionists who either actually served in the field, or actively aided the Insurgents with their money and influence."[97] These electoral victories sent a clear message to the military government: the United States would soon have to fulfill the conditions of the Teller Amendment by ending the military occupation and allowing for an independent Cuban republic.[98]

Historians have interpreted the nationalist electoral victories in June 1900 as evidence of the triumph of revolutionary values over the US imperialistic efforts to restrict suffrage along class and racial lines.[99] Evidence of modest cross-racial political patronage in certain areas of Santa Clara Province supports this interpretation. New Men relied to a significant degree on black veteran voters to secure electoral victory. As such, it was no coincidence that white Republican candidates in cities with strong black populations, like Trinidad, Camajuaní, and Palmira, included men of African descent among their city council picks. Even some conservative and Democratic Union candidates had employed the same tactics to win over black veteran voters, though with less success.

Though troubled by the election of veterans, what preoccupied opponents of separatist rule most of all was what they saw as the deterioration of the racial purity of political power. Once these cross-racial Republican tickets secured victory at the polls, opponents of separatist rule quickly protested what they saw as impending "Negro Rule." However, these claims were clearly hyperbolic at best. The vast majority of the men elected to municipal office

Table 7.3. White mayors of selected cities in Santa Clara, elected in June 1900

Santa Clara	**Gerardo Machado Morales**
Calabazar	Leopoldo Ramos
Ranchuelo	José Grau
Trinidad	**Charles Lynn**
Sancti-Spíritus	**Fernando Cancio Madrigal**
Cienfuegos	**Leopoldo Figueroa Martí**
Abreus	Arturo Aulet
Palmira	Jacinto Portela
San Fernando de Camarones	Jorge Rodríguez
Cruces	Julio Domínguez
Lajas	Tomás Velasco
Rodas	Tomás Aroiz Etchandy
Cartagena	Mariano Pino
Sagua	**Manuel Alberdi**
Santo Domingo	Gustavo Casanova
Cifuentes	Juan Díaz
Rancho Veloz	Alfredo Leiseca
Quemado de Güines	Antonio López
Ceja de Pablo	Adalberto Billers
Remedios	**Enrique Malaret**
Caibarién	Próspero Pérez
Camajuaní	Casimiro Naya
Yaguajay	Martín Barrero
Placetas	Juan Fuste

Note: Bold font indicates a major city.
Source: José Miguel Gómez, "Enclosing Electoral Returns for his Province," June 17, 1900, Box 72, File 1305, USNAII/MGC/RG 140/E 3.

were prominent white veterans, and every single mayor in the province was a white man (see table 7.3).

Nonetheless, framing the election as a revolutionary triumph neglects the fierce negotiations over the racial and gendered parameters of public authority that defined the electoral races across the province. As much as the local elections revealed the expected tensions between advocates of absolute independence and supporters of strong ties with the United States, they also exposed profound cleavages among the men of the revolution. The vast majority of major candidates were white men. Moreover, the dubious revolutionary credentials of some white veteran candidates suggests that whiteness trumped military honor as a qualifier for office, even as New Men vocally advocated for broad enfranchisement for veterans. Even more revealing, white veteran candidates struggled among themselves for political power. Although this fact itself is not shocking, the way they engaged in these struggles suggests a disturbing shift away from the racially inclusive premise of revolutionary masculinity. As New Men invoked black veteran criminality to prove their own political fitness, they evinced a growing reluctance to maintain ties of cross-racial military patronage.

Part of this active denial of cross-racial patronage was undoubtedly performative. Although white veterans relied on black veteran voters for their electoral victories, some of these men had also learned how quickly allegations of racial disorder could lead US military authorities to question their political fitness. Civil governor Gómez's emphasis on how peaceful the election was illustrates this. He reported on June 16 that "the election is taking place throughout the province without the slightest sign of disorder," even through allegations of banditry, crime, uprisings, and voter intimidation swirled across Santa Clara.[100] Yet, US military officials still launched an investigation into his conduct, following allegations that he had failed to keep order during the elections. Clearly upset by the allegations, Gómez wrote to Military Governor of Cuba Leonard Wood, appealing to his "unbiased mind" to rectify what he termed certain "misrepresentations" of his conduct during the elections. "I swear upon my honor as a gentleman," wrote Gómez, "that I have, ever since the Government distinguished me with its confidence, ever attempted to be guided in all my acts by a strict sence [sic] of justice. I may have erred, for such is the lot of man, but I do most solemnly assert that upon such occasions no malice or bias has prevailed in my actions." Gómez depicted himself as "the victim of circumstances unfortunately turned against me." He denied that any disturbances had afflicted election day, but noted that there were only "petty ambitions here and there that have never been encouraged by me." He swore that during the elections, he had "only fulfilled my duty," and had "been most prudent, most circumspect" and was assured of the "propriety" of his conduct.[101] The almost pleading tone of his letter underscored his recognition of the conditionality of his political power.

Striking a delicate balance between securing popular support and maintaining the approval of US military officials seemed to shape New Men's approach to the upcoming August elections for the Constitutional Convention. One way New Men reconciled these two seemingly contradictory constituencies was by curbing, though not yet eliminating, the explicit ties between black veterans and the Republican Party. For instance, the Las Villas

"Because One Happens to Belong to the Male Species" 209

branch of the party initially proposed the black veteran and Rural Guard officer José González Planas as a candidate for the Constitutional Convention. However, military officials seemed to oppose his candidacy. US officials ordered him to organize one of the recently formed Rural Guard corps, an activity that essentially removed him from the race. Eventually the party dropped his candidacy, but continued to support a more conservative black revolutionary and politician, Martín Morúa Delgado.[102]

Just two months after the Republican landslide in the municipal elections, voters across Santa Clara once again elected Republicans as the vast majority of delegates to the Constitutional Convention. All seven of the delegates from Santa Clara Province belonged to the Republican Party and possessed the highest revolutionary credentials. Most had served in key leadership roles in the Fourth Corps. One of the province's delegates, Morúa Delgado, was black.[103]

The repeat Republican victory in the August elections again catalyzed widespread unrest among opponents of separatist rule. After all, they recognized that the convention's pro-independence majority would invariably vote to end US rule, which they believed to be critical for preserving order. One annexationist disparaged the new delegates as a bunch of "revolutionary bandits," who were bound to abuse their power over such significant decisions and throw the island into perpetual disorder.[104] Turning once more to familiar tactics, these men expressed their anxieties by alleging that an end of US rule would plunge the island into race war.

Between the August 1900 elections and the first meeting of the Constitutional Convention on November 5, opponents of separatist rule alleged that racialized crime pervaded the central Cuban countryside. Amid rumors of "a great many bandits" terrorizing the countryside, "armed groups" marauding about, and the abundance of "nocturnal thieves," were also more dramatic reports of impending racial unrest.[105] Allegations surfaced that black men were smuggling arms in the vicinity of Trinidad in preparation for an attack against US rule. One white veteran and captain of the Rural Guard of Trinidad, who failed to secure a political position in the June elections, allegedly spoke at a "negro club." There, he allegedly promised black veterans that "for every man you take to the woods after the Americans I have one who will go after you.'"[106] Like the majority of other reports of crime, this allegation combined two key claims: first, that radical separatists were inherently anti-American and threatened to express their discontent with political disenfranchisement through violent uprising; and second that radical white separatists drew their support from black veterans, who formed the majority of the alleged anti-American forces.

Other opponents of separatist rule speculated that the election of pro-independence candidates had set Cuba on a path toward independence, which would invariably result in race war. One prominent Autonomist wrote: "I frequently hear in all public places the colored race saying—'Wait until the Americans leave then they will see who are the people with the most rights to govern the country.'"[107] Others argued that allowing black political participation was not "*real* patriotism." Rather, it would lead to catastrophe for whites: "What delirium!" exclaimed one Matanzas man. "Given our deficient education, our bad habits [*resabios*] and our *formidable racial antagonism that dominates us*," independence would lead us "straight and quickly to the abyss!"[108] Others complained of labor shortages as "idle negroes" roamed the countryside in "a restless, half nomadic condition traceable to the recent war."[109] These complaints harnessed a familiar assumption: that radical white nationalists, if left unattended by US authorities, were incapable or at very least unwilling to maintain racial order in Cuba.

Opponents of separatist rule had demonstrated that their preferred form of protest was the weaponization of race to dismantle the masculinity of black and white veterans in racially specific ways. They deployed two interrelated discourses to counter the cross-racial implications of revolutionary masculinity. First, they invoked racialized notions of crime to dismantle black veterans' claims to masculinity by discursively transforming them from war heroes to actual or potential criminals. Second, opponents of separatist rule effectively applied these racialized notions of criminality to redefine the responsibilities of local and provincial authorities as pivoting on their ability to preserve (racial) order. Together, they deployed these discourses to produce racially specific qualifications for manhood. Black men, by virtue of their supposed criminal tendencies could not claim manhood, and thus were to be excluded from the political privileges it entailed. In turn, white men could demonstrate their manhood and their political fitness by relinquishing their ties of military patronage with black veterans and by suppressing the political participation of individuals who failed to conform to these racialized gendered expectations. Through these powerful racialized gendered counterpoints to revolutionary masculinity, opponents of separatist rule were able to exert some degree of influence over the mostly white veterans who they viewed as their political antagonists.

As they had been during the June and August elections, the reports of racial unrest that surfaced in anticipation of the convention were hyperbolic at best. They framed New Men's political views as radical, socially revolutionary, and as un-American. Opponents of separatist rule exaggerated most of their claims, but they were right about one thing: most of the convention delegates adhered to a radically pro-independence agenda, and would soon begin to write these values into the constitution of the emerging republic. The next chapter charts the ways the contentious national conversations over the island's political future played out at the local and provincial level.

CHAPTER EIGHT

"The Colored Patriot and His Box of Matches"

Black Criminality, White Radicalism, and the Redefinition of the New Man in an Era of Universal Manhood Suffrage

THE INAUGURATION OF THE CUBAN CONSTITUTIONAL CONVENTION afforded New Men the unprecedented opportunity to exert their influence on some of the most important questions defining the future republic. Most significantly, they had to write a constitution and articulate the desired relationship between the United States and Cuba. Almost immediately after the convention convened its first meeting on November 5, 1900, a debate emerged over elections and the parameters of suffrage.[1] One of several proposals for universal manhood suffrage was introduced on January 25, 1901, by delegates from Santa Clara Province: José Braulio Alemán, José de Jesús Monteagudo, José Luis Robau, José Miguel Gómez, and Martín Morúa Delgado. The amendment they introduced proposed that the constitution "recognize universal suffrage, which will be exercised by all the citizens who enjoy their civil and political rights."[2] Other delegates introduced similar proposals, some of which clarified that suffrage would be limited to adult men. One delegate specifically noted that the proposed amendment was not "true universal suffrage" because it did not apply to women.[3]

Central Cuban delegates, like their former compatriots-in-arms from other parts of the island, defended universal manhood suffrage as the foundation of a "popular and democratic" republic. Alemán, for example, described it as one of the "legs" that "maintain the political-social body erect." He added that "if we are honorable, the Constitution will protect universal suffrage." He reminded his fellow delegates that they represented the people and that it was unfair to disparage them as "inferior," or attempt to deny them their rights, thereby creating a new "oppressed class." He proclaimed, "I want universal suffrage because I know the virtues of my people and I have faith in their discretion."[4] By June 1901 delegates wrote universal manhood suffrage into the provisional electoral law that would govern the upcoming local and general elections in June and December, respectively.[5] By July, they approved the new electoral law that guaranteed universal manhood suffrage by a vote of 17 to 6.[6]

As white political elites basked in the glory of their selfless commitment to cross-racial citizenship, black men ultimately struggled to see the practical results of universal manhood suffrage. Rather, universal manhood suffrage quickly became a "mechanism of historic inequality."[7] This was in part because black political authority now remained as inconceivable as it had been to many white men during the war. And it was also significant that racial silence defined the political platforms of the few black political elites in national government.[8] Yet, understanding the failure of universal manhood suffrage requires that we look beyond the actions of a handful of black political elites to the everyday experiences of the numerous black and working-class men who struggled for political inclusion, even if it was just to cast their vote in support of their white patrons.

This chapter interrogates the limits of manhood suffrage for black men's citizenship between the beginning of the Constitutional Convention in November 1900 and the inauguration of the Cuban republic in May 1902. I show that the approval of universal manhood suffrage actually further marginalized most black men from political authority. In central Cuba, men from nearly every social and political orientation closely watched the convention as they debated and ultimately decided these important questions. While veterans, workers, and the poor celebrated the prospect of universal manhood suffrage as a triumph of revolutionary values, opponents of separatist rule and US military officials were deeply troubled by it. If Republicans had swept the 1900 election under restricted suffrage, universal manhood suffrage promised to favor the success of pro-independence candidates in politics for the foreseeable future.

Opponents of separatist rule sought to derail universal suffrage by depicting the masses as black and criminal. Once they failed to derail universal manhood suffrage, however, opponents of separatist rule targeted the political careers of specific New Men. Recognizing that New Men relied on black and working-class constituencies for their political power, opponents of separatist rule exploited the specter of black criminality to exert indirect control over the electoral process. At the core of their agenda was prolonging US rule, which they knew white pro-independence candidates opposed. Seeking to ward off their electoral victory, opponents of separatist rule used the specter of black crime to support pro-US Democratic Union candidates, initially by advocating for restricted suffrage, and later by invoking notions of order. They also used the specter of crime to force white Republican Nationalist Party candidates to accept a more significant US presence and take a tougher stance on "order."

US military authorities also delivered a swift response to the revolutionary potential of universal manhood suffrage by introducing an amendment that would curtail Cuban sovereignty even before the republic was born. As early as January 1901 US Secretary of War Elihu Root proposed the imposition of restrictions on the convention's ability to dictate the nature of its relationship with the United States. This vision became a reality when Connecticut Senator Orville Platt introduced a bill, drafted in large part by Root himself, which would require the Constitutional Convention to accept a series of sovereignty-limiting conditions on Cuban independence in order to secure US withdrawal. Among the most important of these conditions were the provisions allowing for future US intervention to protect US economic interests, requiring Cubans to obtain permission from the United States before signing international treaties, leasing certain lands and naval stations to the United States indefinitely, and enforcing all military orders already imposed.[9] The Platt Amendment, as this bill came to be known, passed as an attachment to the Army Appropriations Bill in the US Senate without the consent or input of the Cuban Constitutional Convention.

Just as soon as delegates successfully secured universal manhood suffrage, the Platt Amendment, even before it went into effect, vested US officials and opponents of separatist rule with unprecedented power to influence local and provincial politics. These two groups immediately set out to curtail the practical authority of New Men elected to office. Opponents of separatist rule resumed their hyperbolic claims of black criminality, but went even further by claiming that a black rebellion against US rule threatened to plunge the island into race war. These allegations undermined the political fitness of New Men, who faced mounting pressures to preserve order. US authorities, for their part, overrode democratically elected officials, replacing them with men they handpicked for their conservatism and pliancy. In so doing, they sent a clear message to the hundreds of New Men who had recently secured or hoped to win election: the power of the newly expanded electorate, not to mention the autonomy enjoyed by elected officials themselves, had little meaning if it went against the interests of the United States. Quite simply, the sources of New Men's political legitimacy shifted from the popular classes of workers, men of African descent, and veterans, to the wealthiest and most powerful members of society—US military officials and wealthy planters.

Amid the overwhelming conditionality of New Men's political authority, ongoing rumors of black criminality pushed some of these men to perform their political fitness upon the bodies of black men. I argue that these conditions catalyzed a fundamental shift in what it meant to be a New Man. Under restricted suffrage, the enfranchisement of black veterans forced New Men to be at least minimally accountable to the racially inclusive nature of revolutionary masculinity, even as they had to prove their political fitness to US military officials. Yet, under universal manhood suffrage, US military officials directly influenced local elections to favor their preferred candidates and essentially forced New Men to secure US military support for their candidacy as an absolute precondition to their success at the polls. Some New Men responded to the unprecedented conditionality of their political power by modifying their platforms, practically eliminating their public support for racial inclusion and cooperating more openly with US authorities. These transformations allude to a shift in the values to which political men had access in constructing their political legitimacy, which I call neocolonial masculinity—a conditional state of manhood in which political elites could boast formal national self-determination but were constantly subject to US approval.

"The Element of Color, Whose Tendencies Are Racist"

When discussion over the possible revision of the electoral law erupted in the Constitutional Convention, opponents of separatist rule quickly characterized any attempt at universal manhood suffrage as tantamount to encouraging "Negro Rule." Rumors of black criminality immediately surfaced throughout Santa Clara Province.[10] Many of these rumors originated with an anonymous informant to US military authorities, who later revealed himself to be Javier Medina Escalona, a former Spanish volunteer in Cienfuegos and vehement critic of the revolution. In a series of anonymous letters to military officials, Medina alleged that the two black delegates to the Constitutional Convention, Juan Gualberto Gómez and Martín Morúa Delgado, were organizing an uprising of "the colored race" against US rule.[11] Medina's claims were baseless. If there was anything that Morúa and Gómez were *not*, it was conspirators for black rule. Neither of these political leaders espoused particularly radical racial views. Morúa had argued that racial issues had been "perfectly resolved by the Revolution." Gómez largely eschewed discussions of racial inequality after securing legal equality for black men in the constitution.[12]

When his outlandish claims failed to attract the desired attention from US military officials, Medina invoked what he believed to be a more plausible scenario. He claimed to have intelligence about a new racial uprising, even more sinister than the last—one led by a known "racial agitator," the black veteran Quintín Bandera. Medina claimed that the black veteran chief was "marauding from village to village . . . preparing the terrain for rebellion."[13] This rumor, though still clearly fictional, seemed more probable than the last. Bandera faced chronic unemployment after the war, after being denied a political appointment in line with his rank.[14] He earned his living selling ads for newspapers, traversing the country collecting donations for his subsistence, and selling soap to black laundresses. The very mobility Bandera gained from his unemployment and underemployment triggered anxiety among planters and Spaniards who linked his supposed vagrancy to potential criminal violence.[15]

By December Medina alleged that Bandera was "the Chief of the colored forces of [Las] Villas." He had already recruited over one thousand men to rise up immediately in a military coup against US rule.[16] Within three days, Medina claimed, Bandera could gather seven thousand men "who will meet in the town of La Sierra or in Cumanayagua at the foot of the hills."[17] These country towns had been revolutionary strongholds during the war, and would supposedly become the headquarters of the impending armed black uprising. Medina reported that these black rebels acquired artillery, sixty thousand Remingtons, ten thousand bayonets, boxes of grenades, pots of shrapnel, and other weapons and munitions used by the mobilized forces and volunteers and auctioned by the Spanish government at the end of the war. Moreover, Medina claimed that "in all the country towns there are arms deposits under the care of determined insurgent chiefs," most of whom were reportedly black. By early 1901 Medina claimed that the rebellion had spread to encompass Cuba's entire "black belt," where "the colored race is most numerous and is

Figure 8.1. Quintín Bandera. Source: "Quintín Bandera and his mule," in Thomas R. Dawley Jr., "Campaigning with Gómez," *American Magazine* 47 (November 1898–April 1899), 541.

already organized." This dangerously black zone encompassed the provinces of Santiago, Matanzas, and most importantly, Santa Clara.[18]

Medina was not content simply to label the fictitious rebels as black; he claimed that they were "racist." He alleged that "the element of color, whose tendencies are racist, and are very united, work with much activity in plain daylight." In a letter to the US military governor of Cuba, Leonard Wood, Medina wrote that "it is an undeniable fact that the revolutionary movement will have a racist character."[19] By labeling the fictional uprising "racist," Medina conflated the very existence of blackness with an active and virulent movement of anti-whiteness. In so doing, he invoked longstanding fears that black men would take over the island and strip white men of their "rightful" positions at the apex of society. He urged the military governor to reinforce US troops on the island in anticipation of this black uprising.[20] The revolution, Medina claimed, would likely take place in February or March 1901, a period that would coincide with the initial discussions surrounding the Platt Amendment.[21]

Medina's persistent letters caught the attention of military authorities, who launched an investigation of the "conditions" in Santa Clara Province. The supervisor of police claimed that a "complete state of agitation exists in the province of Santa Clara, hard times are being felt and there is a general feeling of inquietude." Armed gangs abounded throughout the province, numerous kidnappings had occurred for ransom, and at least one murder was reported in the second half of November 1900. He noted that "considerable hard feeling exists between the blacks and whites" in Cienfuegos. In the neighboring town of Caibarién, there was evidence of "considerable discontent among the 'n*s#&rs,'" as one US observer phrased it.[22] Most ominously of all, he found that Bandera was exploiting these racial tensions to fuel his impending uprising. The police supervisor claimed that the black general was indeed in Cienfuegos "collecting contributions" to fund "a war against the Americans."[23] Contrary to this police supervisor's conclusions, with six children to feed and no formal employment, it is unlikely that Bandera was using the donations for anything other than subsistence.[24]

Later, Medina alleged that Bandera had recruited black men from Haiti and various British Caribbean islands to overthrow white rule in Cuba. "It is said in Jamaica, the Caiman Islands, and other English islands close to the[se] coasts that several thousand Negro[e]s will come to take part in the war. They will also come from Haiti, and from what I have found out, they are collaborating with this last Republic."[25] These allegations conjured memories of the Antilles League, a transnational black secret society supposedly aimed at consolidating black rule in the Caribbean and to which Antonio Maceo allegedly had belonged. Medina implied that if the US did not intervene to crush the movement, Cuba would become another Haiti.

Nor was Medina alone in using Bandera to induce fear of black uprising. One Cuban-born annexationist proposed a plan to expel black veterans like Bandera, Isidro Acea, Juan Gualberto Gómez, "and other agitators [*perturbadores*] and pernicious men from the Country." He also advocated for the disbandment of the Constitutional Convention on the erroneous premise that the delegates were overwhelmingly "negroes, mulattoes, and depraved whites." Although he blamed men of African descent most severely, he also implicated radical whites in the unrest, seemingly holding them responsible for failing to preserve the social order from which they benefited. He declared that "there is a need in Cuba for an American Weyler"—a claim he used to challenge the US military governor of Cuba, Leonard Wood, to crush prominent black veterans.[26]

In January 1901 as the predominantly white delegates continued to debate the merits of universal manhood suffrage, planters and merchants across central Cuba joined in the chorus of reports of racial unrest. One of these men, Esteban Cacicedo, a Cienfuegos-based merchant, denounced the presence of menacing black men on his estate. Among the alleged agitators was the black man Luis Carrillo, who reportedly threatened to put workers "to the machete" if they did not join a labor union for sugar workers that he was organizing.[27] Cacicedo complained that the incident harmed his business because his workers reportedly "feared the negro" so much that they refused to work. He appealed to military authorities, claiming that the police had failed to suppress the crime with sufficient force.[28]

The timing and tone of these reports of crime suggest that they had little to do with actual conditions in the countryside. Key leaders in the Rural Guard exposed most of the reports as either false or incidents of personal dispute.[29] After inspecting the entire province, the acting chief of the Santa Clara Rural Guard reported that the "news" of banditry "are false, I can vouch for it." He argued that Santa Clara Province lacked organized banditry or other crime "with the exception of petty thievery and some horse stealing."[30] He concluded that "people who give alarming news are residents who want the establishment there of a post of Rural Guards."[31] Simply put, they used allegations of crime to secure their political ends.

Prominent veterans and military officials alike suspected that opponents of separatist rule used the specter of crime to prolong US rule. Wilson himself noted that "there are a few, principally the owners of large estates, who are urging delay and would delay [the end of US rule] indefinitely so long as the measures proposed do not lead positively to the realization of their wishes."[32] White Cuban veteran Gerardo Machado noted that the former guerrillas "constitute the muddy sediment of all the big political commotions." He claimed that "in order to satiate their rapacious instincts and habits of pillage, they would bring about this or another uproar, as some sinister plot against the governance or independence of Cuba."[33] As ludicrous as these claims seemed, New Men recognized that even fictitious reports of black criminality could have real political consequences for the Constitutional Convention and for their own political futures because the specter of racial disorder undermined political elites' public reputations as agents of order.

Seeking to avoid the encroachment of US military officials on their increasingly fragile political authority, provincial officials ordered a public campaign to protect property owners against the banditry and disorder they already admitted did not exist. In December 1900 they published a circular calling for greater vigilance during the sugar harvest, when "the greatest amount of capital is exposed" and when it is "most profitable for the evil doers to try to meddle with the threat or harm to the property owners." They also renewed emphasis on preventive policing, ordering rural law enforcement to "anticipate" crime during the harvest, using "their good judgment and zeal to prevent banditry from perturbing public order and [jeopardizing] the safety of people and things."³⁴ These mandates clarified that the Rural Guard's main function was to protect the property of the wealthiest members of society.

Rural Guardsmen implemented preventive policing in ways that underscored the conflation of blackness and criminality. In late 1900 and early 1901 white Rural Guardsmen contributed to a rising tide of state violence against rural laborers, many of whom were black. Around that time, Rural Guardsmen responded to reports that "two colored men, colonels of the disbanded Cuban army," were "behaving improperly" and "abusing of an authority which they do not have" around a sugar plantation. Once on the scene Rural Guardsmen could not justify their detention because they had not committed any crimes, but their chief set up Rural Guard posts in the vicinity "to exercise a constant outlook for these two men and to arrest them the moment they trespass the Law." Captain Avelino Sanjenis, a white veteran and guardsmen with a reputation for ruthless violence against black men, was assigned to watch "these undesirable characters" at one of the posts.³⁵ In the weeks thereafter, the two black veterans went missing and were later found dead.

Over the next few months, similar incidents played out in other areas of the province, usually at or in the vicinity of major sugar mills. Some rural dwellers, prominent veterans, and even US military authorities began to suspect foul play. Another incident involving the disappearance of two laborers from Central Narcisa confirmed these suspicions. In this case, Sanjenis assumed "all responsibility" for their disappearance, but claimed that he merely ordered them to leave. Initially civil authorities "gave full weight" to his explanation. However, after more than two weeks, no one had seen the men, who had worked and lived on the plantation for many years. They reportedly did not even return to their respective residences to collect their belongings. One US official reported that "the situation is a serious one," because "the people insist very reasonably" that Sanjenis was lying. Rural laborers reportedly were in "mortal terror," suspecting that Sanjenis and other Rural Guardsmen colluded with wealthy planters to murder, disappear, or otherwise allow their employees to assassinate rural workers deemed to be problematic.³⁶

In other cases, planters themselves, likely emboldened by their recently expanded access to arms permits for their private guard forces, did not even consult with Rural Guardsmen before exercising violent force against black veterans and other men they deemed problematic. In early 1901 Atkins arranged "a man hunt" against his longtime nemesis, the black veteran Claudio

Sarría, claiming that he was a member of a group of bandits responsible for ransom letters, threats, and cane fires at a number of nearby plantations: "I think Claudio is in this gang, and would like to catch him," wrote Atkins without offering any evidence to support the claim.[37] Although it is unlikely that Sarría perpetrated the depredations, Atkins invoked supposed acts of banditry to justify violence against the black veteran, likely to punish him for burning his cane and destroying his property during the war. His private guard caught Sarría and brought him to the estate. Atkins wrote that he "never saw a more frightened negro." In a rather emasculating narrative, he recounted the way Sarría pleaded for his life, seemingly nullifying his image as a brave veteran, while emphasizing the power differential between the two men. "He dropped on his knees before me, threw his arms around my legs and begged for his life, promising to be good in future," remembered Atkins. "I told him he ought to be shot but that I would spare his life that time. If, however, he was caught on the property again he would be shot on sight by my orders."[38] In this incident, strikingly reminiscent of the lynchings plaguing the US South at around the same time, Atkins, a northerner, presented himself as benevolent in allowing Sarría to live.

If Atkins boasted of his own mercy toward Sarría, he showed little sympathy on hearing news of the black veteran's subsequent murder by Rural Guardsmen. He wrote without the slightest emotion in his diary that Claudio "died of 'rope disease,' meaning that they had hanged him in the woods, where his skeleton was afterwards found."[39] The murder of Sarría not only demonstrated the emergence of white violence against black men as a mechanism for reinforcing the old social hierarchy. The fact that Rural Guardsmen—most of whom were themselves veterans—perpetrated the murder implied a certain level of state complicity in this project, not to mention the disintegration of what remaining cross-racial ties military service had forged.

New Men and "A Government Resting upon a Supposition of Incapacity"

Amid all the uproar over universal suffrage, delegates to the Constitutional Convention received the text of the Platt Amendment on March 2. The response was a mix of anger, indignation, and resignation. Some delegates argued for disbanding the convention in protest, but US officials quickly made it clear that this course of action would incur severe consequences, including the possible withholding of tariff concessions. Although most delegates retreated from their desires to disband the convention, they refused to concede in their opposition to the amendment. In their formal response to the United States in late March 1901, the delegates rejected the amendment as a violation of the Teller Amendment and the Treaty of Paris. They especially resented Article 3, which afforded the United States the right to intervene in Cuba. By mid-April delegates voted 18 to 10 to reject the Platt Amendment.[40] Delegates from eastern and central Cuba had been some of the most vocal opponents of the Platt Amendment. José Braulio Alemán and José Luis Robau were among the "no" votes.

Opponents of separatist rule and even some conservative white Cubans disdained men who fought against the Platt Amendment, claiming they cared little for the prosperity of Cuba. One white Rural Guard officer who wrote to military officials in May 1901, characterized opposition to the Platt Amendment as ignorant, radical and detrimental to the nation, arguing that honorable men supported it: "All, I mean every single one of the individuals of good will, everyone who desires that this country be rich, prosperous and happy as soon as possible dreams, requests, begs and accepts" US protection.[41]

Opponents of separatist rule, for their part, initially expressed their disappointment with the delegates' opposition to the Platt Amendment in the usual form—by emphasizing black criminality. Former Spanish volunteer Javier Medina argued that only the "radical element" was in favor of immediate withdrawal, whereas the "reasonable classes" favored annexation. Another man noted that "all persons having an interest in order and the welfare of the country are partisans of the Platt Amendment."[42] An American investigator noted that "the Spanish Element and the Cubans of good judgment are of the opinion that the withdrawal of the American Army from this country will bring its entire ruin."[43] Reasonable classes (that is, conservative whites), then, became defined in terms of the annexationist political position.

Although they initially panicked at the prospect the Platt Amendment might be rejected, opponents of separatist rule eventually understood that the United States had no intention of allowing the convention to make such a decision. According to former Spanish volunteer Javier Medina, Cuban self-government would be devastating to wealthy property owners: "The government should be happy that the Platt Amendment was rejected. If absolute independence is conceded to the country" anarchy will reign, "instigated by all the local authorities . . . and the assassinations, robberies and fires will be of the order of the day. Here in this town they are setting fire to the houses often, and it is said publically that it is ordered by the authorities."[44] Foreign property owners sought to maintain US rule in Cuba to secure their property and racial privilege against black outlaws and veterans, because the Cubans, they argued, were not fulfilling this requirement. The forced imposition of the Platt Amendment, it seemed, offered the only way to preserve US influence and save Cuba from the race war that supposedly awaited it. Indeed, the US government would not take no for an answer.

At the core of these responses to the Constitutional Convention's opposition to the Platt Amendment were racial ideas defining political fitness as an exclusively white domain—views that tended to buttress the racial logic of US rule in Cuba. In one US political cartoon, these ideas emerged with startling clarity. A smiling black *guajiro* child in the image of a Sambo sits barefoot atop a rickety mule-drawn wagon labeled "Cuba," as a disappointed-looking Uncle Sam, hat in hand, gives him the reins of government. The racial and age difference between the black child and Uncle Sam connote a definite hierarchy, implying the foolishness of relinquishing control over Cuba to Cubans. The conflation of Negro Rule and Cuban independence conveyed in the political cartoon communicated in no uncertain terms the inconceivability of a Cuban republic completely independent of the United States. The implication was not only that independence entailed allowing black people to rule Cuba, but also that Cuban rule would inevitably produce destitution (see fig. 8.2).

Not everyone took seriously the convention's decision however. Days after the convention rejected the Platt Amendment, a political cartoon was published in the US magazine *Puck* conveying confidence that Cubans would eventually come to embrace the United States. The cartoon depicted a seemingly obvious choice between an honorable *man* who could provide security and comfort to his woman and a selfish, impassioned seducer, who would presumably neglect his manly duties of protecting his family. Appearing as a curvaceous woman of swarthy complexion, Lady Cuba coyly fans herself as she is confronted with the ultimate decision of two suitors: one a tall, gentlemanly, and indisputably white Uncle Sam, and the other a sinister-looking, mustached insurgent with dark skin and furrowed brow, donning a sash with the label of revolutionist, though the final three letters are barely visible. Almost as if requesting protection, the sensuous woman leans toward Uncle Sam, grasping his extended arm. She glances timidly out of the side of her eye at the humiliated insurgent, suggesting a careful mixture of fear and disdain. The dichotomous representation of good and evil is compounded by the indomitable jungle behind the insurgent, an allusion to the war and

"The Colored Patriot and His Box of Matches"

Figure 8.2. "Here you are." Caricature of American views of Cuban independence. Source: "Here you are," newspaper clipping, [n.d.], Volume II.61, folio 72, Massachusetts Historical Society/Atkins Family Papers. Courtesy of Massachusetts Historical Society.

to the lack of productivity that would supposedly define Cuban society under Cuban rule. In contrast, Uncle Sam stands before lush but manicured greenery with both a pristine lake and a flowing fountain, representing both renewal and peace.

This cartoon offered a powerfully gendered metaphor for the Platt Amendment. Lady Cuba's acceptance of Uncle Sam over the Revolutionist alludes to the ultimate decision of the Constitutional Convention to accept the humiliating amendment to their constitution, severely limiting Cuban sovereignty and perpetually condemning Cuban political elites to subordinate status. Moreover, the union of Lady Cuba and Uncle Sam foreshadows the potential marriage of the two, and subsequently the penetration of the former by the latter in the name of racial "betterment" from which the darker Lady Cuba's offspring would benefit. This metaphor held clear economic significance, but also rendered the darker-skinned insurgent man as

Figure 8.3. "Good Government vs. Revolution—An Easy Choice." Source: Udo J. Keppler, "Good Government vs. Revolution—An Easy Choice," *Puck*, April 17, 1901, Library of Congress, Prints and Photographs Division.

symbolically humiliated for having his woman stolen away and ravaged by another man (see fig. 8.3).

Although the political cartoon presented Cuba *choosing* close relations with the United States, in actuality, the delegates of the Constitutional Convention had little control over the matter. Indeed, the decision of a slight majority of delegates to reject the Platt Amendment in April 1901 proved only temporary. If delegates continued to reject the amendment, the United States would simply refuse to grant independence, some feared.⁴⁵ As a result, some veterans who initially opposed it began to emphasize the need for "consensus," a euphemism that implied acceptance of the amendment. White convention delegate Enrique Villuendas wrote that "it terrifies me to think that the occupation could be prolonged one or two more years because I know that at the end of those, we will not have left dignity nor ideals in the shocking chaos of the absolute moral ruin. What choice do we have?" he wrote in despair.⁴⁶

Beyond the convention, other veterans mused that any resistance to US rule merely offered greater justification for its prolongation. White veteran Gerardo Machado noted that it was "critical for all Cubans" and "doubly so for those who fought in the ranks of the Revolution" to "demonstrate the utmost calm, serenity and composed judgment, so that the defense of our ideals results to be doubly amenable, regardless of future emergencies." Machado called for absolute order, castigating any effort of protest against the controversial amendment. "Any isolated attempt to resort in these moments to the means of force would not only result [to be] ineffective because of its own weakness but would also serve as a pretext" to extend the occupation. "We need to demonstrate not only to the United States but to the entire world with our conduct and civic virtue, that in this land we do not need any 'guard body,' rather that the people and the property will be always be sufficiently guaranteed by our patriotism."[47] Perhaps unsurprisingly Machado called for complete obedience to the separatist chiefs and implied that the absolute suppression of disorder was the key to securing US withdrawal.

Debate was fierce, but ultimately the acceptance of the amendment was a product of what one white veteran called "the will of the American government" and our need to "cede to force."[48] By mid-June 1901 the majority of delegates voted to accept the Platt Amendment verbatim as Congress had passed it earlier that year.[49] After initial controversy subsided, Robau abstained, leaving Alemán the only representative of Santa Clara to continue his opposition. The decreasing resistance to the Platt Amendment between its announcement in March and its final approval in June suggests that Cubans increasingly viewed its implementation as their only choice for continued political power, as US pressure made the acceptance of the amendment a condition of establishing a Cuban republic.

The Platt Amendment was not only a blow to Cuban sovereignty at the national level; it had profound consequences on the political and racial parameters of public authority at the local and provincial levels. The case of José Braulio Alemán illustrates how perceived political radicalism served to disqualify otherwise elite New Men from political power. Other than being a veteran, Alemán garnered the attention of US military authorities during his editorship of the radical nationalist newspaper *La Tribuna*, which periodically ran inflammatory articles criticizing US rule. During the Constitutional Convention, he emerged as one of the staunchest supporters of universal manhood suffrage and one of the fiercest critics of the Platt Amendment. This supposedly "radical" political view attracted considerable disdain on the part of US military officials, opponents of separatist rule, and conservative Cubans.

For some critics Alemán's established links to black veterans made his political radicalism particularly suspect. Although he belonged to Santa Clara's white urban elite, he had advocated for the multiracial rank and file of the defunct Liberating Army during his tenure as president of the Cienfuegos

Veterans' Center. Responding to popular outcry, he demanded a more thorough investigation of the murder of black general Dionisio Gil in December 1899. His reputation as a racial agitator only grew when he reportedly gave a speech in August 1900 urging resistance against US rule and informing "the negroes that they were as good as the whites." Apparently, US military authorities found these remarks "offensive" enough to warrant an investigation into his conduct.[50] Ironically, the same man who had openly appealed to racial divisions to oppose the authority of black men in the Cuban army had now emerged as one of the more outspoken advocates of racial inclusion, at least in theory.

Unsurprisingly, Alemán's name appeared in several vitriolic denunciations of the so-called white radicals. One former Spanish volunteer speculated that Alemán threatened to mobilize "radical elements" at the Constitution Convention to overturn any decision he deemed unsatisfactory.[51] This kind of radical talk was alarming to US officials, especially Wood, who wished "to avoid making Cuba into a second Haiti."[52] Medina urged military officials to monitor this "famous revolutionist" (*famoso revoltoso*), as he was equally as dangerous as the black leaders Quintín Bandera, Juan Gualberto Gómez, and Martín Morúa Delgado.[53] The reaction to Alemán's intransigence (used in the Cuban sense to mean a man of principle) highlighted the subtle conflation of opposition to US rule and political and social radicalism.

Following the passage of the Platt Amendment, Alemán's ongoing public invocation of revolutionary masculinity proved increasingly detrimental to his political aspirations. Although he continued to defend the equalizing principles of revolutionary masculinity, he also recognized that his political future hinged on moderating his public rhetoric on race and performing the role of conservator of order. This subtle shift in his enactment of New Man status manifested in his response to the military government's attempt to exclude black men from the newly formed Artillery Corps.

In summer 1901 the military government created the Artillery Corps, a reduced and state-controlled replacement for the more robust Liberating Army. The order initially sought to limit enlistment to white men. From the perspective of many veterans, this attempt to exclude nonwhites from the military was a direct attack on military service as the historic foundation of veterans' citizenship.[54] After all, the entire discourse of revolutionary masculinity was premised on military service as a demonstration of manliness and later as a qualifier for martial manhood.

Black veterans recognized immediately the ways this racial exclusion undermined the discursive foundations of their manhood and by extension their claims to citizenship. The order allegedly provoked "serious agitation" among black veterans, but also drew the immediate condemnation of white political elites and the popular press. One white critic wrote that "not opposing such a resolution would make us accomplices of the military government."[55] In response to the protests, US military officials modified the original order to include a separate company for men of African descent.[56]

One of the most outspoken critics of the proposed racial division of the Artillery Corps was Alemán himself. In a lengthy and impassioned letter to US military authorities, he criticized the policy as an attempt to impose Jim Crow-style racial segregation on Cubans. For Alemán this was problematic for two reasons. First, it dishonored "our democratic and revolutionary tradition," of which a long history of black military service and legal equality were core parts. He reminded US officials that black men had demonstrated their "love for liberty" during the wars. Neither in war nor in peace, Alemán proclaimed, had black men desired anything but "the disinterested liberation of the country, its welfare and prosperity." For that reason, the convention created the constitution to "not recognize any privileges," be they "by virtue of birth, color of the skin, nor in view of any circumstantial incident of life."[57] The newly approved Constitution of Cuba "accepts equality among all Cubans" and "equally calls upon all citizens to render military service." By invoking the cross-racial premise of revolutionary masculinity, Alemán critiqued US efforts to exclude black men from the Artillery Corps.

Alemán's appeals to raceless manhood provided a palatable framing for a much more cynical argument—one that foregrounded white men's supposed responsibility to preserve order. He claimed that implementing a racially restrictive policy in the military would inhibit white veterans from preserving "harmony" and ensuring "stable government." Alemán anticipated "disastrous" consequences if US officials left the policy intact. It would create "a political-social problem ... of such gravity" that it would eclipse whatever "good intentions" the military government might have had. Alemán even denounced the "tenebrous political intention" behind the segregationist policy, implying that the military government sought to foment divisions among the Cuban separatists that would likely cause the emerging government to falter. US military officials could then conveniently blame "Cuban incapacity" for any failure in government. These comments suggested that what really mattered to Alemán and other white veterans were the potentially catastrophic political consequences this policy of explicit racial exclusion would have for their own political futures.⁵⁸

Alemán revealed himself to be more concerned with his own public reputation regarding racial issues than the actual principle of racial equality. If he and other New Men refused to denounce the policy publically, they risked damaging their electoral prospects with voters. He noted that the policy constituted a "political imprudence," because it would divide "the Cuban family" thereby inhibiting white political elites like himself from enjoying unfettered popular support. As Alemán explained to US military officials, in Cuba, "prejudices do not require such discrimination." Unofficial and unspoken systemic prejudice accomplished this almost as well as explicit racial exclusion, without jeopardizing the public reputations of political elites.

Alemán proposed a more politically expedient policy, one that would assuage veterans' concerns about explicit racial discrimination, but ultimately have the same exclusionary result. Requiring all candidates to "pass similar examinations of enlistment," he claimed, would allow the evaluation of "the merits of the Cuban applicants of both races."⁵⁹ Herein lay the essence of how revolutionary masculinity enabled racial discrimination. While the meritocratic tone of Alemán's proposed policy seemed to offer black and white men an equal opportunity to enter the Artillery Corps, in actuality, it systematized racial silence. By refusing to acknowledge the ways historic white privilege (presumptions of honor, preferential access to formal education, among other benefits) cumulatively advantaged white men over their black counterparts, the policy would effectively reproduce existing inequalities and perpetuate ongoing exclusions. Although the military government tacitly agreed to open the Artillery Corps to black men, they remained firm in keeping the officer ranks exclusively white.⁶⁰

The combined implications of universal manhood suffrage and the Platt Amendment had rendered the delicate balancing act around racial inclusion even more challenging. Radical white separatists like Alemán faced a catch-22: their political legitimacy and to a certain extent their electoral viability depended on securing the black vote through a public commitment to racial equality, yet any association with this radical ideal disqualified them as real contenders for political power because social radicalism was construed as anti-Americanism. The rising importance of collaboration with US officials increasingly favored conservatism among political elites. Unlike other prominent white veterans like José Miguel Gómez, José de Jesús Monteagudo, or Carlos Mendieta, Alemán would not obtain prominent government positions at the national level in the years to come. Alemán's failure to adequately transform himself into a convincing agent of order likely contributed to his marginalization from national politics.

As much as white men risked being labeled radicals for supporting independence and nominal racial inclusion, black men who expressed similar views faced even harsher sanctions. One black veteran suspected that his race and anti-Platt Amendment political views landed him in prison. From his cell, he pleaded for help exposing the "criminal lowliness of the enemies of the colored race, principally against those who demonstrate their rank."[61] Opposition to the Platt Amendment, formerly the definition of intransigent commitment to Cuban independence, increasingly became a dangerous and unpatriotic proposition for political hopefuls, one for which black men were judged more harshly than whites.

The Myth of Democracy: Patronage, Fraud, and the Birth of the New Veteran-Politician

The unprecedented conditionality of New Men's political power following the acceptance of the Platt Amendment likewise informed a shift in local electoral politics. A careful examination of electoral races in central Cuba's major cities in 1901 suggests that cooperation with the US military government was a precondition for maintaining political power. Consequently, white political elites could no longer downplay or ignore the vocal allegations of annexationists that the end of US rule would beget black rule. Whereas some white veterans had initially rejected the conditionality of their political authority toward the beginning of the military occupation, the increasing intervention of US military officials in local politics fostered greater cooperation from New Men, whose acknowledgment of US authority earned them greater political security.

Nowhere is this evolving response to conditional political power more evident than the 1901 mayoral race in the city of Cienfuegos. US officials handpicked Leopoldo Figueroa as their preferred candidate for mayor in the June 1901 elections. This was the same man they had installed to replace prestigious separatist mayor José Antonio Frías in early 1900 after a series of major conflicts between veterans and US officials (see chapter 7).[62] Figueroa held all the revolutionary credentials of the most prestigious Cuban patriots, leading many (though not all) of his compatriots to vote for him in the municipal elections.[63] He also stacked his city council with men of his same social status, individuals with the most illustrious names of the city.[64] Over the course of his first term as mayor, Figueroa had garnered the support of the "best elements of the community." After all, he was the favorite of annexationists such as Edwin F. Atkins.[65]

One of the key reasons Figueroa gained support among these conservative sectors was because during his tenure as mayor in 1900 and early 1901, he carried out a series of policies that benefited the wealthiest members of society and marginalized veterans and workers of African descent. He bowed to pressure from wealthy planters to suppress the predominantly black dockworkers, who had formed one of the most powerful labor unions on the island. Figueroa also complied with demands of US military officials to relocate the red light district from the central urban waterfront to the peripheral neighborhood of Reina, a policy that effectively dismantled the historically black community that had taken root there since the 1820s.[66] Numerous urban residents favored the mayor's campaign to "cleanse" the city center, and US military officials and opponents of separatist rule renewed their support for Figueroa's reelection.

These same policies earned Figueroa staunch opposition from workers and veterans. He was known among the urban masses by such unflattering nicknames as "Majá," "The Great Mogol," and the "Weyler of Cienfuegos," references to his cowardice during the war and his draconian policies toward the masses.[67] One worker expressed his support of Republican opposition candidate Gonzalo García Vieta, a doctor and veteran, as a rejection of the self-serving and pro-US policies of Figueroa: "we sealed the ballots with the shit of Platt Amendment cows," because "the Republican Party united with the Worker has decreed the departure from the city council of Figueroa and his gang, AND THEY WILL LEAVE, because it is just that they get out to cleanse themselves of their guilt and of the sin of allowing themselves to be guided by their greedy bellies and not by the voices of their consciences."[68] These lines revealed popular discontent with Figueroa for his perceived antagonism against the lower classes.

His conservative support base and his prior service in the Sanitary Corps (as opposed to combat) also led certain radical veterans to question his revolutionary credentials. José Braulio Alemán published a scathing critique of the mayor in his newspaper, *La Tribuna*, in which he condemned Figueroa as a collaborator of US rule, no better than the Autonomists, Spaniards, and annexationists who appealed to delay Cuban independence.[69] Supporters of Figueroa crushed Alemán's criticisms as unpatriotic. Dozens of prominent white veterans gathered in the Tomás Terry theater and censured Alemán for his "anti-revolutionary and despotic expressions." One veteran exclaimed that "this community does not need intrusive intermediaries. General Alemán has committed an outrage against the people of Cienfuegos."[70] Although framed as a defense of revolutionary unity and an appeal to democracy, the language betrayed clear intolerance for dissenting views.

Figueroa's supporters dismissed critiques that his low-rank and service in the Sanitary Corps disqualified him for the high office of mayor. They retorted that his military service was the principal foundation for his masculine honor, demonstrated his fitness for political power and proved his commitment to independence. In his address to the audience, prominent white veteran Carlos Trujillo praised Figueroa for his patriotism, arguing that all contributions to the war effort were "equally" valuable: "The war ended, and for the people, neither generals nor soldiers exist, but rather revolutionaries," he claimed. Trujillo simultaneously downplayed the importance of rank and military achievement to place his medical service on equal footing with the military honor of less prestigious but more meritorious veterans. He eulogized revolutionary unity, proclaiming that "the warrior of one hundred battles and that warrior who, suffering, risked his life to save the wounded or to secure the sustenance of the Chief during the fateful days of persecution and misery are equally worthy of the honor and greatness of the fatherland [patria]."[71] This reference to military service as a marker of manhood transformed it from a true reflection of military rank to a hollow justification for political eligibility.

With white veterans divided, and black veterans and workers firmly supporting Vieta, Figueroa's supporters knew that their preferred candidate was unlikely to win a fair democratic election. So both annexationists and US military officials set out to engineer his victory. One of the ways they attempted to favor Figueroa was by undermining his opponent's political fitness.[72] Critics accused Vieta of being soft on race, allegations that fit within a well-established pattern of racializing and criminalizing political agendas perceived as insufficiently deferential to US interests.[73] Indeed, critics were quick to point out that Vieta's platform foregrounded absolute and immediate independence, his mayoral ticket included several black men, and that he enjoyed the endorsement of local labor leaders. Opponents of separatist rule labeled Vieta's supporters as "blacks and mulattos in the majority and vicious corrupted whites who desire absolute Independence to live by stealing from honorable men."[74] Barker described Vieta as "a very popular and conscientious man," and "comparatively if not strictly honest," but noted that his "principle support is from the rabble; for instance, on his ticket are four negroes for councilmen. This fact alone creates serious fear among the property holders, who are almost unanimously supporters either openly or tacitly of Figueroa."[75] The racialization and criminalization of radical nationalist candidates, like Vieta, characterized their election as dishonorable and illegitimate.

Another way Vieta's critics attempted to undermine his political fitness was by accusing him and his supporters of electoral fraud and voter intimidation. US military officials claimed that the electoral campaign was shrouded in controversy and plagued by a "great number of personal incidents." They accused Vieta of "*caudillaje*," alleging that he exploited his networks of revolutionary patronage to secure political support. Some of his political opponents alleged that Vieta enlisted his supporters in the Rural Guard in terrorizing local residents to ensure they voted as they were told. Local veteran chiefs, or "caudillos," as Barker called them, canvassed their areas of influence to ensure that voters turned out for Vieta. Former Cienfuegos mayor José Antonio Frías, known for his early opposition to US authority, apparently mobilized his revolutionary network on behalf of Vieta, further solidifying US opposition. Frías pressured one white veteran officer to "control his district for Vieta, which he did." A Spanish merchant reported to US military officials that this white veteran had been "terrorizing the country" to influence the elections.[76] These accusations channeled fears about the hypermasculinity of veterans to depict Vieta as dishonorable and to undermine his campaign as illegitimate.

For all the accusations levied against Vieta, most evidence suggests that electoral fraud was actually committed by supporters of Figueroa, the less popular candidate. US military officials even enlisted their influential allies to ensure that Figueroa won. Bostonian planter Edwin F. Atkins, for one, admitted to tampering directly in the Cienfuegos mayoral race to ensure the victory of "a very respectable man," who had garnered the support of military governor Leonard Wood.[77] He recounted: "I sent for one of the alcaldes de barrio, and told him my wishes. He told me to have no anxiety; the man I suggested would be elected." When asked how the man would do this, he replied that "they would take possession of the ballot boxes and destroy the ballots of the opposition candidates." Atkins "told him it was a magnificent idea and worthy of Tammany Hall," glorifying the political machines of late nineteenth-century New York.⁷⁸ Clearly neither the military government nor local property owners wished to leave control over Cienfuegos up to a democratic vote.

Nor was electoral fraud in favor of Figueroa limited to opponents of separatist rule and US military officials. One of Figueroa's most powerful allies was recently appointed police chief Juan José Campillo y D'Wolf, a prominent white veteran who had turned the municipal police force into a political machine in favor of the pro-US candidate. Campillo allegedly pressured his subordinates to vote for Figueroa and fired those who did not. The sixty-three men Campillo removed from the force were mostly veterans, at least some of them black, including Inocencio Sarría, José González González, Francisco Fernández, José Bermúdez, and Benigno Ortiz. Figueroa himself even publically thanked "the chiefs and officers and individuals who *today* form part of [the municipal police force]," and who "have constituted true safeguards of Society proceeding always with justice and with the severest energy." Figueroa ended by praising the upstanding services of the police "for the magnificent and commendable behavior they have observed in the fulfillment of their delicate duties, in which they have recognized exactly the sacred mission they have to fulfill."⁷⁹ Those who no longer formed part of the force, Figueroa implied, had not fulfilled their duties. In July 1901 the former police officers complained that Campillo had denounced them to Figueroa, resulting in their dismissal "for the good of the force." In addition, Campillo withheld their pay, as a form of "revenge."⁸⁰

Despite the political maneuvering of his powerful allies, Figueroa lost the election. Barker had lamented that "the situation here is extremely unfortunate," because "with Figueroa as alcalde, good order would have been maintained." He noted the disappointment of planters: "I did not realize until it became a fact, how deeply the better classes of people irrespective of nationality regretted Figueroa's defeat." US military authorities pressed the local board of scrutiny to review the election results concerning the fraud, placing one of their own officers in charge. When it was clear that Figueroa failed to garner the popular vote, Barker urged his superiors to offer him "some State position," this "being so much in the interest of decency and manliness." Vindicating Figueroa would serve as "a justification of him in the eyes of the people, which would be much appreciated by himself and friends."⁸¹ Whereas during the war, military service became a symbol of manhood that would render the individual eligible for citizenship, the 1901 elections proved that political conservatism, which was critical to US support, had become a critical qualifier for US support.

Indeed, the power of the newly expanded electorate was no match for the preferences of US military officials and opponents of separatist rule. Vieta assumed the office of mayor only to confront a full-blown crisis of mayoral authority. One of the key conflicts emanated from the police force. Vieta reinstated the policemen Campillo had fired for refusing to vote for Figueroa. However, public outcry against Campillo's ongoing abuses of police and local residents provoked public protests. Radical separatists and veterans including the black officer José Camacho, clamored against Campillo, who had abused his power while in office. Some of these protesters allegedly carried arms and "openly declare[d] that in order to disarm them they will have to be killed." US military authorities feared an impending attack upon Campillo by "the wors[t] element of this city."[82] Vieta ordered one of his police officers to disarm the protesters, while the Rural Guard from various stations in the province helped preserve order.[83] He also removed Campillo and several other pro-Figueroa officers from the force. In their place, Vieta installed his own allies, ones who did not secure the approval of US authorities. One of the newly hired policemen allegedly had given an inflammatory speech right before the election "denouncing Americans and proclaiming that he was ready to drive them out of the Island." According to Barker, Vieta had made other "equally discreditable" appointments.[84]

His adjustments to the police force provoked an uproar from wealthy residents and recently dismissed police officers. In early July several residents presented a petition to the city council, protesting the dismissal of Campillo and his subordinates. Vieta adamantly defended his decision to fire Campillo, claiming to have "more than enough reason," for doing so. He declared that "far from deserving protest or censure," the decision "should have been considered as the most brilliant, just and necessary act that could ever have been realized."[85] Vieta enumerated a long list of justifications for the termination which centered on Campillo's masculine failures, such as his tendency toward excessive force and the dishonor of his abuses of power. For example, he cited Campillo's "violent temper"—likely a subtle invocation of what US military authorities understood as the "excitable" temperament of the Latin race. Certainly, his lack of control had been abundantly evident in his behavior during a legal suit levied against him by local black activist Nicolás Valverde. Campillo had been known for occasionally abusing innocent citizens. Vieta also accused him of disrespecting his authority by appointing men to the police force without his approval.⁸⁶ Moreover, Campillo allegedly condoned and even attended cockfights, which the US military government had outlawed at the beginning of the occupation.⁸⁷

One of the most severe indictments Vieta hurled at Campillo was his alleged inability to preserve order. He claimed that notwithstanding his "revolutionary achievements" during the war, Campillo "failed completely" as police chief. Vieta cited the "repeated and unnecessary summoning" of US authorities, whom Campillo and Figueroa "bothered without cause, and to the detriment of the town, for which the former police chief was responsible."⁸⁸ In Vieta's opinion, only a man who had failed in his function would have to resort to US authorities.

US military authorities dismissed Vieta's indictments of Campillo. Barker claimed that Vieta had fired Campillo not because of his unfitness for the job, but rather as a political favor to his patron, former Cienfuegos mayor José Antonio Frías, who allegedly "controls the entire administration."⁸⁹ US officials also defended Campillo, declaring that "while the private life of the chief of police is not what it should be, he is undoubtedly strong with all the best people."⁹⁰ Prominent planters like Edwin F. Atkins and Elias Ponvert even wrote on his behalf, assuring US military authorities that Campillo held the "respect of the business community of Cienfuegos."⁹¹ Campillo also maintained close correspondence with high-ranking US military officials, including military governor Leonard Wood.⁹² Military officials favored Campillo to such a degree that they reinstated him, citing Military Order Number 156 of June 12, 1901, which required the investigation of complaints before approving a public employee's dismissal. When Vieta refused to comply, they forced him to resign as mayor.

The reaction to the municipal election, on all fronts, demonstrated the increasing political value of conservatism at the same time as it demonstrated the immense power of groups opposing radical separatists. Even though Vieta had won the election, US military officials unilaterally removed him from office. In his place, they installed Higinio Esquerra, the celebrated white brigadier general.⁹³ Although Esquerra was supposedly a "neutral" choice, he was "a warm personal friend and supporter of Campillo," and had long been held in high esteem by US authorities.⁹⁴ Certainly, his tenure as chief of the Cienfuegos Rural Guard prepared him well for the demands of the office of mayor, not least of which were the preservation of social order and collaboration with US military officials.

The removal of Vieta did not erase tensions between the Frías faction

Figure 8.4. Higinio Esquerra. Courtesy of Archivo Histórico Municipal de Remedios.

and the Figueroa coalition, and violent protest subsumed during the first days of Esquerra's term as mayor.[95] The police force remained at the center of this conflict. Under Esquerra, chief Campillo continued Figueroa's policy of refusing to pay the policemen who had been suspended for not voting for him. Esquerra also ordered major pay cuts for police officers, and even prohibited police from negotiating their salaries, allegedly "for the purpose of forcing them to relinquish their positions." Esquerra's administration also withheld pay from policemen for several consecutive months in order to "deprive them of the means of subsistence," and "compel them by hunger" to resign from the force.[96]

Efforts to remove Campillo continued, but ultimately failed in the face of US military support for him. One city councilman brought charges against Campillo for insubordination after a dispute over police uniforms.[97] However, Campillo's supporters retaliated, alleging that the councilman and several other "spiritists," obliged a young girl "to commit immoral acts" through spiritist suggestions. These allegations of sexual immorality combined attacks against the manhood of Campillo's political enemies as well as references to supposed magical practices, likely understood to mean African-influenced religion.[98] The accusations led to the temporary removal of Campillo from his position as chief, although US military officials again quickly restored him.⁹⁹

By supporting veterans like Esquerra and Campillo, who simultaneously boasted the highest revolutionary credentials and demonstrated a history of harmonious and cooperative conduct with the military government, US military officials set a powerful precedent for conservative political predominance in Cienfuegos. US officials' preference for Figueroa, Esquerra, and Campillo over Frías and Vieta demonstrates just how important a pro-US platform had become for New Men's ability to secure local political power. When US officials assessed a candidate's posture toward the military government, the racial composition of their networks of political patronage mattered. Whereas US authorities condemned Frías and Vieta for their connections to black veterans, they celebrated Figueroa, whose administration had defended the interests of the wealthiest residents by suppressing poor and working-class blacks.

The Consolidation of Conservatism and the Eclipse of Revolutionary Masculinity

Watching the presidential elections from Santa Clara Province in late 1901, black veterans realized just how completely some of their white compatriots had abandoned revolutionary masculinity in pursuit of their own political ambitions. The two candidates Bartolomé Masó and Tomás Estrada Palma, both formally educated, prominent white men, represented the civil branch of Cuba Libre, a group of separatists recognizably more conservative than most veterans. Yet, the candidates espoused remarkably diverging approaches to relations with the United States, which in turn had significant implications for the racial inflections of their candidacies. Even though neither Estrada Palma nor Masó openly favored racial equality, their posture toward the United States became a powerful determinant of the sectors from which each man drew support. The clear favorite of the US military government was Estrada Palma, a longtime New York resident, converted Quaker and naturalized US citizen, who alienated the popular sectors—and with them many black men—because of his strong commitment to the US.

In contrast, Masó's irrevocable revolutionary credentials and pro-independence platform attracted broad support from the Cuban masses, despite his ambivalence on issues of race. After all, at the outset of military rule, he had assured US officials that the racial order would remain intact, as black men would continue to work in the cane fields.[100] By 1901 Masó declared "absolute impartiality on the race question" as his official political platform.[101] Yet, the occupation government's secret police reported that Masó commanded "the *unanimous support of the colored race*."[102] Masó reportedly also relied on the support of workers who argued that by "fighting against Estrada Palma they f[ou]ght against the American government."[103] US military officials speculated that black voters would only vote for the pro-independence candidate, and that Masó used this to his advantage. One US military official explained that "the negroes have been led to believe that the American is not the friend of the negro and should American control continue, the negro will suffer." He believed that "this anti-American feeling is merely for the purpose of getting negro votes."[104] Conflating pro-independence ideas with racial radicalism, US military authorities labeled Masó disparagingly as the pro-black candidate.

The alleged racial agitation in Santa Clara Province on behalf of Masó proved to be one of the more worrisome aspects of the presidential campaign. The military government dispatched secret police to investigate the mobilization of workers in support of Masó's candidacy in Cienfuegos in September 1901. Anarchists and workers gathered in the Tomás Terry theater, allegedly insulting the United States. One worker reportedly proclaimed that "Americans violate rights and law and do not violate [rape] their mothers because they had none, that having them they [would] do it." Another man declared that workers "should not wait any longer, but should rise up to the realization of their divine rights and make the moneyed power abandon its capital and humiliate itself at the feet of honest workingmen."[105] Workers from across the island joined in celebrating the meeting, which US officials characterized as an "accentuated explo[i]tation of the anarchistical creed and a marked hatred of everything American."[106] In this context of heightened political stakes, local authorities in Santa Clara Province interpreted the supposed racial agitation on behalf of Masó as a threat to order. In Camajuaní the mayor disbanded one *masoísta* political rally, evoking the consternation of Juan Gualberto Gómez, a member of Masó's campaign committee.[107]

Similar to what had transpired during the June 1901 local election, a candidate's posture toward US rule became one of the most important determinants of their political fitness in the December general elections. US military officials had already concluded that a government under Masó would be largely unsuitable for US interests. So they manipulated the political terrain in favor of Estrada Palma, ousting openly pro-Masó mayors across the island and appointing partisans of Estrada Palma to the electoral supervision committee. Local black activist Félix Dorticós explained the general demoralization in Cienfuegos with the presidential election. The opposition party employed the specter of war with the United States to undermine the agenda of absolute and immediate independence, supposedly supported by Masó. They argued that "there is no point in voting against Estrada Palma as the candidate the United States would impose." Dorticós characterized this position of indifference as "inconsequential, false, and cowardly."[108] In the face of seemingly insurmountable odds against him, Masó withdrew his candidacy and Estrada Palma obtained the presidency.[109]

Masó's withdrawal marked the culmination in a series of defeats of pro-independence candidates in 1901. He had ultimately failed in his negotiation of the contentious political situation of the military occupation. He distanced himself from political and racial radicalism, occasionally invoking Cuba Libre to retain popular support. This appeal, however empty, marked him as radical in the eyes of US authorities.

Importantly, Masó's withdrawal told of an ominous shift in the definition of political fitness. The ideal man in this emerging neocolonial order was a white man, just like it had been after the war. However, the impending birth of the Cuban republic rendered whiteness necessary but insufficient to qualify a man for political authority. Cuba's new guardians were charged with ensuring order on the island, lest the United States intervene once again. Maintaining order in Cuba meant abandoning revolutionary masculinity's cross-racial implications and accepting that conditional sovereignty was necessary for these white men to remain in power. Consequently political and social conservativism were crucial qualities that defined political fitness in neocolonial Cuba.

Alemán's political marginalization and subsequent appeals to order, Vieta's removal from office, and Masó's renunciation as presidential candidate illustrate just how critical US approval was for securing political power, even as military rule drew to a close. Access to political power increasingly required appeasing US military authorities, who often controlled elections behind the scenes. Silence on racial issues and decidedly more self-interested cooperation with US authorities had emerged as the essential currency of political authority and formed a core part of what it meant to be a political elite in Cuba.

Figure 8.5. White rural guardsmen patrol a celebration of the republic in Sagua, May 1902. Source: "Sesión Extraordinaria del 20 de mayo de 1902," *Ayuntamiento de Sagua la Grande*, May 20, 1902, Biblioteca Provincial de Santa Clara, Sala de Fondos Raros.

If revolutionary masculinity had become politically dangerous, neocolonial masculinity had emerged in its place. This new vision of political fitness hinged on the consolidation of national self-determination, embodied in the inauguration of a Cuban republic. Yet, in contrast to revolutionary masculinity, neocolonial masculinity dismissed intransigent commitment to absolute and immediate independence as impractical, rather emphasizing cooperation with US authorities as a more pragmatic route to independence. New political men viewed this as the most expedient way to bring an end to direct US rule, rendering it a more appropriate translation of patriotic military service in the political realm. Due to the centrality of whiteness and racial order in this new political landscape, neocolonial political men effectively abandoned the socially equalizing function of military service.

In May 1902 men and women across central Cuba welcomed the birth of the Cuban republic. White Rural Guardsmen patrolled the streets, warding off any potential display of disorder that could taint the culmination of New Men's political authority. However, the increasingly repressive tenor of the local state illustrated just how conditional that political power was.

While outwardly authoritative and patriarchal, conservative Cuban political elites were but middlemen in an ongoing negotiation of what it meant to be a Cuban man at the interstices of anticolonial struggle and neocolonial consolidation. In part this subordination was premised on US perceptions of white Cubans' racial inferiority as members of the so-called Latin race. Cuban authorities straddled their domestic masculine image of political authority over a largely neutralized multiracial populace with inwardly effeminate status buckling beneath the weight of US empire. Black and working-class Cuban veterans, now largely excluded from dominant visions of masculinity, clung to the potentially radical meanings of their military service. They silently commemorated the contribution of black men to the emerging republic, occasionally demanding a greater role in the republic they helped win. But seldom did they frame their arguments explicitly in terms of race, but rather on their merits as men and revolutionaries.

CONCLUSION

The Racial Limits of Revolutionary Masculinity

DURING THE TRANSITION FROM COLONY TO REPUBLIC, PREVAILING discourses of masculinity were fundamentally transformed. Under Spanish rule, masculinity hinged on notions of honor as an in-born status that privileged whiteness, legitimate birth, and peninsular origin. This colonial masculinity served as the ideological foundation for colonial social and racial hierarchies that placed peninsular Spanish men over white Cuban Creole men, and white men over men of African descent.

The outbreak of anticolonial struggle in 1868 initiated a protracted process by which Cuban-born men chipped away at their feminized colonial subordination. Calling themselves citizens, these insurgents laid the foundation for a new vision of Creoles as free men. However, these challenges to the established order did not go uncontested. The soldiers and officers of the Spanish army deployed colonial notions of masculinity to disparage insurgents as illegitimate because of the multiracial character of the insurrection. In turn, this gendered logic enabled them to dismiss the revolution as banditry—that is, as racialized crime—rather than acknowledging it as a legitimate political act. The deployment of colonial masculinity successfully undermined not one, but two anticolonial insurrections.

It was not until the eruption of the War of Independence in 1895 that

Cuban insurgents consolidated their emergent masculine sensibility into a coherent discourse and applied it to contest Spanish counterinsurgency propaganda. Building on the legacies of two failed revolutions, insurgents shattered longstanding associations between European birth and political manhood. They rejected their seemingly effeminate status of political and economic subordination to the supposedly masculine Spanish colonizer. In the throes of battle, Cuban insurgents constructed a new vision of masculinity that privileged their own military service as its foundation. Revolutionary masculinity posited that Cuban veterans demonstrated their superior manhood in two interrelated ways. As soldiers, Cuban men claimed military honor through bravery and self-abnegation on the battlefield. Simultaneously, they translated their patriarchal roles to the rebel camps, protecting Cuban women from Spanish cruelties and controlling their bodies and labor despite their absence from the home front. Insurgents' emphasis on merit rather than inherited status as a measure of manliness called into question the logic of Cuban men's colonial subordination under Spanish rule.

The meritocratic thrust of revolutionary masculinity also destabilized prevailing notions that masculinity was the exclusive domain of white men. This emerging discourse offered men of diverse racial and class backgrounds a powerful tool to challenge their racial and class subordination. Citing their military achievements and fulfillment of patriarchal duties, these men could theoretically overcome the historic devaluation of blackness as an immutable marker of subordinate status. Black and working-class men, especially those in officer ranks, harnessed this emergent discourse to lay claim to the military prestige, authority, and resources they believed their achievements had entitled them.

The practical results of black men's claims to revolutionary masculinity were mixed. Certainly, the prospect of gaining inclusion and even citizenship in a free Cuba proved appealing to black and working-class men, who joined the insurrection en masse. Moreover, the notion that military rank measured tangible achievements on the battlefield propelled a number of talented black soldiers to positions of leadership in the Liberating Army. Nevertheless, revolutionary masculinity failed to produce lasting changes in racial and class hierarchies. In part, the failure resulted from the persistence of social hierarchies among veterans themselves—a continuity that stemmed from the racial silence defining revolutionary masculinity. Whereas white men were presumed to be honorable and meritorious, black men had to prove their manhood constantly. Not only did black men face greater scrutiny than white men over their conformity to masculine ideals, they also were subject to higher standards. White insurgent leaders often applied the supposedly raceless ideals of revolutionary masculinity unevenly, holding black men accountable for transgressions while allowing white men to commit the same acts with impunity. Although military service remained the cornerstone of insurgent honor, white insurgents defended their own racial privilege by coding their racist assumptions and actions in a language of masculinity.

In the army white insurgents perpetuated racial hierarchy through implicit racial assumptions undergirding two key pillars of manhood: patriarchal authority and military merit. First, white insurgents emphasized their own patriarchal honor on the basis of their chivalric protection of an idealized image of chaste, self-abnegating, patriotic Cuban womanhood. Because prevailing ideals of women's sexual morality implicitly privileged whiteness, white insurgents benefited disproportionately from this source of masculine claims-making. Black men's claims to patriarchy were often unsuccessful due to the unspoken devaluation of black womanhood. Second, white insurgents redefined military merit in terms of racially tinged measures of honor, including respect for authority, orderliness, and sexual morality. They applied the emergent image of the bad soldier (majá) to name and punish presumed transgressions against proper military conduct. Yet in practice, the very notion of what constituted a good soldier (mambí) had become racialized. Mambises were implicitly coded as white. By contrast, the label of majá, disproportionately applied to men of African descent, became a way to punish black soldiers' infractions against racial etiquette, without explicitly naming the grievance as racial. The implicit racial undertones of this gendered language were crucial in undermining black officers' claims to military merit, especially their enjoyment of officer rank. Thus white insurgents deployed gendered language to reproduce white privilege within the very structures of military rank, which many optimistically assumed to be a crucial stepping stone to postwar political power.

The discursive universality of insurgent appeals to manhood tended to obscure the uneven ways white insurgent leaders implemented them on their black counterparts. Because this language erased race, black men struggled to challenge its very real racial implications using the same discourse. The abolition of explicit racial language prevented black men from naming racial discrimination within these discursive parameters and therefore inhibited their ability to dismantle the racial double standard. Moreover, even though racial silence was a key pillar of revolutionary masculinity, access to racial language was also racialized. Black men could not name anti-black racism without being labeled as racist and unpatriotic. Yet, white men periodically invoked race to invalidate the perspectives of their black counterparts, appeals that often successfully derailed black men's efforts to combat racial discrimination.

As insurgents became veterans after the war, the racial hierarchy of military rank became the basic premise of martial manhood. Indeed, many white officers envisioned themselves as the rightful bearers of postwar political power precisely because of their privileged position within the military hierarchy. The prevailing idea of Cuba's New Man, like that of mambí, was implicitly white. Yet, under US rule, even the most prestigious white veterans initially struggled to translate their military rank into parallel postwar political authority. At the center of this struggle was a fundamental disagreement about the definition of whiteness. White veterans claimed martial manhood on the unspoken premise of their whiteness. Although New Men envisioned their own racial privilege within Cuban society as sufficient to prove their political fitness, many US military officials did not recognize these men as white. Rather, Cuba's self-proclaimed New Men were of a supposedly inferior Latin racial stock that rendered them unfit for political power. Moreover, US officials suspected that white veterans' alleged political and racial radicalism would beget black political power and antagonism against US rule in Cuba. US officials were much more inclined to recognize the whiteness of white men who were politically and socially conservative and who favored close ties with the United States. Consequently, revolutionary masculinity failed to emerge as post-colonial hegemonic masculinity, the set of masculine norms and practices most highly valued by the dominant social class, which could be deployed to produce or reinforce the position of elites.[1]

When US officials finally conceded that they could not exclude all Cuban separatists and veterans from political power, racial exclusion became the key condition on which they could assume local office. New Men perpetuated the racial exclusivity of political power in nearly every aspect of local government. However, they subtly maintained their public commitment to the racially inclusive implications of revolutionary masculinity through racially selective employment policies. They included a small number of their black compatriots in the lowest ranks of public employment, namely in the poorly remunerated law enforcement bodies. White political elites simultaneously celebrated black veterans' military service and justified their political exclusion through appeals to the need for productive labor, formal credentials, and orderliness—implicitly racial qualities that black men supposedly lacked.

Despite the severe limitations of black men's access to public authority, US military authorities cited the employment of black veterans as evidence of New Men's political and racial radicalism. After a series of violent confrontations between municipal police and white US soldiers and employees, New Men realized that maintaining even limited commitments to their cross-racial networks of military patronage and refusing to cooperate with US military authorities threatened their political futures. Some civil authorities attempted to redeem themselves by presenting themselves as agents of order and distancing themselves from revolutionary masculinity's racial inclusivity. Although these changes ameliorated tensions with US military officials, they proved insufficient to salvage these New Men's political careers. US officials swiftly implemented changes in local politics, appointing men who they could trust to obey their authority.

Ultimately, the protracted transition from war to peace demonstrated that military service was an inadequate argument to guarantee black veterans political influence on par with their military achievements. It even proved insufficient to earn working-class black veterans the social and physical space to claim just working conditions. Among white men, the capacity to preserve order increasingly became the ultimate test of a man's political fitness. Only men who supported close ties with the United States and those who demonstrably favored the preservation of order and the priorities of the capitalists of the sugar industry could be entrusted with political power.

With the establishment of a Cuban civil government under US military rule and the announcement of local elections in 1900, white veterans were torn between two competing constituencies to secure political power in the upcoming elections: their cross-racial networks of military patronage and the US officials who had the power to make or break their political futures. Securing electoral victory hinged on support from men of the revolution, and later of the black and working-class masses. These men demanded an outspoken commitment to revolutionary masculinity, including racial inclusion and absolute independence. However, white veterans had learned that securing US approval was crucial for their political futures, a requirement at odds with their public commitment to revolutionary virtues. After all, securing US support was fundamentally about using political authority to preserve order, a euphemism for the repression of black men.

In this context, two interrelated racialized discourses on manhood emerged as powerful challenges to the cross-racial dimensions of revolutionary masculinity: criminality and order. In central Cuba, Spanish military officials' racialization of banditry during the previous wars of independence and the periodic hysteria of white sugar planters about the ebbs and flows of a highly mobile post-emancipation labor force came together as a foundation for early twentieth- century discourses of racialized criminality. Opponents of separatist rule drew on longstanding tropes of black hypermasculinity rooted in hemispheric experiences of colonialism and slavery to criminalize black veterans for claiming public authority and enfranchisement. The result was the consolidation of a new criminal type: the black veteran. Even as allegations of black criminality were often demonstrably false, they exerted a powerful influence over the racial parameters of the postwar Cuban public sphere. The criminalization of black veterans compelled New Men to assume the role of agents of order by suppressing perceived or potential black criminals. Only New Men who could effectively preserve (racial) order could lay claim to the degree of masculine authority necessary for political power.

White veterans balanced their political obligations to their competing constituencies by publically supporting an expansive vision of citizenship, while curtailing black men's practical ability to enjoy the rights of citizenship. As they publically demanded universal manhood suffrage, many white veterans internalized the notion that black men constituted the single biggest impediment to Cuban self-government. This threat *warranted*, indeed *demanded*, state intervention. Implicitly racialized discourses of criminality offered white political elites the perfect foil to reconcile their repression of black men with their public appeals to revolutionary masculinity. This critical shift helped crystallize the criminalization of black men among Santa Clara's—and indeed Cuba's—political elite, even before the nation's criminologists and intellectuals were able to rationalize these ideas with their faulty racial "science."[2] The consequences of criminalization were measured in the blood of black men, on whose corpses white men stepped to secure their conditional political power.

Over the course of three and a half years of US military rule, New Men had transformed themselves from reluctant defenders of a limited cross-racial manhood to the local executors of racial violence in the name of US neocolonialism. The late 1899 murder of black general Dionisio Gil and the 1902 slaying of black captain Claudio Sarría form the symbolic bookends of Cuban men's violent renegotiation of racial hierarchy during the politically tumultuous period of US military occupation. In 1895 both these men figured strongly in a broader pattern of emerging black leadership in the Cuban army's Fourth Corps. By the end of the war, a handful of their white compatriots violently rejected their presumption that this military leadership would somehow translate into a semblance of authority following the cessation of hostilities. The fact that both men met their deaths at the hands of white veterans who exercised their functions as law enforcement officials highlights the willingness of these so-called patriots to defend their own privileged access to public authority even by means of violence.

Yet, there is a key difference distinguishing these two murders. Although New Men and local US officials attacked the black general's military record and accused him of vagrancy, these criminalizing efforts were not systematic enough to justify the murder. Popular outcry following the assassination of Gil resulted in follow-up investigations and eventually a conviction of the murderer. In contrast, no such outcry seems to have followed the murder of Sarría, whose murderers walked away with impunity.[3] This is no coincidence. Rather, it underscores how criminality provided a powerful gendered justification to legitimize this racial violence as a warranted state response to black men's transgression of their subordinate status. By the end of US military rule in 1902, a visibly and rhetorically whitened Cuban political manhood hinged upon the continued subordination of black men. The internalization of this new masculine ideal by white political elites consolidated state violence as a quintessential feature of maintaining the supposed color-blindness of Cuban nationality, simultaneously marking the hypocrisy and hollowness of the ideal as well as its faltering legitimacy among the popular classes. The gendered implications of criminalizing discourses allowed white veterans to justify a rising tide of state and vigilante violence against their black former compatriots-in-arms.

These two examples are instructive for at least two reasons. First, they remind us that the prevailing narrative of Cuba as a racial democracy could not be further from the realities lived by people of African descent, as scholars have previously suggested.[4] Yet, this book's analysis of the broader developments leading to the murders of Gil and Sarría, and the persecution and violence afflicting so many other black men, offers a new perspective by exposing the ways a racially universalizing concept of manhood helped white men reproduce and solidify racial hierarchy. The gendered dynamics of criminalization provided the foundation for future racial violence.

In this sense, gender is key to understanding how racial democracy could coexist with racial discrimination.[5] In the case of central Cuba, masculinity offered a metalanguage for both challenging and reproducing racial hierarchy in a context in which racial silence became an implicit requirement of patriotism. In particular, revolutionary masculinity—by way of racially charged concepts like mambí, majá, New Man, criminal, and radical—enabled diverse groups of insurgent men to police hierarchy without ever having to mention race explicitly. Although black veterans attempted to appropriate concepts of masculinity to claim political and social authority, the profound limitation of their success in many cases confirms the truth in Patricia Hill Collins's insight that unequal access to power produces unequal access to the production of truth.[6] The very idea of being a Cuban man was subsumed in a racially and class-specific set of values associated most closely with white middle-class patriots, even as it was framed as a universalist and theoretically meritocratic concept. Honor, as a terrain on which race and gender intersected—whether harnessed in service of patriarchal or political objectives—allowed for the simultaneous coexistence, as Peter Wade might call it, of racial brotherhood and racial inequality in the same moment, through the same actions, and in the same context.[7]

Second, the murders of Gil and Sarría underscore both the limits and the totalizing power of dominant notions of masculinity in validating racism. Drawing on the writings of Italian intellectual Antonio Gramsci, scholars have adapted the concept of hegemony to explain the seemingly inexplicable popular acceptance of—even consent for—their own subordination. Classic definitions of hegemony emphasize the power of non-violent mechanisms of control like ideology and culture as ways to constitute and legitimize an existing social or political order.[8] Those non-violent, often implicit forms of control are usually reinforced by violence or the threat of violence by the state, including measures such as policing, arrest, and imprisonment—the other major mechanisms of preserving the status quo.

When applied to masculinity, this insight implies that the need to resort to violence connotes the incomplete hegemony of dominant ideas about being a man. R. W. Connell notes that the hegemony of a particular set of masculine ideals, though not incompatible with violence, usually is reproduced through ingrained cultural practices. The deployment of violence to enforce the dominant position of a particular set of masculine ideals sometimes reveals the failures of contestations of its hegemony.[9]

On the one hand, forms of protest precipitating the murders of Gil and Sarría elucidate the precariousness of racially exclusive visions of masculinity.

Black veterans continually appropriated revolutionary masculinity to validate their claims to military rank, and later to employment, political participation, and local authority. The racial consciousness of a small number of black veterans, such as Gil and Sarría, but also of others, like Pedro P. Mutos y Juan Sardiñas y Villa, explicitly challenged the gendered bases of racial silence. The increasing state violence against black men following the war, thus, can be interpreted as a response to dissent against the emerging neocolonial masculine idea, which marginalized military service as an equalizing foundation of masculinity and emphasized cooperation with US authorities.

On the other hand, we may have underestimated the role hegemonic masculinities play in justifying and legitimizing the state use of force in ways that effectively erase the violence inherent in the process. Remembering the essentially contested nature of hegemony suggests that it is defined not so much by consent as by constant struggle and negotiation.[10] In this sense, state violence to suppress crime constitutes not the failure of hegemony, but rather its power in creating discourses that validate and legitimize violence against a certain person or group as just and productive. As I have suggested elsewhere, the significance of criminalization for consolidating an existing social and political order is twofold.[11] First, the state retains the power to codify in law the dominant definitions of criminality. In this way, dominant, state-sponsored ideas about crime contribute toward the construction of hegemony by structuring the limits of what is possible, defining which behaviors are unacceptable, and clearly demarcating how good citizens *should* behave.[12] But law, as the codification of dominant ideas of order and criminality, draws its validity from "science," as intellectuals create theories to explain who commits crimes and why, and also from popular perception, which is shaped by media. Indeed, in December 1899 US military government ordered sweeping reforms of the University of Havana, including the formation of the Department of Anthropology and Anthropometric Exercises, which was closely tied to the production of racial and criminological "science." The intellectuals in those incipient academic disciplines later produced the social scientific logics guiding law enforcement and incarceration, which were key to projecting the emergent Cuban state as modern, civilized, orderly, and most importantly, white.[13] Moreover, sensationalized media reports of black criminality, whether the alleged black bandits setting cane fields ablaze during the occupation or the murderous negro brujo, inspired white anxiety during the early republic. These images in turn helped consolidate popular internalization of these racialized criminal tropes as these discourses of power filtered through Cuban society.[14]

The other important aspect of criminalization is that it provides an air of legitimacy to state violence against marginal social groups demanding greater degrees of access to the rights and privileges of citizenship and against the supposed internal enemies threatening the nation. In the case of racial protest, criminalization depoliticizes the claim to inclusion and renders the black male protester illegitimate—not a real man—which in turn facilitates his subordination to state interests. Ordinary citizens may view policing, punishment, incarceration, and even the impunity of vigilante violence as legitimate, so long as they are convinced that this form of state violence is in service of order, progress, modernity, or national security. In these instances, police (as agents of the state) and even witnesses cease to see this use of force as violence. The increasing crystallization of ideas criminalizing black veterans' displays of authority may help explain the drastically different public reactions to the murders of Gil and Sarría.

The very same white veterans who orchestrated the criminalization of black men in Santa Clara also dominated Cuba's national political scene for decades to come. Thus, it is no coincidence that the rising tide of anti-black violence in US-occupied Santa Clara also shaped Cuba's early republican years, particularly in historical moments defined by the conditionality of New Men's political power. In 1906 white Rural Guardsmen assassinated black veteran general Quintín Bandera during the so-called August Revolution, a protest against the fraudulent reelection of Tomás Estrada Palma. In 1912 thousands of black men met their deaths at the hands of white Rural Guardsmen and vigilantes in a massacre of Independent Party of Color activists, a catastrophe that in part justified the third US military intervention that year. These were far from anomalies; they marked particular, though not altogether unprecedented, episodes of state-sponsored anti-black violence in service of racial silence, and most importantly, they benefited the political aspirations of a small number of white men.

The violent silencing did not eliminate racially conscious mobilization. However, some black veterans and activists responded to the violence by developing alternative forms of dissent, often framed in non-racial terms in order to elude criminalization and repression. The continuing salience of military service as a marker of masculine honor among black and working-class veterans offers a glimpse into these racially silent forms of protest. By recognizing the racial protest embedded in these gendered claims, an entirely new story of social inequality emerges. This narrative is defined by muffled cries for recognition and inclusion, by marginalized assertions of honor, and by dissenting visions of manhood that creatively dodged violent suppression through racelessness. Exposing these critical intersections of gendered hierarchy and racial inequality not only unveils a new set of evidence about the actions of black men (and women). It also challenges historians to look beyond the most overt, the most violent, the most infamous episodes of racism. The mechanisms enabling these overt forms of violence in neocolonial Cuba originated in the manipulation and dismantling of revolutionary masculinity. The evolving gendered codes of race undercut black claims to honor and buttressed the emergence of a neocolonial masculinity that cast political manhood as contingent on the suppression of black men.

Notes

INTRODUCTION

1. Martí, "My Race," 313; Guerra, *Myth of José Martí*, 25–26; Ferrer, *Insurgent Cuba*, 3.
2. Appelbaum, MacPherson, and Alejandra, "Introduction: Racial Nations," 2; Lasso, *Myths of Harmony*.
3. Iglesias Utset, *Las metáforas del cambio*, 159–60; 221–25; Guerra, *Myth of José Martí*, 96–99; Helg, *Our Rightful Share*; De la Fuente, *A Nation for All*; Lucero, "Civilization before Citizenship."
4. De la Fuente, *A Nation for All*, 6.
5. Helg, *Our Rightful Share*, 98; Ferrer, *Insurgent Cuba*, 7–10; De la Fuente, *A Nation for All*, 33. For later periods, see Fernández, *Revolutionizing Romance*, 4–8; Sawyer, *Racial Politics in Post-Revolutionary Cuba*, xviii.
6. In his theory of language, Roland Barthes posited that metalanguage offered a vocabulary by which to describe a natural language. Barthes, *Mythologies*.
7. Higginbotham, "Metalanguage of Race."
8. Stoner, *Cuban Woman's Movement*, 10.
9. Sippial, *Prostitution*, 26–27.
10. Ocasio, *Afro-Cuban Costumbrismo*, 60–86; 120–158; Lane, *Blackface Cuba*; Kutzinski, *Sugar's Secrets*.
11. Lane, *Blackface Cuba*, 76; Thomas, *Cuban Zarzuela*, 84–86.
12. Ferrer, *Insurgent Cuba*, 37–42.
13. Hill Collins, *Black Feminist Thought*; Crenshaw, "Mapping the Margins"; Anzaldúa and Moraga, *Bridge Called My Back*; Hull, Scott, and Smith, *Some of Us are Brave*.
14. Martínez-Alier, *Marriage, Class and Colour*.
15. Dudink and Hagemann, "Masculinity in Politics and War," 3–4.
16. On the concept of men as gendered subjects, see Connell, *Masculinities*, 44, 54, 75; Bederman, *Manliness and Civilization*; Gilmore, *Gender and Jim Crow*; Brown, *Good Wives, Nasty Wenches*.
17. For conceptions of honor in Latin America, see Caulfield, *In Defense of Honor*, 3–4; Johnson and Lipsett-Rivera, *Faces of Honor*, 3–6; Martínez-Alier, *Marriage, Class and Colour*; Stern, *Secret History of Gender*, 302; Twinam, *Public Lives, Private Secrets*, 30; Twinam, *Purchasing Whiteness*; Wiegman, *American Anatomies*, 64.

18. De la Fuente, *A Nation for All*; Guerra, *Myth of José Martí*; Ferrer, *Insurgent Cuba*; Helg, *Our Rightful Share*.
19. On the rise of slavery in Cuba, see Knight, *Slave Society in Cuba*, 22; Reid Vázquez, *Year of the Lash*. For more on slavery in Cuba during British abolitionism, see Corwin, *Abolition of Slavery in Cuba*; Schmidt-Nowara, *Empire and Antislavery*; Murray, *Odious Commerce*; Marquese, Parron, and Berbel, *Slavery and Politics*; Graden, *Disease, Resistance, and Lies*.
20. Ferrer, *Freedom's Mirror*; Naranjo Orovio et al., *Rumor de Haití*; Fischer, *Modernity Disavowed*.
21. Ferrer, *Insurgent Cuba*.
22. Scott, *Slave Emancipation in Cuba*; Sartorius, *Ever-Faithful*, 61–62; Ferrer, *Insurgent Cuba*, 173–87.
23. Ferrer, *Insurgent Cuba*.
24. De la Fuente, *A Nation for All*, 6–7.
25. Pérez, *On Becoming Cuban*, 91–95; Weston, *Racism in U. S. Imperialism*, 1–3, 139–41; Appelbaum et. al., "Introduction," 4–5; Pike, *United States and Latin America*, 168–71.
26. Pappademos, *Black Political Activism*, 17–62.
27. United States War Department, Cuban Census Office, *Census of Cuba*, 153, 164, 138–39, 545.
28. Helg, *Our Rightful Share*, 194–226; Pappademos, *Black Political Activism*, 78–79.
29. Stoner, *From the House to the Streets*; Vinat de la Mata, *Las cubanas*; Prados-Torreira, *Mambisas*; Pérez, *Imitations of Modernity*.
30. Cowling, *Conceiving Freedom*; Sippial, *Prostitution*; Morrison, *Cuba's Racial Crucible*. Also see Juncker, *Espiritismo and Santería*. For one of the only discussions of black women's political activism, see Pappademos, *Black Political Activism*, 189–96. For earlier periods, see Finch, *Rethinking Slave Rebellion*.
31. For a similar critique of scholarship on the West, see Nagel, "Masculinity and Nationalism," 242–3.
32. Sierra Madero, *La sexualidad*; Sierra Madero, "Cuerpos En Venta"; Hamilton, *Sexual Revolutions*. For theoretical reflections, see González Pagés, *Macho, Varón, Masculino*. For a discussion of scholarly work on masculinity in Cuba, see Da Silva and Guerra, "Study of Masculinities in Cuba"; Formental Hernández, Hernández Pita, and Fernández de Juan, "Masculinities in Cuba." For later periods, see Allen, *¿Venceremos!*
33. Ferrer, *Insurgent Cuba*, 174–75; "Rustic Men, Civilized Nation," 663–86.
34. Bronfman, *Measures of Equality*, 37–65; Helg, "Black Men"; Colón Pichardo, *Masculinidad*.
35. Nagel, "Masculinity and Nationalism."
36. Scott, "Gender: A Useful Category."
37. Anderson, *Imagined Communities*. For studies of people of African descent with

regard to the Cuban nation, see De la Fuente, *A Nation for All*, 99–171; Scott, *Degrees of Freedom*, 178–188; Pappademos, *Black Political Activism*, 41–46; Guerra, *Myth of José Martí*, 108–151; Whitney and Chailloux Laffita, *Subjects or Citizens*; Queeley, *Rescuing Our Roots*; Howard, *Black Labor, White Sugar*.

38. Ferrer, *Insurgent Cuba*.
39. Guerra, *Myth of José Martí*, 15–18.
40. After the revolution launched an aggressive yet contradictory campaign against racial discrimination in 1959, scholars on both sides of the Straights of Florida have produced a politically polarized historiography on race in Cuba. For a critique of the campaign, see Benson, *Antiracism in Cuba*. For some exceptions to the silence, see Fernández Robaina, *El negro en Cuba*; Corvalán, *Raza: Documental* (2008); Morales Domínguez, *Race in Cuba*; Roberto Zurbano, "For Blacks in Cuba, the Revolution Hasn't Begun," *New York Times*, March 23, 2013. The resurgence of theories dating to the 1940s about Latin America's supposedly benign race relations enabled US revisionist historians to condemn the pro-imperialist tenor of some 1960s and 1970s scholarship on Cuba, express political solidarity with the Revolution, or subtly critique US race relations. For pro-imperialist scholarship, see Hitchman, *Leonard Wood*; Healy, *United States in Cuba*. For critiques, see Ring, *Race Discrimination*; Duke, "Idea of Race." Despite the nuance of the best recent work on race in Cuba, echoes of the raceless nationalist argument continue to appear in some US and Cuban scholarly works. See Rodríguez, *La conspiración*; Horne, *Race to Revolution*; Fountain, *José Martí*. For an overview of the persisting scholarly engagement with the Tannenbaum thesis, see de la Fuente, "From Slaves to Citizens?"
41. For an overview of the objectives and methods of microhistory as well as some critiques of it, see Putnam, "Microhistory," 615; Struck, Ferris, and Revel, "Transnational History," 578–79; Swett, "Everyday Life."
42. United States War Department, *Census of Cuba*, 82.
43. United States War Department, *Census of Cuba*, 179, 192, 702.
44. Diamond News Co., *Standard Guide to Cuba*, 163.
45. Tone, *Genocide in Cuba*, 88–96.
46. Tone, *Genocide in Cuba*, 81–83, 119–20.
47. Tone, *Genocide in Cuba*, 194–95, 198–99.
48. Zeuske, "Los negros hicimos la independencia," 193. Other examples include fifth president and dictator Santa Clara-native Gerardo Machado, Santo Domingo-native Carlos Mendieta, and Remedios-native Federico Laredo Brú.
49. For a critique of scholarly (mis)use of racial terms for Latin America, see Bourdieu and Wacquant, "Imperialist Reason"; on the valorization of whitening in the early republican period, see Wade, *Race and Ethnicity in Latin America*, 30–35; On the "mulatto escape hatch," see Degler, *Neither Black Nor White*.
50. For an overview of the ways white normativity has informed discourses of race in Latin America, see Miller, *Cosmic Race*. Also see Bonnett, "Whiteness."

CHAPTER ONE

1. See Gilmore, *Manhood in the Making*.
2. Martínez-Alier, *Marriage, Class and Colour*; Lavrin, *Colonial Latin America*; Stern, *Secret History*; Chambers, *Subjects to Citizens*; Johnson and Lipsett-Rivera, *Faces of Honor*.
3. Strasser and Tinsman, "Masculinity," 85; Anderson, *Imagined Communities*, 50; Nagel, "Masculinity and Nationalism," 248.
4. For other studies of colonial masculinity, see Sinha, *Colonial Masculinity*; Brown, *Good Wives, Nasty Wenches*, 107–36.
5. Vicente Tejera, "Conferencia dada a los obreros cubanos emigrados durante la última Guerra de independencia, en la 'Sociedad de Trabajadora' de Key West," December 12, 1897, in *Cuba Contemporánea* 28, no. 3 (1922): 176.
6. Martínez-Alier, *Marriage, Class and Colour*; Martínez-López, *Genealogical Fictions*; Twinam, *Public Lives, Private Secrets*; Twinam, *Purchasing Whiteness*, 127–138; Burkholder, "Honor and Honors," in Johnson and Lipsett-Rivera, *Faces of Honor*, 34–37.
7. Martínez-Alier, *Marriage, Class and Colour*.
8. Sartorius, *Ever-Faithful*, 61–62.
9. Opartný, *Historical Pre-Conditions*.
10. García Martínez, "Brigada de Cienfuegos," 170. SOA is an acronym for "Sin otro apellido," (without another last name) commonly used to identify the formerly enslaved people in Cuba. See Zeuske, "Names of Slavery." 51–80.
11. García Martínez, "La Brigada de Cienfuegos," 183; Tone, *Genocide in Cuba*, 95.
12. García Martínez, "La Brigada de Cienfuegos," 174; Zeuske, "'Los negros hicimos la independencia.'"
13. United States War Department, *Census of Cuba*, 97, 713; Instituto de Geográfico y Estadístico, *Censo de población de España*, 771.
14. Atkins, *Sixty Years in Cuba*, 179.
15. Barnet, *Biografía*, 188.
16. Carlos Betancourt to Maximo Gómez, November 17, 1899, Legajo 35, Expediente 4434 new (4997 old), Archivo Nacional de Cuba, Fondo Personal Máximo Gómez (hereafter, ANC/FPMG).
17. "Testimony of Paulino Castro Rodríguez," February 24, 1904, Case 293, Box 142, Part 3, Folder 1, folio 30, United States Archives II, College Park, MD, Spanish Treaty Claims Commision Records, Record Group 76, Entry 352 (hereafter, USNAII/STCC/RG 76/E 352).
18. Majors and Billson, *Cool Pose*, 17; Vinson, *Bearing Arms*, 224–225; Beattie, *Tribute of Blood*, 274; Scott, *Slave Emancipation*.
19. Ferrer, *Insurgent Cuba*, 70–89.
20. General Luque to Civil Governor of Santa Clara, "Telegram," Febraury 24, 1895, Fondo Ultramar, Archivo Histórico Nacional de España, Madrid (hereafter, AHNE/FU). Thank you to Orlando García Martínez for sharing this document.

21. Polavieja y del Castillo, *Relación documentada*, 97.
22. Helg, *Our Rightful Share*, 82.
23. "Newspaper Clipping," [n.d.], Volume II.57, folio 30, Massachusetts Historical Society, Edwin F. Atkins Papers (hereafter, MHS/EFAP).
24. Arsenio Martínez Campos, "Discurso," March 9, 1895, *El Correo* in Box 88, Exhibit 23, USNA/SCC/RG 76/E 352.
25. Halstead, *Story of Cuba*, 95.
26. *Diario de la Marina*, April 18, 1895, quoted in Helg, *Our Rightful Share*, 80.
27. Halstead, *Story of Cuba*, 104.
28. Naranjo Orovio et al., *Rumor de Haití*, 130–40.
29. "Testimony of Antonio Betancourt Díaz," March 25, 1904, Case 293, Box 142, Part 4, Folder 3, folio 31, USNAII/STCC/RG 76/E 352.
30. García Martínez, "La Brigada de Cienfuegos," 172–173; José Braulio Alemán to Máximo Gómez, April 20, 1896, Box 6, File 867, ANC/FPMG.
31. D. Agustín Luque, "Bando," July 17, 1895, *Diario Nuevo*, Dispatches of the US Consulate in Cienfuegos, Microfilm Reel #5, Cienfuegos, Walter Royal Davis Library, University of North Carolina, US Consul in Cuba (hereafter, WRD/UNC/USCC).
32. "Testimony of Enrique Ubieta," May 24, 1904, Case 293, Box 144, Part 7, Folder 2, USNAII/STCC/RG 76/E 352.
33. Fernando Gómez, *La insurrección*, 17–18.
34. "Diario de Operaciones de José B. Alemán," June 18, 1897, Box 104, File 171, Archivo Nacional de Cuba Fondo Donativos y Remisiones (hereafter, ANC/FDR); "Testimony of Francisco Esquerro Solano," June 3, 1904, Case 293, Box 144, Part 7, Folder 2, USNAII/STCC/RG 76/E 352; "Testimony of Constantino March y Ferra," May 28, 1904, Case 293, Box 144, Part 7, Folder 3, USNAII/STCC/RG 76/E 352.
35. Loynaz del Castillo, *Memoirias de la guerra*, 135. Also see Balboa, "*Bandidos*, Patriots or Delinquents?"
36. Fischer, *Poverty of Rights*, 103; Frazer, *Bandit Nation*, 8; Hobsbawm, *Primitive Rebels*; Slatta, *Latin American Banditry*.
37. Pérez, *Lords of the Mountain*; Schwartz, *Lawless Liberators*; de Paz, Fernández and López, *El bandolerismo en Cuba*; Balboa Navarro, *La protesta rural*.
38. Interview of General Sabás Marín, quoted in Halstead, *Story of Cuba*, 91–92.
39. Interview of General Sabás Marín, quoted in Halstead, *Story of Cuba*, 91–92; Sinha, *Colonial Masculinity*.
40. Bronfman, *Measures of Equality*, 30–33.
41. Flint, *Marching with Gómez*, 98.
42. Flint, *Marching with Gómez*, 93.
43. Helg, "Black Men"; Palmié, *Wizards and Scientists*.
44. Sartorius, *Ever-Faithful*, 62–63.
45. Flint, *Marching with Gómez*, 80; Juan Casanova, Vice United States Consul at Cienfuegos to Department of State, United States, "Report on the Insurrection," October 12, 1896, Dispatches of the US Consulate in Cienfuegos, Microfilm Reel

#5, WRD/UNC/USCC; Edwin F. Atkins, "Petition before the Spanish Treaty Claims Commission," December 1905, Box II.4, folio 121, MHS/EFAP.
46. "Testimony of Bibián Fernández," October 28, 1907, Case 196, Box 86, Part 4, folio 6, USNAII/STCC/RG 76/E 352; "Testimony of Enrique García," November 5, 1907, Case 196, Box 87, Part 5, folio 7, USNAII/STCC/RG 76/E 352.
47. Love, *Race Over Empire*, 7, 20–25; Pérez, *Cuba between Empires*, 128–132.
48. "Newspaper Clipping," [n.d.], Volume II.57, folio 30, MHS/EFAP.
49. "A Woman's Reply to 'American,'" newspaper clipping, November 6, 1896, Volume II.57, folio 59, MHS/EFAP.
50. "A Woman's Reply to 'American,'" newspaper clipping, November 6, 1896, Volume II.57, folio 59, MHS/EFAP; "Newspaper Clipping," [n.d.], Volume II.57, folio 30, MHS/EFAP.
51. Collazo, *Cuba independiente*, 86. A remarkably similar passage appears in Collazo's subsequent work: Collazo, *Cuba heróica*, 106–07.
52. Flint, *Marching with Gómez*, 226–27.
53. Boza, *Mi diario*, 34–35.
54. José Rogelio Castillo to Villareños, July 1895, in Castillo y Zúñiga, *Autobiografía del General*, 288.
55. "Comunicación dirigida a Salvador Cisneros, Pres del Consejo de Gobierno, firmada por JB Alemán, referida a envío y proclama dirigida a los villareños," July 17, 1896, Legajo 17, Exp. 2475, Archivo Nacional de Cuba, Fondo Revolución del '95 (hereafter, ANC/R95).
56. "Comunicación dirigida a Salvador Cisneros, Pres del Consejo de Gobierno, firmada por JB Alemán, referida a envío y proclama dirigida a los villareños," July 17, 1896, Legajo 17, Exp. 2475, ANC/R95.
57. Ferrara, *Memorias*, 97.
58. Pérez, *Structure of Cuban History*, 78–79; 87.
59. Moreno Fraginals and Moreno Masó, *Guerra*, 132.
60. Navarro García, *Las guerras*, 137.
61. Juan J. Casanova (US Consul at Cienfuegos) to Edwin F. Uhl, November 11, 1895, Dispatches of the US Consulate in Cienfuegos, Microfilm Reel #5, document 48, WRD/UNC/USCC; Navarro García, *Las guerras*, 144. Estimates as high as twelve thousand insurgents in Santa Clara likely include the men of the Invasion Force.
62. "Testimony of José Miguel Gómez," April 27, 1904, Case 293, Box 144, Part 7, Folder 1, USNAII/STCC/RG 76/E 352.
63. "Testimony of José Miguel Gómez," April 27, 1904, Case 293, Box 144, Part 7, Folder 1, USNAII/STCC/RG 76/E 352.
64. "Testimony of Marcos García Castro," June 11, 1904, Case 293, Box 145, Part 9, Folder 2, USNAII/STCC/RG 76/E 352; "Testimony of Enrique Ubieta," May 24, 1904, Case 293, Box 144, Part 7, Folder 2, USNAII/STCC/RG 76/E 352; Boza, *Mi diario*, 108–10.

65. "Testimony of José Miguel Gómez," April 27, 1904, Case 293, Box 144, Part 7, Folder 1, USNAII/STCC/RG 76/E 352.
66. "Testimony of Jorge Rodríguez," January 24, 1904, Case 293, Box 141, Part 3, Folder 1, USNAII/STCC/RG 76/E 352; García Martínez, "La Brigada de Cienfuegos," 173.
67. "Testimony of Eduardo Guzmán," April 13, 1904, Case 293, Box 143, Part 5, Folder 3, USNAII/STCC/RG 76/E 352; "Testimony of Higinio Esquerra," April 18, 1904, Case 293, Box 143, Part 5, Folder 3, USNAII/STCC/RG 76/E 352.
68. "Testimony of Julián Valdés Sierra," December 7, 1904, Case 293, Box 145, Part 8, Folder 3, USNAII/STCC/RG 76/E 352.
69. Ferrara, *Memorias*, 75.
70. "Testimony of Julián Valdés Sierra," December 7, 1904, Case 293, Box 145, Part 8, Folder 3, USNAII/STCC/RG 76/E 352.
71. Tone, *War and Genocide in Cuba*, 127.
72. "Testimony of Julián Valdés Sierra," December 7, 1904, Case 293, Box 145, Part 8, Folder 3, USNA/STCC/RG 76/E 352.
73. Testimony of Julián Valdés Sierra," December 7, 1904, Case 293, Box 145, Part 8, Folder 3, USNA/STCC/RG 76/E 352.
74. No Title," in *Las Villas*, April 10, 1897, Box 290, File 11, ANC/FDR.
75. Moreno Fraginals and Moreno Masó, *Guerra*, 132; No Title, in *Las Villas*, April 10, 1897, Box 290, File 11, ANC/FDR.
76. Enrique Villuendas to Máximo Gómez, January 3, 1897, Box 7, File 937, ANC/FPMG.
77. "Diario de Operaciones de José B. Alemán," May 12, 1897, Box 104, File 171, ANC/FDR.
78. "Testimony of Eduardo Guzmán," April 13, 1904, Case 293, Box 143, Part 4, Folder 3, USNAII/STCC/RG 76/E 352.
79. "Testimony of José Miguel Gómez," April 27, 1904, Case 293, Box 144, Part 7, Folder 1, USNAII/STCC/RG 76/E 352.
80. "Testimony of Arturo Aulet," April 29, 1904, Case 293, Box 143, Part 5, Folder 3, USNAII/STCC/RG 76/E 352.
81. "Un Astro," in Máximo Gómez to Francisco Carrillo, December 14, 1898, in Gómez, *Cartas a Francisco Carrillo*, 258.
82. "Testimony of Julián Valdés Sierra," December 7, 1904, Case 293, Box 145, Part 8, Folder 3, USNAII/STCC/RG 76/E 352.
83. José B. Alemán to Máximo Gómez, August 25, 1896, Box 6, File 903, ANC/FPMG.
84. Collazo, *Cuba heróica*, 10; Pérez, *To Die in Cuba*, 84.
85. José Rogelio Castillo to Cuartel General, November 20, 1896, in Castillo y Zúñiga, *Autobiografía*, 306.
86. José Rogelio Castillo to Cuartel General, November 20, 1896, in Castillo y Zúñiga, *Autobiografía*, 306.

87. Anonymous to Rita Suárez del Villar, [n.d.], Box 1, file 22, Archivo Provincial Histórico de Cienfuegos, Fondo Rita Suárez del Villar (hereafter AHPC/RSV).
88. Carlos Trujillo to Rita Suárez del Villar, December 21, 1898, Box 1, file 33, AHPC/RSV.
89. Alfredo Rego to Máximo Gómez, December 3, 1896, Box 6, File 850, ANC/FPMG.
90. "Testimony of José de J. Monteagudo," March 4, 1904, Case 293, Box 146, Part 9, Folder 1, USNAII/STCC/RG 76/E 352.
91. "Relación de Oficiales del Cuarto Cuerpo," [n.d.] 1896, Legajo 2, Archivo Provincial de Sancti Spíritus, Fondo Serafín Sánchez (hereafter, APSS/FSS).
92. García Martínez, "La Brigada de Cienfuegos," 178, 182–83; Zeuske, "'Los negros hicimos la independencia,'" in Martínez Heredia, Scott, and García Martínez, *Espacios*, 203.
93. "Relación de Oficiales del Cuarto Cuerpo," [n.d.] 1896, Legajo 2, APSS/FSS.
94. García Martínez, "La Brigada de Cienfuegos," 178.
95. Leopoldo Figueroa to Sr. Presidente del Club Federico de la Torre, January 23, 1898, Sancti Spíritus, Biblioteca Provincial de Santa Clara, Fondos Raros y Valiosos (hereafter BPSC/FRV).
96. Flint, *Marching with Gómez*, 226–27.
97. Carlos Trujillo to Rita Suárez del Villar, January, 27 1898, Box 1, file 33, AHPC/RSV.
98. Fischer, *A Poverty of Rights*, 8.
99. García Martínez, "La Brigada de Cienfuegos," in Martínez Heredia, Scott, and García Martínez, *Espacios*, 182–83.
100. For western militaries, see Adams, *Frontier Army*.
101. Ferrara, *Memorias*, 65.
102. Thomas Dawley, Jr., "Campaigning with Gómez," *American Magazine* 47 (November 1898–April 1899), 536. My emphasis.
103. Gómez, *La insurrección por dentro*, 94.
104. Diario del brigadier José González Planas, August 20, 1895, Museo Histórico Municipal de Remedios; Máximo Gómez to José González Planas, April 13, 1896, Museo Histórico Municipal de Remedios.
105. Scott, "Reclaiming Gregoria's Mule."
106. Rosell y Malpica, *Diario del Teniente*, vol. 2, 108.
107. Ferrara, *Memorias*, 65.
108. See Scott, *Degrees of Freedom*, 94–153.

CHAPTER TWO

1. For an overview of the consequences of reconcentration on the Cuban population, see García, "Urban Guajiros."
2. Tone, *War and Genocide*, 212.
3. Balch Lewis, "Report on Sanitary Condition at Cienfuegos," December 22, 1898, Box 1, File 12, Records of the United States Army Overseas, Record Group 395,

United States National Archives, Washington DC (hereafter, USNAI/RUSA/RG 395/E 1466); Wilson, *Annual Report*, 1899, 66.
4. For an analogous argument, see Brown, "Soldiers and Strawberries," 733.
5. Martínez-Alier, *Marriage, Class and Colour*, 66–70.
6. Tone, *War and Genocide*, 194.
7. "Una hazaña española," *Las Villas*, June 10, 1897, Box 290, File 5, ANC/FDR.
8. Coronel Victor Ramos al Cuartel General de la Brigada de Jiguaní, Carreras, March 3, 1896, Archivo Histórico Provincial de Santa Clara, Fondo Ejército Libertador, Legajo 2, Expediente 69.
9. J. W. Aguirre to Máximo Gómez, September 21, 1896, Box 6, File 920, ANC/FPMG.
10. No Title, in *Las Villas*, April 10, 1897, Box 290, File 11, ANC/FDR.
11. Flint, *Marching with Gómez*, 101–08.
12. Flint, *Marching with Gómez*, 76.
13. José B. Alemán to Máximo Gómez, September 21, 1896, Box 6, File 912, ANC/FPMG.
14. García, "Urban Guajiros," 224–26.
15. Francisco Carrillo to Máximo Gómez, June 23, 1897, Box 7, File 1020, ANC/FPMG; Valdés-Domínguez, *Diario de un soldado*, III, 89.
16. Sylvester Henry Scovel, "Sickened by Horrors, Consul Barker Resigned," *World*, March 14, 1898. Newspaper clipping available in Missouri History Museum, Sylvester Henry Scovel Papers, Box 2. See reproduction of this and other articles by Scovel in Andreu, "Sylvester H. Scovel," 173.
17. Miguel J. Monteavaro on behalf of Cándido Álvarez to Máximo Gómez, January 16, 1897, Box 7, File 943, ANC.FPMG; José J. Monteagudo to Máximo Gómez, January 17, 1897, Box 7, File 944, ANC/FPMG.
18. "Una hazaña española," *Las Villas*, June 10, 1897, Box 290, File 5, ANC/FDR.
19. "Diario de Operaciones de José B. Alemán," April 17, 1897, Box 104, File 171, ANC/FDR.
20. "Testimony of Sixto Roque del Sol," February 16, 1904, Case 293, Box 142, Part 4, Folder 2, USNA/STCC/RG 76/E 352.
21. Alejandro Rodríguez to Máximo Gómez, March 5, 1897, Box 7, File 964, ANC/FPMG.
22. Valdés-Domínguez, *Diario de un soldado*, III, 95.
23. Antonio Maceo to Valeriano Weyler, February 27, 1896, in de Quesada and Northrop, *War in Cuba*, 222–24.
24. "Testimony of José Pelaez Cardiff," June 1, 1904, Case 293, Box 144, Part 7, Folder 2, USNAII/STCC/RG 76/E 352; "Testimony of Francisco Esquerro Solano," June 3, 1904, Case 293, Box 144, Part 7, Folder 2, USNAII/STCC/RG 76/E 352; "Testimony of Enrique Ubieta," May 24, 1904, Case 293, Box 144, Part 7, Folder 2, USNAII/STCC/RG 76/E 352.
25. Tone, *War and Genocide*, 213–15.

26. "Relación de las familias reconcentradas en esta cabecera con derechos a la ración de la etapa," December 1897, Legajo 163, Expediente 1832, Archivo Provincial de Sancti Spíritus, Fondo Ayuntamiento (Hereafter, APSS/FA).
27. Emilio Terry, "Relación de los individuos reconcentrados a quienes se le ha repartido el donativo de $100 plata por orden del Sor. D. Emilio Terry," December 10, 1897, Legajo 67, Expediente 89, ANC/FDR.
28. Nazario Viamonte, "Requests aid for poor families in vicinity," February 10, 1899, Box 5, File 885, USNAI/RUSA/RG 395/E1466.
29. Stoner, *Cuban Woman's Movement*, 13–14.
30. Pérez, *Structure of Cuban History*, 90–93.
31. Collazo, 86. A remarkably similar passage appears in Collazo's subsequent work, *Cuba heróica*, 174.
32. Miró Argenter, *Crónicas de la Guerra*, 55.
33. Collazo, *Cuba independiente*, 86.
34. Antonio Maceo to Valeriano Weyler, February 27, 1896, in de Quesada and Northrop, *The War in Cuba*, 222–24.
35. Clete Hernández to Máximo Gómez, June 19, 1896, BPSC/FRV.
36. Joaquín Plana to Marta Abreu de Estévez, March 7, 1897, No. 234, v. 2, Biblioteca Nacional "José Martí, Havana, Fondo Marta Abreu (hereafter BNJM/FMA).
37. Boza, *Mi diario*, 109–10.
38. Francisco Carrillo to Máximo Gómez, June 23, 1897, Box 7, File 1020, ANC/FPMG; Valdés-Domínguez, *Diario de un soldado*, III, 89.
39. Carlos Trujillo to Rita Suárez del Villar, February 10, 1898, Box 1, file 33, AHPC/RSV.
40. "Diario de Operaciones de José B. Alemán," May 12, 1897, Box 104, File 171, ANC/FDR.
41. "Diario de Operaciones de José B. Alemán," May 12, 1897, Box 104, File 171, ANC/FDR.
42. "Diario de Operaciones de José B. Alemán," May 12, 1897, Box 104, File 171, ANC/FDR.
43. Piccato, *Tyranny of Opinion*, 242–43; Parker, "Gentlemanly Responsibility," 111–15; Stern: *Secret History*, 162.
44. "Diario de Operaciones de José B. Alemán," May 12, 1897, Box 104, File 171, ANC/FDR.
45. "Diario de Operaciones de José B. Alemán," May 12, 1897, Box 104, File 171, ANC/FDR.
46. "Diario de Operaciones de José B. Alemán," May 12, 1897, Box 104, File 171, ANC/FDR.
47. "Diario de Operaciones de José B. Alemán," May 12, 1897, Box 104, File 171, ANC/FDR.
48. "Diario de Operaciones de José B. Alemán," May 12, 1897, Box 104, File 171, ANC/FDR.

49. Tosh, *Manliness and Masculinities*, 43; Donaldson, "What is Hegemonic Masculinity?," 648; Tosh, "Hegemonic Masculinity," 46–47.
50. Sinha, *Colonial Masculinity*.
51. "Diario de Operaciones de José B. Alemán," May 12, 1897, Box 104, File 171, ANC/FDR.
52. Cabrales Nicolarde, *Epistolario de héroes*, 81.
53. Valdés-Domínguez, *Diario de un Soldado*, II, 207; Gómez, *Diario de campaña*, 421–22.
54. General Loynaz del Castillo en defensa de la gloriosa memoria del Mayor General José María Rodríguez," [n.d.], Box 524, File 1, p. 59, ANC/FDR.
55. General Loynaz del Castillo en defensa de la gloriosa memoria del Mayor General José María Rodríguez," [n.d.], Box 524, File 1, p. 59, ANC/FDR.
56. Martínez-Alier, *Marriage, Class and Colour*; Twinam, *Private Secrets*.
57. Martínez-Alier, *Marriage, Class and Colour*, 63–70; 115–19.
58. Flint, *Marching with Gómez*, 160–61.
59. Fernando Gómez, *La insurrección*, 118. Emphasis in original.
60. Morrison, *Cuba's Racial Crucible*, 170–74.
61. United States War Department, *Census of Cuba*, 123–35; Libro 2, Santíssima Iglesia Catedral de Cienfuegos/Libro de Matrimonios de Pardos y Morenos, (hereafter, SICC/LMPM).
62. Martínez-Alier, *Marriage, Class and Colour*; Morrison, *Cuba's Racial Crucible*, 106–30; Lucero, "Esclavos y comerciantes."
63. Zeuske, "Postemancipación y trabajo."
64. United States War Department, *Census of Cuba*, 119–25; 140.
65. Martinez-Alier, *Marriage, Class and Colour*, xiv.
66. Libros de Bautizos de Pardos y Morenos, Santíssima Iglesia Catedral de Cienfuegos/Libro de Bautizos de Pardos y Morenos, (hereafter, SICC/LBPM).
67. Stoler, *Carnal Knowledge*, 43.
68. "Historial del Reg de Caballeria 'Villa Clara,'" September 21, 1895, Legajo 2, Expediente 114, Archivo Histórico Provincial de Villa Clara, Fondo Ejército Libertador (hereafter, AHPVC/FEL).
69. Boza, *Mi diario*, 84.
70. Flint, *Marching with Gómez*, 47.
71. Rosell y Malpica, *Diario del Teniente*, II, 127.
72. Crenshaw, "Mapping the Margins."
73. For further examples of mambisas, see Prados-Torreira, *Mambisas*.
74. Pérez, *Structure of Cuban History*, 95–97.
75. "Una hazaña española," *Las Villas*, June 10, 1897, Box 290, File 5, ANC/FDR.
76. Eduardo M. Enríquez to Rita Suárez del Villar, May 8, 1898, Box 1, file 33, AHPC/RSV.
77. "Expediente que contiene documentos relativos al Club Patriótico 'Hermanas de Juan Bruno Zayas' Santa Clara, April 6, 1898-July 25, 1919, Legajo 7, Expediente

415, Archivo Histórico Provincial de Villa Clara, Fondo Manuel García Garófalo (hereafter, AHPVC/FMGG); Valdés-Domínguez, *Diario de un soldado*, III, 187.
78. Anonymous to Rita Suárez del Villar, [n.d.], Box 1, file 22, AHPC/RSV.
79. Rosell y Malpica, *Diario del Teniente*, II, 107.
80. Wiegman, *American Anatomies*, 9–13; Messerschmidt, *Crime as Structured Action*, 38.
81. Flint, *Marching with Gómez*, 88, nt 1; Prados-Torreira, *Mambisas*.
82. Collazo, *Cuba heróica*, 9.
83. Flint, *Marching with Gómez*, 75.
84. Flint, *Marching with Gómez*, 76–77.
85. Gómez, *La insurrección por dentro*, 83–84.
86. Rosell y Malpica, *Diario del Teniente*, II, 42.
87. Flint, *Marching with Gómez*, 85.
88. Tone, *War and Genocide*, 143.
89. Prados-Torreira, *Mambisas*, 135.
90. Boza, *Mi diario*, 114.
91. Prados-Torreria, *Mambisas*, 135–36.
92. Scott, *Degrees of Freedom*, 149.
93. Flint, *Marching with Gómez*, 88, nt 1.
94. Scott, 149.
95. Rosell y Malpica, *Diario del Teniente*, II, 130.
96. Piedra Martel, *Mis primeros treinta años*, 234.
97. Rosell y Malpica, *Diario del Teniente*, II, 130.
98. Quesada, *War in Cuba*, 226; on racialized gender tropes, see Weigman, *American Anatomies*, 45.
99. Crenshaw, "Mapping the Margins."
100. Ferrer, *Insurgent Cuba*, 175.
101. Flint, *Marching with Gómez*, 88, nt 1.
102. For analogous cases, see Olcott, *Revolutionary Women*, 6–7; Chambers, *From Subject to Citizen*, 161–88.
103. Hill Collins, *Black Feminist Thought*, 77.
104. Fraiman, *Unbecoming Women*, 73–74.
105. Flint, *Marching with Gómez*, 84.
106. Flint, *Marching with Gómez*, 84–85.

CHAPTER THREE

1. Tone, *War and Genocide*, 160.
2. Tone, *War and Genocide*, 186.
3. Tone, *War and Genocide*, 172.
4. Anonymous to Rita Suárez del Villar, [n.d.], Box 1, file 22, AHPC/RSV.
5. Pérez, *Cuba between Empires*, 128–32.

6. Alejandro Rodríguez to Máximo Gómez, October 11, 1896, Box 8, File 1149, ANC/FPMG.
7. Pérez, *Cuba between Empires*, 115–17.
8. José B. Alemán, "Diario de Operaciones" in Guerra Alemán, *Juro pero no prometo*, 244–45; Tone, *War and Genocide*, 187; Valdés-Domínguez, *Diario de un soldado*, III, 184; Valdés-Domínguez, 43–60; Gómez, *Diario de Campaña*, 412–13, 417.
9. Zeuske, "'Los negros hicimos la independencia,'" 203–04; Tone, *War and Genocide*, 96; Francisco Carrillo to Máximo Gómez, May 20, 1897, in Gómez, *Cartas a Francisco Carrillo*, 163; Alejandro Rodríguez to Máximo Gómez, June 5, 1897, Box 7, File 1018, ANC/FPMG.
10. Nagel, "Masculinity and Nationalism," 242–43.
11. Máximo Gómez to Francisco Carrillo, February 2, 1897, in Gómez, *Cartas a Francisco Carrillo*, 148.
12. Collazo, *Cuba heróica*, 9; Consuegra y Gúzman, *Mambiserías*, 112–13.
13. Máximo Gómez to Francisco Carrillo, May 9, 1898, in Gómez, *Cartas a Francisco Carrillo*, 226.
14. Máximo Gómez to José Rogelio Castillo, May 1, 1897, in Castillo y Zúñiga, *Autobiografía*, 323.
15. Máximo Gómez to Rita Suárez del Villar, January 28, 1898, Box 2, file 26, AHPC/RSV. Also see Era and Díaz Roque, *Cartas desconocidas*, 31.
16. Máximo Gómez to Rita Suárez del Villar, January 28, 1898, Box 2, file 26, AHPC/RSV. Also see Era and Díaz Roque, *Cartas desconocidas*, 31; Máximo Gómez to Francisco Carrillo, May 9, 1898, in Gómez, *Cartas a Francisco Carrillo*, 226; Máximo Gómez to José Rogelio Castillo, April 27, 1897, April 28, 1897, and April 30, 1897 in Castillo y Zúñiga, *Autobiografía*, 319–322.
17. Máximo Gómez to José Rogelio Castillo, April 11, 1896, in Castillo y Zúñiga, *Autobiografía del General*, 298; Antonio Maceo to José Rogelio Castillo, October 29, 1896, in Castillo y Zúñiga, 306; Máximo Gómez to José Rogelio Castillo, April 6, 1897, in Castillo y Zúñiga, 315; Máximo Gómez to José Rogelio Castillo, April 27, 1897, April 28, 1897, and April 30, 1897 in Castillo y Zúñiga, 319–322.
18. Máximo Gómez to Rita Suárez del Villar, January 28, 1898, Box 2, file 26, AHPC/RSV. Also see Era and Díaz Roque, *Cartas desconocidas*, 31.
19. Miguel J. Monteavaro on behalf of Cándido Álvarez to Máximo Gómez, January 16, 1897, Box 7, File 943, ANC/FPMG.
20. José B. Alemán to Serafín Sánchez, April 17, 1896, Legajo 2, Expediente 121, Archivo Provincial Histórico de Villa Clara, Fondo José Braulio Alemán (hereafter, AHPVC/FJBA).
21. Colonel Rafael Cabrera to José B. Alemán, quoted in José B. Alemán to Máximo Gómez, December 6, 1896, Box 8, File 1165, ANC/FPMG.
22. José Lacret Morlot to Máximo Gómez, January 25, 1897, Box 7, File 947, ANC/FPMG.
23. Máximo Gómez to Francisco Carrillo, July 30, 1897, in Gómez, *Cartas a Francisco Carrillo*, 172.

24. "Comunicación dirigía al Tte Cor en Comisión, firmada por Antonio Rojas (a nombre de Porfirio Sánchez) al parecer del Regimiento J B Zayas, referente a queja por problemas de alimentación," n.d.-late November 1896, Legajo 18, Exp. 2508, ANC/R95.
25. "Comunicación dirigida al brig Silverio Sánchez, firmada por el tte cor Acea, referente al exceso de atribuciones y falta de obediencia en el incidente surgido entre el comandante Alfredo Ramírez y el teniente cor. en comisión Isidro Acea, adjunto causa instruida, November 21–22, 1896," Legajo 17, Exp. 2482 ANC/R95.
26. Rosell y Malpica, *Diario del Teniente*, II, 109; Pérez, *Radiografía*, 87. Also see pp. 146–149 for a discussion of conflicts over military authority in this encounter.
27. "Diario de Operaciones de José B. Alemán," April 30, 1897, Box 104, File 171, ANC/FDR. This diary was published in an abridged and edited form in Guerra Alemán, *¡Juro, pero no prometo!*, 217–67.
28. "Diario de Operaciones de José B. Alemán," April 30, 1897, Box 104, File 171, ANC/FDR.
29. Gould, *Mismeasure of Man*; Jackson and Weidman, *Race, Racism, and Science*.
30. Máximo Gómez to José B. Alemán, May 4, 1897, Legajo 1, Expediente 22, AHPVC/FJBA.
31. "Diario de Operaciones de José B. Alemán," May 1897, Box 104, File 171, ANC/FDR.
32. "Testimony of José Miguel Gómez," April 27, 1904, Case 293, Box 144, Part 7, Folder 1, USNAII/STCC/RG 76/E 352.
33. Álvarez Pitaluga, *Revolución, hegemonía y poder*, 91.
34. Castillo y Zúñiga, *Autobiografía del General*, 149.
35. Boza, *Mi diario de la guerra*, 39.
36. Ferrer, *Insurgent Cuba*, 166–67.
37. Consuegra y Guzmán, 32–33.
38. Rosell y Malpica, *Diario del Teniente*, II, 114.
39. "Circular," Najasa, July 1, 1895, and "Circular," Sancti Spíritus, November 6, 1895, in Gómez, *Cartas a Francisco Carrillo*, 127–28.
40. José B. Alemán to Gerardo Machado, July 30, 1896, Legajo 1, Expediente 11, AHPVC/FJBA; Tone, *War and Genocide*, 176–76.
41. Alejandro Rodríguez to Máximo Gómez, March 5, 1897, Box 7, File 964, ANC/FPMG.
42. José B. Alemán to Máximo Gómez, December 6, 1896, Box 8, File 1165, ANC/FPMG.
43. José B. Alemán to Máximo Gómez, April 10, 1897, Box 7, File 983, ANC/FPMG.
44. Clete Hernández to Máximo Gómez, June 19, 1896, BPSC/FRV.
45. Rosell y Malpica, *Diario del Teniente*, II, 123.
46. Rosell y Malpica, *Diario del Teniente*, 123.
47. José B. Alemán to Máximo Gómez, September 17, 1896, Box 6, File 905, ANC/FPMG.
48. José B. Alemán to Gerardo Machado, July 30, 1896, Legajo 1, Expediente 11, AHPVC/FJBA.

49. José B. Alemán to Máximo Gómez, September 21, 1896, Box 6, File 903, ANC/FPMG.
50. José B. Alemán to Máximo Gómez, August 7, 1896, Box 6, File 903, ANC/FPMG.
51. José B. Alemán to Máximo Gómez, date illegible and August 7, 1896, Legajo 1, Expediente 45, AHPVC/FJBA.
52. José B. Alemán to Máximo Gómez, date illegible and August 7, 1896, Legajo 1, Expediente 45, AHPVC/FJBA.
53. José B. Alemán to Máximo Gómez, September 15, 1896, Box 6, File 912, ANC/FPMG.
54. José B. Alemán to Máximo Gómez, August 24, 1896, Box 6, File 903, ANC/FPMG; José B. Alemán to Máximo Gómez, September 15, 1896, Box 6, File 912, ANC/FPMG; José B. Alemán to Máximo Gómez, August 7, 1896, Box 6, File 903, ANC/FPMG.
55. Atkins, *Sixty Years in Cuba*, 186.
56. Atkins, *Sixty Years in Cuba*, 202, 229; Edwin F. Atkins, Petition before the Spanish Treaty Claims Commission," December 1905, Box II.4, folio 3, MHS/EFAP.
57. "El Ciudadano Claudio Sarría y Sarría to Máximo Gómez," [n.d.], Box 22, File 3083, folio 18, ANC/FPMG.
58. Flint, *Marching with Gómez*, 178.
59. Diario del brigadier José González Planas, August 20, 1895, December 1, 1895, and January 20, 1896, Museo Histórico Municipal de Remedios (hereafter MHMR); Máximo Gómez to José González Planas, April 13, 1896, MHMR.
60. Francisco Carrillo to José González Planas, July 22, 1897 in Martínez-Fortún y Foyo, *Anales y Efemérides*, 57–58.
61. Máximo Gómez to José González Planas, July 30, 1897, in Martínez-Fortún y Foyo, *Anales y Efemérides*, 59; Quoted in Máximo Gómez to Francisco Carrillo, May 11, 1897 in *Cartas a Francisco Carrillo*, 160.
62. Sartorius, "Limits of Loyalty," 251.
63. Vulcano to Vencedor, December 19, 1897, MHMR.
64. Máximo Gómez to Francisco Carrillo, March 8, 1898, in Gómez, *Cartas a Francisco Carrillo*, 206.
65. Máximo Gómez to Francisco Carrillo, March 8, 1898, in *Cartas a Francisco Carrillo*, 206.
66. Manuel José Delgado to Juan Gualberto Gómez, February 9, 1899, Caibarien, Legajo 18, Expediente 1092, Archivo Nacional de Cuba, Fondo Adquisiciones (hereafter, ANC/FA).
67. Diario de José González Planas, April 18–April 20, 1898, MHMR.
68. Manuel José Delgado to Juan Gualberto Gómez, February 9, 1899, Caibarien, Legajo 18, Expediente 1092, ANC/FA.
69. Batrell Oviedo, *Para la historia*, 33–34.
70. Batrell Oviedo, *Para la historia*, 22–23.
71. García Martínez, "La Brigada de Cienfuegos," 185–86.

72. Flint, *Marching with Gómez*, 80; Balboa Navarro, *La protesta rural en Cuba*, 13; García Martínez, "La Brigada de Cienfuegos," 164; Pérez, *Lords of the Mountain*, 29, 47; Schwartz, *Lawless Liberators*, 226; "Testimony of Avelino Sanjenis," February 11, 1908, Case 196, Box 90, Part 9, folio 4, USNAII/STCC/RG 76/E 352.
73. Flint, *Marching with Gómez*, 91–92.
74. Gómez, *Diario de campaña*, 434.
75. Máximo Gómez to Francisco Carrillo, May 20, 1897 in Gómez, *Cartas a Francisco Carrillo*, 163.
76. Padrón, *Quintín Bandera*, 56–57.
77. Máximo Gómez to Lieutenant Colonel Armando Sánchez, Jefe de Reg, "Expedicionaria," July 8, 1897 in "Expediente formado para el esclarecimiento de hechos que se dicen cometidos por el Brigadier Quintín Bandera," July 1897, Legajo 16, Exp. 2157 (new 2277), Archivo Nacional de Cuba, Fondo Máximo Gómez (hereafter, ANC/FMG).
78. Valdés-Domínguez, *Diario de un soldado*, IV, 193; Máximo Gómez to Francisco Carrillo, May 20, 1897 in Gómez, *Cartas a Francisco Carrillo*, 163.
79. Padrón, *Quintín Bandera*, 236.
80. Ferrer, *Insurgent Cuba*, 174–75; Ferrer, "Rustic Men, Civilized Nation"; Ferrer, "Quintín Bandera" in Martínez Heredia, Scott, and García Martínez, *Espacios*, 141–62.
81. Alejandro Rodríguez to Máximo Gómez, March 5, 1897, Box 7, File 964, ANC/FPMG.
82. Tone, *War and Genocide*, 95.
83. On performative self-representation, see Kelley, *Race Rebels*, 50–51; Butler, *Gender Trouble*. On resistance, see Scott, *Weapons of the Weak*, 282, 334.
84. Juan Masó Parra to Máximo Gómez, May 26, 1897, in "Expediente formado para el esclarecimiento de hechos que se dicen cometidos por el Brigadier Quintín Bandera," July 1897, Legajo 16, Exp. 2157 (new 2277), ANC/FMG.
85. Testimony of Quintín Bandera, in "Expediente formado para el esclarecimiento de hechos que se dicen cometidos por el Brigadier Quintín Bandera," July 1897, Legajo 16, Exp. 2157 (new 2277), ANC/FMG.
86. Curtin, *Plantation Complex*, 175; Ferrer, "Quintín Bandera" in Martínez Heredia, Scott, and García Martínez, *Espacios*, 150; Manuel Moreno Fraginals, *El Ingenio*; Knight, *Slave Society in Cuba*, 25–46.
87. Gómez, *La insurrección por dentro*, 103. Emphasis in original.
88. Gómez, *La insurrección por dentro*, 130. Emphasis mine.
89. Alfredo Rego to José Rogelio Castillo, January 25, 1896, in Castillo y Zúñiga, *Autobiografía*, 295.
90. José María Rodríguez to Máximo Gómez, June 26, 1897, Legajo 7, Exp. 1022, ANC/FPMG.
91. Quintín Bandera to Máximo Gómez, May 4, 1897, Legajo 7, Exp. 996, ANC/FPMG.
92. Valdés-Domínguez, *Diario de un soldado*, IV, 47.

93. Testimony of Quintín Bandera, in "Expediente formado para el esclarecimiento de hechos que se dicen cometidos por el Brigadier Quintín Bandera," July 1897, Legajo 16, Exp. 2157 (new 2277), ANC/FMG.
94. Padrón, *Quintín Bandera*, 286.
95. D'ou and De Oraá, *Papeles del teniente coronel*, 88–89; Savignón, *Quintín Bandera*, 10–11; Gómez, *La insurrección por dentro*, 118. Emphasis in original.
96. D'ou, and De Oraá, *Papeles del teniente coronel*, 91.
97. Ferrer, "Rustic Men," 682.
98. Ferrer, "Rustic Men," 670–71.
99. Helg, "Black Men," 583.
100. Helg, "Black Men," 130.
101. Helg, "Black Men," 66.
102. Tone, *War and Genocide*, 179.
103. Tone, *War and Genocide*, 179–180; Valdés-Domínguez, *Diario de un soldado*, II, 40.
104. Collazo, *Cuba heróica*, 9; Consuegra y Gúzman, *Mambiserías*, 112–13.
105. José B. Alemán to Máximo Gómez, April 10, 1897, Box 7, File 983, ANC/FPMG.
106. Valdés-Domínguez, *Diario de un soldado*, II, 301.
107. Valdés-Domínguez, *Diario de un soldado*, II, 301.
108. Rosell y Malpica, *Diario del Teniente*, II, 65.
109. Ferrara, *Memorias*, 92.
110. "Testimony of Juan Piñol," May 11, 1906, Case 387, Box 167, Part 2, Folder 2, folio 17, USNAII/STCC/RG 76/E 352.
111. Gómez, *Diario de campaña*, 434.
112. Halstead, *Story of Cuba*, 273–74.
113. Flint, *Marching with Gómez*, 93.
114. Fermín Valdez-Domínguez to José Braulio Alemán, June 3, 1897, Legajo 1, Exp. 8, AHPVC/FJBA; Máximo Gómez to Fermín Valdez-Domínguez, quoted in Fermín Valdez-Domínguez to José Braulio Alemán, June 3, 1897, Legajo 1, Expediente 8, AHPVC/FJBA.
115. Máximo Gómez to Francisco Carrillo, May 29, 1896, May 20, 1897 and May 9, 1898 in Gómez, *Cartas a Francisco Carrillo*, 276, 163; Mayor General Loynaz del Castillo en defensa de la gloriosa memoria del Mayor General José María Rodríguez," [n.d.], B 524, File 1, folio 59, ANC/FDR. This manuscript seems to be an earlier version of his published memoir, with some sections crossed out and not appearing in the later version. Loynaz del Castillo, *Memorias de la guerra*, 491. Also see Boza, *Mi diario*, 34–35.
116. Gómez, *Cartas a Francisco Carrillo*, 284.
117. Martí, "El plato de lentejas," *Patria*, January 6, 1893.
118. The delegates for the Fourth Army Corps were Domingo Méndez Capote, Ernesto Fonts Sterling, José B. Alemán Urquía, Nicolás Alberdi Golzari, and Eusebio Hernández Pérez (alternate).

119. Tone, *War and Genocide*, 234–35.
120. Benjamin, *Cuban Revolution*, 7–9.
121. For an overview of the debates in US Congress over the Teller Amendment, see Foner, *Spanish-Cuba-American War*, 261–80. On Cuban views of the Teller Amendment, see Pérez, *Cuba between Empires*, 185–86.
122. Roloff, *Indice alfabético*.
123. "Comunicación sin destino firmada por el Gral de Div Jefe Accidental del Quinto Cuerpo referente a traslado de circular sobre la política a seguir con presentados y desertores que regresen a las fueras y conducta de respeto hacia los pacíficos," May 5, 1898, Legajo 16, Exp 2700, ANC/FMG; Alejandro Rodríguez to unknown, May 22, 1898 Miscellaneous documents from the 5to Cuerpo, Legajo 16, Exp 2700, ANC/FMG.
124. Leopoldo Figueroa to Sr. Presidente del Club Federico de la Torre, January 23, 1898, Sancti Spíritus, BPSC/FRV.
125. García Martínez, "La Brigada de Cienfuegos," 186; Higinio Esquerra, *Diario de Operaciones, 1896–1898*, Museo Histórico Provincial de Cienfuegos (hereafter, MPHC); Ferrer, *Insurgent Cuba*, 186–188; De la Torre, *Conflictos y cultura política*, 129–31; Ferrer, 184–85. For a compelling analysis of the ways education serves as a coded reference to race, class and gender, and functions to reinforce hierarchies based on these, see de la Cadena, *Indigenous Mesitzos*.
126. Roloff, *Indice alfabético*.
127. Helg, "Afro-Cubans in Cuba's War for Independence, 1895–1898," in Foote and Horst, *Military Struggle*, 68; Tone, *War and Genocide*, 95; Carlos Roloff to José Rogelio Castillo, October 7, 1898, José Rogelio Castillo to Sr. Director de "La Lucha," May 6, 1899, in Castillo y Zúñiga, *Autobiografía*, 354, 378–79; "Inspección General del Ejército del Departamento occidental," September 2, 1898, Box 71, File 4246, ANC/FA; Manuel José Delgado to Juan Gualberto Gómez, February 9, 1899, Caibarien, Legajo 18, Expediente 1092, ANC/FA; Máximo Gómez to Francisco Carrillo, February 28, 1898, in Gómez, *Cartas a Francisco Carrillo*, 204; "Testimony of Higinio Esquerra," April 18, 1904, Case 293, Box 143, Part 5, Folder 3, USNAII/STCC/RG 76/E 352; "Testimony of Arturo Aulet," April 29, 1904, Case 293, Box 143, Part 5, Folder 3, USNAII/STCC/RG 76/E 352; Máximo Gómez to Francisco Carrillo, February 28, 1898, in Gómez, *Cartas a Francisco Carrillo*, 204; Batrell Oviedo, *Para la historia*, 171; García Martínez, "La Brigada de Cienfuegos," 189.

CHAPTER FOUR

1. Diego Vicente Tejera, "Conferencia dada a los obreros cubanos emigrados durante la última Guerra de independencia, en la 'Sociedad de Trabajadora' de Key West," December 12, 1897, in *Cuba Contemporánea* 28: 3 (1922): 171.
2. Castillo y Zúñiga, *Autobiografía del General*, 332.

3. On the concept of martial manhood in Western societies, see Snyder, *Citizen-Soldiers*. For martial manhood in the United States, see Greenberg, *Manifest Manhood*; Gilmore, *Gender and Jim Crow*. For martial manhood in Europe, see Dudink, Hagemann, and Tosh, *Masculinities in Politics and War*; Streets, *Martial Races*. For martial manhood in the Caribbean, see Smith, *Jamaican Volunteers*.
4. On the racial, social, and political views of the PRC as compared to insurgents, see Guerra, *Myth of Jose Martí*, 62–82; Perez, *Cuba between Empires*, 110–12.
5. Pappademos, *Black Political Activism*, 38.
6. Benjamin, *Cuban Revolution*, 8–9.
7. On late nineteenth-century US visions of manhood in relation to race, see Bederman, *Manliness and Civilization*, 23, 25–29; Hoganson, *Fighting for American Manhood*, 10–12.
8. Pérez, *Cuba between Empires*, 202.
9. Wilson, *Annual Report*, 1899, 66, 72.
10. José de Jesús Monteagudo to Gonzalo de Quesada, February 17, 1899, in *Archivo de Gonzalo de Quesada, Epistolario II*, Academia de la Historia de Cuba (Havana: Imprenta El Siglo XX, 1948), 91–92.
11. Alfredo Lewis to Rita Suárez del Villar, August 22, 1898, Box 1, AHPC/RSV
12. Manuel Aramo to Rita Suárez del Villar, May 4, 1898, Box 1, file 22, AHPC/RSV.
13. Amparo Hernández to Presidente Club Federico de la Torre, August 8, 1897, Fondos Raros y Valiosos, BPSC; Eloisa O'Halloran to Presidente Club Federico de la Torre, July 27, 1897, Fondos Raros y Valiosos, BPSC.
14. Carlos Trujillo to Rita Suárez del Villar, January, 27 1898, Box 1, file 33, AHPC/RSV.
15. Carlos Trujillo to Rita Suárez del Villar, April 12, 1898, Box 1, file 33, AHPC/RSV.
16. Antío Cuevas y Rodríguez to Rita Suárez del Villar, February 22, 1900, Box 1, file 33, AHPC/RSV; Col. José Camacho to Rita Suárez del Villar, October 9, 1899, Box 1, file 3, AHPC/RSV.
17. As chief of the Brigade of Remedios, González Planas maintained direct communication with María Escobar Laredo, known as Vencedor. Vulcano to Vencedor, 1897–1898, MHMR.
18. Manuel José Delgado to Juan Gualberto Gómez, January 31, 1899, Caibarien, Legajo 18, Expediente 1092, ANC/FA.
19. José González Planas to Juan Gualberto Gómez, February 8, 1899, Caibarien, Legajo 23, Expediente 1675, ANC/FA.
20. Leopoldo Figueroa to Sr. Presidente del Club Federico de la Torre, January 23, 1898, Sancti Spíritus, BPSC/FRV.
21. Juan B. Medina to Marta Abreu, Cienfuegos, May 6, 1899; Antonio Gutiérrez Alseny to Marta Abreu, Cienfuegos August 30, 1899, No. 357, V. 11, BNJM/FMA; Various Letters to Rita Suárez del Villar, 1898, in AHPC/RSV.
22. Thomas R. Dawley, Jr., "Campaigning with Gómez," *American Magazine* 47 (November 1898–April 1899), 536; "Testimony of Eduardo Guzmán," April 13,

1904, Case 293, Box 143, Part 5, Folder 3, USNAII/STCC/RG 76/E 352; "Testimony of Higinio Esquerra," April 18, 1904, Case 293, Box 143, Part 5, Folder 3, USNAII/STCC/RG 76/E 352.

23. Magdalena Peñarredonda, president of the Patriotic Association of Cuban Women to Carmen Gutierrez, President of the Club Hermanas de Juan Bruno Zayas, April 17, 1900, Legajo 7, Expediente 415, AHPVC/FMGG; Assorted newspaper clippings in Citizens' Permanent Relief Committee, "Cuban Relief Work," 1898–1899, Volume 7, Pennsylvania Historical Society, Citizens' Permanent Relief Committee Collection (hereafter, PHS/CPRC); Home Mission Board, Original Minute Book (July 1, 1875-November 29, 1898), 1897–1898, Box 2, Item 1, Southern Baptist Historical Library and Archive (hereafter, SBHLA); Wilson, *Annual Report*, 1899, 156.

24. "Testimony of Ramón Sánchez Varona," July 27, 1907, Case 196, Box 85, Part 1, USNAII/STCC/RG 76/E 352. Emphasis mine.

25. Wilson, *Annual Report*, 1899, 74.

26. J. D. Hickey, "Report of his investigation between Cárdenas and Cienfuegos," January 26, 1899, Box 1, No File, Records of the Military Government of Cuba, Record Group 140, Entry 3, USNAII/MGC/RG 140/E 3.

27. Wilson, *Annual Report*, 1899, 74.

28. "The Situation in Cienfuegos," *New York Times*, January 15, 1899.

29. For a discussion of social death in relation to slavery, see Patterson, *Slavery and Social Death*.

30. Martínez Ortiz, *Cuba: los primeros años*, 107.

31. For a discussion of similar arguments of economic autonomy as essential for political masculinity, see Díaz, *Female Citizens*.

32. Commander of Trinidad, "Makes report with recommendations on condition of affairs in his district," January 4, 1899, Box 2, No File, USNAI/RUSA/RG 395/E 1466.

33. "Testimony of Ramón Sánchez Varona," July 27, 1907, Case 196, Box 85, Part 1, USNAII/STCC/RG 76/E 352. Emphasis mine.

34. Grant Hamilton, "'War is Hell'—Sherman [but] Peace in Cuba under Spanish rule is Worse than Hell," April 30, 1898, Color lithograph, Library of Congress, Prints and Photographs Division (hereafter, LOC/PPD).

35. "Testimony produced in the case of C. P. Johnson, 1st Lieutenant, USA and Doctor Maximilian Lund," Arroyo Blanco, Las Villas, July 28, 1898, Fondo Máximo Gómez, Legajo 16, Expediente 2158 #nuevo 2278, ANC/FMG; José M. Estrada y Abreu to Marta Abreu, [n.d.], BNJM/FMA, No. 315; Miscellaneous Court cases and reports, September 26, 1898-December 26, 1898, Legajo 99, Expediente 22, ANC/DR.

36. Bolton, *Illinois Volunteer Infantry*, 122

37. Wheeler, *Santiago Campaign*, 157–59.

38. Bolton, *Illinois Volunteer Infantry*, 127

39. Appelbaum, MacPherson, and Alejandra, "Introduction: Racial Nations," in Appelbaum, MacPherson, and Alejandra, 4; Beattie, *Tribute of Blood*, 274; Smith, *Jamaican Volunteers*; Chambers, *From Subjects to Citizens*, 172, 179–80; Lipsett-Rivera, *Daily Life*, 13–14; Stern, *Secret History*, 168; Vinson, *Bearing Arms*, 224–25.
40. Diego Vicente Tejera, "Conferencia dada a los obreros cubanos emigrados durante la última Guerra de independencia, en la 'Sociedad de Trabajadora' de Key West," December 12, 1897, in *Cuba Contemporánea* 28: 3 (1922): 176–77.
41. Wilson, *Annual Report*, 1899, 74.
42. Rafael M. Portuondo to John R. Brooke, January 26, 1899, Box 2, File 504, USNA/MGC/RG 140/E 3.
43. José Rogelio Castillo to Sr. Director de "El Porvenir," September 7, 1898, in Castillo y Zúñiga, *Autobiografía*, 341–42.
44. Excerpt from *La Lucha*, March 21, 1898, quoted in Sylvester Henry Scovel, "Special Cable," *World*, March 22, 1898. Newspaper clipping available in Missouri History Museum, Sylvester Henry Scovel Papers, Box 2; Manuel Aramo to Rita Suárez del Villar, May 4, 1898, Box 1, file 22, AHPC/RSV.
45. "Al Trabajo," in *La Nación*, September 1, 1898, Box 291, File 41, ANC/FDR; José Miguel Gómez, "Submits a list of recommendations for the most important of Public Works needed in the Province of Santa Clara," June 4, 1899, Box 9, File 4643, USNAI/RUSA/RG 395/E 1331.
46. Edwin F. Atkins vs. United States of America, Case 250, USNAII/STCC/RG 76/E 352; E. Atkins & Company vs. United States of America, Case 387, USNAII/STCC/RG 76/E 352; Wood, *Final Report*, 58–59, 76–77. Other American citizens with properties in Cienfuegos claimed hundreds of thousands of dollars in losses. Andrés L. Terry and estate administrator Francis Egerton Webb claimed over $611,000 in damages to the properties of the deceased Antonio E. Terry in Cruces and Cienfuegos. Constancia Sugar Company of New York claimed nearly $4,178,000 in damages. Hormiguero Central Company assessed their damages at nearly $769,000. Andrés L. Terry vs. United States of America, Case 90, USNAII/STCC/RG 76/E 352; Wood, *Final Report*, 32–35; Constancia Sugar Co vs. United States of America, Case 196, USNAII/STCC/RG 76/E 352; Wood, *Final Report*, 48–49; Homiguero Central Company vs. United States of America, Case 293, USNAII/STCC/RG 76/E 352; Wood, *Final Report*, 64–65; Wood, *Final Report*. Also see USNAII/STCC/RG 76/E 352. These property owners included Luis Mayoline, Manuel Antón Recio de Morales, Gabriel M. Landa, Domingo J. Álvarez, Carlos J. Marsillán, María Sánchez de la Torre, Emilio Fernández Cabada and Ynés, Ambrosia, Nicolás, and Antonio Suárez del Villar, Victor Virgilio Vila González, Victoria Fowler de Cabada, Patricio Ponce de Leon, Agnes de Béquer, Joeseph R. Lombard and María Josefa Sánchez de Lombard.
47. Wilson, *Annual Report*, 1900, 118; Lane, *Armed Progressive*, 239, 287.
48. Pepper, *To-Morrow in Cuba*, 151; Scott and Zeuske, "Property in Writing."
49. Musgrave, *Under Three Flags*, 163.

50. James H. Wilson to Adjutant General, "Reports on agricultural conditions," February 3, 1900, Box 31, File 665, USNAI/RUSA/RG 395/E 1331.
51. James H. Wilson to Adjutant General, February 8, 1900, Box 31, File 665, USNAII/MGC/RG 140/E 3; Wilson, *Annual Report*, 1899, 72; Clark, "Labor Conditions in Cuba," 679.
52. United States War Department, *Census of Cuba, 1899*, 403–33.
53. James H. Wilson to Adjutant General, "Reports on agricultural conditions," February 3, 1900, Box 31, File 665, USNAI/RUSA/RG 395/E 1331.
54. Wilson, *Annual Report*, 1899, 72; Clark, "Labor Conditions in Cuba," 679.
55. Edwin F. Atkins to Brooks," January 30, 1899, Volume II.19, folio 87, MHS/EFA.
56. Edwin F. Atkins to L O'Brien Esq., January 16, 1899, Volume II.19, folio 23, MHS/EFA.
57. Major General Bates to Adjutant General, March 11, 1899, Box 6, File 1911, USNA/RG 140/E 3.
58. Wilson, *Annual Report*, 1899, 47; Major General Bates to Adjutant General, April 24, 1899, Box 11, File 2601, USNA/RG 140/E 3; William Wright to John C. Bates, "Report of visit to Ingenio Soledad," January 16, 1899, Box 5, File 132, USNAI/RUSA/RG 395/E 1466.
59. José de Jesus Monteagudo to Gonzalo de Quesada, February 17, 1899 in *Archivo de Gonzalo de Quesada, Epistolario II*, 91–92; Wilson, *Annual Report*, 1899, 47; Major General Bates to Adjutant General, April 24, 1899, Box 11, File 2601, USNAII/MGC/RG 140/E 3; Major General Bates to Adjutant General, March 11, 1899, Box 6, File 1911, USNAII/MGC/RG 140/E 3.
60. Oliver Agramonte to John C. Bates, "Requests that a detachment of American troops be stationed at the Central Juragua," February 22, 1899, Box 6, File 1199, USNAI/RUSA/RG 395/E 1466.
61. Edwin F. Atkins to L O'Brien Esq., January 16, 1899, Volume II.19, folio 23, MHS/EFA.
62. "Daily Journal of Brigadier General James H. Wilson," May 11, 1899, Box 53, Library of Congress, Manuscripts Division, James H. Wilson Papers (hereafter, LOC/MD/JHW); Wilson, *Annual Report*, 1899, 225.
63. A. Castellanos, "States that acts of violence have been committed," January 16, 1899, Box 1, File 130, USNAI/RUSA/RG 395/E 1466.
64. A. Castellanos, "States that acts of violence have been committed," January 16, 1899, Box 1, File 130, USNAI/RUSA/RG 395/E 1466.
65. Geo P. Barker to Adjutant General, "Explains deeds of violence," March 4, 1899, Box 6, File 1699, USNAI/RUSA/RG 395/E 1466.
66. "Brigands Murder a Spaniard," *New York Times*, May 6, 1899; "Principio del Final," newspaper clipping, August 3, 1899, Volume II.60, folio 79, MHS/EFA; Edwin F. Atkins to James H. Wilson, October 5, 1899, Box 2, LOC/MD/JHW; Alfredo López Miró to General Leonard Wood, August 14, 1899, Box 28, File 5799, USNAII/MGC/RG 140/E 3.

67. Merchants, "Asks for American soldiers to preserve better order," January 27, 1899, Box 3, File 323, USNAI/RUSA/RG 395/E 1466; José de la Torre, "A Spanish citizen asks for protection of the Spanish element in Cuba for the sake of prosperity," February 12, 1899, Box 6, File 1867, USNAII/MGC/RG 140/E 3.
68. "Edwin F. Atkins, Petition before the Spanish Treaty Claims Commission," December 1905, Box II.4, folio 83, MHS/EFA.
69. "Edwin F. Atkins, Petition before the Spanish Treaty Claims Commission," December 1905, Box II.4, folio 83, MHS/EFA.
70. William Wright to John C. Bates, "Report of visit to Ingenio Soledad," January 16, 1899, Box 5, File 132, USNAI/RUSA/RG 395/E 1466.
71. William Wright to John C. Bates, "Report of visit to Ingenio Soledad," January 16, 1899, Box 5, File 132, USNAI/RUSA/RG 395/E 1466.
72. William Wright to John C. Bates, "Report of visit to Ingenio Soledad," January 16, 1899, Box 5, File 132, USNAI/RUSA/RG 395/E 1466.
73. "Edwin F. Atkins, Petition before the Spanish Treaty Claims Commission," December 1905, Box II.4, folio 83, MHS/EFA; Foner, *Spanish-Cuba-American War*, 422.
74. For an analysis of the gendered dimensions of US civilizing projects, see Gilmore, *Gender and Jim Crow*, 62–63; Hoganson, *Fighting for American Manhood*, 24–26.
75. Helg, *Our Rightful Share*, 92–93; Pérez, *Cuba between Empires*, 198–201.
76. "Please for Suffering Cubans," *New York Times*, February 7, 1898; "Ex-Consul Barker Blessed by People at Sagua," *Chicago Tribune*, December 1, 1898; Rowland, *Mississippi: Contemporary Biography*, vol. 3, 166.
77. Walter B. Barker, Correspondence with Various Individuals, 1895–1898, Dispatches from U.S. Consuls in Sagua La Grande, 1878–1900, Microfilm Reels #5–6, WRD/UNC/USCC; Machado, *¡Piedad!*, 30–33.
78. Walter B. Barker to Orville H. Platt, January 4, 1900, Folder 5, Mississippi State University, Mitchell Memorial Library, Special Collections, Frank Archibald Critz Family Papers, Family and Business Papers, 1880–1915 (hereafter, MSU/MML/FACF).
79. Walter B. Barker to John Addison Porter, November 28, 1899, Library of Congress, Manuscripts Division, William McKinley Papers (hereafter, LOC/MD/WMP).
80. Walter B. Barker to General John C. Bates, January 15, 1900, Folder 5, MSU/MML/FACF. On the gendered dimensions of US-Indian policy, see Simonsen, *Making Home Work*, 71–110; For more on the continental precedents of US imperialism and racial views, see Weston, *Racism in U. S. Imperialism*; Williams, "United States Indian Policy"; Rydell, *All the World's a Fair*; McFerson, *Racial Dimension*.
81. "Testimony of José Miguel Gómez," April 27, 1904, Case 293, Box 144, Part 7, Folder 1, USNAII/STCC/RG 76/E 352.
82. José Antonio Frías, "States that citizens have protested against appointment of Mr. Trinidad Martínez," March 16, 1899, Box 6, File 2917, USNAII/MGC/RG 140/E 3.
83. Wilson, *Annual Report*, 1899, 225.
84. James H. Wilson to J. B. Foraker, August 12, 1899, Box 44, LOC/MD/JHW.

85. Santiago Dod, "letter in which he certified that Juan Venancio Schweiss [sic], during the blockade of the Island of Cuba, by his courageous and determined attitude allayed public excitement," August 14, 1898, Box 7, File 2096, USNAII/MGC/RG 140/E 3; Pelayo García to Cosme de la Torriente, December 9, 1900, Legajo 570, Expediente 22, Academa de Historia, Asociación de Veteranos, Colección Cosme de la Torriente; Juan Venancio Schwiep to John C. Bates, "Wishes to be maintained as General attorney of Santa Clara," January 20, 1899, Box 7, File 2096, USNAII/MGC/RG 140/E 3; Geo P. Barker, "3rd Endorsement," March 20, 1899, Box 7, File 2096, USNAII/MGC/RG 140/E 3; Walter B. Barker to Major Hoyt, "States does not know that anyone has been recommended to take the place of the Municipal Judge," November 23, 1900, Box 118, File 6088, USNAII/MGC/RG 140/E 3; General John R. Brooke to Juan Venancio Schwiep, "4th Endorsement," September 14, 1899, Box 7, File 2096, USNAII/MGC/RG 140/E 3.
86. Leon Ichasso, "Statement of Affairs in Café Central," March 20, 1899, Box 5, File 2081, USNAI/RUSA/RG 395/E 1466.
87. Cienfuegos City Council Minutes, January–April, 1899, Volume 42, Actas Capitulares, Archivo Provincial Histórico de Cienfuegos (Hereafter, AHPC/AC); Santa Clara City Council Minutes, January-April, 1899, Actas Capitulares, Archivo Provincial Histórico de Villa Clara (hereafter, AHPVC/ACSC); Sagua la Grande City Council Minutes, January-April, 1899, Actas Capitulares, Archivo Provincial Histórico de Villa Clara (hereafter, AHPVC/ACSLG); Trinidad City Council Minutes, January-April, 1899, Actas Capitulares, Archivo Municipal Histórico de Trinidad (hereafter, AMHT/ACT); "Edwin F. Atkins to Brooks," January 30, 1899, Volume II.19, folio 85, MHS/EFAP; Wilson, *Annual Report*, 1899, 225; "The Situation in Cienfuegos," in *New York Times*, January 15, 1899.
88. "Nuevo Ayuntamiento de Trinidad," *La Verdad* (Cienfuegos), reproduced in *El Telégrafo* (Trinidad), July 9, 1899, Archivo Municipal Histórico de Trinidad, Fondo Hemeroteca (hereafter, AMHT/FH).
89. "The Situation in Cienfuegos," in *New York Times*, January 15, 1899; Bolton, *Illinois Volunteer Infantry*, 126.
90. "Vicios de oríjen [sic], *Unión Cubana* (Santa Clara), January 20, 1899, in Juan V. Schwiep, "Takes exception to a newspaper article," January 20, 1899, Box 2, File 906, USNAI/RUSA/RG 395/E 1422.
91. "Nuestros Hombres," *La Protesta: Diario Independiente (Periódico suprimido por el Gobierno Español el día 10 de Octubre 1894)*, September 3, 1899, Instituto de Historia de Cuba.
92. José de Jesús Monteagudo to Gonzalo de Quesada, February 17, 1899, in *Archivo de Gonzalo de Quesada*, II, 91, 92.
93. José Miguel Tarrafa to Gonzalo de Quesada, February 20, 1899, in *Archivo de Gonzalo de Quesada*, II, 283.
94. "Daily Journal of Brigadier General James H. Wilson," May 12, 1899, Box 53, LOC/MD/JHW.

95. Miguel Gener, "Ladrón de su propia dádiva," *Cárdenas Herald*, April 26, 1899, Box 1, No File, USNAI/RUSA/RG 395/E 1340.
96. "Nuevo Ayuntamiento de Trinidad," *La Verdad* (Cienfuegos), reproduced in *El Telégrafo* (Trinidad), July 9, 1899, AHMT/FH.
97. Cienfuegos City Council Minutes, January 31, 1899, Volume 42, folio 72, AHPC/AC.
98. Pérez Guzmán, *Radiografía*; Álvarez Pitaluga, *Revolución, hegemonía y poder*; García Martínez, "Caciques, elites, clientelas."
99. Bronfman, "Más allá del color," in Martínez Heredia, Scott, and García Martínez, *Espacios*, 292.
100. "City Council Minutes," April 28, 1899, Volume 43, folio 68, AHPC/AC.
101. For understandings of post-revolutionary male honor, see Chambers, *From Subjects to Citizens*, 187; Wade, *Race and Sex*, 123–24.
102. "City Council Minutes," May 18, 1899, Volume 43, folio 82, AHPC/AC.
103. "City Council Minutes," March 23, 1899, Volume 43, folio 41, AHPC/AC.
104. Capt. C. J. Stevens, "Report relative to the rural police of the Province of Santa Clara," June 9, 1899, Box 11, File 5062, USNAI/RUSA/RG 395/E 1331.
105. "City Council Minutes," March 9, 1899, Volume 43, folios 27–28, AHPC/AC.
106. Máximo Gómez to Rita Suárez del Villar, January 28, 1898, Box 2, file 26, AHPC/RSV. Also see Era and Díaz Roque, *Cartas desconocidas*, 31.
107. Oviedo, *Para la historia*, 170–72; Barnet, *Biografía de un Cimarrón*, 188.
108. José Camacho to Rita Suárez del Villar, October 9, 1899, Box 1, file 3, AHPC/RSV.
109. John C. Bates to Adjutant General, January 28, 1899, Box 1, File 196, USNAI/RUSA/RG 395/E 1331.
110. José Miguel Gómez to John C. Bates, April 4, 1899, Box 9, File 2344, USNAII/MGC/RG 140/E 3.
111. Cienfuegos City Council Minutes, February 7, 1899; April 28, 1899, Volume 43, folios 10, 68, AHPC/AC.
112. C. J. Stevens to Adjutant General, May 6, 1899, Box 7, No File, RUSA/RG 395/E 1331; Judge Advocate's Office to Adjutant General, Dept. of Matanzas and Santa Clara, July 3, 1899, Oversize Box 1, File 2, USNAI/RUSA/RG 395/E 1331.
113. Judge Advocate's Office to Adjutant General, Dept. of Matanzas and Santa Clara, July 3, 1899, Oversize Box 1, File 2, USNAI/RUSA/RG 395/E 1331; Cienfuegos City Council Minutes, April 28, 1899, Volume 43, folio 68, AHPC/AC.
114. Juan B. Cabrera, "Reports officers and men of Cuban army employed by the US," March 26, 1899, Box 2, File 2337, USNAI/RUSA/RG 395/E 1466. To determine the racial backgrounds of the police, I cross-referenced the March 1899 list of veterans from the Brigade of Cienfuegos with military pension records, notarial records, military diaries and journals, and a database of Cienfuegos veterans created by Orlando García Martínez.
115. "The Engineering and Sanitary Renovation of Havana under U. S. Military Government," *Engineering News* 42: 15 (1899): 243; Sacks, "Police Repression," 800–801; "Americanizing Havana's Police," *Leslie's Weekly*, March 19, 1899, Volume 88, 184.

116. "List of officers selected for police force, Cienfuegos," January 29, 1899, Box 2, File 383, USNAI/RUSA/RG 395/E 1466.
117. José de Jesús Monteagudo to General James H. Wilson, May 31, 1899, Box 11, File 5221, USNAI/RUSA/RG 395/E 1331.
118. José de Jesús Monteagudo to General James H. Wilson, May 31, 1899, Box 11, File 5221, USNAI/RUSA/RG 395/E 1331; Major General Bates to Adjutant General, April 24, 1899, Box 11, File 5062, USNAI/RUSA/RG 395/E 1331; Capt. C. J. Stevens, "Submits report relative to the rural police of the Province of Santa Clara," June 9, 1899, Box 11, File 5062, USNAI/RUSA/RG 395/E 1331.
119. "Major General Bates to Adjutant General," April 24, 1899, Box 11, File 2601, USNAII/MGC/RG 140/E 3.
120. "Capt. C. J. Stevens submits report relative to the rural police of the Province of Santa Clara," June 9, 1899, Box 11, File 5062, USNAI/RUSA/RG 395/E 1331; "José de Jesús Monteagudo to General James H. Wilson," May 31, 1899, Box 11, File 5221 USNAI/RUSA/RG 395/E 1331.
121. E. I. Helmick to Adjutant General, "Submits reports of the operations of his officer[s] for the year ending June 30, 1900," July 11, 1900, File 6367, Box 41, USNA/RUSA/RG 395/E 1331.
122. "Historia Militar del Mayor General Jefe de las Fuerzas Armadas José de Jesús Monteagudo y Consuegra," [n.d.], Legajo 4, Expediente 318, Fondo de Manuel García Garófalo, AHPVC.
123. José de Jesús Monteagudo, "List of Individuals from the Cuban Army Employed, April 1, 1899, Box 2, File 2337, USNAI/RUSA/RG 395/E 1466; Capt. C. J. Stevens, "Report relative to the rural police of the Province of Santa Clara, June 9, 1899, Box 11, File 5062, USNAI/RUSA/RG 395/E 1331; Zeuske, "'Los Negros hicimos la independencia.'" in Martínez Heredia, Scott. and García Martínez, *Espacios*, 218; García Martínez, "La Brigada de Cienfuegos," in Martínez Heredia, Scott, and García Martínez, *Espacios*, 175, 188; Roloff, *Indice alfabético*; Capt. C. J. Stevens, "Report relative to the rural police of the Province of Santa Clara, June 9, 1899, Box 11, File 5062, USNAI/RUSA/RG 395/E 1331; Wilson, *Annual Report*, 1899, 217; "Remigio González," [n.d.], RG 165/E 92.
124. Capt. C. J. Stevens, "Submits report relative to the rural police of the Province of Santa Clara," June 9, 1899, Box 11, File 5062, USNAI/RUSA/RG 395/E 1331.
125. Edwin F. Atkins to General James H. Wilson, October 5, 1899, Box 2, File Atkins, LOC/MD/JHW; Wilson, *Annual Report*, 1899, 108.
126. Breu, *Hard-Boiled Masculinities*, 6; Nurse, "Masculinities in Transition," in Reddock, *Interrogating Caribbean Masculinities*, 8–11; Viveros Vigoya, "Contemporary Latin American Perspectives on Masculinity," in Gutmann, *Changing Men and Masculinities*, 36–37.
127. Edwin F. Atkins to L O'Brien Esq., January 16, 1899, Volume II.19, folio 23, MHS/EFA; Carlos Betancourt to Maximo Gómez, November 17, 1899, Legajo 35, Exp. 4434

new (4997 old), ANC/FPMG; Atkins, *Sixty Years in Cuba*, 179; Barnet, *Biografía de un Cimarrón*, 188.
128. Edwin F. Atkins to L. Darlyshrie, March 3, 1899, Volume II.19, folio 209, MHS/EFA.
129. Atkins, *Sixty Years in Cuba*, 302.
130. Edwin F. Atkins to Brooks, April 4, 1899, Volume, II.19, folio 304, MHS/EFA.
131. "Towns held by Cuban Brigands," *New York Herald*, June 6, 1899, Volume II.60, folio 47, MHS/EFA.
132. Balboa Navarro, *La protesta rural en Cuba*; Ferrer, *Insurgent Cuba*; Pérez, *Lords of the Mountain*; Schwartz, *Lawless Liberators*; Ramón Sánchez Varona, "Testimony in the Case of Constancia Sugar Co.," Box 85, Part 1, folio 6, USNAII/STCC/RG 76/E 352.
133. "Towns Held by Cuban Brigands," *New York Herald*, June 6, 1899, Volume II.60, folio 47, MHS/EFA.
134. "News is Suppressed," newspaper clipping, May 11, 1899, Volume II.60, folio 16, MHS/EFA.
135. "Terrorized by Cuban Bandits," *New York Herald*, June 7, 1899, Volume II.60, folio 49, MHS/EFA; "News is Suppressed," *Boston Herald*, May 11, 1899, Volume II.60, folio 16, MHS/EFA; "Towns Held by Cuban Brigands," *New York Herald*, June 6, 1899, Volume II.60, folio 47, MHS/EFA.
136. Buffington, *Criminal and Citizen*, 3-8; Chambers, *From Subjects to Citizens*, 172-73, 190.
137. Bronfman, *Measures of Equality*, 124-134; Colón Pichardo, *¿Es fácil ser hombre y difícil ser negro?*, 73-91; Helg, "Black Men," 576-604; Stepan, *"Hour of Eugenics,"* 50-54.

CHAPTER FIVE

1. On US officials' opposition to the Teller Amendment during the early occupation, see Pérez, *Cuba between Empires*, 271-78.
2. James H. Wilson to Captain Arthur Murray, May 25, 1899, Box 44, LOC/MD/JHW.
3. James H. Wilson to Colonel Bluford Wilson, July 15, 1899, Box 44, LOC/MD/JHW.
4. James H. Wilson to William Potter, February 22, 1899, Box 43, Volume 2, LOC/MD/JHW.
5. James H. Wilson to J. B. Foraker, May 12, 1899, Box 44, LOC/MD/JHW.
6. James H. Wilson to J. B. Foraker, May 12, 1899, Box 44, LOC/MD/JHW.
7. James H. Wilson to Colonel Bluford Wilson, July 15, 1899, Box 44, LOC/MD/JHW.
8. James H. Wilson to Warren Green, Esq, January 21, 1899, Box 43, LOC/MD/JHW; James H. Wilson to Asa P. Potter, Esq., January 14, 1899, Box 43, LOC/MD/JHW; "Affairs at Matanzas," January 11, 1899, *Los Angeles Herald*.
9. James H. Wilson to Honorable Anthony Higgins, Matanzas, July 15, 1899, Box 44, LOC/MD/JHW.

10. Similar riots erupted in other parts of Santa Clara, Matanzas, and elsewhere. See "Los sucesos de anoche," *La Patria*, Sagua, September 14, 1899, Box 1, No File, USNAI/RUSA/RG 395/E 1340; "El Colmo," *El Pensamiento Español*, Cárdenas, June 7, 1899, Box 22, File 5460, USNAII/MGC/RG 140/E 3.
11. I use the term US civilian employees to denote US citizens who worked for the military government in a civilian capacity, as opposed to forming part of the US military.
12. United States War Department, *Census of Cuba*, 403–33.
13. "Españoles y Cubanos," *Ecos Populares*, August 4, 1900 (Cienfuegos: Tipografía de B Valero, 1900," 118, Legajo 90, Expediente 4425, ANC/FA.
14. On intersectionality, see Crenshaw, "Mapping the Margins."
15. On the relationship between public and private masculine authority, see for example, Miller Lubbock, *Contested Communities*, 72.
16. Francisco de Ostolaza, "Transmits depositions in the shooting affair at the office of Capt. W. B. Barker (Deposition of Andrés Herrera y Fernández)," May 17, 1899, Box 7, File 3915, USNAI/RUSA/RG 395/E 1331. For a more detailed discussion of race and labor mobilization, see Lucero, "'In this Matter of Dignity,'" in Hoyer and Falola, *Human Rights, Race and Resistance*.
17. Dr. Vieta to Superintendent Correctional and Charitable Institutions of Matanzas, June 6, 1900, Box 36, File 3118, USNAI/RUSA/RG 395/E 1331.
18. Walter B. Barker to Chief Quartermaster, "Reports having no funds to pay laborers," February 3, 1899, Box 5, File1562, USNAI/RUSA/RG 395/E 1466. Emphasis in original.
19. Walter B. Barker to J. H. Dorst, Adjutant General, "Deposition of Eligio A. Brunet," June 19, 1899, Box 12, File 5573, USNAI/RUSA/RG 395/E 1331.
20. Vice United States Consul at Cienfuegos to Assistant Secretary of State, July 3, 1897, Dispatches of the US Consulate in Cienfuegos, Microfilm Reel #5, WRD/UNC/USCC.
21. Walter B. Barker to J. H. Dorst, Adjutant General, "Deposition of Eligio A. Brunet," June 19, 1899, Box 12, File 5573, USNAI/RUSA/RG 395/E 1331.
22. Walter B. Barker to J. H. Dorst, Adjutant General, "Deposition of Charles H. Evans," June 19, 1899, Box 12, File 5573, USNAI/RUSA/RG 395/E 1331.
23. "A Fighting Consul was Barker, of Sagua," *New York Journal*, April 11, 1898; "The Cause of Cuba," *Washington Evening Star*, May 17, 1897; "Gunboats for Cuba," *Washington Post*, May 17, 1897.
24. Walter B. Barker to C. E. Dempsey, May 18, 1899, Box 7, File 3868, USNAI/RUSA/RG 395/E 1331.
25. Walter B. Barker to J. H. Dorst, Adjutant General, "Deposition of Luis Lewis," June 19, 1899, Box 12, File 5573, USNAI/RUSA/RG 395/E 1331.
26. Walter B. Barker to J. H. Dorst, Adjutant General, "Deposition of Eligio A. Brunet," June 19, 1899, Box 12, File 5573, USNAI/RUSA/RG 395/E 1331.

27. Walter B. Barker to J. H. Dorst, Adjutant General, "Deposition of F. N. Alduncin," June 19, 1899, Box 12, File 5573, USNAI/RUSA/RG 395/E 1331; "Report on Matter of Disturbance," 18 May 1899, Box 7, File1636 RUSA/RG 395/E 1331.
28. Francisco de Ostolazo, "Transmits depositions in the shooting affair at the office of Capt. W. B. Barker," May 17, 1899, Box 7, File 3915, USNAI/RUSA/RG 395/E 1331; Walter B. Barker to J. H. Dorst, Adjutant General, "Deposition of Charles H. Evans," June 19, 1899, Box 12, File 5573, USNAI/RUSA/RG 395/E 1331.
29. Francisco de Ostolazo, "Transmits depositions in the shooting affair at the office of Capt. W. B. Barker," May 17, 1899, Box 7, File 3915, USNAI/RUSA/RG 395/E 1331; Walter B. Barker to J. H. Dorst, Adjutant General, "Deposition of Charles H. Evans," June 19, 1899, Box 12, File 5573, USNAI/RUSA/RG 395/E 1331.
30. James H. Wilson to Colonel Bluford Wilson, July 15, 1899, Box 44, LOC/MD/JH. On the notion of gratitude, see Pérez, "Incurring a Debt of Gratitude."
31. Judge Advocate's Office to Adjutant General, Dept. of Matanzas and Santa Clara, July 3, 1899, Oversize Box 1, File 2, folios 32–37, USNAI/RUSA/RG 395/E 1331.
32. On critiques, Luis, "Politics of Memory," 478. Although questions about the historical accuracy of Barnet's *Cimarrón* have rightly criticized the heavy editorial hand of the "mediator" in shaping the narrative, ample historical documentation seems to corroborate Montejo's presence in this event. Zeuske, "Cimarrón in the Archives."
33. "Foky, Foky," seemingly a perversion of the American expression and vulgar euphemism for sex—"fuck"—seemed to be a phrase widely used in communication between Americans and prostitutes, pimps, or madams. See, for example, "Court-Martial of James B. Hughes," August 31, September 5, 1899, Case number 13738, USNA/CMR/RG 153/E 15.
34. José Antonio Frías to Walter B. Barker, June 2, 1899, Libro Copiador de Cartas, Aarchivo Histórico Municipal de Trinidad/Fondo Ayuntamiento (hereafter, AHMT/FA).
35. Barnet, *Biografía de un Cimarrón*, 190–91.
36. Barnet, *Biografía de un Cimarrón*, 190–91.
37. Barnet, *Biografía de un Cimarrón*, 191.
38. Judge Advocate's Office to Adjutant General, Dept. of Matanzas and Santa Clara, July 3, 1899, Oversize Box 1, File 2, folio 19, USNAI/RUSA/RG 395/E 1331.
39. Newspaper Clipping, *La Tribuna*, July 5, 1899, Box 13, File 6092, USNAI/RUSA/RG 395/E 1331; "Court-Martial of Frank D. Bennett," August 28-September 9, 1899, Case number 13333, USNA/CMR/RG 153/E 15; James H. Wilson to William L. Bull, August 12, 1899, Box 44, Volume V, folio 47, LOC/MD/JHW.
40. E. B. Fenton to General James H. Wilson, July 16, 1899, Box 15, File 7021, USNAI/RUSA/RG 395/E 1331.
41. "The Cienfuegos Affair," *Havana Herald*, June 30, 1899, Box 21, File 6059, USNAII/MGC/RG 140/E 3.

42. Francisco de Ostolazo, "Submits papers bearing on the 'inquest carried on for assault to agents of the authority' believing that he has no jurisdiction in the case," May 17, 1899, Box 7, File 4243, USNAI/RUSA/RG 395/E 1331.
43. Walter B. Barker, "Reply yours 15th requesting to be informed of the facts about the trouble between Q. M. employees and Cienfuegos police," June 19, 1899, Box 12, File 5573, USNA/RUSA/RG 395E 1331.
44. Francisco de Ostolazo, "Submits papers bearing on the 'inquest carried on for assault to agents of the authority' believing that he has no jurisdiction in the case," May 17, 1899, Box 7, File 4243, USNAI/RUSA/RG 395/E 1331.
45. Walter B. Barker to J. H. Dorst, Adjutant General, "Deposition of Charles H. Evans," June 19, 1899, Box 12, File 5573, USNAI/RUSA/RG 395/E 1331.
46. Walter B. Barker to J. H. Dorst, Adjutant General, "Deposition of Luis Lewis," June 19, 1899, Box 12, File 5573, USNAI/RUSA/RG 395/E 1331.
47. Walter B. Barker to C. E. Dempsey, May 18, 1899, Box 7, File 3868, USNAI/RUSA/RG 395/E 1331.
48. C. J. Stevens to Adjutant General, 6 May 1899, Box 7, No File, RUSA/RG 395/E 1331.
49. José Miguel Gómez to James H. Wilson, June 3, 1899, Box 9, File 4667, USNAI/RUSA/RG 395/E 1331;
50. Eli A. Helmick to A. W. Corliss, April 2, 1900, Box 36, File 2867, USNAI/RUSA/RG 395/E 1331.
51. José Antonio Frías to John C. Bates, April 10, 1899, Libro Copiador de Cartas, AHMT/FA.
52. José Antonio Frías to John C. Bates, April 14, 1899, Libro Copiador de Cartas, AHMT/FA; José Antonio Frías to Chief of Police of the Department of Santa Clara, May 6, 1899, Libro Copiador de Cartas, AHMT/FA.
53. Judge Advocate's Office to Adjutant General, Dept. of Matanzas and Santa Clara, July 3, 1899, Oversize Box 1, File 2, folios 32–33, USNAI/RUSA/RG 395/E 1331, 32.
54. Judge Advocate's Office to Adjutant General, Dept. of Matanzas and Santa Clara, July 3, 1899, Oversize Box 1, File 2, folio 7, USNAI/RUSA/RG 395/E 1331, 32.
55. Judge Advocate's Office to Adjutant General, Dept. of Matanzas and Santa Clara, July 3, 1899, Oversize Box 1, File 2, folios 32–33, USNAI/RUSA/RG 395/E 1331, 32.
56. Judge Advocate's Office to Adjutant General, Dept. of Matanzas and Santa Clara, July 3, 1899, Oversize Box 1, File 2, folios 47, 64, USNAI/RUSA/RG 395/E 1331, 32.
57. Major Bowman, "Makes report on the disturbance at Cienfuegos," June 24, 1899, Box 12, File 4389, USNAI/RUSA/RG 395/E 1331.
58. Major Bowman, "Makes report on the disturbance at Cienfuegos," June 24, 1899, Box 12, File 4389, folio 123, USNAI/RUSA/RG 395/E 1331; J. M. Rodriguez, "Certificate," July 18, 1899," Oversize Box 1, File 2, USNAI/RUSA/RG 395/E 1331.
59. Judge Advocate's Office to Adjutant General, Dept. of Matanzas and Santa Clara, July 3, 1899, Oversize Box 1, File 2, USNAI/RUSA/RG 395/E 1331, 11; "Wilson demoliendo," *La Tribuna*, Cienfuegos, August 23, 1899, Box 1, No File, USNAI/RG 395/RUSA/E 1352.

60. Major 2nd Infantry to Mayor, June 24, 1899, Oversize Box 1, File 2, USNAI/RUSA/RG 395/E 1331.
61. Judge Advocate's Office to Adjutant General, Dept. of Matanzas and Santa Clara, July 3, 1899, Oversize Box 1, File 2, folio 28, USNAI/RUSA/RG 395/E 1331.
62. C. J. Stevens to Adjutant General, 6 May 1899, Box 7, No File, RUSA/RG 395/E 1331.
63. Wilson, *Annual Report*, 1899, 230, 25.
64. C. J. Stevens, "Report on the Municipal Police of the Department," September 5, 1899, Box 21, File 8062, RUSA/RG 395/E 1331.
65. Judge Advocate's Office to Adjutant General, Dept. of Matanzas and Santa Clara, July 3, 1899, Oversize Box 1, File 2, folios 38, 74, USNAI/RUSA/RG 395/E 1331.
66. Judge Advocate's Office to Adjutant General, Dept. of Matanzas and Santa Clara, July 3, 1899, Oversize Box 1, File 2, folios 27–28, 32, 46, USNAI/RUSA/RG 395/E 1331; Walter B. Barker to C. E. Dempsey, May 18, 1899, Box 7, File 3868, USNAI/RUSA/RG 395/E 1331.
67. Judge Advocate's Office to Adjutant General, Dept. of Matanzas and Santa Clara, July 3, 1899, Oversize Box 1, File 2, folio 24, USNAI/RUSA/RG 395/E 1331.
68. Judge Advocate's Office to Adjutant General, Dept. of Matanzas and Santa Clara, July 3, 1899, Oversize Box 1, File 2, folios 27–28, 32, 46, USNAI/RUSA/RG 395/E 1331.
69. For an analysis of how the US Southerners envisioned race and authority, see Gilmore, *Gender and Jim Crow*, 72–74.
70. Francisco de Ostolazo, "Submits papers bearing on the 'inquest carried on for assault to agents of the authority' believing that he has no jurisdiction in the case," May 17, 1899, Box 7, File 4243, USNAI/RUSA/RG 395/E 1331.
71. Orestes Ferrara, "Forwards copy of report of Mayor of Cienfuegos on the disorder occurring at that place," May 16, 1899, Box 7, File 3869, USNAI/RUSA/RG 395/E 1331. In the testimonies, the interim mayor's name appears as Pedro Hernández, but the acting mayor during that time was Pablo Modesto Hernández, the fifth deputy mayor under the last city council appointed under Spanish rule in 1898.
72. Judge Advocate's Office to Adjutant General, Dept. of Matanzas and Santa Clara, July 3, 1899, Oversize Box 1, File 2, folios 27–28, 32, 46, USNAI/RUSA/RG 395/E 1331.
73. Judge Advocate's Office to Adjutant General, Dept. of Matanzas and Santa Clara, July 3, 1899, Oversize, p. 42.
74. J. M. Rodriguez, "Certificate," July 18, 1899, Oversize Box 1, File 2, USNAI/RUSA/RG 395/E 1331.
75. Orestes Ferrara, "Forwards copy of report of Mayor of Cienfuegos on the disorder occurring at that place," May 16, 1899, Box 7, File 3869, USNAI/RUSA/RG 395/E 1331.
76. James H. Wilson to Edwin F. Atkins, June 13, 1899, Box 44, LOC/MD/JHW.
77. "El General Wilson y los empleados civiles y militares. Buena Disposición.

Reconociendo errores. Censuras oficiales," *La Tribuna*, Cienfuegos, July 14, 1899, Box 1, No File, USNAI/RUSA/RG 395/E 1340.
78. Walter B. Barker to Senator Redfield Proctor, May 24, 1899, Folder 5, MSU/MML/FACF; Walter B. Barker to Orville H. Platt, January 4, 1900, Folder 5, MSU/MML/FACF.
79. Walter B. Barker to Senator Redfield Proctor, May 24, 1899, Folder 5, MSU/MML/FACF; Walter B. Barker to Orville H. Platt, January 4, 1900, Folder 5, MSU/MML/FACF; Walter B. Barker to C. E. Dempsey, May 18, 1899, Box 7, File 3868, USNAI/RUSA/RG 395/E 1331.
80. Major 2nd Infantry to Mayor, June 24, 1899, Oversize Box 1, File 2, USNAI/RUSA/RG 395/E 1331.
81. Walter B. Barker to Adna R. Chaffee, December 2, 1899, Folder 5, MSU/MML/FACF.
82. Walter B. Barker to J. H. Dorst, Adjutant General, "Deposition of Eligio A. Brunet," June 19, 1899, Box 12, File 5573, USNAI/RUSA/RG 395/E 1331.
83. Walter B. Barker to J. H. Dorst, Adjutant General, "Deposition of Eligio A. Brunet," June 19, 1899, Box 12, File 5573, USNAI/RUSA/RG 395/E 1331.
84. Judge Advocate's Office to Adjutant General, Dept. of Matanzas and Santa Clara, July 3, 1899, Oversize Box 1, File 2, folio 9, USNAI/RUSA/RG 395/E 1331; Third United States Volunteer Engineers, *David DuBose Gaillard* (Saint Louis, 1916), 15.
85. Rudyard Kipling, "The White Man's Burden," *McClure's Magazine* 12 (February 1899).

CHAPTER SIX

1. Foner, *Spanish-Cuba-American War*, 433–51.
2. Pérez, *Cuba between Empires*, 255–57.
3. José Antonio Frías to James H. Wilson, June 17, 1899, Libro Copiador de Cartas, Fondo Ayuntamiento, AHMT/FA; Major General John C. Bates to Adjutant, Division of Cuba, March 18, 1899, Box 7 File 2020, USNAI/RUSA/RG 395/E 1331.
4. James H. Wilson to General John Rutter Brooke, June 19, 1899, Box 44, folio 327, LOC/MD/JHW.
5. "Refuse to Disband: Cubans May Attempt an Armed Demonstration," newspaper clipping, May 15, 1899, Volume II.60, folio 21, MHS/EFA.
6. "Reunión de Libertadores," periódico no identificado, November 16, 1899, Legajo 292, Expediente 35, ANC/DR.
7. "Ni limosna, ni propina," *El Pueblo* (Santa Clara), May 22, 1899, Box 1, No File, USNAI/RUSA/RG 395/E 1340.
8. Ni limosna, ni propina," *El Pueblo* (Santa Clara), May 22, 1899, Box 1, No File, USNAI/RUSA/RG 395/E 1340.
9. Ni limosna, ni propina," *El Pueblo* (Santa Clara), May 22, 1899, Box 1, No File, USNAI/RUSA/RG 395/E 1340.

10. "Provocación. Deslindemos los campos," *La Tribuna*, Cienfuegos, May 22, 1899, Box 1, No File, USNAI/RUSA/RG 395/E 1340.
11. Adna R. Chaffee to General James H. Wilson, "Translation of manifesto 'To the Valiant Army of Las Villas,'" June 12, 1899, Box 11, No File, USNAI/RUSA/RG 395/E 1331.
12. "Fuera Caretas!" in *El Siglo Semanario*, Cienfuegos, September 13, 1899, Legajo 575, Expediente 1, ANC/DR
13. James H. Wilson to Colonel Frank J. Hecker, May 25, 1899, Box 44, Volume III, folio 156, LOC/MD/JHW.
14. James H. Wilson to Colonel Frank J. Hecker, May 25, 1899, Box 44, Volume III, folio 156, LOC/MD/JHW.
15. "Provocación: Deslindemos los campos," *La Tribuna*, May 22, 1899, Box 1, No File, USNAI/RUSA/RG 395/E 1340.
16. "Tonos subidos," *La Correspondencia*, May 22, 1899, Box 1, No File, USNAI/RUSA/RG 395/E 1340.
17. "Provocación: Deslindemos los campos," *La Tribuna*, May 22, 1899, Box 1, No File, USNAI/RUSA/RG 395/E 1340.
18. Pérez, *Cuba between Empires*, 255–57; Máximo Gómez to John R. Brooke, May 13, 1899, Box 15, File 3151, USNAII/MGC/RG 140/E 3; For a detailed account of the role and criticism of Máximo Gómez in the disbandment of the Cuban Army, see Foner, *Spanish-Cuba-American War*, 433–51.
19. Foner, 434.
20. "Military Order No. 53," May 9, 1899, Box 14, No File, USNAI/RUSA/RG 395/E 1331.
21. "Fuera Caretas!" in *El Siglo Semanario*, Cienfuegos, September 13, 1899, Legajo 575, Expediente 1, ANC/DR.
22. A Mexican, "Regarding collection of arms by Cuban police," April 6, 1899, Box 3A, File 3019, USNAI/RUSA/RG 395/E 1466. Captain Beal, the manager of Soledad estate also protested when Lieutenant Colonel Machado arrived to the estate to disarm "all people about the colony." Captain Beal, "Protests and request[s] to be allowed to carry arms," April 3, 1899, Box 3A, File 425, USNAI/RUSA/RG 395/E 1466.
23. Captain Fenton to Adjutant General, June 24, 1899, Box 12, File 5347, USNAI/RUSA/RG 395/E 1331.
24. "Bowman, Maj. 2nd Infty, telegram states that about two hundred ex Cuban soldiers arrived in city . . . ," June 20, 1899, Box 12, File 5367, USNAI/RUSA/RG 395/E 1331; In Quemado de Güines, a ball celebrating the entry of the Cuban forces into the city had one ballroom for whites, and a separate hall for blacks. In Rancho Veloz, the Club Maceo put on a celebration for black soldiers. Sanjenis, *Mis cartas*, 414, 406.
25. Domingo Méndez Capote, "Report of the Alcalde Santa Isabel de las Lajas . . . ," November 29, 1899, Box 35, File 6462, USNAII/MGC/RG 140/E 3; José Miguel

Gómez to Secretary of Government, November 28, 1899, Box 35, No File, USNAII/ MGC/RG 140/E 3; Consejo Territorial de los veteranos de la independencia de la provincia de Matanzas, "A los amantes de la independencia de Cuba," November 29, 1899, Box 35, File 8815, USNAII/MGC/RG 140/E 3.

26. F. J. Kernan, Captain and Adjutant 2nd Infantry to The Adjutant, Rowell Barracks, January 27, 1900, Box 42, File 86, USNAII/MGC/RG 140/E 3.
27. A. H. Bowman, "Reports circumstances attending the Death of General Gil (negro) late of the Cuban Army," 4 January 1900, Box 42, File 136, USNAII/MGC/ RG 140/E 3.
28. Brigadier General James H. Wilson to Adjutant General Hugh L. Scott, January 1, 1900, Box 42, File 86, USNAII/MGC/RG 140/E 3; Mayor J. A. Frías, "States that the lower class of colored people asked to have the body of General Gil turn over to them for embalming, guarding and burial with honors . . . ," December 30, 1899, 6th Endorsement, February 3, 1900, Box 29, File 20, USNAI/RUSA/RG 395/ E 1331.
29. Perfecto Gil to Máximo Gómez, [n.d.], Box 9, File 1265-B, ANC/FMG.
30. General Máximo Gómez to General Leonard Wood, March 1, 1900. Courtesy of Orlando F. García Martínez.
31. "Hechos Lamentables," in *El Telégrafo: Periódico Político*, January 1900, AHMT/FH.
32. "The Mayor J. A. Frías states that the lower class of colored people asked to have the body of General Gil turn over to them for embalming, guarding and burial with honors . . . ," December 30, 1899, Box 29, File 20 USNAI/RUSA/RG 395/E 1331.
33. Perfecto Gil to Máximo Gómez, [n.d.], Box 9, File 1265-B ANC, ANC/FMG.
34. Nicolás Valverde to Juan Gualberto Gómez," October 26, 1901, Box 48, File 32, Number 3831, ANC/FA; Cienfuegos City Council Minutes, January 10, 1902, Volume 50, AHPC/AC; Nicolás Valverde to Juan Gualberto Gómez," May 18, 1902, Box 48, File 32, Number 3831, ANC/FA.
35. A. H. Bowman to Adjutant General, Department of Matanzas and Santa Clara, January 4, 1900, Box 42, File 136, USNAII/MGC/RG 140/E 3.
36. "The Mayor J. A. Frías states that the lower class of colored people asked to have the body of General Gil turn over to them for embalming, guarding and burial with honors . . . ," December 30, 1899, Box 29, File 20 USNAI/RUSA/RG 395/E 1331; García Martínez, "Caciques, elites, clientelas," 106.
37. Musgrave, *Under Three Flags in Cuba*, 163.
38. "Hechos Lamentables," in *El Telégrafo: Periódico Político*, January 1900, AHMT/FH.
39. José B. Alemán, "La muerte de Gil," in *La Tribuna*, newspaper clipping, [n.d.], File 382, Box 42, USNAII/MGC/RG 140/E 3.
40. F. J. Kernan, Captain and Adjutant 2nd Infantry to The Adjutant, Rowell Barracks, January 27, 1900, Box 42, File 86, USNAII/MGC/RG 140/E 3; "La Muerte de Gil," in *El Telégrafo: Periódico Político*, 21 January 1900, AHMT/FH.
41. "Mayor J. A. Frías states that the lower class of colored people asked to have the

body of General Gil turn over to them for embalming, guarding and burial with honors ...," December 30, 1899, 6th Endorsement, February 3, 1900, Box 29, File 20, USNAI/RUSA/RG 395/E 1331.
42. Tribunal Supremo, *Jurisprudencia del Tribunal Supremo*, vol. III, 70.
43. Brigadier General James H. Wilson to Adjutant General Hugh L. Scott, January 1, 1900, Box 42, File 86, USNAII/MGC/RG 140/E 3.
44. Tribunal Supremo, *Jurisprudencia del Tribunal Supremo*, 70.
45. F. J. Kernan, Captain and Adjutant 2nd Infantry to The Adjutant, Rowell Barracks, January 27, 1900, Box 42, File 86, USNAII/MGC/RG 140/E 3; Tribunal Supremo, *Jurisprudencia del Tribunal Supremo*, 70.
46. Possibly refers to officer Ambrosio Hernández, as no officer by the name of Antonio Hernández appears on the roster. José Miguel Gómez, "States that the Mayor of Cienfuegos has notified him of the killing by a policeman of the ex-general Gil of the Cuban Army," December 30, 1899, Box 31, File 24, USNAI/RUSA/RG 395/E 1331.
47. "Hechos Lamentables," in *El Telégrafo: Periódico Político*, January 1900, AHMT/FH.
48. "La Muerte de Gil," *El Telégrafo: Periódico Político*, January 21, 1900, AMHT/FH.
49. F. J. Kernan, Captain and Adjutant 2nd Infantry to The Adjutant, Rowell Barracks, January 27, 1900, Box 42, File 86, USNAII/MGC/RG 140/E 3.
50. "La Muerte de Gil," in *El Telégrafo: Periódico Político*, January 21 1900, AHMT/FH.
51. Tribunal Supremo, *Jurisprudencia del Tribunal Supremo*, 72.
52. F. J. Kernan, Captain and Adjutant 2nd Infantry to The Adjutant, Rowell Barracks, January 27, 1900, Box 42, File 86, USNAII/MGC/RG 140/E 3.
53. "La Muerte de Gil," in *El Telégrafo: Periódico Político*, January 21, 1900, AHMT/FH.
54. F. J. Kernan, Captain and Adjutant 2nd Infantry to The Adjutant, Rowell Barracks, January 27, 1900, Box 42, File 86, USNAII/MGC/RG 140/E 3.
55. F. J. Kernan, Captain and Adjutant 2nd Infantry to The Adjutant, Rowell Barracks, January 27, 1900, Box 42, File 86, USNAII/MGC/RG 140/E 3.
56. Captain Pedro P. Mutos and Commandant Juan Sardiñas y Villa, "To the Colored Race, Glory to General Gil," January 27, 1900, Box 42, File 86, USNAII/MGC/RG 140/E 3.
57. Captain Pedro P. Mutos and Commandant Juan Sardiñas y Villa, "To the Colored Race, Glory to General Gil," January 27, 1900, Box 42, File 86, USNAII/MGC/RG 140/E 3.
58. El Ciudadano Pedro P. Mutos, "A Los Ciudadanos Cubanos," September 8, 1898, Legajo 106, Expediente 267, Archivo Nacional de Cuba, Fondo Academia de Historia (hereafter, ANC/FAH).
59. Captain Pedro P. Mutos and Commandant Juan Sardiñas y Villa, "To the Colored Race, Glory to General Gil," January 27, 1900, Box 42, 86, USNAII/MGC/RG 140/E 3.
60. Captain Pedro P. Mutos and Commandant Juan Sardiñas y Villa, "To the Colored Race, Glory to General Gil," January 27, 1900, Box 42, 86, USNAII/MGC/RG

140/E 3; José Antonio Frías to A. J. Coriles, January 25, 1900, Libro Copiador de Cartas, Fondo Ayuntamiento, AHMT/FA.
61. "Expediente relativo a la comisión del cónsul de Santo Domingo solicitando detalles sobre la muerte del General del Ejército Libertador dominicano Dionisio Gil," 26 April–9 June 1900: May 10, 1900, Archivo Nacional de Cuba, Fondo Secretario de Estado y Gobernación (Hereafter cited as ANC/FSEG).
62. Perfecto Gil to Máximo Gómez, [n.d.], Box 9, File 1265-B ANC, ANC/FMG.
63. Nicolás Valverde to Juan Gualberto Gómez, May 18, 1902, Box 48, File 32, Number 3831, ANC/FA.
64. García Martínez, "Caciques, elites, clientelas."
65. James H. Wilson, "5th Endorsement," January 11, 1900, Box 49, File 220, USNAII/MGC/RG140/E 3; A. M. Jimenez, "Complains of treatment he has received from mayor of Cienfuegos, September 22, 1899, Box 31, File 8736, USNAII/MGC/RG 140/E 3; José Antonio Frías, "States that no fear has ever existed of a duel between Yznaga and Alemán," September 9, 1899, Box 18, File 8236, USNAI/RUSA/RG 395/E 3.
66. José Antonio Frías to A. H. Bowman, September 23, 1899, Box 19, File 8670, USNAI/RUSA/RG 395/E 1331.
67. Atkins, *Sixty Years in Cuba*, 316; José Miguel Gómez, "Telegram advising that Doctor Frías delivered office to Leopoldo Figueroa," March 2, 1900, Box 55, File 347, USNAII/MGC/RG 140/E 3.
68. Dr. José Antonio Frías, "Petitions repeal of Order 280, these headquarters," July 24, 1900, Box 94, File 2763, Box 94, File 2823, USNAII/MGC/RG 140/E 3.
69. Parker, *Cubans of To-Day*; Roloff, *Indice alfabético*.
70. Bustamante, *Diccionario Biográfico Cienfueguero*.
71. Nicolás Valverde, "Cienfuegos: Tipografía de B Valero, 1900," *Ecos Populares*, August 4, 1900, pp. 116–18, Box 90, File 4425, ANC/FA.
72. Unknown Author to Máximo Gómez, [n.d.], Box 38, File, 4719 (new 5392), ANC/FMG; García Martínez, "Caciques, elites, clientelas," 107.
73. Captain Pedro P. Mutos and Commandant Juan Sardiñas y Villa, "To the Colored Race, Glory to General Gil," January 27, 1900, Box 42, 86, USNAII/MGC/RG 140/E 3; Also see Barnet, *Biografía de un Cimarrón*, 188.
74. Barnet, *Biografía de un Cimarrón*, 188.
75. J. Kernan, Captain and Adjutant 2nd Infantry to The Adjutant, Rowell Barracks, January 27, 1900, Box 42, File 86, USNAII/MGC/RG 140/E 3
76. "Summary of Relevant Facts of the Matanzas Municipal Police," September 30, 1899, Box 19, no file, RUSA/RG 395/E 1331.
77. "The Engineering and Sanitary Renovation of Havana under U. S. Military Government," *Engineering News* 42: 15 (1899): 243.
78. Sacks, "'To Show Who was in Charge,'" 800–801.
79. "Americanizing Havana's Police," *Leslie's Weekly*, March 19, 1899, Volume 88, p. 184.

80. Unknown Author to Máximo Gómez," [n.d.], Box 38, File, 4719 (new 5392), ANC/FMG.
81. Unknown Author to Máximo Gómez," [n.d.], Box 38, File, 4719 (new 5392), ANC/FMG.
82. Unknown Author to Máximo Gómez," [n.d.], Box 38, File, 4719 (new 5392), ANC/FMG.
83. Nicolás Valverde, "Cienfuegos: Tipografía de B Valero, 1900," *Ecos Populares*, August 4, 1900, pp. 116–118, Box 90, File 4425, ANC/FA.
84. Nicolás Valverde, "Cienfuegos: Tipografía de B Valero, 1900," *Ecos Populares*, August 4, 1900, pp. 116–118, Box 90, File 4425, ANC/FA.
85. Henry A. Bailing to Commanding Officer, Rowell Barracks, August 7, 1900, Box 109, File 244, USNAII/MGC/RG 140/E 3; Geo C. Saffarans to Adjutant 10th Infantry, August 9, 1900, Box 109, File 244, USNAII/MGC/RG 140/E 3.
86. José López de Campillo to Leopoldo Figueroa, September 8, 1900, Box 109, File 244, USNAII/MGC/RG 140/E 3.

CHAPTER SEVEN

1. James H. Wilson to Colonel Bluford Wilson, June 24, 1899, Box 44, LOC/MD/JHW.
2. See Free, *Suffrage Reconstructed*.
3. Wilson, *Annual Report*, 1899, 88–89.
4. Wilson, *Annual Report*, 1899, 88–89.
5. United States War Department, *Census of Cuba*, 101.
6. Enrique Parrodi, "Protests against order of Gen. Wood allowing all soldiers of the Cuban army to vote in Municipal elections," January 8, 1900, Box 67, File 1327, USNAII/MGC/RG 140/E 3
7. "Hand Bill advising the negroes and laborers to assert themselves for suffrage without restriction," February 15, 1900, Box 72, File 1036, USNAII/MGC/RG 140/E 3.
8. "¡Más verdad y patriotismo!" February 7, 1900, Box 72, File 1036, USNAII/MGC/RG 140/E 3.
9. "Documents relative to the resolutions adopted by the Ayuntamientos [. . .] requesting that suffrage be granted in the coming elections," March 6, 1900, Box 72, File 1305, USNAII/MGC/RG 140/E 3; Enrique Malaret, "Expressing the protest of the Ayuntamiento [of Remedios] against the restriction of suffrage in the next election," March 12, 1900, Box 72, File 1305, USNAII/MGC/RG 140/E 3; M. Lechuga, "Essay on the right to unrestricted suffrage," March 10, 1900, Box 72, File 1305, USNAII/MGC/RG 140/E 3.
10. Ayuntamiento de Cuevitas, "Protesta," February 27, 1900, Box 72, File 1305, USNAII/MGC/RG 140/E 3.
11. Ayuntamiento de Camajuaní, "Protesta," February 27, 1900, Box 72, File 1305, USNAII/MGC/RG 140/E 3

12. "Protesta del Partido Republicano Democrático Federal de la Habana. Libertad, Fraternidad, Igualdad," March 24, 1900, Havana, Legajo 106, Expediente 222, ANC/FAH.
13. Ernest Hamlin Abbott, Lyman Abbott, Francis Rufus Bellamy, and Hamilton Wright Mabie, "The Cuban Elections," *Outlook* 65 (1900): 423.
14. De la Fuente, *A Nation for All*, 57.
15. On convict labor in the US, see Blackmon, *Slavery by Another Name*.
16. "Daily Journal of Brigadier General James H. Wilson," May 12, 1899, Box 53, LOC/MD/JHW.
17. Mayor José Antonio Frías to Dorst, June 13, 1899, Box 11, File 5354, USNAI/RUSA/RG 395/E 1331; Capt. C. J. Stevens, "Report relative to the rural police of the Province of Santa Clara," June 9, 1899, Box 11, File 5062, USNAI/RUSA/RG 395/E 1331; "El Crímen de Cruces," *El Pueblo* (Cienfuegos), June 12, 1899, Box 1, No File, USNAI/RUSA/RG 395/E 1340.
18. "Daily Journal of Brigadier General James H. Wilson," May 12, 1899, Box 53, LOC/MD/JHW; Mayor José Antonio Frías to Dorst, June 13, 1899, Box 11, File 5354, USNAI/RUSA/RG 395/E 1331; Capt. C. J. Stevens, "Report relative to the rural police of the Province of Santa Clara," June 9, 1899, Box 11, File 5062, USNAI/RUSA/RG 395/E 1331; "El Crímen de Cruces," *El Pueblo* (Cienfuegos), June 12, 1899, Box 1, No File, USNAI/RUSA/RG 395/E 1340.
19. "Daily Journal of Brigadier General James H. Wilson," May 12, 1899, Box 53, LOC/MD/JHW.
20. "Edwin F. Atkins, Petition before the Spanish Treaty Claims Commission," December 1905, Box II.4, folio 83, MHS/EFA.
21. Edwin F. Atkins to General James H. Wilson, October 5, 1899, Box 2, LOC/MD/JHW.
22. James H. Wilson to The Editor of *the Herald* of New York City, 22 June 1899, Box 44, JHW/MS/LOC.
23. James H. Wilson to General O. H. Ernst, April 25, 1899, Box 44, LOC/MD/JHW.
24. "La guardia rural," unknown newspaper, Santa Clara, May 9, 1899, USNAI/RG 395/RUSA/E 1352, Box 1, File 3304; James H. Wilson to Colonel John J. McCook, April 23, 1899, Box 44, LOC/MD/JHW; James H. Wilson, "Telegram stating he is considering the advisability of disbanding the rural police on July 1st," June 11, 1899, USNAII/MGC/RG 140/E 3, Box 17, File 3758.
25. "Wilson demoliendo," *La Tribuna*, Cienfuegos, August 23, 1899, Box 1, No File, USNAI/RG 395/RUSA/E 1352.
26. "Wilson demoliendo," *La Tribuna*, Cienfuegos, August 23, 1899, Box 1, No File, USNAI/RG 395/RUSA/E 1352.
27. "El clavo del fraile," *La Tribuna*, Cienfuegos, May 22, 1899, Box 1, No File, USNAI/RUSA/RG 395/E 1340.
28. "La guardia rural," unknown newspaper, Santa Clara, May 9, 1899, USNAI/RG 395/RUSA/E 1352, Box 1, File 3304.

29. "Guardia Rural: necesidad de aumentarla," *La Tribuna*, May 4, 1899, Box 7, File 3339, USNAI/RUSA/RG 395/E 1331; "Wilson demoliendo," *La Tribuna*, Cienfuegos, August 23, 1899, Box 1, No File, USNAI/RG 395/RUSA/E 1352.
30. Edwin F. Atkins to L. Darlyshrie, March 3, 1899, Volume II.19, folio 209–10, MHS/EFA; José de la O. García to John C. Bates, "Requests the authority to carry firearms," March 17, 1899, Box 6, File 1958, USNAI/RUSA/RG 395/E 1466; José Antonio Frías to James H. Wilson, June 19, 1899, Libro Copiador de Cartas, AHMT/FA.
31. Wilson, *Annual Report*, 1899, 225, 86.
32. Wilson, *Annual Report*, 1899, 231.
33. Guillermo Hernández to General James H. Wilson, "States that a party of 25 men, negroes, armed with short [sic] guns and machetes were yesterday on the estate 'Bonachea,'" August 14, 1899, Box 33, File 5997, USNAII/MGC/RG 140/E 3; José de Jesús Monteagudo to General James H. Wilson, May 18, 1899, Box 8, File 4010, USNAI/RUSA/RG 395/E 1331; José Miguel Gómez to General James H. Wilson, "Telegram," May 11, 1899, Box 7, File 3428, USNAI/RUSA/RG 395/E 1331; Mayor of Camarones, Jorge Rodríguez to José Miguel Gómez, November 6, 1899, Box 23, File 9860, USNAI/RUSA/RG 395/E 1331.
34. "Capt. C. J. Stevens submits report relative to the rural police of the Province of Santa Clara," June 9, 1899, Box 11, File 5062, USNAI/RUSA/RG 395/E 1331.
35. Capt. C. J. Stevens, "Submits report relative to the rural police of the Province of Santa Clara," June 9, 1899, Box 11, File 5062, USNAI/RUSA/RG 395/E 1331. Emphasis added. "Rectificando un error," *La Lucha*, July 22, 1899, Box 1, No File, USNAI/RUSA/RG 395/E 1352; Colón Pichardo, *¿Es fácil ser hombre y difícil ser negro?*, 48–49.
36. Capt. C. J. Stevens, "Submits report relative to the rural police of the Province of Santa Clara," June 9, 1899, Box 11, File 5062, USNAI/RUSA/RG 395/E 1331.
37. Capt. C. J. Stevens, "Submits report relative to the rural police of the Province of Santa Clara," June 9, 1899, Box 11, File 5062, USNAI/RUSA/RG 395/E 1331.
38. Wilson, *Annual Report*, 1899, 230; "Capt. C. J. Stevens submits report relative to the rural police of the Province of Santa Clara," June 9, 1899, Box 11, File 5062, USNAI/RUSA/RG 395/E 1331; Casimiro Palacio and 36 others, "State that they have learned to their great surprise of the withdrawal of the Rural Guard from that Municipality," August 28, 1899, Box 18, File 874, USNAI/RUSA/RG 395/E 1331.
39. "Regulations for the Rural Police of the Province of Santa Clara, Cuba," 29 August 1899, Box 31, No File, USNAII/MGC/RG 140/E 3.
40. Capt. C. J. Stevens, "Submits report relative to the rural police of the Province of Santa Clara," June 9, 1899, Box 11, File 5062, USNAI/RUSA/RG 395/E 1331.
41. José Balseiro on behalf of José Denis Rodriguez, "Sentenced to 8 months in Cienfuegos jail for homicide," November 8, 1901, Box 208, File 4724, USNAII/MGC/RG 140/E 3.
42. Capt. C. J. Stevens, "Report relative to the rural police of the Province of Santa Clara," June 9, 1899, Box 11, File 5062, USNAI/RUSA/RG 395/E 1331.

43. Capt. C. J. Stevens, "Submits report relative to the rural police of the Province of Santa Clara," June 9, 1899, Box 11, File 5062, USNAI/RUSA/RG 395/E 1331; José de Jesús Monteagudo "Distribution of [Rural Guard in] the Province" 30 April 1899, Box 31, No File, MGC/RG 140/E 3.
44. "Regulations for the Rural Police, Province of Santa Clara, Cuba, approved by Brigadier General James H. Wilson," August 29, 1899, Box 17, File 8064, USNAI/RUSA/RG 395/E 1331.
45. E. I. Helmick to Adjutant General, "Submits reports of the operations of his officer[s] for the year ending June 30, 1900," July 11, 1900, File 6367, Box 41, USNA/RUSA/RG 395/E 1331.
46. E. I. Helmick to Adjutant General, "Submits reports of the operations of his officer[s] for the year ending June 30, 1900," July 11, 1900, File 6367, Box 41, USNA/RUSA/RG 395/E 1331.
47. E. I. Helmick to Adjutant General, "Submits reports of the operations of his officer[s] for the year ending June 30, 1900," July 11, 1900, File 6367, Box 41, USNA/RUSA/RG 395/E 1331.
48. José de Jesús Monteagudo to Fitzhugh Lee, October 31, 1900, Box 118, File 6105 USNAII/MGC/RG 140/E 3; "O.P. y Policía, Circular," *Boletín Oficial de la Provincia de Santa Clara*, December 16, 1900; E. I. Helmick to Adjutant General, "Submits reports of the operations of his officer [sic] for the year ending June 30, 1900," July 11, 1900, File 6367, Box 41, USNAI/RUSA/RG 395/E 1331.
49. "Regulations for the Rural Police of the Province of Santa Clara, Cuba," 29 August 1899, Box 31, No File, MGC/RG 140/E 3.
50. Pérez, "Supervision of a Protectorate," 258–60.
51. García Martínez, "Caciques, elites, clientelas, y los problemas raciales," 107.
52. José de Jesús Monteagudo to General James H. Wilson, May 18, 1899, Box 8, File 4010, USNAI/RUSA/RG 395/E 1331; José de Jesús Monteagudo, "News from the Chief of the Rural Guard, District of Cienfuegos," May 12, 1899, Box 7, File 3419, USNAI/RUSA/RG 395/E 1331; José Miguel Gómez to General James H. Wilson, "States that the Chief of Police informed him . . . ," August 5, 1899, Box 15, File 7238, USNAI/RUSA/RG 395/E 1331.
53. Manuel Fernández Labrada to Marta Abreu, [n.d., likely 1899], BNJM/FMA, No. 313.
54. "Regulations for the Rural Police of the Province of Santa Clara, Cuba," 29 August 1899, Box 31, No File, MGC/RG 140/E 3. Also in Box 17, File 8064, USNAI/RUSA/RG 395/E 1331.
55. For an examination of race, gender, and vagrancy in Rio de Janeiro, see Gomes da Cunha, "The Stigmas of Dishonor,'" in Caulfield, Chambers, and Putnam, *Honor, Status, and Law*.
56. Pedro E. Betancourt, "Gives his Opinion in regard to the "Evil of Vagrancy" as denounced in a Sagua paper," February 12, 1900, Box 31, File 870, USNA/RUSA/RG 395/E 1331.

57. "Regulations for the Rural Police of the Province of Santa Clara, Cuba," 29 August 1899, Box 31, No File, MGC/RG 140/E 3. Also in Box 17, File 8064, USNAI/RUSA/RG 395/E 1331.
58. "Ejecutoria recaída en causa contra Apolonio Hernández @ Siete por atentados a agentes de la autoridad, July 9, 1899-August 10, 1900, Legajo 1, Expediente 2, AHMT/FJMT; Juicio de faltas el pardo Eulogio Sánchez contra el pardo José Ruíz Varona, Otober 31, 1899 APHC/JMC/JF, legajo 17, escritura 1389.
59. United States War Department, *Census of Cuba*, 198–99.
60. "Una Disposicion contra la Ley," *La Patria*, Sagua, May 18, 1899, Box 1, No File, USNAI/RUSA/RG 395/E 1340.
61. José López y López, "Complaint of abuse and ill treatment," February 10, 1901, Box 155, File 1110, USNAII/MGV/RG 140/E 3.
62. "Malos procedimientos," Unknown newspaper, Cárdenas, November 16, 1899, Box 1, No File, USNAI/RUSA/RG 395/E 1340.
63. "Ejecutoria en causa contra Claudio Sarría por hurto," January 12–October 25, 1901, Legajo 2, Expediente 29, AMHT/FJMT.
64. García Martínez, "La Brigada de Cienfuegos," in Martínez Heredia, Scott, and García Martínez, *Espacios*, 166–69.
65. Averhoff Purón, *Los primeros partidos políticos*, 29–38.
66. A. H. Bowman to Adjutant General, 'Answering letter of April 27th," May 1, 1900, Box 35, File 2460, USNAI/RUSA/RG 395/E 1331.
67. United States Congress, *Receipts and Expenditures in Cuba*, 21.
68. Anonymous to General Leonard Wood, "Complains of the negro Martín Morúa Delgado," April 27, 1900, Box 92, File 2547, USNAII/MGC/RG 140/E 3.
69. Anonymous to General Leonard Wood, "Complains of the negro Martín Morúa Delgado," April 27, 1900, Box 92, File 2547, USNAII/MGC/RG 140/E 3.
70. Gen. Monteagudo, "Telegram stating that the two men who had taken horses and gone to the woods had surrendered themselves and their arms to him and returned the stolen horses," May 11, 1900, Box 94, File 2823, USNAII/MGC/RG 140/E 3.
71. Pres. Veterans Association Baracoa, "Enclosing protest against the revolutionary actions there of Col. Juan Carreras and 40 men," May 17, 1900, Box 94, File 2823, USNAII/MGC/RG 140/E 3.
72. Carlos Roloff, "Telegram stating that he has protests from various people against the attempt to injure the reputation of Lt. Col. Carreras . . . ," May 18, 1900, Box 94, File 2832, USNAII/MGC/RG 140/E 3; President of Veterans Association of Baracoa, "protests against the revolutionary actions of Lt. Col. Carreras and 40 men," May 17, 1900, Box 94, File 2832, USNAII/MGC/RG 140/E 3.
73. Gen. Carlos Roloff, "Telegram stating that Lt. Col. Carreras is reported to him as being quietly attending to his own business at Nibujon, and is well throught [sic] of," May 21, 1900, Box 94, File 2823, USNAII/MGC/RG 140/E 3.
74. José Miguel Gómez, "Enclosing herewith documents bearing on the questions that have produced misrepresentations," May 24, 1900, Box 94, File 2758, USNAII/

MGC/RG 140/E 3; Anonymous, "Letter stating that there will be trouble at Matanzas during the election," April 27, 1900, Box 72, File 1305, USNAII/MGC/RG 140/E 3; Diego de Rojas Sánchez, "States that owing to his being assaulted by the chief of police and abused by various relatives of the present mayor who is candidate for re-election, he has withdrawn his candidacy . . . ," June 2, 1900, Box 35, File 3052, USNAI/RUSA/RG 395/E 1331.

75. José Miguel Gómez, "Enclosing herewith documents bearing on the questions that have produced misrepresentations," May 24, 1900, Box 94, File 2758, USNAII/MGC/RG 140/E 3; Anonymous, "Letter stating that there will be trouble at Matanzas during the election," April 27, 1900, Box 72, File 1305, USNAII/MGC/RG 140/E 3; Diego de Rojas Sánchez, "States that owing to his being assaulted by the chief of police and abused by various relatives of the present mayor who is candidate for re-election, he has withdrawn his candidacy . . . ," June 2, 1900, Box 35, File 3052, USNAI/RUSA/RG 395/E 1331; Eli A. Helmick, "Submits report giving probable causes for the so-called uprising of bandits in Santa Clara province," May 24, 1900, Box 35, File 3574, USNAI/RUSA/RG 395/E 1331.

76. Eli A. Helmick, "Submits report on investigation made at Camajuaní," June 10, 1900, Box 35, File 3248, USNAI/RUSA/RG 395/E 1331.

77. James H. Wilson, "1st Endorsement," June 13, 1900, Box 35, File 3254, USNAI/RUSA/RG 395/E 1331.

78. Eli A. Helmick, "Submits report giving probable causes for the so-called uprising of bandits in Santa Clara province," May 24, 1900, Box 35, File 3574, USNAI/RUSA/RG 395/E 1331.

79. Eli A. Helmick, "Submits report on investigation made at Camajuaní," June 10, 1900, Box 35, File 3248, USNAI/RUSA/RG 395/E 1331.

80. The mulatto carpenter, Arturo Zanyo, the mulatto café owner, Guillermo Pérez, and the mulatto shoemaker, Gerónimo Reguera Batista, ran with Vidal. The black worker and workshop owner Juan Rojas Rodríguez, the mulatto silversmith, Faustino González, and the mulatto workshop owner, Tomas Matarama Rodríguez ran with Naya. José Miguel Gómez, "States that owing to his visit to Santo Domingo, he has been able to make peace between the two candidates," June 10, 1900, Box 35, File 3254, USNAI/RUSA/RG 395/E 1331.

81. José Miguel Gómez, "Enclosing herewith documents bearing on the questions that have produced misrepresentations," May 24, 1900, Box 94, File 2758, USNAII/MGC/RG 140/E 3.

82. José Miguel Gómez, "Enclosing herewith documents bearing on the questions that have produced misrepresentations," May 24, 1900, Box 94, File 2758, USNAII/MGC/RG 140/E 3.

83. José Miguel Gómez, "Enclosing herewith documents bearing on the questions that have produced misrepresentations," May 24, 1900, Box 94, File 2758, USNAII/MGC/RG 140/E 3.

84. José Miguel Gómez, "Enclosing herewith documents bearing on the questions

that have produced misrepresentations," May 24, 1900, Box 94, File 2758, USNAII/MGC/RG 140/E 3.
85. James H Wilson, "Telegram stating action he has taken as to Rural Guard on election day," June 14, 1900, Box 72, File 1305, USNAII/MGC/RG 140/E 3; James H Wilson, "Encloses correspondence with Civil Governor and Chief of Rural Guard of Santa Clara province outlining the position to be taken as to Rural Guard on election day," June 14, 1900, Box 72, File 3246, USNAII/MGC/RG 140/E 3.
86. Anonymous, "Anonymous letter stating that there will be trouble at Matanzas during the election," April 26, 1900, Box 72, File 1305, USNAII/MGC/RG 140/E 3.
87. Lino Pérez, José M. Maurí, Teodoro Lara, Arturo Roja, Alfredo Fernández de Cueto y Codina, and others, "Desde Trinidad," *La Tribuna*, June 3, 1900, Box 31, File 3256, USNAI/RUSA/RG 395/E 1331.
88. Wilson, *Annual Report*, 1899, 242.
89. Carlos Yznaga, "States that he is a candidate for mayor, and outlines the political situation in that town," May 29, 1900, Box 35, File 3182, USNAI/RUSA/RG 395/E 1331.
90. Rousseau and Díaz de Villegas, *Memoria descriptiva*, 272.
91. Captain Barker, "Telegram reporting very quiet and orderly election in Cienfuegos," June 17, 1900, Box 73, File 1305, USNAII/MGC/RG 140/E 3.
92. L. Casanova to Marta Abreu, February 23, 1900, BNJM/FMA No. 357, V. 12.
93. José Miguel Gómez to Marta Abreu, March 5, 1900, BNJM/FMA No. 156.
94. "¡Pueblo de Cienfuegos!" January 11, 1900, Box 49, File 220, USNAII/MGC/RG 140/E 3.
95. De la Fuente and Casey, "Race and the Suffrage Controversy," in McCoy and Scarano, *Colonial Crucible*, 220–29; Pérez, *Cuba between Reform and*, 182; Averhoff Purón, *Los primeros partidos políticos*, 52–53.
96. Chapman, *History of the Cuban Republic*, 130–31.
97. Wilson, *Annual Report*, 1900, 19.
98. Pérez, *Cuba between Empires*, 312.
99. De la Fuente, *A Nation for All*, 56–57; Pérez, *Cuba between Empires*, 309–12; Benjamin, *Origins of the Cuban Revolution*, 63.
100. Commanding General, Dept. Matanzas & Santa Clara, "Telegram stating that the Civil Governor of Santa Clara informs him that the election is taking place throughout the Province without the slightest sign of disorder," June 16, 1900, Box 72, File 1305, USNAII/MGC/RG 140/E 3.
101. José Miguel Gómez, "Enclosing herewith documents bearing on the questions that have produced misrepresentations," May 24, 1900, Box 94, File 2758, USNAII/MGC/RG 140/E 3.
102. Miguel Ricardo González Pérez, "El General José González Planas y la brigada de Remedios en la guerra de 1895," unpublished manuscript, AHMR.
103. "Sección de elecciones," *Boletín Oficial de la Provincia de Santa Clara*, September 29, 1900, Box 104, File 4000, USNAII/MGC/RG 140/E 3. Santa Clara's

delegates were: José Miguel Gómez, José de Jesus Monteagudo, Pedro González Llorente, Martín Morúa Delgado (one of the few black delegates), Enrique Villuendas, José Luis Robau, and José B. Alemán.

104. Camilo Suárez García to William McKinley, July 7, 1900, Box 105, File 4267, USNAII/MGC/RG 140/E 3.

105. Javier Medina Escalona to General Leonard Wood, October 28, 1900, Box 114, File 5583, USNAII/MGC/RG 140/E 3; Francisco Pujol Carbonell to Leonard Wood, November 28, 1900, Box 118, File 6308 USNAII/MGC/RG 140/E 3; Colonel Noyes, "Telegram stating that the report from Capt. Foltz informs that the owner of Santa Gertrudis has had one of his employees arrested," December 8, 1900, Box 119, File 6390, USNAII/MGC/RG 140/E 3.

106. Van S. Chamberlain, "States that he has information to the effect that the negroes in the vicinity have been smuggling arms," October 1, 1900, Box 113, File 5314, USNAII/MGC/RG 140/E 3.

107. "E Meeting de Tacón. Montoro. AH. Lo que Dijo," *Suplemento de la Tarde*, August 18, 1900, Box 110, File 4592, USNAII/MGC/RG 140/E 3.

108. Un matancero, "Complains against the proceeding of the party who were successful in the elections, and against its elected candidates," [n.d.], Box 3, File 3740, USNAI/RUSA/RG 395/E 1331. Emphasis mine.

109. A. H. Bowman to Adjutant, Rowell Barracks, July 18, 1900, Box 41, File 6265, USNAI/RUSA/RG 395/E 1331.

CHAPTER EIGHT

1. Sesión del Lunes 12 de noviembre de 1900, *Diario de Sesiones de la Convención Constituyente de la Isla de Cuba* 4 (1900): 25–26.
2. Sesión del Lunes 29 de enero de 1901, *Diario de Sesiones de la Convención Constituyente de la Isla de Cuba* 4 (1900): 273.
3. Sesión del Lunes 29 de enero de 1901, *Diario de Sesiones de la Convención Constituyente de la Isla de Cuba* 4 (1900): 283.
4. Sesión del Lunes 29 de enero de 1901, *Diario de Sesiones de la Convención Constituyente de la Isla de Cuba* 4 (1900): 274.
5. Apéndice al número 35 de 30 de julio de 1901, *Diario de Sesiones de la Convención Constituyente de la Isla de Cuba* 4 (1900): 499–509.
6. Sesión del Miércoles 31 de julio de 1901, *Diario de Sesiones de la Convención Constituyente de la Isla de Cuba* 4 (1901): 511.
7. Pappademos, *Black Political Activism*, 3.
8. Pappademos, 23, 24–33.
9. Foner, *Spanish-Cuba-American War*, Vol. II, 560–64.
10. Sesión del Lunes 12 de noviembre de 1900, *Diario de Sesiones de la Convención Constituyente de la Isla de Cuba* 4 (1900): 25–26.
11. Javier Medina Escalona to General Wood, "5th Endorsement," November 7, 1900,

Box 117, File 5980, USNAII/MGC/RG 140/E 3; Javier Medina Escalona to General Wood, October 10, 1900, Box 114, File 5583, USNAII/MGC/RG 140/E 3; J. M. E. to General Wood, April 16, 1901, Box 156, File 1186, USNAII/MGC/RG 140/E 3.
12. Sanjenis, *Mis cartas*," 433–34; Pappademos, *Black Political Activism*, 13.
13. Javier Medina Escalona to General Leonard Wood, October 10, 1900, Box 114, File 5583, USNAII/MGC/RG 140/E 3.
14. Quintín Bandera to Máximo Gómez, October 13, 1904, Box 25, File 3265 (new 3526), ANC/FPMG.
15. "Quintín Bandera," June 7, 1903, Box 26, File 3308 (new 3589), ANC/FPMG; Antonio Govín publically disparaged Quintín Bandera for his radical agenda and the popular support their supposedly garnered. "Govín y los negros," *El Cubano*, August 28, 1900, Box 110, File 4592, USNAII/MGC/RG 140/E 3.
16. Javier Medina Escalona to General Leonard Wood, November 7, 1900, Box 117, File 5980, USNAII/MGC/RG 140/E 3.
17. Javier Medina Escalona to General Leonard Wood, October 10, 1900, Box 114, File 5583, USNAII/MGC/RG 140/E 3.
18. Javier Medina Escalona to General Wood, February 18, 1901, Box 156, File 1186, USNAII/MGC/RG 140/E 3.
19. Javier Medina Escalona to General Wood, December 2, 1900, Box 120, File 6489, USNAII/MGC/RG 140/E 3.
20. Javier Medina Escalona to General Leonard Wood, November 7, 1900, Box 117, File 5980, USNAII/MGC/RG 140/E 3.
21. Javier Medina Escalona to General Wood, December 2, 1900, Box 120, File 6489, USNAII/MGC/RG 140/E 3.
22. Supervisor of Police, "Report in matter of unrest and hard times in the province of Santa Clara," December 4, 1900, Box 119, File 6390, USNAII/MGC/RG 140/E 3. I have chosen to censor this racial slur to limit the spread of the hate it signifies.
23. Supervisor of Police, "Report in matter of unrest and hard times in the province of Santa Clara," December 4, 1900, Box 119, File 6390, USNAII/MGC/RG 140/E 3.
24. Padrón, *Quintín Bandera*, 2.
25. Javier Medina Escalona to General Wood, February 18, 1901, Box 156, File 1186, USNAII/MGC/RG 140/E 3.
26. Alejo García to Leonard Wood, August 29, 1901, Box 193, File 2229, USNAII/MGC/RG 140/E 3.
27. Esteban Cacicedo to Walter B. Barker, January 6, 1901, Box 131, File 223, USNAII/MGC/RG 140/E 3.
28. Esteban Cacicedo to Walter B. Barker, January 6, 1901, Box 131, File 223, USNAII/MGC/RG 140/E 3; Raiborne to Adjutant, 10th U. S. Infantry, January 6, 1901, Box 131, File 223, USNAII/MGC/RG 140/E 3.
29. Esteban Cacicedo to Walter B. Barker, January 6, 1901, Box 131, File 223, USNAII/MGC/RG 140/E 3; Raiborne to Adjutant, 10th U. S. Infantry, January 6, 1901, Box 131, File 223, USNAII/MGC/RG 140/E 3.

30. W. I. Consuegra, "Submits monthly report for November 1900," December 14, 1900, Box 118, File 6105, USNAII/MGC/RG 140/E 3.
31. Captain Rasco (on behalf of W. I. Consuegra), "Telegram regarding his investigation of the Tahon affair," December 9, 1900, Box 119, File 6390, USNAII/MGC/RG 140/E 3.
32. Wilson, *Annual Report*, 1900, 18.
33. Gerardo Machado, "Proclamation addressed by said president to committees and sub-committees of the association," March 14, 1901, Box 192, File 3051, USNA/MGC/RG 140/E 3.
34. "O.: P.: y Policía: Circular," *Boletín Oficial de la Provincia de Santa Clara*, December 16, 1900, Box 118, File 6308, USNAII/MGC/RG 140/E 3.
35. W. I. Consuegra, "Submits report of an inspection he made through the Province," December 13, 1900, Box 118, File 6105, USNAII/MGC/RG 140/E 3.
36. Sanjenis reportedly executed several compatriots accused of banditry during the war, and was tried for the murder of several workers in 1901. Federico García Ramis, "Three telegrams relating to the arrest of Capt. Avelino Sanjenis, of the Rural Guard," February 28, 1901, Box 155, File 1080, USNAII/MGC/RG 140/E 3.
37. Atkins, *Sixty Years in Cuba*, 323–4.
38. Atkins, *Sixty Years in Cuba*, 323–24.
39. Atkins, *Sixty Years in Cuba*, 324–25.
40. Atkins, *Sixty Years in Cuba*, 593–612.
41. Luis Vega, "Letter stating that he is under the impression that the majority of the inhabitants of the rural wards of Santa Clara approved the politic of American Government," May 4, 1901, Box 192, File 3051, USNAII/MGC/RG 140/E 3.
42. Francisco Gutierrez, "Information in connection with matters of general interest in the city of Santiago," April 3, 1901, Box 154, File 1029, USNAII/MGC/RG 140/E 3.
43. Supervisor of Police to Chief of Detective Bureau, "Report of a trip made through Santa Clara province, y a special agent," February 19, 1901, Box 156, File 1209, USNAMGC/G 140/E 3.
44. J. M. E. to General Wood, April 16, 1901, Box 156, File 1186, USNA/MGC/RG 140/E 3.
45. "The Platt Amendment Rejected Again," April 14, 1901, *New York Times*; Edwin F. Atkins to Mr. Kholy, April 12, 1901, Volume II.23, folio 133, MHS/EFA; J. M. E. to General Wood, April 16, 1901, Box 156, File 1186, USNA/MGC/RG 140/E 3.
46. Enrique Villuendas to Cosme de la Torriente, April 24, 1901, Legajo 570, Expediente 8, Academia de Historia, Asociación de Veteranos, Colección Cosme de la Torriente.
47. Gerardo Machado, "Proclamation addressed by said president to committees and sub-committees of the association," March 14, 1901, Box 192, File 3051, USNAII/MGC/RG 140/E 3.
48. "Sesión del Viernes 16 de Agosto de 1901," *Diario de Sesiones de la Convención Constituyente de la Isla de Cuba* 4 (1901): 602.

49. Foner, *Spanish-Cuban-American War*, 625; Also see Perez, *Cuba under the Platt Amendment*, 47–55.
50. Fred Van S. Chamberlain to Adjutant General, Department of Occidente, "Submits report of offensive speeches made by General Alleman [*sic*]," August 25, 1900.
51. "Supervisor of Police, Report in matter of unrest and hard times in the province of Santa Clara," December 4, 1900, Box 119, File 6390, USNAII/MGC/RG 140/E 3.
52. General Leonard Wood, Speech at Santiago, quoted in Pérez, *Cuba between Empires*, 314.
53. J. M. E. to General Wood, April 16, 1901, Box 156, File 1186, USNAII/MGC/RG 140/E 3; Javier Medina Escalona to General Leonard Wood, October 28, 1900, Box 114, File 5583, USNAII/MGC/RG 140/E 3.
54. For a similar argument in the case of US-occupied Puerto Rico, see Franqui-Rivera, "'Porto Rico's Jibaro,'" 185–206; 186–87.
55. "Havana Detective Bureau Report," August 19, 1901, Box 129, File 193, USNAII/MGC/RG 140/E 3; "We Don't Want Privileges," *La Opinión*, August 18, 1901, Box 129, File 193, USNAII/MGC/RG 140/E 3.
56. Orum, "Politics of Color," 62.
57. José B. Aleman, "Communication protesting in the name of the "Centro de Veteranos" against the resolution of the Government in reference to the creation of an Artillery Corps in Cuba, excluding therefrom the colored Cubans," October 12, 1901, Box 205, File 4327, USNA/MGC/RG 140/E 3.
58. Luciano Derouville y Ronaló to Juan Gualberto Gómez, October 16, 1901, Legajo 18, Expediente 1170, ANC/FA; Serapio Arteaga, "Communication stating that the Center of Veterans has adopted the resolution of requesting that the Order providing for an Artillery Corps be revoked," September 12, 1901, Box 205, File 4327 USNAII/MGC/RG 140/E 3.
59. José B. Aleman, "Communication protesting in the name of the "Centro de Veteranos" against the resolution of the Government in reference to the creation of an Artillery Corps in Cuba, excluding therefrom the colored Cubans," October 12, 1901, Box 205, File 4327, USNAII/MGC/RG 140/E 3.
60. Orum, "The Politics of Color," 62.
61. Simón Díaz to Máximo Gómez, June 24, 1901, Legajo 18, Expediente 1134, ANC/Fondo Adquisiciones.
62. José Miguel Gómez, "Telegram advising that Doctor Frías delivered office to Leopoldo Figueroa," March 2, 1900, Box 55, File 347, USNAII/MGC/RG 140/E 3.
63. Leopoldo Figueroa to James H. Wilson, April 25, 1900, Box 35, File 3182, USNAI/RUSA/RG 395/E 1331. Dr. Joaquín H. Hernández y Carbó, Juan Avilés y Dorticós, Julio González y Capote, Dr. Juan Torrabla y Quesada, Manuel Carbonell y Pascual, among others all sat on the city council.
64. Cienfuegos City Council Minutes, July 1, 1900, Volume 44, folio 1, AHPC/AC.
65. Atkins, *Sixty Years in Cuba*, 322.
66. S. H. Lincoln to Leopoldo Figueroa, July 5, 1900, Box 39, File 4528, USNAI/RUSA/

RG 395/E 1331; Leopoldo Figueroa to S. H. Lincoln, July 18, 1900, Box 39, File 4528, USNAI/RUSA/RG 395/E 1331.

67. "Los ñequitos mintiendo," *La Opinión*, June 10, 1901, Box 196, File 182, USNAII/MGC/RG 140/E 3.
68. "Los ñequitos mintiendo," *La Opinión*, June 10, 1901, Box 196, File 182, USNAII/MGC/RG 140/E 3. Emphasis in original.
69. Leopoldo Figueroa, "Replies to telegram of even date, referring to trouble between *La Tribuna* and Joaquín de la Peña," April 25, 1900, Box 35, File 3162, USNAI/RUSA/RG 395/E 1331.
70. Leopoldo Figueroa, "Replies to telegram of even date, referring to trouble between *La Tribuna* and Joaquín de la Peña," April 25, 1900, Box 35, File 3162, USNAI/RUSA/RG 395/E 1331.
71. Leopoldo Figueroa, "Replies to telegram of even date, referring to trouble between *La Tribuna* and Joaquín de la Peña," April 25, 1900, Box 35, File 3162, USNAI/RUSA/RG 395/E 1331.
72. Antonio Tomás, "Statement that several men belonging to the Republican party have threatened to kill Leopoldo Figueroa, and that on behalf of his family he request protection for him," June 6, 1901, Box 169, File 1846, USNAII/MGC/RG 140/E 3; Leopoldo Figueroa, "States the Board of Scrutiny refuses to count the ballot there one by one, they resolving to make the scrutiny of the certificates of the electoral boards," June 10, 1901, Box 169, File 1846, USNAII/MGC/RG 140/E 3; Captain F. S. Foltz, "Report on progress of the Junta in making the count, as well as on the general situation," June 22, 1901, Box 169, File 1846, USNAII/MGC/RG 140/E 3; Esquerra, Hernández, Trujillo, and other residents of Cienfuegos to General Leonard Wood, "Complaining of the anarchical condition prevalent in said city in consequence of frictions arising from the elections between the rival candidates," June 5, 1901, Box 169, File 1846, USNAII/MGC/RG 140/E 3; Juan Suárez, "Letter referring to the incidents that have taken place at Cienfuegos on occasion of the elections," June 7, 1901, Box 169, File 1846, USNAII/MGC/RG 140/E 3; Joaquín de la Peña, "Protests against the legality of the recent elections in the Municipality of Cienfuegos," June 14, 1901, Box 169, File 1846, USNAII/MGC/RG 140/E 3, Walter B. Barker, "Wires in regard to the situation in Cienfuegos in connection with the election frauds at that place," June 12, 1901, Box 169, File 1846, USNAII/MGC/RG 140/E 3.
73. Rousseau and Díaz de Villegas, *Memoria descriptiva*, 278.
74. "Statement of the platforms of various political parties in the Island of Cuba," August 2, [1901], Box 198, File 3500, USNAII/MGC/RG 140/E 3; Alejo García to Leonard Wood, August 29, 1901, Box 193, File 2229, USNAII/MGC/RG 140/E 3.
75. Walter B. Barker to General Leonard Wood, "Report on Election situation there," June 10, 1901, Box 169, File 1846, USNAII/MGC/RG 140/E 3.
76. Walter B. Barker to General Leonard Wood, "Report on Election situation there," June 10, 1901, Box 169, File 1846, USNAII/MGC/RG 140/E 3.

77. Pérez, *Cuba between Empires*, 312; Averhoff Purón, *Los primeros partidos políticos*, 51–52.
78. Atkins, *Sixty Years in Cuba*, 322. It should be noted that there is a discrepancy between Atkins's account of the 1901 election and the civil and military records on the same. Although Atkins claimed that his electoral fraud was successful in electing the man he wanted, Figueroa was defeated in 1901 and did not re-enter the office of mayor subsequently, despite the maneuverings of American military officials in his favor. He was successful in ousting Vieta from office in favor of a more conservative veteran, however.
79. Cienfuegos City Council Minutes, July 20, 1901, Volume 49, AHPC/AC. Added emphasis.
80. Inocencio Sarría, Lorenzo Cabrera, José Ayala, Gavino Crespo, Herminio Quirós, Manuel Sánchez, R. Rodríguez, Pastor Ruíz, Florentino Leon, Aniceto Soto, José López, Narciso P. Blanco, José González, Gustavo Lescano, José Pagola, Andrés Díaz, Marcelino Cabrera, Adalio Torre, Alejandro Torres, Abelardo González, Manuel Alduncin, Francisco Fernández, and others, "Application stating they have been discharged," June 17, 1901, Box 195, File 1846, USNAII/MGC/RG 140/E 3.
81. Walter B. Barker, "Enclosing letter recommending that Dr. Fugueredo [*sic*], late Mayor of Cienfuegos be offered some State position," June 30, 1901, Box 195, File 3161, USNAII/MGC/RG 140/E 3; Walter B. Barker to General Leonard Wood, "Report on Election situation there," June 10, 1901, Box 169, File 1846, USNAII/MGC/RG 140/E 3.
82. Roger Frank to Hugh L. Scott, "Letter stating that an excursion leaves tonight for Havana," July 14, 1901, Box 195, File 3243, USNAII/MGC/RG 140/E 3.
83. Federico Rasco to Adjutant General, July 6, 1901, Box 183, File 2698, USNAII/MGC/RG 140/E 3.
84. Walter B. Barker to Adjutant General, July 9, 1901, Box 183, File 2698, USNAII/MGC/RG 140/E 3.
85. Cienfuegos City Council Minutes, July 3, 1901, Volume 49, AHPC/AC.
86. Gonzalo García Vieta to Walter B. Barker, July 6, 1901, Box 183, File 2648, USNAII/MGC/RG 140/E 3.
87. Civil Governor of Santa Clara, "Enclosing a communication addressed by him to the Mayor of Cienfuegos relative to some grave charges of irregularities preferred against the chief of police of that town," March 8, 1902, Box 243, File 945, USNAII/MGC/RG 140/E 3.
88. Cienfuegos City Council Minutes, July 3, 1901, Volume 49, AHPC/AC.
89. Walter B. Barker to Hugh L. Scott, March 21, 1902, Box 243, File 945, USNAII/MGC/RG 140/E 3; José Miguel Gómez to Leonard Wood, March 8, 1902, Box 243, File 945, USNAII/MGC/RG 140/E 3.
90. Walter B. Barker to Hugh L. Scott, March 21, 1902 Box 243, File 945, USNAII/MGC/RG 140/E 3.
91. Edwin F. Atkins to Hugh L. Scott, March 11, 1902, Box 243, File 945, USNAII/

MGC/RG 140/E 3; Elias Ponvert to Hugh L. Scott, March 13, 1902, Box 243, File 945, USNAII/MGC/RG 140/E 3.
92. Juan L. Campillo to Leonard Wood, November 6, 1900, Box 118, File 6088, USNAII/MGC/RG 140/E 3.
93. Pérez, *Cuba between Empires*, 340–342.
94. José Miguel Gómez to Municipal Mayor of Cienfuegos, 8 March 1902, Box 243, File 945, USNAII/MGC/RG 140/E 3.
95. "Gran Escándalo en Cienfuegos," *La Lucha*, August 7, 1901, Box 183, File 2648, USNAII/MGC/RG 140/E 3; Report of the Havana Detective Bureau, August 17, 1901, on affairs at Cienfuegos, August 17, 1901, Box 183, File 2648, USNAII/MGC/RG 140/E 3. Police officers who supported Vieta allegedly attempted to assassinate the editor of the newspaper *La República* for praising American military authorities.
96. "Report of irregularities at Cienfuegos- wrongs committed in the Hospital management and in the Ayuntamiento, etc.," October 17, 1901, Box 176, File 2363, USNAII/MGC/RG 140/E 3.
97. Cienfuegos City Council Minutes, March 29, 1902, Volume 49, AHPC/AC.
98. José Miguel Gómez to Municipal Mayor of Cienfuegos, 8 March 1902, Box 243, File 945, USNAII/MGC/RG 140/E 3.
99. José Miguel Gómez to Municipal Mayor of Cienfuegos, 8 March 1902, Box 243, File 945, USNAII/MGC/RG 140/E 3; Civil Governor of Santa Clara, "Enclosing a communication addressed by him to the Mayor of Cienfuegos relative to some grave charges of irregularities preferred against the chief of police of that town," March 8, 1902, Box 243, File 945, USNAII/MGC/RG 140/E 3.
100. Musgrave, *Under Three Flags*, 163.
101. Secret Police of Havana, "Report on Presidential campaign," September 12, 1901, Box 129, File 192, USNAII/MGC/RG 140/E 3.
102. Secret Police of Havana, "Report on Presidential campaign," September 12, 1901, Box 129, File 192, USNAII/MGC/RG 140/E 3; Pérez, *Cuba between Empires*, 372.
103. Secret Police of Havana, "Report on Presidential campaign," September 12, 1901, Box 129, File 192, USNAII/MGC/RG 140/E 3; Secret Service, "Report of a meeting of the society 'el Pilar,'" September 26, 1901, Box 129, File 193, USNAII/MGC/RG 140/E 3.
104. Superintendant of the Rural Guard, "Statement of circumstances in Ramírez conviction, Santiago," December 1, 1901, Box 129, File194, USNAII/MGC/RG 140/E 3.
105. Havana Secret Service Bureau, "Report on Anarchy existing in the Island of Cuba," September 12, 1901, Box 129, File 193, USNAII/MGC/RG 140/E 3.
106. Secret Service, "Report of a meeting of the society 'El Pilar,'" September 26, 1901, Box 129, File 193, USNAII/MGC/RG 140/E 3.
107. Emilio del Junco and Juan Gualberto Gómez to Leonard Wood, December 4, 1901, Box 208, File 4779, USNAII/MGC/RG 140/E 3.

108. Félix Dorticós to Juan Gualberto Gómez, December 2, 1901, Cienfuegos, Legajo 18, Expediente 1169, ANC/FA.
109. Pérez, *Cuba between Empires*, 372.

CONCLUSION

1. For early theorizations of hegemonic masculinity, see Connell, *Gender and Power*, 183–89, and Connell, *Masculinities*. For an overview of the origins definitions, and critiques of the concept of hegemonic masculinity see Connell and Messerschmidt, "Hegemonic Masculinity," 829–859; Tosh, "Hegemonic Masculinity and the History of Gender," in Dudink, Tosh, and Hagemann, *Masculinities in Politics and War*, 48–48; 41–60; Donaldson, "What is Hegemonic Masculinity?"
2. It was not until the 1910s that Cuban ethnologist Fernando Ortiz was able to apply the ideas of his mentor, Italian criminologist Cesar Lombroso, to the unique racial context in Cuba. On Ortiz and Lombroso, see Bronfman, *Measures of Equality*, 31, 46–47.
3. Atkins, *Sixty Years in Cuba*, 325.
4. De la Fuente, *A Nation for All*; Ferrer, *Insurgent Cuba*; Helg, *Our Rightful Share*.
5. Suárez Findlay, *Imposing Decency*, 206–07. For a similar articulation of the ways gender "became a conceptual sphere" for the production of other social identities, see de la Cadena, *Indigenous Mestizos*, 148.
6. Hill Collins, *Black Feminist Thought*, 251–53.
7. Wade, *Race and Sex in Latin America*, 178.
8. Litowitz, "Gramsci, Hegemony, and the Law," 525–26.
9. Connell, *Gender and Power*, 183–89.
10. Roseberry, "Hegemony and the Language of Contention," 355–66, 357.
11. Lucero, "Conclusions: Towards an Intersectional History of Crime," in Huertas, Lucero, and Swedberg, *Voices of Crime*.
12. Litowitz, "Gramsci, Hegemony, and the Law," 546.
13. Bronfman, *Measures of Equality*, 7–9.
14. Bronfman, *Measures of Equality*, 37–53; Foucault, *Discipline and Punish*; Helg, "Black Men"; Colón Pichardo, *¿Es fácil ser hombre y difícil ser negro?*; Román, *Governing Spirits*, 23–50.

Bibliography

Archives and Libraries

Archivo Histórico Nacional de España, Madrid, Spain (AHNE)
Archivo Histórico Municipal "Capitán Joaquín Llaverías Martínez," Trinidad, Cuba (AHMT)
Archivo Histórico Municipal de Remedios, Remedios, Cuba (AHMR)
Archivo Histórico Provincial de Cienfuegos "Rita Suárez del Villar," Cienfuegos, Cuba (AHPC)
Archivo Histórico Provincial de Sancti Spíritus, Sancti Spíritus, Cuba (AHPSS)
Archivo Histórico Provincial de Villa Clara, Santa Clara, Cuba (AHPVC)
Archivo Nacional de Cuba, Havana, Cuba (ANC)
Biblioteca Nacional José Martí, Havana, Cuba (BNJM)
Biblioteca Provincial de Cienfuegos, Cienfuegos, Cuba (BPC)
Biblioteca "José Martí" de Santa Clara, Santa Clara, Cuba (BSC)
Cuban Heritage Collection, University of Miami Libraries, Miami, FL (CHC)
Emory University Manuscripts, Archives and Rare Book Library, Atlanta, GA (MARBL)
Harvard University Archives and Special Collections, Cambridge, MA (HUA)
Library of Congress, Manuscripts Division, Washington, DC (LCMD)
Massachusetts Historical Society, Boston, MA (MHS)
Mississippi State University Library, Special Collections, Mississippi State, MS (MSUL)
Museo Histórico Provincial de Cienfuegos, Cienfuegos, Cuba (MHPC)
Museo Histórico Municipal de Remedios, Remedios, Cuba (MHMR)
Pennsylvania Historical Society, Philadelphia, PA (PHS)
Southern Baptist Historical Library and Archive, Nashville, TN (SBHLA)
United States National Archives I, Washington, DC (USNAI)
United States National Archives II, College Park, MD (USNAII)
Walter Royal Davis Library, University of North Carolina (WRDL)

Newspapers and Periodicals

American Magazine (New York)
Boston Herald
Cárdenas Herald
Cuba Contemporánea (Havana)
Diario de la Marina (Havana)
Diario de Sesiones de la Convención Constituyente de la Isla de Cuba (1900–1901) (Havana)
Ecos Populares (Cienfuegos)
El Imparcial (Cienfuegos)
El Heraldo de Cienfuegos
El Siglo Semanario (Cienfuegos)
El Telégrafo: Periódico Político (Trinidad)
Engineering News (New York)
Havana Herald
La Discusión (Havana)
La Lucha (Havana)
La Protesta: Diario Independiente (Havana)
La República (Cienfuegos)
Las Villas (Santa Clara)
La Tribuna (Cienfuegos)
La Verdad (Cienfuegos)
Leslie's Weekly (New York)
McClure's Magazine (New York)
New York Times
New York Herald
Outlook (New York)
Patria (New York)
Puck (New York)
World (New York)

Published Primary Sources

Academia de la Historia de Cuba, *Archivo de Gonzalo de Quesada, Epistolario*, 2 vols. Havana: Imprenta El Siglo XX, 1948.

Atkins, Edwin F. *Sixty Years in Cuba*. Cambridge, MA: Riverside Press, 1926.

Barnet, Miguel. *Biografía de un Cimarrón*. Havana: Ediciones Ariel, 1966.

Batrell Oviedo, Ricardo. *Para la historia: Apuntes autobiográficos de la vida de Ricardo Batrell Oviedo*. Havana: Seoane y Alvarez, 1912.

Bolton, Horace Wilbert. *History of the Second Regiment Illinois Volunteer Infantry*. Chicago: R. R. Donelley & Sons Company, 1899.

Boza, Bernabé. *Mi diario de la guerra: desde Baire hasta la intervención americana.* 2 vols. Havana: Imprenta Propagandista, 1900.
Bustamante, Luis J. *Diccionario Biográfico Cienfueguero.* Cienfuegos, 1931.
Cabrales Nicolarde, Gonzalo. *Epistolario de héroes: cartas y documentos históricos.* Havana: Editorial de Ciencias Sociales, 1996.
Cámara de Representantes. *Memoria de los trabajos realizados durante la primera legislatura ordinaria.* Havana: Imprenta de Rambla y Bouza, 1917.
Castillo y Zúñiga, José Rogelio. *Autobiografía del General.* Havana: Rambla y Bouza, 1910.
Céspedes, Benjamín de. *La prostitución en la ciudad de la Habana.* Havana: O'Reilly, 1888.
Chapman, Charles E. *A History of the Cuban Republic: A Study in Hispanic American Politics.* New York: Macmillan, 1927.
Clark, Victor S. "Labor Conditions in Cuba," *Bulletin of the Department of Labor* 41 (July 1902): 663–793.
Collazo, Enrique. *Cuba heróica.* Havana: Impr. La Mercantil de Suárez, Solana y ca, 1912.
——. *Cuba independiente.* Havana: La Moderna Poesía, 1900.
Consuegra y Guzmán, Israel. *Mambiserías: Episodios de la Guerra de Independencia, 1895–1898.* Havana: Impr. del Ejercito, 1930.
Diamond News Company, *Standard Guide to Cuba.* New York: Foster & Reynolds, 1905.
Era, Doris and José Díaz Roque, *Cartas desconocidas de Máximo Gómez a Rita Suárez del Villar.* Cienfuegos: Ediciones Mecena, 1992.
Ferrara, Orestes. *Memorias, una mirada sobre tres siglos.* Havana: Ediciones Universal, 1975.
Flint, Grover. *Marching with Gómez: A War Correspondent's Field Note-Book Kept During Four Months with the Cuban Army.* Boston: Lamson, Wolffe and Company, 1898.
Gómez, Fernando. *La insurrección por dentro: Apuntes para la historia.* Havana: M Ruiz y Compañía, 1897.
Gómez, Máximo. *Cartas a Francisco Carrillo.* Havana: Editorial de Ciencias Sociales, 1986.
——. *Diario de campaña.* Havana: Instituto del Libro, 1969.
Gómez Núñez, Severo. *La guerra hispano-americana: El bloqueo y la defensa de las costas con grabados y planos.* Madrid: Imprenta del Cuerpo de Artillería: 1899.
Guerra Alemán, José. *Juro pero no prometo (Biografía del general José Braulio Alemán y otros relatos de la Guerra y la paz).* Mexico City: Costa-Amic Editores, 1989.
Halstead, Murat. *The Story of Cuba: Her Struggles for Liberty; The Cause, Crisis and Destiny of the Pearl of the Antilles.* Chicago: National Publishing Co., 1896.
Instituto de Geográfico y Estadístico, *Censo de población de España según el empadronamiento hecho el 31 de diciembre de 1887.* Madrid, 1891.
Loynaz del Castillo, Enrique. *Memorias de la guerra.* Havana: Editorial de Ciencias Sociales, 1989.

Machado, Francisco P. *¡Piedad! Recuerdos de la Reconcentración*. Sagua la Grande: Imprenta de P. Montero, 1917.
Martí, José. *Our America*. Reprint, New York: Monthly Review Press, 1977.
Martínez-Fortún y Foyo, José Andrés. *Anales y Efemérides de San Juan de los Remedios y su Jurisdicción*. Havana: Editorial Ed. Mimeografiada, 1959.
McIntosh, Burr William. *The Little I Saw of Cuba*. New York: F. Tennyson Neely, 1899.
Miró Argenter, José. *Crónicas de la Guerra: La Campaña de Invasión*. Santiago de Cuba: Imprenta El Cubano Libre, 1899.
Musgrave, George Clarke. *Under Three Flags in Cuba: A Personal Account of the Cuban Insurrection and Spanish-American War*. Boston: Little, Brown and Company, 1899.
Parker, William Belmont, ed. *Cubans of To-Day*. New York: G. P. Putnam's Sons, 1919.
Pepper, Charles M. *To-Morrow in Cuba*. Reprint, New York: Young People's Missionary Movement of the United States and Canada, 1910.
Piedra Martel, Manuel. *Mis primeros treinta años: memorias, infancia y adolescencia, la guerra de independencia*. Havana: Minerva, 1945.
Pinilla, Alejo, and José Camejo P. *Bocetos biográficos de los generales José Lacret Morlot y Quintín Bandera*. Havana: Imprenta El Crisol, 1910.
Polavieja y del Castillo, Camilo García de. *Relación documentada de mi política en Cuba: lo que ví, lo que hice, lo que anuncié*. Madrid: Imprenta Emilio Minuesa, 1898.
Quesada, Gonzalo de, and Henry Davenport Northrop. *The War in Cuba, Being a Full Account of her Great Struggle for Freedom, Containing a Complete Record of Spanish Tyranny and Oppression*. Chicago: Wabash Publishing House, 1896.
Roloff, Carlos. *Indice alfabético y defunciones del Ejército Libertador de Cuba, guerra de independencia, iniciada el 24 de febrero de 1895 y terminada oficialmente*. Havana: Imprenta de Rambla y Bouza, 1901.
Rosell y Malpica, Eduardo. *Diario del Teniente Eduardo Rosell y Malpica (1895–1897)*. 2 vols. Havana: Academia de Historia, 1977.
Rousseau, Pablo L., and Pablo Díaz de Villegas. *Memoria descriptiva, historia y biográfica de Cienfuegos y las fiestas del primer centenario de la fundación de esta ciudad*. Havana: Establecimiento tipográfico "El siglo XX," 1920.
Rowland, Dunbar, ed. *Mississippi: Contemporary Biography*. 3 vols. Atlanta: Southern Historical Publication Association, 1907.
Sanjenis, Avelino. *Mis cartas: memorias de la revolución de 1895 por la independencia de Cuba*. Sagua la Grande: Imprenta "El Comercio," 1900.
Suárez del Villar, Rita. *Mis Memorias*. Cienfuegos, 1955.
Tribunal Supremo, *Jurisprudencia del Tribunal Supremo en material criminal*. Vol. 3. Havana: Rambla y Bouza, 1908.
Trujillo, José. *Los criminales de Cuba y D. José Trujillo: Narración de los servicios prestados en el cuerpo de policía de La Habana, historia de los criminales impresos por él en las diferentes épocas de los distintos empleos que ha desempeñado hasta el 31 de diciembre de 1881*. Barcelona: Establecimiento Tipográfico de Fidel Giró, 1882.

United States Congress, *Receipts and Expenditures in Cuba from Jan. 1, 1899, to Apr. 30, 1900*, Vol. 1. Washington, DC: Government Printing Office, 1900.

United States Surgeon-General's Office, *Report of the Surgeon-General of the Army to the Secretary of War for the Fiscal Year ending June 30, 1899*. Washington, DC: Government Printing Office, 1899.

United States War Department, Cuban Census Office, *Report on the Census of Cuba, 1899*. Washington, DC: Government Printing Office, 1900.

Valdés-Domínguez, Fermín. *Diario de un soldado*. 4 vols. Transcribed by Hiram Dupotey Fideaux. Havana: Centro de Información Científica y Técnica de la Universidad de la Habana, 1973.

Vice Commission of Chicago, *The Social Evil in Chicago*. Chicago: American Vigilance Association, 1911.

Wheeler, Joseph. *The Santiago Campaign, 1898*. Philadelphia: Drexel Biddle, 1899.

Wilson, James H. *Annual Report of Brigadier General James H. Wilson, U.S.V., Commanding the Dept. of Matanzas and Santa Clara*. Matanzas, 1899.

———. *Annual Report of Brigadier General James H. Wilson, U.S.V., Commanding the Dept. of Matanzas and Santa Clara*. Matanzas, 1900.

Wood, James P. *Final Report of the Spanish Treaty Claim Commission*. Washington, DC: Government Printing Office, 1910.

Books and Articles

Adams, Kevin. *Class and Race in the Frontier Army: Military Life in the West, 1870–1890*. Norman: University of Oklahoma Press, 2009.

Agamben, Giorgio. *State of Exception*. Chicago: Chicago University Press, 2005.

Aguirre, Carlos. *The Criminals of Lima and Their Worlds: The Prison Experience, 1850–1935*. Durham, NC: Duke University Press, 2005.

Alfonso y García, Ramón María. *La prostitución en Cuba y especialmente en La Habana*. Havana: P. Fernández & Cía, 1902.

Allen, Jafari. *¿Venceremos! The Erotics of Black Self-Making in Cuba*. Durham, NC: Duke University Press, 2011.

Anderson, Benedict. *Imagined Communities*. London: Verso, 1983.

Álvarez Pitaluga, Antonio. *Revolución, hegemonía y poder: Cuba, 1895–1898*. Havana: Fundación Fernando Ortiz, 2012.

Anzaldúa, Gloria, and Cherríe Moraga. *This Bridge Called My Back: Writings by Radical Women of Color*. New York: Persephone Press, 1981.

Appelbaum, Nancy P., Anne S. MacPherson, and Karin Alejandra, "Introduction: Racial Nations." In *Race and Nation in Modern Latin America*, edited by Nancy P. Appelbaum, Anne S. MacPherson, and Karin Alejandra, 1–31. Chapel Hill: University of North Carolina Press, 2003.

Averhoff Purón, Mario. *Los Primeros Partidos Políticos*. Havana: Instituto Cubano del Libro, 1971.

Balboa Navarro, Imilcy. *La protesta rural en Cuba. Resistencia cotidiana, bandolerismo y revolución (1878–1902)*. Madrid: CSIC, 2003.
Barthes, Roland. *Mythologies*. Translated by Annette Lavers. New York: Hill & Wang, 1972.
Beattie, Peter. *The Tribute of Blood: Army, Honor, Race and Nation in Brazil, 1864–1945*. Durham, NC: Duke University Press, 2001.
Bederman, Gail. *Manliness and Civilization: A Cultural History of Gender and Race in the United States, 1880–1917*. Chicago: University of Chicago Press, 1995.
Benjamin, Jules. *The United States and the Origins of the Cuban Revolution: An Empire of Liberty in an Age of National Liberation*. Princeton, NJ: Princeton University Press, 1990 [1977].
Bennett, Herman L. *Africans in Colonial Mexico: Absolutism, Christianity, and Afro-Creole Consciousness, 1570–1640*. Bloomington: Indiana University Press, 2003.
Benson, Devyn Spence. *Antiracism in Cuba: The Unfinished Revolution*. Chapel Hill: University of North Carolina Press, 2016.
Bonnett, Alastair. "A White World? Whiteness and the Meaning of Modernity in Latin America and Japan." In *Working through Whiteness: International Perspectives*, edited by Cynthia Levine-Rasky, 69–106. Albany: SUNY Press, 2002.
Bourdieu, Pierre, and Loïc Wacquant. "On the Cunning of Imperialist Reason." *Theory, Culture, and Society* 16, no. 1 (1991): 41–58.
Breu, Christopher. *Hard-Boiled Masculinities*. Minneapolis: University of Minnesota Press, 2005.
Bronfman, Alejandra. "Más allá del color: clientelismo y conflicto en Cienfuegos, 1912." In *Espacios, silencios y los sentidos de la libertad. Cuba entre 1878 y 1912*, edited by Fernando Martínez Heredia, Rebecca J. Scott, and Orlando F. García Martínez, 285–294. La Habana: Ediciones Unión, 2001.
———. *Measures of Equality: Social Science, Citizenship, and Race in Cuba, 1902–1940*. Chapel Hill: University of North Carolina Press, 2004.
Brown, Kathleen. *Good Wives, Nasty Wenches, and Anxious Patriarchs: Gender, Race and Power in Colonial Virginia*. Chapel Hill: University of North Carolina Press, 1996.
Brown, Matthew. "Soldiers and Strawberries: Questioning Military Masculinity in 1860s Colombia." *Bulletin of Hispanic Studies* 87, no. 6 (2010): 725–44.
Buffington, Robert M. *Criminal and Citizen in Modern Mexico*. Lincoln: University of Nebraska Press, 2000.
Burkholder, Mark A. "Honor and Honors in Colonial Spanish America." In *The Faces of Honor: Sex, Shame, and Violence in Colonial Latin America*, edited by Lyman L. Johnson and Sonya Lipsett-Rivera, 18–44. Albuquerque: University of New Mexico Press, 1998.
Butler, Judith. *Gender Trouble: Feminism and the Subversion of Identity*. New York: Routledge, 1990.
Campi, Daniel. "Historia regional. ¿Por qué?" In *Lugares para la historia: espacio, historia regional, e historia local en los estudios contemporáneos*, edited by Sandra Fernández and Gabriela Dalla Corte, 83–90. Rosario: UNR Editora, 2001.

Caulfield, Sueann. *In Defense of Honor: Sexual Morality, Modernity, and Nation in Early-Twentieth-Century Brazil*. Durham. NC: Duke University Press, 2000.
Chambers, Sarah C. *From Subjects to Citizens: Honor, Gender, and Politics in Arequipa, Peru*. University Park: Pennsylvania State University Press, 1999.
Chasteen, John Charles. "Fighting Words: The Discourse of Insurgency in Latin American History." *Latin American Research Review* 28, no. 3 (1993): 83–111.
Childs, Matt D. *The 1812 Aponte Rebellion and the Struggle Against Atlantic Slavery*. Chapel Hill: University of North Carolina Press, 2006.
Clark, Anna. "The Rhetoric of Masculine Citizenship: Concepts and Representations in Modern Western Culture." In *Representing Masculinity: Male Citizenship in Modern Western Culture*, edited by Stefan Dudink, Karen Hagemann, and Anna Clark, 3–24. New York: New York University Press, 2007.
Cohen, Deborah. "From Peasant to Worker: Migration, Masculinity, and the Making of Mexican Workers in the US." *International Labor and Working-Class History* 69 (2006): 81–103.
Colón Pichardo, Maikel. *¿Es fácil ser hombre y difícil ser negro? Masculinidad y estereotipos raciales en Cuba (1898–1912)*. Havana: Asociación Hermanos Saíz, 2014.
Connell, R. W. *Masculinities*. Berkeley: University of California Press, 1995.
Connell, R. W., and James W. Messerschmidt. "Hegemonic Masculinity: Rethinking the Concept." *Gender and Society* 19, no. 6 (2005): 829–59.
Cooper, Frederick, Thomas C Holt, and Rebecca Jarvis Scott. *Beyond Slavery: Explorations of Race, Labor, and Citizenship in Postemancipation Societies*. Chapel Hill: University of North Carolina Press, 2000.
Cooper, Frederick, and Ann L. Stoler. "Introduction: Tensions of Empire: Colonial Control and Visions of Rule." *American Ethnologist* 16, no. 4 (1989): 609–21.
Corwin, Arthur F. *Spain and the Abolition of Slavery in Cuba, 1817–1886*. Austin: University of Texas Press, 1967.
Cowling, Camillia. *Conceiving Freedom: Women of Color, Gender, and the Abolition of Slavery in Havana and Rio de Janeiro*. Chapel Hill: University of North Carolina Press, 2013.
Crenshaw, Kimberlé. "Mapping the Margins: Intersectionality, Identity Politics, and Violence Against Women of Color." *Stanford Law Review* 43, no. 6 (1991): 1241–99.
Curtin, Philip D. *The Rise and Fall of the Plantation Complex: Essays in Atlantic History*. Cambridge: Cambridge University Press, 1998.
Degler, Carl N. *Neither Black Nor White: Slavery and Race Relations in Brazil and the United States*. New York: Macmillan, 1971.
De la Cadena, Marisol. *Indigenous Mestizos: The Politics of Race and Culture in Cuzco, Peru, 1919–1991*. Durham, NC: Duke University Press, 2000.
De la Fuente, Alejandro. "From Slaves to Citizens? Tannenbaum and the Debates on Slavery, Emancipation, and Race Relations in Latin America." *International Labor and Working-Class History* 77 (2010): 154–73.

———. *Havana and the Atlantic in the Sixteenth Century.* Chapel Hill: University of North Carolina Press, 2008.

———. "Myths of Racial Democracy: Cuba, 1900–1912." *Latin American Research Review* 34: 3 (1999), 39–73.

———. *A Nation for All: Race, Inequality, and Politics in Twentieth-Century Cuba.* Chapel Hill: University of North Carolina Press, 2001.

De la Fuente, Alejandro, and Matthew Casey. "Race and the Suffrage Controversy in Cuba, 1898–1901." In *Colonial Crucible: Empire in the Making of the Modern American State*, 220–29, edited by Alfred W. McCoy and Francisco A. Scarano. Madison: University of Wisconsin Press, 2009.

De la Torre, Mildred. *Conflictos y cultura política: Cuba, 1878–1898.* Havana: Editora Política, 2006.

Díaz, Arlene J. *Female Citizens, Patriarchs, and the Law in Venezuela, 1786–1904.* Lincoln: University of Nebraska Press, 2009.

Díaz, María Elena. *The Virgin, the King, and the Royal Slaves of El Cobre: Negotiating Freedom in Colonial Cuba, 1670–1780.* Stanford, CA: Stanford University Press, 2000.

Dietz, Mary G. "Citizenship with a Feminist Face: The Problem with Maternal Thinking." In *Feminism: The Public and the Private*, edited by Joan Landes, 45–64. Oxford: Oxford University Press, 1998.

Donaldson, Mike. "What is Hegemonic Masculinity?" *Theory and Society* 22, no. 5 (1993): 643–57.

D'ou, Lino, and Pedro de Oraá, *Papeles del teniente coronel Lino D'ou.* Havana: UNEAC, 1983.

Dudink, Stefan, Karen Hagemann. and John Tosh, eds. *Masculinities in Politics and War: Gendering Modern History.* Manchester: Manchester University Press, 2004.

Duke, Cathy. "The Idea of Race: The Cultural Impact of the American Intervention in Cuba, 1898–1912." In *Politics, Society and Culture in the Caribbean*, edited by Blanca E. Silvestrini, 87–109. San Juan: University of Puerto Rico, 1983.

Fanon, Franz. *The Wretched of the Earth.* Translated by Richard Philcox with commentary by Jean-Paul Sartre and Homi K. Bhabha. New York: Grove Press, 2003 [1961].

Fernández, Nadine. *Revolutionizing Romance: Interracial Couples in Contemporary Cuba.* New Brunswick, NJ: Rutgers University Press, 2010.

Fernández Robaina, Tomás. *El negro en Cuba, 1902–1958: Apuntes para la historia de la lucha contra la discriminación racial.* Havana: Editorial de Ciencias Sociales, 1994.

Ferrer, Ada. *Freedom's Mirror: Cuba and Haiti in the Age of Revolution.* Cambridge: Cambridge University Press, 2014.

———. "Haiti, Free Soil, and Antislavery in the Revolutionary Atlantic." *American Historical Review* 117, no. 1 (2012): 40–66.

———. *Insurgent Cuba: Race, Nation and Revolution, 1868–1898* Chapel Hill: University of North Carolina Press, 1999.

———. "Raza, región y género en la Cuba rebelde: Quintín Bandera y la cuestión del liderazgo político." In *Espacios, silencios y los sentidos de la libertad. Cuba entre 1878 y 1912*, edited by Fernando Martínez Heredia, Rebecca J. Scott, and Orlando F. García Martínez, 141–162. La Habana: Ediciones Unión, 2001.

———. "Rustic Men, Civilized Nation: Race, Culture, and Contention on the Eve of Cuban Independence." *Hispanic American Historical Review* 78, no. 4 (1998): 663–86.

Finch, Aisha K. *Rethinking Slave Rebellion in Cuba: La Escalera and the Insurgencies of 1841–1844*. Chapel Hill: University of North Carolina Press, 2015.

———. "What Looks Like a Revolution: Enslaved Women and the Gendered Terrain of Slave Insurgencies in Cuba, 1843–1844." *Journal of Women's History* 26, no. 1 (2014): 112–34.

Fischer, Brodwyn. *A Poverty of Rights: Citizenship and Inequality in Twentieth-Century Rio de Janeiro*. Stanford, CA: Stanford University Press, 2008.

Fischer, Sibylle. *Modernity Disavowed: Haiti and the Cultures of Slavery in the Age of Revolution*. Durham, NC: Duke University Press, 2004.

Foner, Philip S. *The Spanish-Cuban-American War and the Birth of American Imperialism, 1895–1902*. 2 vols. New York: Monthly Review Press, 1972.

Foote, Lorien. *The Gentlemen and the Roughs: Manhood, Honor, and Violence in the Union Army*. New York: New York University Press, 2010.

Formental Hernández, Soura, Iyamira Hernández Pita, and Teresa Fernández de Juan. "Masculinities in Cuba: Description and Analysis of a Case Study from a Gender Perspective." *Masculinities and Social Change* 3, no. 3 (2014): 220–47.

Foucault, Michel. *Discipline and Punish: The Birth of the Prison*. New York: Vintage Books, 1979.

Fountain, Anne. *José Martí, the United States, and Race*. Gainesville: University Press of Florida, 2014.

Fraiman, Susan. *Unbecoming Women: British Women Writers and the Novel of Development*. Columbia: Columbia University Press, 1994.

Frazer, Chris. *Bandit Nation: A History of Outlaws and Cultural Struggle in Mexico, 1810–1920*. Lincoln: University of Nebraska Press, 2006.

Francois, Marie Eileen. *A Culture of Everyday Credit: Housekeeping, Pawnbroking, and Governance in Mexico City, 1750–1920*. Lincoln: University of Nebraska Press, 2006.

Franqui-Rivera, Harry. "'So a New Day has Dawned for Porto Rico's Jíbaro': Military Service, Manhood and Self-Government during World War I." *Latino Studies* 13, no. 2 (2015), 185–206.

Free, Laura E. *Suffrage Reconstructed: Gender, Race, and Voting Rights in the Civil War Era*. Ithaca, NY: Cornell University Press, 2015.

García, Guadalupe. "Urban Guajiros: Colonial Reconcentración, Rural Displacement and Criminalization in Western Cuba, 1895–1902," *Journal of Latin American Studies* 43, no. 2 (2011), 209–35.

García Martínez, Orlando. "Caciques, elites, clientelas, y los problemas raciales: veteranos negros en Cienfuegos entre 1902 y 1912." *Op. Cit. Revista del Centro de Investigaciones Históricas* 15 (2004): 101–22.

———. *Esclavitud y colonización en Cienfuegos, 1819–1879.* Cienfuegos: Ediciones Mecena, 2008.

———. "La Brigada de Cienfuegos: un análisis social de su formación." In *Espacios, silencios y los sentidos de la libertad. Cuba entre 1878 y 1912*, edited by Fernando Martínez Heredia, Rebecca J. Scott and Orlando F. García Martínez, 163–92. Havana: Ediciones Unión, 2001.

Gilmore, David D. *Manhood in the Making: Cultural Concepts of Masculinity.* New Haven, CT: Yale University Press, 1990.

Gilmore, Glenda Elizabeth. *Gender and Jim Crow: Women and the Politics of White Supremacy in North Carolina, 1896–1920.* Chapel Hill: University of North Carolina Press, 1996.

Gomes da Cunha, Olivia Maria. "The Stigmas of Dishonor: Criminal Records, Civil Rights, and Forensic Identification in Rio de Janeiro: 1903–1940." In *Honor, Status, and Law in Modern Latin America*, edited by Sueann Caulfield, Sarah C. Chambers, and Lara Putnam, 295–315. Durham: Duke University Press, 2005.

González Pagés, Julio César. *Macho, Varón, Masculino: Estudios de Masculinidades en Cuba.* Havana: Editorial de la Mujer, 2010.

Gould, Stephen Jay. *The Mismeasure of Man.* Revised and Expanded, New York: W. W. Norton, 1992.

Graden, Dale T. *Disease, Resistance, and Lies: The Demise of the Transatlantic Slave Trade to Brazil and Cuba.* Baton Rouge: Louisiana State University Press, 2014.

Graubart, Karen B. *With Our Labor and Sweat: Indigenous Women and the Formation of Colonial Society in Peru, 1550–1700.* Stanford, CA: Stanford University Press, 2007.

Green, Anna. "The Work Process." In *Dock Workers*, Vol. 1, edited by Sam Davies, Colin J. Davis, David e Vries, Lex Heerma van Voss, Lidewij Hesselink, and Klaus Weinhauer, 560–579. Burlington, VT: Ashgate, 2000.

Greenfield. Anne, ed., *Interpreting Sexual Violence, 1660–1800.* London: Pickering & Chatto, 2013.

Gregory, Brad S. "Is Small Beautiful? Microhistory and the History of Everyday Life." *History and Theory* 38, no. 1 (1999): 100–110.

Guerra, Lillian. *The Myth of José Martí: Conflicting Nationalisms in Early Twentieth-Century Cuba.* Chapel Hill: University of North Carolina Press, 2005.

Guerra y Sánchez, Ramiro, José M. Pérez Cabrera, Juan J. Remos, and Emeterio S. Santovenia. *Historia de la nación cubana. Tomo VII: cambio de soberanía. Desde 1868 hasta 1902.* Havana: Editorial Historia de la nación cubana, S. A. 1952.

Guridy, Frank Andre. *Forging Diaspora: Afro-Cubans and African Americans in a World of Empire and Jim Crow.* Chapel Hill: University of North Carolina Press, 2010.

Gutmann, Matthew C., ed. *Changing Men and Masculinities in Latin America.* Durham, NC: Duke University Press, 2003.

Hamilton, Carrie. *Sexual Revolutions in Cuba: Passion, Politics, and Memory.* Chapel Hill: University of North Carolina Press, 2012.
Hanisch, Carol. "The Personal Is Political." *Notes From the Second Year: Women's Liberation.* New York: Radical Feminism, 1970.
Harwich Vallenilla, Nikita. "La historia patria." In *De Los Imperios a Las Naciones: Iberoamérica,* edited by Antonio Annino, Luis Leiva Castro, and François-Xavier Guerra, 427–37. Zaragoza: IberCaja Obra Cultural, 1994.
Healy, David. "One War from Two Sides: The Cuban Assessment of U.S.-Cuban Relations." *Cercles* 5 (2002): 31–38.
———. *The United States in Cuba, 1898–1902: Generals, Politicians and the Search for Policy.* Madison: University of Wisconsin Press, 1963.
Helg, Aline. "Afro-Cubans in Cuba's War for Independence, 1895–1898." In *Military Struggle and Identity Formation in Latin America: Race, Nation and Community during the Liberal Period,* edited by Nicola Foote and René D. Harder Horst, 59–82. Gainesville: University Press of Florida, 2010.
———. "Black Men, Racial Stereotyping, and Violence in the U. S. South and Cuba at the Turn of the Century." *Comparative Studies in Society and History* 12, no. 3 (2000): 576–604.
———. *Our Rightful Share: The Afro-Cuban Struggle for Equality, 1886–1912.* Chapel Hill: University of North Carolina Press, 1995.Hellwig, David J. *African-American Reflections on Brazil's Racial Paradise.* Philadelphia: Temple University Press, 1992.
Higginbotham, Evelyn Brooks. "African-American Women's History and the Metalanguage of Race." *Signs* 17, no. 2 (1992), 251–74.
Hill Collins, Patricia. *Black Feminist Thought: Knowledge, Consciousness, and the Politics of Empowerment.* New York: Routledge, 2010.
Hitchman, James H. *Leonard Wood and Cuban Independence, 1898–1902.* The Hague: Martinus Nijhoff, 1971.
Hobsbawm, Eric J. *Bandits.* New York: Penguin, 1969.
———. *Primitive Rebels: Studies of Archaic Forms of Social Movement in 19th and 20th Centuries.* Manchester: Manchester University Press, 1959.
———. "Social Criminality: Distinctions between Socio-Political and Other Forms of Crime." *Bulletin of the Society for the Study of Labour History* 25 (1972): 5–6.
Hoganson, Kristin L. *Fighting for American Manhood: How Gender Politics Provoked the Spanish-American and Philippine-American Wars.* New Haven, CT: Yale University Press, 1998.
Holston, James, and Arjun Appadurai. "Cities and Citizenship." *Public Culture* 8 (1996): 187–204.
hooks, bell. *Teaching to Transgress: Education as the Practice of Freedom.* New York: Routledge, 1994.
Horne, Gerald. *Race to Revolution: The United States and Cuba under Slavery and Jim Crow.* New York: Monthly Review Press, 2014.

Howard, Phillip A. *Black Labor, White Sugar: Caribbean Braceros and their Struggle for Power in the Cuban Sugar Industry*. Baton Rouge: Louisiana State University Press, 2015.

Hull, Gloria T., Patricia Bell Scott, and Barbara Smith. *All the Women are White, All the Blacks are Men, but Some of Us are Brave—Black Women's Studies*. Old Westbury, NY: Feminist Press, 1982.

Iglesias Utset, Marial. *Las metáforas del cambio en la vida cotidiana: Cuba, 1898–1902*. Havana: Ediciones Unión, 2003.

Instituto de Historia. *Historia de Cuba, la neocolonia: Organización y crisis desde 1899 hasta 1940*. Havana: Editorial Félix Varela, 2004.

Jackson, John P., and Nadine M. Weidman. *Race, Racism, and Science: Social Impact and Interaction*. New Brunswick, NJ: Rutgers University Press, 2004.

Johnson, Lyman L., and Sonya Lipsett-Rivera, *The Faces of Honor: Sex, Shame, and Violence in Colonial Latin America*. Albuquerque: University of New Mexico Press, 1998.

Jones-Rogers, Stephanie. "Rethinking Sexual Violence and the Marketplace of Slavery: White Women, the Slave Market and Enslaved People's Sexualized Bodies in the Nineteenth-Century South." In *Sexuality and Slavery: Reclaiming Intimate Histories in the Americas*, edited by Daina Ramey Berry and Leslie Harris. Athens: University of Georgia Press, 2018.

Juncker, Kristine. *Expressions of Cultural Inheritance in Espiritismo and Santería*. Gainesville: University Press of Florida, 2014.

Keire, Mara L. *For Business and Pleasure: Red-Light Districts and the Regulation of Vice in the United States, 1890–1933*. Baltimore, MD: Johns Hopkins University Press, 2011.

Kelley, Robin D. G. *Race Rebels: Culture, Politics, and the Black Working Class*. New York: Free Press, 1994.

Knight, Franklin W. *Slave Society in Cuba during the Nineteenth Century*. Madison: University of Wisconsin Press, 1970.

Labra, Rafael M. *La brutalidad de los negros*. 1876. Reprint, Havana: Ayón, 1950.

Landes, Joan B. "The Public and the Private Sphere: A Feminist Reconsideration." In *Feminism: The Public and the Private*, edited by Joan Landes, 135–64. Oxford: Oxford University Press, 1998.

Lane, Jack C. *Armed Progressive: General Leonard Wood*. Lincoln: University of Nebraska Press, 2009.

Lane, Jill. *Blackface Cuba, 1840–1895*. Philadelphia: University of Pennsylvania Press, 2005.

Lasso, Marixa. *Myths of Harmony: Race and Republicanism during the Age of Revolution, Colombia, 1795–1831*. Pittsburgh: University of Pittsburgh Press, 2007.

Levine, Philippa. "Venereal Disease, Prostitution, and the Politics of Empire: The Case of British India." *Journal of the History of Sexuality* 4, no. 4 (1994): 579–602.

Lipsett-Rivera, Sonya. *Gender and the Negotiation of Daily Life in Mexico, 1750–1856*. Lincoln: University of Nebraska Press, 2012.

Lister, Ruth. *Citizenship: Feminist Perspectives*. New York: New York University Press, 2003.
Litowitz, Douglas. "Gramsci, Hegemony, and the Law." *BYU Law Review* 2 (2000): 515–51.
Love, Eric Tyrone Lowery. *Race Over Empire: Racism and U. S. Imperialism, 1865–1900*. Chapel Hill: University of North Carolina Press, 2004.
Lucero, Bonnie A. "Civilization before Citizenship: Education, Racial Order and the Material Culture of Female Domesticity, Cuba (1899–1902)." *Atlantic Studies: Global Currents* 12, no. 1 (2015): 26–49.
———. "Conclusions: Towards an Intersectional History of Crime." In *Voices of Crime: Constructing and Contesting Social Control in Modern Latin America*, edited by Luz E. Huertas, Bonnie A. Lucero, and Gregory Swedberg. Tucson: University of Arizona Press, 2016.
———. "Entre esclavos y comerciantes: Mujeres negras como intermediarias en la economía colonial Cienfueguera." In *Emergiendo del silencio: Mujeres negras en la Historia de Cuba*, edited by Oilda Hevia Lanier (Havana: Editorial de Ciencias Sociales, 2016).
———. "'In this Matter of Dignity': Black Unionism, Racial Order, and the Struggle for Citizenship in Cienfuegos, Cuba, 1899–1907." in *Human Rights, Race and Resistance in the African Diaspora*, edited by Cacee Hoyer and Toyín Falola. New York: Routledge, forthcoming.
———. "Racial Geographies, Imperial Transitions: Property Ownership and Race Relations in Cienfuegos, Cuba, 1894–1899." *Journal of Transnational American Studies* 3, no. 2 (2011): 1–21.
Luis, William. "The Politics of Memory and Miguel Barnet's *The Biography of a Runaway Slave*." *MLN* 104, no. 2 (1989): 475–91.
Majors, Richard, and Janet Mancini Billson. *Cool Pose: The Dilemmas of Black Manhood in America*. New York: Touchstone Books, 1992.
Mangan, Jane E. *Trading Roles: Gender, Ethnicity, and the Urban Economy in Colonial Potosí*. Durham, NC: Duke University Press, 2005.
Marquese, Rafael, and Tâmis Parron, and Márcia Berbel, *Slavery and Politics: Brazil and Cuba, 1790–1850*. Albuquerque: University of New Mexico Press, 2016.
Martínez-Alier, Verena. *Marriage, Class and Colour in Nineteenth-Century Cuba: A Study of Racial Attitudes and Sexual Value in a Slave Society*. Cambridge: Cambridge University Press, 1974.
Martínez Heredia, Fernando, Rebecca J. Scott, and Orlando F. García Martínez, eds. *Espacios, silencios y los sentidos de la libertad: Cuba entre 1878 y 1912*. Havana: Ediciones Unión, Unión de Escritores y Artistas de Cuba, 2001.
Martínez Ortiz, Rafael. *Cuba: los primeros años de independencia*. 2 vols. Paris: LUX, 1921.
Martínez-Vergne, Teresita. *Shaping the Discourse on Space: Charity and Its Wards in Nineteenth-Century San-Juan, Puerto Rico*. Austin: University of Texas Press, 1991.

McFerson, Hazel M. *The Racial Dimension of American Overseas Colonial Policy.* Westport: Greenwood Press, 1997.
Miller, Marilyn Grace. *The Rise and Fall of the Cosmic Race: The Cult of Mestizaje in Latin America.* Austin, TX: University of Texas Press, 2004.
Miller Lubbock, Thomas. *Contested Communities: Class, Gender, and Politics in Chile's El Teniente Copper Mine, 1904–1951.* Durham, NC: Duke University Press, 1998.
Morales Domínguez, Esteban. *Race in Cuba: Essays on the Revolution and Racial Inequality.* New York: Monthly Review Press, 2013.
Moreno, Paul D. *Black Americans and Organized Labor: A New History.* Baton Rouge: Louisiana State University Press, 2006.
Moreno Fraginals, Manuel. *El Ingenio: Complejo económico social cubano del azúcar.* Havana: Editorial de Ciencias Sociales, 1978.
Moreno Fraginals, Manuel, and José J. Moreno Masó. *Guerra, migración y muerte (El ejército español en Cuba como vía migratoria).* Colombres: Ediciones Júcar, 1993.
Mörner, Magnus. *Race Mixture in the History of Latin America.* Boston: Little Brown, 1967.
Morrison, Karen Y. *Cuba's Racial Crucible: The Sexual Economy of Social Identities, 1750–2000.* Bloomington: Indiana University Press, 2015.
Murray, David R. *Odious Commerce: Britain, Spain, and the Abolition of the Cuban Slave Trade.* Cambridge: Cambridge University Press, 1980.
Myers, Jorge. "Language, History, and Politics in Argentine Identity, 1840–1880." In *Nationalism in the New World*, edited by Don H. Doyle and Marco Antonio Pamplona, 117–42. Athens: University of Georgia Press, 2006.
Nagel, Joane. "Masculinity and Nationalism: Gender and Sexuality in the Making of Nations." *Ethnic and Racial Studies* 21, no. 2 (1998): 242–69.
Naranjo Orovio, Consuelo. "En búsqueda de lo nacional: migraciones y racismo en Cuba (1880–1910)." In *La nación soñada, Cuba, Puerto Rico y Filipinas ante el 98: actas del congreso internacional celebrado en Aranjuez del 2 al 28 de abril de 1995*, edited by Consuelo Naranjo Orovio, Miguel Angel Puig-Samper Mulero, and Luis Miguel García Mora,149–62. Madrid: Doce Calles, 1996.
Naranjo Orovio, Consuelo, Ada Ferrer, Ma. Dolores González Ripoll, Gloria García, and Josef Opartny. *El rumor de Haití en Cuba: Temor, raza y rebeldía.* Madrid: Consejo Superior de Investigaciones Científicas, 2004.
Nash, Gary B. "The Hidden History of Mestizo America," *Journal of American History* 82, no. 3 (1995): 950–62.
Navarro García, Luis. *Las guerras de España en Cuba.* Madrid: Ediciones Encuentro, 1998.
Niethammer, Lutz. "Zeroing in on Change: In Search of Popular Experiences of the Industrial Province in the German Democratic Republic." In *The History of Everyday Life: Reconstructing Historical Experiences and Ways of Life*, edited by Alf Lüdtke, 252–311. Princeton: Princeton University Press, 1995.
Nurse, Keith. "Masculinities in Transition: Gender and the Global Problematique." In

Interrogating Caribbean Masculinities Theoretical and Empirical Analyses, edited by Rhoda E. Reddock, 3–33. Kingston: University of the West Indies Press, 2004.
Ocasio, Rafael. *Afro-Cuban Costumbrismo from Plantations to the Slums*. Gainesville: University Press of Florida, 2012.
Olcott, Jocelyn. *Revolutionary Women in Post-Revolutionary Mexico*. Durham, NC: Duke University Press, 2005.
Opatrný, Josef. *Antecedentes históricos de la formación de la nación cubana*. Prague: Universidad Carolina, 1986.
Orum, Thomas T. "The Politics of Color: The Racial Dimension of Cuban Politics during the Early Republican Years." PhD Dissertation, New York University, 1975.
Padrón, Abelardo. *General de tres guerras*. Havana: Editorial de Letras Cubanas, 1991.
Palmié, Stephen. *Wizards and Scientists: Explorations in Afro-Cuban Modernity and Tradition*. Durham, NC: Duke University Press, 2002.
Pappademos, Melina. *Black Political Activism and the Cuban Republic*. Chapel Hill: University of North Carolina Press, 2011.
Parker, David. "Gentlemanly Responsibility and Insults of a Woman: Dueling and the Unwritten Rules of Public Life in Uruguay, 1860–1920," In *Gender, Sexuality, and Power in Latin America Since Independence*, edited by Katherine Bliss and William French, 109–32. Lanham: Rowman and Littlefield, 2006.
Paton, Diana. "The Penalties of Freedom: Punishment in Postemancipation Jamaica." In *Crime and Punishment in Latin America: Law and Society since Late Colonial Times*, edited by Ricardo D. Salvatore, Carlos Aguirre, and Gilbert M. Joseph, 275–307. Durham, NC: Duke University Press, 2001.
Paz, Manuel de, José Fernández, and Nelson López, *El bandolerismo en Cuba: Presencia canaria y protesta rural*. La Laguna, Tenerife: Centro de Cultura Popular Canaria, 1993–1994.
Pérez, Francisco. *Radiografía Del Ejército Libertador 1895–1898*. Havana: Editorial de Ciencias Sociales, 2005.
Pérez, Jr., Louis A. *On Becoming Cuban: Identity, Nationality, and Culture*. Chapel Hill: University of North Carolina Press, 2008.
———. *Cuba and the United States: Ties of Singular Intimacy*. Athens: University of Georgia Press, 2003.
———. *Cuba between Empires, 1878–1902*. Pittsburgh, PA: University of Pittsburgh Press, 1983.
———. *To Die in Cuba: Suicide and Society*. Chapel Hill: University of North Carolina Press, 2005.
———. *Imitations of Modernity: Culture and Society in Nineteenth-Century Cuba*. Chapel Hill: University of North Carolina Press, forthcoming.
———. "Incurring a Debt of Gratitude: 1898 and the Moral Sources of United States Hegemony in Cuba." *American Historical Review* 104, no. 2 (1999): 356–98.
———. *Lords of the Mountain: Social Banditry and Peasant protest in Cuba, 1878–1918*. Pittsburgh, PA: University of Pittsburgh Press, 1989.

———. *The Structure of Cuban History: Meanings and Purpose of the Past*. Chapel Hill: University of North Carolina, 2013.

———. "Supervision of a Protectorate: The United State and the Cuban Army, 1898–1908." *Hispanic American Historical Review* 52, no. 2 (1972): 250–71.

Piccato, Pablo. *The Tyranny of Opinion: Honor in the Construction of the Mexican Public Sphere*. Durham, NC: Duke University Press, 2010.

Pike, Fredrick B. *The United States and Latin America: Myths and Stereotypes of Civilization and Nature*. Austin: University of Texas Press, 1992.

Prados-Torreira, Teresa. *Mambisas: Rebel Women in Nineteenth-Century Cuba*. Gainesville: University Press of Florida, 2005.

Putnam, Lara. "To Study the Fragments/Whole: Microhistory and the Atlantic World." *Journal of Social History* 39, no. 3 [Special Issue on the Future of Social History] (2006): 615–630.

Quaresma Da Silva, Denise, and Oscar Ulloa Guerra, "The Study of Masculinities in Cuba." *Cuban Studies* 42 (2011): 227–38.

Queeley, Andrea J. *Rescuing Our Roots: The African Anglo-Caribbean Diaspora in Contemporary Cuba*. Gainesville: University Press of Florida, 2015.

Reid Vázquez, Michelle. *The Year of the Lash: Free People of Color in Cuba and the Nineteenth-Century Atlantic World*. Athens: University of Georgia, 2011.

Ring, Harry. *How Cuba Uprooted Race Discrimination*. New York: Merit Publishers, 1969.

Roberts, Mary Louise. *What Soldiers Do: Sex and the American G. I. in World War Two France, 1944–1946*. Chicago: University of Chicago Press, 2013.

Rodríguez, Rolando. *La conspiración de los iguales: la protesta de los Independientes de Color en 1912*. Havana: Ediciones Imagen Contemporánea, 2010.

Roig de Leuchsenring, Emilio. *La Lucha Cubana por la República, contra la Anexión y la Enmienda Platt*. Havana: Oficina del Historiador de la Ciudad de La Habana, Colección Histórica Cubana Americana, 1952.

Román, Reinaldo L. *Governing Spirits: Religion, Miravles, and Spectables in Cuba and Puerto Rico, 1898–1956*. Chapel Hill: University of North Carolina Press, 2007.

Roseberry, William. "Hegemony and the Language of Contention." On *Everyday Forms of State Formation: Revolution and the Negotiation of Rule in Modern Mexico*, 355–66. Durham, NC: Duke University Press, 2004.

Rosenberg, Daniel. *New Orleans Dockworkers: Race, Labor, and Unionism, 1892–1923*. Albany: State University of New York Press, 1988.

Rowland, Dunbar, ed., *Mississippi: Contemporary Biography*, 3 vols. Atlanta: Southern Historical Publication Association, 1907.

Rydell, Robert W. *All the World's a Fair: Visions of Empire at American International Expositions, 1876–1916*. Chicago: University of Chicago Press, 1984.

Sacks, Marcy S. "'To Show Who was in Charge': Police Repression of New York City's Black Population at the Turn of the Twentieth Century." *Journal of Urban History* 31 (2005): 799–819.

Sartorius, David A. *Ever-Faithful: Race Loyalty and the Ends of Empire in Spanish Cuba.* Durham, NC: Duke University Press, 2013.

———. "Limits of Loyalty: Race and the Public Sphere in Cienfuegos, Cuba, 1845–1898." PhD Dissertation, University of North Carolina at Chapel Hill, 2003.

Savignón, Tomás. *Quintín Bandera: el mambí sacrificado y escarnecido.* Havana: Ministerio de Defensa Nacional, 1948.

Sawyer, Mark Q. *Racial Politics in Post-Revolutionary Cuba.* Cambridge: Cambridge University Press, 2005.

Schmidt-Nowara, Christopher. *Empire and Antislavery: Spain, Cuba, and Puerto Rico, 1833–1874.* Pittsburgh, PA: University of Pittsburgh Press, 1999.

Schwartz, Rosalie. *Lawless Liberators: Political Banditry and Cuban Independence.* Durham, NC: Duke University Press, 1989.

Scott, James C. *Weapons of the Weak: Everyday Forms of Peasant Resistance.* New Haven, CT: Yale University Press, 1985.

Scott, Joan Wallach. "The Evidence of Experience." *Critical Inquiry* 17, no. 4 (1991): 773–97.

———. "Gender: A Useful Category of Historical Analysis." *American Historical Review* 91, no. 5 (1986): 1053–75.

Scott, Rebecca J. *Degrees of Freedom: Louisiana and Cuba after Slavery.* Cambridge: Harvard University Press, 2005.

———. *Freedom Papers: An Atlantic Odyssey in the Age of Emancipation.* Cambridge: Harvard University Press, 2012.

———. "Race, Labor, and Citizenship in Cuba: A View from the Sugar District of Cienfuegos, 1886–1909." *Hispanic American Historical Review* 78, no. 4 (1998): 687–728.

———. "Reclaiming Gregoria's Mule: The Meanings of Freedom in the Arimao and Caunao Valleys, Cienfuegos, Cuba, 1880–99." *Past & Present* 170 (2001): 181–216.

———. *Slave Emancipation in Cuba: The Transition to Free Labor, 1860–1899.* Princeton, NJ: Princeton University Press, 1986.

———. "Small-Scale Dynamics of Large-Scale Processes." *American Historical Review* 105, no. 2 (2000): 472–79.

Scott, Rebecca J., and Michael Zeuske, "Property in Writing, Property on the Ground: Pigs, Horses, Land, and Citizenship in the Aftermath of Slavery, Cuba, 1880–1909." *Comparative Studies in Society and History* 44, no. 4 (2002): 669–99.

Seed, Patricia. "The Social Dimensions of Race: Mexico City, 1753." *Hispanic American Historical Review* 62, no. 4 (1982): 569–606.

Sierra Madero, Abel. "Cuerpos En Venta: Pinguerismo y Masculinidad Negociada En La Cuba Contemporánea." *NÓMADAS* 38 (2013): 166–83.

———. *Del otro lado del espejo: La sexualidad en la construcción de la nación cubana.* Havana: Casa de las Americas, 2006.

Simonsen, Jane E. *Making Home Work: Domesticity and Native American Assimilation in the American West, 1860–1919.* Chapel Hill: University of North Carolina Press, 2006.

Sinha, Mrinalini. *Colonial Masculinity: The 'Manly Englishman' and the 'Effeminate Bengali' in the Late Nineteenth Century*. Manchester: Manchester University Press, 1995.
Sippial, Tiffany A. *Prostitution, Modernity, and the Making of the Cuban Republic, 1840–1920*. Chapel Hill: University of North Carolina, 2013.
Slatta, Richard W., ed. *Bandidos: The Varieties of Latin American Banditry*. Westport, CT: Greenwood Press, 1987.
Smith, Robert Freeman. "Twentieth-Century Cuban Historiography." *Hispanic American Historical Review* 44, no.1 (1964): 44–73.
Smith, Richard. *Jamaican Volunteers in the First World War: Race, Masculinity and the Development of National Consciousness*. Manchester: Manchester University Press, 2004.
Snyder, R. Claire. *Citizen-Soldiers and Manly Warriors: Military Service and Gender in the Civic Republican Tradition*. Lanham, MD: Rowman & Littlefield, 1999.
Sommer, Doris. "Irresistible Romance." In *Foundational Fictions: The National Romances of Latin America*, edited by Doris Sommer, 1–30. Berkeley: University of California Press, 1991.
Spongberg, Mary. *Feminizing Venereal Disease: The Body of the Prostitute in Nineteenth-Century Medical Discourse*. New York: New York University Press, 1997.
Steege, Paul, Andrew Stuart Bergerson, Maureen Healy, and Pamela E. Swett. "The History of Everyday Life: A Second Chapter." *Journal of Modern History* 80, no. 2 (2008): 358–78.
Stepan, Nancy Leys. *"The Hour of Eugenics": Race, Gender and Nation in Latin America*. Ithaca, NY: Cornell University Press, 1991.
Stern, Steve J. *Secret History of Gender: Women, Men, and Power in Late Colonial Mexico*. Chapel Hill: University of North Carolina Press, 1995.
Stoler, Ann Laura. *Carnal Knowledge and Imperial Power: Race and the Intimate in Colonial Rule*. Berkeley: University of California Press, 2010.
Stoner, K. Lynn. *From the House to the Streets: The Cuban Woman's Movement for Legal Reform, 1898–1940*. Durham, NC: Duke University Press, 1991.
Strasser, Ulrike, and Heidi Tinsman. "It's a Man's World? World History Meets the History of Masculinity, In Latin American Studies, for Instance." *Journal of World History* 21, no. 1 (2010): 75–96.
Struck, Bernhard, Kate Ferris, and Jacques Revel, "Introduction: Space and Scale in Transnational History." *International History Review* 33, no. 4 (2011): 573–84.
Suárez Findlay, Eileen J. *Imposing Decency: The Politics of Sexuality and Race in Puerto Rico, 1870–1920*. Durham, NC: Duke University Press, 1999.
Swett, Pamela E. "The History of Everyday Life: A Second Chapter." *Journal of Modern History* 80, no. 2 (2008): 358–78.
Tannenbaum, Frank. *Slave and Citizen: The Negro in the Americas*. New York, A. A. Knopf, 1947.
Thomas, Susan. *Cuban Zarzuela: Performing Race and Gender on Havana's Lyric Stage*. Urbana-Champaign: University of Illinois Press, 2009.

Thomas-Woodard, Tiffany A. "Desiring Nation: Prostitution, Citizenship, and Modernity in Cuba, 1840–1920." PhD Dissertation, University of New Mexico, 2007.
Tone, John Lawrence. *War and Genocide in Cuba, 1895–1898*. Chapel Hill: University of North Carolina Press, 2006.
Torres-Cuevas, Eduardo. *En busca de la cubanidad*. Havana: Editorial de Ciencias Sociales, 2006.
Tosh, John. "Hegemonic, Masculinity and the History of Gender." In *Masculinities in Politics and War: Gendering Modern History*, edited by Stefan Dudink, John Tosh, and Karen Hagemann, 41–60. Manchester: Manchester University Press, 2004.
———. *Manliness and Masculinities in Nineteenth-Century Britain: Essays on Gender, Family and Empire*. New York: Pearson/Longman, 2005.
Twinam, Ann. *Public Lives, Private Secretes: Gender, Honor, Sexuality, and Illegitimacy in Colonial Spanish America*. Berkeley: University of California Press, 1999.
———. *Purchasing Whiteness: Pardos, Mulattos, and the Quest for Social Mobility in the Spanish Indies*. Stanford, CA: Stanford University Press, 2015.
Unzueta, Fernando, "Scenes of Reading: Imagining Nations/Romancing History in Spanish America." In *Reading and Writing the Nation in Nineteenth-Century Latin America*, edited by Castro Klarén and John C. Chasteen, 115–60. Baltimore: Johns Hopkins University Press, 2003.
Vinat de la Mata, Raquel. *Las cubanas en la posguerra (1898–1902): Acercamiento a la reconstrucción de una etapa olvidada*. Havana: Editora Política, 2001.
Vinson III, *Bearing Arms for His Majesty: The Free-Colored Militia in Colonial Mexico*. Stanford, CA: Stanford University Press, 2001.
Viveros Vigoya, Mara. "Contemporary Latin American Perspectives on Masculinity," In *Changing Men and Masculinities in Latin America*, edited by Matthew Gutmann, 27–57. Durham, NC: Duke University Press, 2006.
Wade, Peter. *Race and Ethnicity in Latin America*, 2nd ed. London: Pluto, 2010.
———. *Race and Sex in Latin America*. New York: Pluto, 2009.
Weston, Rubin Francis. *Racism in U. S. Imperialism: the Influence of Racial Assumptions on American Foreign Policy, 1893–1946*. Columbia: University of South Carolina Press, 1972.
Whitney, Robert, and Graciela Chailloux Laffita, *Subjects or Citizens: British Caribbean Workers in Cuba, 1900–1960*. Gainesville: University Press of Florida, 2014.
Wiegman, Robyn. *American Anatomies: Theorizing Race and Gender*. Durham, NC: Duke University Press, 1995.
Wierling, Dorthee. "The History of Everyday Life and Gender Relations: On Historical and Historiographical Relationships." In *The History of Everyday Life: Reconstructing Historical Experiences and Ways of Life*, edited by Alf Lüdtke, 149–68. Princeton: Princeton University Press, 1995.
Williams, Walter L. "United States Indian Policy and the Debate over Philippine Annexation: Implications for the Origins of American Imperialism." *Journal of American History* 66, no. 4 (1980): 810–31.

Zeuske, Michael. "The Cimarrón in the Archives: A Re-Reading of Miguel Barnet's Biography of Esteban Montejo." *New West Indian Guide/ Nieuwe West-Indische Gids* 71, nos. 3–4 (1997), 265–79.

———. "Die diskrete Macht der Sklaven zur politischen Partizipation von Afrokubanern während des Kubanischen Unabhängigkeitskrieges und der ersten Jahre der Republik (1895–1908)—eine regionale Perspektive." *Comparativ* 1 (1997), 32–98.

———. "'Los negros hicimos la independencia': Aspectos de la movilización afrocubana en un hinterland cubano. Cienfuegos entre colonia y República." In *Espacios, silencios y los sentidos de la libertad: Cuba entre 1878 y 1912*, edited by Fernando Martínez Heredia, Rebecca J. Scott, and Orlando F. García Martínez, 193–234. Havana: Ediciones Unión, 2001.

———. "The Names of Slavery and Beyond: the Atlantic, the Americas and Cuba." In *The End of Slavery in Africa and the Americas: A Comparative Approach*, edited by Ulrike Schmieder, Katja Füllberg-Stolberg, and Michael Zeuske, 51–80. Münster-Hamburg-Berlin-Wien-London: LIT-Verlag, 2011.

———. "Postemancipación y trabajo en Cuba." *Boletín Americanista* 68 (2013): 77–99.

———. "'Sin otro apellido': Nombres esclavos, marcadores raciales e identidades en el proceso de la emancipación de la esclavitud en el Caribe (Cuba 1870–1940)." Paper presented at *Seminario Memorias* V (2001).

———. "Two Stories of Gender and Slave Emancipation in Cienfuegos and Santa Clara, Central Cuba—Microhistorical Approaches to the Atlantic World." In *Gender and Slave Emancipation in the Atlantic World*, edited by Pamela Scully and Diana Paton, 181–198. Durham, NC: Duke University Press, 2005.

Other Media

Eric Corvalán, *Raza: Documental* (2008).

Index

Page numbers in italic text indicate illustrations.

Abreu, Marta, 66, 204
Acea, Isidro, 82
Acea, Victor, 27
Achón, Antonio, 167
Acosta, Gonzalo, 144–46
age distribution, *15*
agricultural bank, 117–18
agriculture, 115–17
Aguilar, Pepe, 101
Aguirre, J. W., 49
aid distribution, 112
Aldave, José García, 57–59
Alemán, José B., 34, 166, 196; alleged political radicalism of, 227–28; characterization of enemy women by, 59; and confrontation with Spanish officer, 59; duel challenge by, 57–58; majasería campaign by, 83; and opposition to Platt Amendment, 223; and political dissention, 233; prosecution of black officer by, 87–89; racial politics of, 230; racial segregation criticized by, 229; revolutionary masculinity invoked by, 228; on Spanish cowardice, 53; on suffrage, 214
Álvarez Arteaga, José, 31
Americans, US, 20

Anderson, Benedict, 12
annexationists, 204, 232
anti-black violence, 2, 11, 189; assassination and, 167, 169, 177, 251; criminalization and, 156, 185–86, 250–54; murder, 164–70, 250–51; and *ñáñigos*, 31, 183; New Men and, 250–51; Race War and, 11; racial stereotypes and, 11, 29; rope disease (lynching) as, 222; and Spanish forces, 30–32; state as perpetrator of, 164–70, 177, 221, 253–54; and US personnel, 11, 119, 137, 140–41; vigilante, 251, 254; white veterans and, 12
anticolonial struggle, 4, 27–29, 42, 245
Antilles League, 33
armed gangs, 218–19
Army Appropriations Bill, 215
Arroyo Blanco, 56
Artillery Corps, 228–29
assassination, 254
Atkins, Edwin F., 89, 132, 237; annexationism and, 232; mayoral race tampering by, 234–35; 1901 election account of, 305n78; and violence against black veterans, 187–88
August Revolution, 254

Autonomists, 122–23
Azcárraga Ugarte, Marcelo de, 103

bad soldier (*majá*), 247
ballroom celebration, racial segregation of, 289n24
Bandera, Quintín, 2, 50, 90, *218*; as alleged chief of black insurgents, 217; assassination of, 254; among black orientales, 27; as brigadier general, 42; challenges to authority of, 95–97; claims of racism against, 218; court-martial of, 11, 94–96; Govín disparaging, 301n15; material comfort and, 96–97; Mayía's unfair treatment of, 98; racial discrimination against, 97–98
banditry: among insurgents, 86–93; partisan politics and, 200; Rural Guard exposing false reports of, 220; Sanjenis and, 302n36; during sugar harvest, 220–21
Barker, Walter B., *121*, 139–40, 151, 171; racialized characterizations of Cuban men by, 120–21; on suffrage restriction, 182–83; white US employees working for, 152
Barroso Lazo, Agripina, 100
Barthes, Roland, 3
Bates, John C., 119, *122*; organization of law enforcement under, 127–28; preference for Autonomists by, 122–23; white separatists appointed by, 125
battlefield: deaths, 40; sexual activity on, 93–94; women on, 67
Battle of Loma del Gato, 76
Battle of Mal Tiempo, 15, 37–38, *38*, 40
battleship (Maine), 103
Benítez, Juan B., 42, 87, 89
Bermúdez, Roberto, 101–2
Betancourt Cisneros, Salvador, 43

Biography of a Runaway Slave (*Biografía de un cimarrón*), 142
black, 18–19; authority, 164–70; bandits, 192–93; community, 14; Cubans, 18; delegates, 217; families, 62–63; insurgents, 7–8, 13–14, 74; leadership, 251; masculinity, 99; rebellion, 28–29; rural labor, 221; suffrage and suppression, 199; vote, 230–31
black criminality, 18; as justification for anti-black violence, 165; Lynn discredited by allegations of, 203; New Men and, 208, 220; opponents of separatist rule and the specter of, 132–33, 152, 199, 215, 223; political fitness and, 216; Rural Guard and presumption of, 192–93, 221; and suffrage, 183; use of force and, 156, 250
black insurgents, 7, 29, 34, 71, 78, 89, 132
black men: alleged criminal deviance of, 31–32, 165; anti-black racism and, 248; challenges to authority of, 95–97; claiming revolutionary masculinity, 246–47; claims of racist, 218; Cuban army enlistment of, 28; firearms allegedly smuggled by, 209–10; Fourth Corps army participation of, 27–28; ideas about manhood and, 133–34; law enforcement targeting, 156; Medina Escalona inducing fears of, 219; in municipal police force, 128–29, 148–49; officer rank attained by, 85; as officers in the Fourth Corps, 42–43, 251; patriotic clubs not benefiting, 112; public jobs and, 174; representations of, 4; in Rural Guard, 131; Rural Guard incarceration of, 193–94; sexual conduct of, 94, 99–100; Spanish army and anxieties about, 29; state violence

INDEX 331

against, 253; universal manhood suffrage results and, 214; well-paid employment lacking for, 138; as witches (*negros brujos*), 11
blackness, 2, 11
black officers, 2; Alemán's prosecutions of, 87–89; challenges to authority of, 82–84; middle-class sexual values and, 102; racial double standards and, 96; white insurgents targeting, 11; white officers anxiety about, 96; white soldier questioning authority of, 85–86
black orientales, 27, 30, 44
black soldiers: aid distribution to, 112; post-war authority of, 112–13; prewar social positions of, 117–19; revolutionary masculinity benefits for, 44–45
black veterans: alienation of, 170; of Brigade of Cienfuegos, 142; and exclusion from political power, 137; law enforcement employment for, 118–19, 151–52; military service and political influence of, 249; New Man status and, 155–56, 167, 176–77; opponents of separatist rule and depiction of, 185–86, 199; police force dismissal of, 173–74; political consequences of employing, 249; political views and imprisonment of, 231; postwar political exclusion of, 127; postwar racial exclusion of, 169; private guards violence against, 221–22; public authority claims of, 141; racial double standards and, 133; Republican Party ties with, 208–9; revolutionary masculinity appropriated by, 253; Rural Guard positions for, 191; Rural Guardsmen killing of, 222; sexually transgressive women and, 144; US military and presumed racial solidarity of, 155; white US employees clashing with, 141–42
black women: alleged dishonor and immorality of, 62, 69–70; as breadwinners, 63; racial double standard for white and, 70; in rebel camps, 71; sexual stereotype of, 64–65; white insurgents and, 71
Blanco, Manuel, 103
Bowman, Alpheus Henry, 165
Boza, Bernabé, 85
bravery, 35–38
Bravo, Juan, 94
Brigade of Cienfuegos, 41–43, 81, 90, 125; archival sources on race and, 281n114; black veterans of, 142
Brigade of Remedios, 43, 90
Brigade of Trinidad, 94–95, 97
brothel incident, 142–44
Brunet, José, 140–41

Cacicedo, Esteban, 219
Calleja, Emilio, 35
Camacho Yera, José, 27, 42, 90, 236
Camajuaní, 199, 202
Campillo y D'Wolf, Juan José López de, 173; insubordination charges against, 238–39; police abuse complaints stifled by, 175–76; police officers removed by, 235; US military defending, 237; Vieta claiming failure of, 237; Vieta removing, 236
Cánovas del Castillo, Antonio, 103
Cardona, Luz, 68
Carreras, Juan, 199
Carrillo, Francisco, 43, 91; concubine of, 101; critiques of reconcentration by, 56; and disbandment, 160; hoarding resources, 112; reprimanding González Planas, 90–91

Carrillo, Luis, 219
Castellón, Pablo, 145
caudillos (local veteran chiefs), 234
cavalry forces, 43–44
Celada Zayas, Rogelio, 128, 168
charity, 113–18, 157
children, in reconcentration camps, *51*
Cienfuegos, 15; Alemán and politics in, 233; black community in, 14; conservative politics in, 239; private guards in, *188*; US citizens property losses in, 277n46
Cienfuegos police force: black veterans dismissal from, 173–74; Campillo y D'Wolf stifling complaints about, 175–76; whitening of, 174; working-class relations with, 175–77
citizenship, 214, 250; black men and second-class, 195, 214, 250; manhood and, 109, 116, 138, 229; military service and, 228, 235–36, 246; suffrage and, 182
civil authorities, 19
civil government, 162–63, *163*
civilian employees, US, 284n11
civilization, 32, 67, 144, 150, 153; laws of, 31; race and, 109–10, 174
civil unrest, 166
Civil War, US, 120
Club Cubanita, 56, 66–67
Coffigny, Julio Oritz y, 204–5, *205*
Collins, Patricia Hill, 252
colonial masculinity, 245
colonial subjugation, 26
color-blind nationalism, 13
concubines, 71, 82, 94–95, 97–98, 100–101
Connell, R. W., 252
conservative politics, 239
Constitución de Jimaguayú (1895), 102
Constitutional Convention: black delegates to, 217; elections for, 208–9;

González Planas as candidate for, 209; Medina Escalona demanding disbandment of, 219; Platt Amendment in, 215
Consuegra y Guzmán, Israel, 85
court-martials, 78, 82, 92, 101–3; of Bandera, 11, 94–96; of Benítez, 87–89; against black officers for sexual misconduct, 94; of González Planas, 92; of Sarría, 89
cowards (*majases*), 61, 77–79
Creoles, 25, 143, 245
crime prevention, 193
criminal deviance, 31–32, 165
criminalization, 156, 185; of black men, 18, 250; gendered dynamics of, 251; racialized, 186; social and political order and, 253; state violence legitimized by, 254
cross-racial citizenship, 214
cross-racial military, 110
cross-racial patronage, 208
Cuba: alleged racial unrest in, 219; anticolonial insurrection in, 27–29, 42, 245; birth of Republic of, 214; civil government in, *163*; dock work in, 138–39; Estrada Palma as first president of, 241; gendered language in, 3; gender in, 3–4; "Good Government vs. Revolution—An Easy Choice" and, *226*; inclusion in, 246–47; independence racial caricature of, *225*; masculine political authority in, 242–43; men outside households in, 6; national identity in, 2; opponents of separatist rule in, 210–11; privileged racial position in, 109–10; race relations in, 259n40; as racial democracy, 251; racialized sexual economy of, 5; racial order in, 210; racial segregation

INDEX 333

in, 229; rise of sugar in, 8–9; sacrifice for freedom of, 40; self-government in, 135, 223–24, 250; Spanish rule in, 9–10, 107–8; US Americans in, 20; US annexation of, 109; US military government and restricted suffrage in, 183; US military intervention in, 103; US military occupation of, 17–18; US relations with, 226; US rule in, 159–60, 220, 224, 228; war laying waste to, 110–11; War of Independence in, 1–2, 7

Cuban army: ballroom celebration by, 289n24; black enlistment in, 28; gendered language used in, 8; Gómez, M., and morality of, 94; high-ranking chiefs lost by, 76–77; infantry of, 43–44; insurgents as soldiers of, 19; majasería allegations in, 77–78; masculinity in, 34; military service bonds from, 26; norms of conduct in, 81–82; postwar economic situation of veterans of, 111; racial hierarchy in, 72–74; racism within, 5–6; sacred ideal of Liberty in, 39; Santa Clara province invaded by, 30; unmanly behaviors in, 78–79; wealthy white men support for, 32–33; women detained by, 59. *See also* Fourth Corps of Cuban army

Cuban Army Party, 202

Cuban cause, 169–70

Cuban delegates (to Constitutional Convention), 213–14

La Cubanita, 111–12

Cuban manhood, 7, 19, 49, 65, 107, 197–98

Cuban men, 25–26; Barker as critic of, 120; and charity, 113–18; and ideas about manhood, 6–7; patriarchal responsibilities of, 23–24, 143–44; white middle-class values and, 252

Cuban Revolutionary Party (PRC), 108

Cuban veterans: and disapproval of disbandment, 157; pay for, 156–57; and requirement to forfeit weapons, 158–59; revolutionary masculinity demonstrated by, 246; in Santa Clara province, 135; US military abuse of, 120–21

Cuban women: Aldave's transgressions against, 57–59; and motherhood, 65; patriotism of, 65–66; Spanish army abusing, 57, 143; US treatment of, 143; virtue of, 60–61

decolonization, 1
dedazo (personal favoritism), 84–85
delegates (to Constitutional Convention): Platt Amendment opposition of, 227; from Santa Clara, 213–14, 299n103; voting on Platt Amendment, 223
delegates (to Yaya Assembly), 102–3
Delgado, Manuel José, 92
Democratic Union Party (*Partido Unión Democrática*), 196
Diario de la Marina (newspaper), 29–30
disbandment, 157–59, 161
La Discusión (newspaper), 160, 162
disorderly conduct, 147
diversity, 246
dock work, 138–39
domestic femininity, 55
domestic ideal, 66
domesticity, 4, 66–67
Dorticós, Félix, 241
"Down with the Intrusive Skirts," 205
draconian policies, 232

easy life (*vida holgada*), 100
elections: Atkins account of 1901,

elections (*continued*)
305n78; for Constitutional Convention, 208–9; Estrada Palma's fraudulent, 254; Figueroa losing, 235–36, 305n78; local, 216; presidential, 239–41; Santa Clara Province, 203–4; US military preserving order after, 200–201
electoral law, 185, 206
electoral races: black veteran voters and, 208; Figueroa and fraud in, 235; US military manipulation of, 231–32, 234; victories in, 206–8
elites, 24–25, 200
employees, US, 152
employment: agricultural, 116–17; black men and well-paying, 138; black veterans' exclusion from government, 125–26; Monteagudo and Fourth Corps, 131; in municipal police force, 148–49; racially selective, 248–49; Rural Guard, 130, 191; US military and black veteran, 249; white social prestige and, 126
Escobar, María Laredo, 92
Esquerra, Higinio, 126, 237, 238
Estrada Palma, Tomás, 76, 125, 239–41, 254
European ancestry, 19
Evans, Charles H., 145
evil-hearted men, 30–31

families, 52, 63
farming, 115
Fecund Truce (1880–1895), 9
femininity, 59–61, 65, 68–69, 72; domestic, 55
Fernández, José, 167
Fernández Labrada, Manuel, 193
Ferrara, Orestes, 37, 150, 196
Ferrer, Ada, 11, 12, 95
Figueroa, Leopoldo, 43, 172, 204, 231; election lost by, 235–36, 305n78; electoral fraud in favor of, 235; nicknames of, 232; threats against, 304n72; as US rule collaborator, 232–33
firearms, 146; black men allegedly smuggling, 209–10; Cuban veterans' forfeiture of, 158–59; Medina Escalona claims about black veterans with, 217–18; promiscuity with, 150; Wilson allowing, 187–88
Fischer, Brodwyn, 43
Fonda Mariposa (café), 167
foreign property owners, 20, 224
Fourth Corps of Cuban army, 13, 17, 76–77; black leadership in, 42–43, 251; black men in, 27–28; majasería campaign in, 80–81; military achievements and, 84–85; Rural Guard employment of veterans of, 131
Fraiman, Susan, 73
Frías, José Antonio, 125, 152, 204; civil authority and, 150; efforts to avoid US interference by, 166; military officials removing, 171–72; opposition to US rule by, 146
Fuller, Andrew E., 142

Galarraga, Roberto, 128
García Martínez, Orlando, 281n114
García Polavieja, Camilo, 29
gender: in Cuba, 3–4; racial democracy and, 251–52; racial inequality and, 11; racialized transgressions of, 29; transgressions, 55–56, 71–72
gendered hierarchy, 255
gendered language, 26–27; in Cuba, 3; Cuban insurgents using, 8; racial inequality and, 5
gendered metalanguage, 8
Gil, Dionisio, 27, 164–65, 228, 250–51;

burial with honors of, 290n28, 290n32, 290n36, 290n41; murder of, 168–71; public skepticism over death of, 167; Quintana encounter with, 168

Gil, Perfecto, 165–66

Gómez, José Miguel, 36, 84, 112, 171, 172; as insurgent officer, 35–36; in national politics, 16; prison labor programs proposed by, 194; as Republican Party founder, 197; on Spanish army, 39; Vidal, J., dispute with, 201–2; Wood letter from, 208

Gómez, Juan Gualberto, 92, 217

Gómez, Máximo, 31, 59; on battlefield deaths, 40; criticizing white chiefs with concubines, 101; criticizing women on battlefield, 67; on Cuban army morality, 94; as General-in-Chief, 27; on Gil, D., as brave soldier, 165; González Planas singled out by, 90–91; and Invasion of the West, 33; majasería allegations by, 77–79; manly bravery of, 36–38; on military virtue, 34–35; on Santa Clara as hub of majasería, 79–80; Spanish army driving back, 76; US rule and, 159–60; on women's sexual virtue, 61–62

Gómez, Panchito, 77

González, Eloy, 131

González Calunga, José, 83–84, 87–89

González Planas, José, 90, 97, 131, 199; acquittal of, 92; allegations against, 91–92; black masculinity and, 99; as Constitutional Convention candidate, 209; as early insurgent, 27; exclusion from patriotic assistance, 112; Gómez, M., singling out, 91; as high-ranking officer, 2; infantry commanded by, 44; as lieutenant colonel, 42–43; military service of, 89–90; as officer in Rural Guard, 191

"Good Government vs. Revolution—An Easy Choice," 226

good soldier (*mambí*), 247

Govín, Antonio, 301n15

Grajales, Mariana, 65

Gramsci, Antonio, 252

Guerra, Lillian, 12

Guerra Chiquita (Little War, 1879–1880), 9, 28, 89

guerrillas, 32

Gutiérrez (Yara), Cármen, 66

Haitian Revolution, 9, 29–30

Harrison, E. H., 145

Havana, 8

hegemony, 252–53

Heredia, Faustina, 70

Hernández, Ambrosio, 291n46

Hernández, Antonio, 168

Hernández, Mateo de Jesús, 70

Hernández, Rosa de, 67–68

Heureaux, Ulises, 165

Higginbotham, Evelyn B., 3

high-ranking chiefs, 76–77

honorable womanhood, 65

horse ownership, 44

imagined communities, 12

imperialistic rule, 163–64, 206

importation of slavery, 8–9

Independent Party of Color, 10, 254

inequality, 5

infant mortality, 15

insubordination charges, 238–39

insurgent officer, 27, 35–36

insurgents, 54–55; black, 7–8, 13–14, 74; bravery of, 35–36, 38; challenges facing, 35–37; critiques of reconcentration by, 51–52; Cuban army soldiers as, 19; domestic femininity

insurgents (*continued*)
preserved by, 55; as evil-hearted men, 30–31; gendered discourse and military service of, 7; Hernández, R., celebrated by, 68; lacking provisions, 37; lamentable condition of, 75–76; as male kin, 55–56, 80; noncombatant collaborating with, 32; patriarchal responsibilities and, 48–49, 56–57; racial differences downplayed by, 4–5; racialized images of, 33; Ruíz and gendered description by, 68–69; on Spanish army incompetence, 39; Spanish army rationalized violence against, 32; Weyler driving back, 75. *See also* black insurgents; white insurgents
insurrection: anticolonial, 27–29, 42, 245; expansion of, 33; majasería problem in, 79; racial hierarchy in, 103
Invasion Campaign, 27, 45, 80, 84, 94
Invasion Force, 37

Kernan, F. J., 169

labor regimes, 25
Lady Cuba, *160*, 161, 224–26
Lafont, Policarpo, 167
Laredo, María Escobar, 66
Latin America, 259n40
Latin race, 148, 152
law enforcement: black men targeted by, 156; opportunities for black veterans in, 118–19, 151–52; opportunities for veterans in, 127–28; reforms to, 188–89; rural, 186–87. *See also* Cienfuegos police force; police force; Rural Guard
laws of civilization, 31
League of the Antilles, 219
Legón, José Rafael, 100
Lewis, Luis, 140, 145–46

Liberating Army, 108–9, 153, 159, 228, 246
Little War (Guerra Chiquita 1879–1880), 9
local: authority, 123–24, 136–37; elections, 216; enlistments, 42; politics, 215–16; veteran chiefs (*caudillos*), 234
"Looking Forward" (cartoon), *162*
Loynaz del Castillo, Enrique, 60, 101
Ludlow, William, 174
Lynn, Charles, 203

Maceo, Antonio, 40, 53, 76–77, 99; Battle of Mal Tiempo with, 15; Cisneros lauding, 43; death of, 94; as high-ranking officer, 2; insults directed at, 31; in Invasion Campaign, 27, 33; as member of League of Antilles, 219
Maceo, José, 76, 100
Machado, Damián, 89
Machado, Gerardo, 87, *88*, 207, 220, 226–27
machetes, 37–39
Maine (battleship), 103
majá (bad soldier), 247
majasería: Alemán launching campaign against, 83; court-martial and allegations of, 102–3; Cuban army allegations of, 77–78; Fourth Corps campaign against, 80–81; Gómez, M., alleging, 77–79; insurrection and problem of, 79; Santa Clara as hub of, 79–80; sexual misconduct as, 93–102; white insurgents alleging, 78
majases (cowards), 61, 77–79
male kin, 55
maleness, 182
male survivor, *52*
mambí (good soldier), 247
mambises, 2, 19, 34, 67–69, 247

manhood: black men and, 133–34; Cuban, 197–98; of Cuban men, 6–7; horse ownership and, 44; martial, 134, 169, 185, 248; raceless, 229; suffrage, 182; white insurgents appeals to, 247–48. *See also* universal manhood suffrage
manliness, 182
Manuel de Céspedes, Carlos, 9
Marín y González, Sabás, 47
marriage, 62–63, 63
Martí, Federico, 145
Martí, José, 1, 4, 109
martial manhood, 134, 169, 185, 248
Martínez Campos, Arsenio, 29, 35, 47
masculine ideal, 34
masculinity: black, 99; blackness link with, 11; colonial, 245; hegemony resorting to violence and, 252–53; machete as symbol of, 37–39; military service, 34; neocolonial, 242; race and, 246; Wilson on, 182
Masó, Bartolomé, 117, 166, 239–41
Massó Parra, Juan, 95–97
Matagás, José, 92
Matanzas Province, 128–29, *129*, 202
Matarama Rodríguez, Tomás, 298n80
Mateo Sagasta, Práxedes, 103
material comforts, 96–97
Matilde Ortega, José, 70, 85, 99
Matos, Desiderio "Tuerto" (one-eyed), 31, 92–93
mayoral office, 236
mayoral race, 234–35; in Camajuaní, 199–202; in Cienfuegos, 203; in Palmira, 198; race and, 198; in Trinidad, 203
May Riot, 138–41, 144–45, 151
McCullough, John, 174
McDowell, Campbell, 142
McKinley, William, 162
Medina Escalona, Javier, 216–19, 223

El Mejicano, 101
men: Cuban households and, 6; evil-hearted, 30–31; hierarchy of, 25; women's subordination to, 4. *See also* black men; Cuban men; white men
Mendieta y Montefur, Carlos, 196, 200, 231
military, US: abuses against Cuban women by, 143; agricultural bank refused by, 117–18; antagonists removed by, 172; black veteran employment criticized by, 249; black veteran solidarity suspected by, 155; in Camajuaní and Santo Domingo, 202; Campillo y D'Wolf defended by, 237; Campillo y D'Wolf not disappointing, 173; civil government promised by, 162–63, *163*; Cuban soldiers attacked by, 114–15; Cubans rejecting restriction of suffrage by, 183; Cuban veterans' abuse by, 120–21; electoral races cooperation with, 231–32, 234; electoral tampering and, 233–35; Estrada Palma favored by, 239; exclusion of veterans from local authority by, 123–24; Figueroa hand-picked by, 231; first shots fired by, 147–50; Frías removed by, 171–72; imperialistic character of, 163–64, 206; local elections influenced by, 216; municipal authorities and, 153; New Man aspirations and, 124, 161, 181–82, 186; occupation of Cuba by, 10; officials on independent agriculture, 116–17; opponents of separatist rule seeking protection by, 119–20; opposition to universal manhood suffrage by, 215; and payment of Cuban veterans, 156–57; on police

military, US (*continued*)
    promiscuity with firearms, 146; political power and, 231; preference for whiteness of, 191–92; preserving order after elections by, 200–201; protest as transgression against authority of, 140; racial hierarchies and, 19, 240; in red light district, 142–43; requiring veterans to forfeit weapons, 158–59; Rural Guard controlled by, 129–30; stevedores pay from, 139; Vieta removed from office by, 237–38; weapons promiscuity of, 150; white municipal leadership and, 151–52
military achievements, 84–85
military officers, 84, 114
Military Order 124, US, 201
Military Order 164, US, 185
military rank, 104, 108, 248
military service: black veteran political influence from, 249; Cuban army bonds from, 26; Cuban army masculinity from, 34; Gómez, M., on virtues of, 34–35; of González Planas, 89–90; honorable, 80; insurgent gendered discourse about, 7; and veterans' demands for suffrage, 183–84
military solidarity, 197
military trenches, 76
Miró Argenter, José, 68, 166
mixed-race population, 15
Modesto Hernández, Pablo, 287n71
Moncada, Guillermo, 99
Monteagudo, José de Jesús, 160, 192, 196, 199–200; employment of Fourth Corps veterans and, 131; as Rural Guard chief, 197; on Spanish domination, 124; on wartime misery, 41
Montejo, Esteban, 142–44
Morales, José, 167

morenos. *See* black; black insurgents; black men; black officers; black soldiers; black veterans
Moret Law, 9
Morúa Delgado, Martín, 10, 16, 198, 209, 217
Morúa Law, 10
motherhood, 65
mujer pública (prostitute), 4
mulatto (*mulatos*), 18
multiracial nature: of Cuban army, 43, 109, 126, 227, 245; of electorate, 196; of police force, 137, 141, 152–53; of Rural Guard, 131–32
municipal authorities, 153
municipal government, 198–99
Muñoz, Ricardo, 203
murder, 166, 168–71
Mutos, Pedro P., 169–70

Najarro, Agustín, 27
Najarro, Benigno, 27
ñáñigos (as derogatory/racialized term for Cuban soldier), 31, 183
national identity, of Cuba, 2
nationalism, 196; color-blind, 13; of Cuban-born men, 25–26; electoral victories and, 206–8; raceless, 3; racial harmony pillar of, 8; racial inequality and, 12–13; white Cuban-born men and, 25
Nationalist Party (*Partido Nacional Cubano*), 196, 215
national politics, 16
Naya y Serrano, Casimiro, 199–201, 298n80
Negro Rule, 216–17, 224
negros brujos (black men as witches), 11
neocolonial masculinity, 242
New Men, 20; black criminality and, 220; black veterans and status of, 155–56, 167, 176–77; as implicitly white,

248; from Liberating Army, 108–9; political power and, 248–49; racial inclusion and, 110; US military and aspirations of, 124, 161, 181–82, 186; US neocolonialism and, 250–51; white officers becoming, 108
newspapers, 159, 172, 306n95; *Diario de la Marina*, 29–30; *La Discusión*, 160, 162; *La Tribuna*, 227, 232
Nodarse, José, 91
noncombatants (*pacíficos*), 32, 50–51
nonwhiteness, 19

officer rank, 85
Olayita Massacre, 50
opponents of separatist rule, 20, 202; criminalizing black veterans, 185–86, 199; Cuban independence and, 210–11; disapproval of Republican Party by, 196; efforts to derail universal manhood suffrage, 214–15; influencing local politics, 215–16; and Platt Amendment, 223; race weaponized by, 210–11; rural crime and, 186–87; unrest among, 209; US military protection demanded by, 119–20
Ordoñez, Epifanio, 128, 147
Oropesa, Joaquín, 146, 149–50, 164, 171–72
Ortiz, Benigno, 73

pacífico (noncombatant), 32
Pact of Zanjón, 28
Partido Nacional Cubano (Nationalist Party), 196, 215
Partido Revolucionario Cubano. *See* Cuban Revolutionary Party
Partido Unión Democrática (Democratic Union Party), 196
patriarchal authority, 73–74
patriarchal responsibilities: of Cuban men, 23–24, 143–44; insurgents and, 48–49, 56–57; white rebel women and, 69
patriotic clubs, 111–12
patriotism, 65–66, 227
pay schedules, *130*
Penal Code, 194
penal settlement, 68
peninsulares, 25
Pérez, Bárbara, 70
personal favoritism (*dedazo*), 84–85
personal honor, 201
Platt, Orville, 215
Platt Amendment, 215–16, 218; angry response to, 222–23; delegates opposition to, 223; delegates voting for, 227; Lady Cuba and, 225–26
police force, *129*; abuses against Vega, E., 176; black men employed in, 128–29, 148–49; black veterans dismissed from, 173–74; employment in, 148–49; racial backgrounds of members of, 281n114; racial composition of, 149–50, 164; San Juan Day riot and, 147–50; in Santa Clara province, 128–29; US military and firearms of, 146; US violence and disrespect against, 145–46, 238; wealthy residents uproar against changes to, 236–37; whiteness and, 174. *See also* Cienfuegos police force
police officers, 235, 306n95
Political cartoons, 224–26, *225–26*
political fitness: black criminality and, 216; US rule and, 240–41; of Vieta, 233–34; whiteness as precondition of, 181–82
political power, 155; black soldiers' worthiness of, 112–13; black veterans' exclusion from, 137; black veterans' military service and, 249;

political power (*continued*)
    conditionality of, 231; exclusion of black men from, 127; New Men and, 248–49; opposition to Yznaga's claim to, 203; US military and, 231
politics, 14, 16, 215–16, 239; Cuban men's rights in, 24–25; order in, 253; radicalism in, 227–28; US influence over local, 231
Pons y Naranjo, José, 160
Ponvert, Elias, 237
Portela, Manuel, 198
postwar political exclusion, 127
postwar racial exclusion, 169
postwar relief effort, 111
PRC. *See* Cuban Revolutionary Party
prejudice, racial, 126, 131
presidential elections (1901), 239–41
preventive imprisonment, 194
prewar occupations, 118
prewar social positions, 117–19
prisoners, 231; forced labor of, 194; by race, *194*; violence faced by, 195
private guards, 187–88, *188*, 221–22
privileged racial position, 109–10
productive labor, 115
professional begging, 113
prostitute (*mujer pública*), 4, 60–61, 143
La Protesta (newspaper), 159
public authority, 137, 141, 204–6
public office, 126–27
Puerto Príncipe, *15*

Quesada, Ciriaco, 27
Quijotesque story, 85–86
Quintana, Enrique, 167–68

Rabasa, Agustín, 164, 168–71
race: Cuban relations of, 259n40; employment selected by, 248–49; opponents of separatist rule weaponizing, 210–11; prisoners by, *194*; relations, 259n40; Spanish propaganda on, 32; wars, 11, 33–34
raceless manhood, 229
racelessness, 3, 10
racial agitation, 217, 228, 240
racial backgrounds, 281n114
racial composition, 149–50, 164
racial democracy, 251–52
racial differences, 4–5
racial discrimination, 18–19, 81–82, 230
racial disorder, 203
racial diversity, 246
racial double standard: black officers and, 96; black veterans and, 133; patriotic motherhood and, 65; and revolutionary masculinity, 102; white privilege and, 108; women and, 72–73
racial equality, 230–31, 239
racial harmony, 8
racial hierarchies, 2, 41, 43–45; colonial subjugation and, 26; in Cuban army, 72–74; in insurrection, 103; martial manhood and, 248; within sugar industry, 42; US military and, 19, 240; white insurgents perpetuating, 247; white separatists support for, 117; white women and, 98
racial inclusion, 110, 249
racial inequality, 11–13, 74, 255
racialized criminalization, 186
racialized gender transgressions, 29
racialized sexual economy, 5
racialized sexual transgressions, 100
racial justice, 20
racially motivated murder, 166
racial order, 210
racial privilege, 71–72
racial segregation, 229
racial stereotypes, 29, 99
racial unrest, 219–20

racism, 5–6, 216–22, 248
Ramírez, Alfredo, 82
rebel troops, 31, 71
reconcentration, 103, 111, 143; camps, 54; Carrillo, F., concerns about, 56; children in, 51; crimes against women and, 48; families in, 52; insurgents on, 51–52; insurgents' vilification of, 54–55; male survivor in, 52; Santa Clara orders for, 47–49; Spanish army enacting, 56; as Spanish gender transgression, 55–56; Weyler expanding, 53; Weyler's orders for, 47, 49–50
Rego, Alfredo, 84, 90, 93, 97
Reinoso, Martín, 125–26
La República (newspaper), 172, 306n95
Republican Party: black veterans ties with, 208–9; cross-racial military solidarity undermining, 197; Gomez, J. M., founder of, 197; opponents of separatist rule against, 196; Santa Clara veterans supporting, 196
revolutionary bandits, 206–11
revolutionary masculinity, 13; Alemán's invocation of, 228; benefits for black soldiers and, 44–45; and black insurgents, 7–8; black men's claim to, 246–47; black veterans appropriating, 253; cross-racial dimensions of, 250; Cuban veterans demonstrating, 246; gendered discourse of, 26–27; meritocratic undertones of, 34; neocolonial masculinity emerging from, 242; public authority and, 137; racial discrimination enabled by, 230; racial double standard in, 102; racial inclusion in, 249. *See also* masculinity
Ricardo, Severino, 92

Robau López, José Luis, 101, 196, 223
Rodríguez, Abelardo, 126
Rodríguez, Alejandro, 86
Rodríguez, José María "Mayía," 98
Rogelio Castillo, José, 40
Roloff, Carlos, 42
Romero Loyola, Antonia, 66
Root, Elihu, 215
rope disease (lynching), 222
Roque del Sol, Sixto, 53
Rosell y Malpica, Eduardo, 71, 86
Ruiz, Paulina, 68–69
rural crime, 186–87
rural families, 49–50, 51
Rural Guard: black bandits pursued by, 192–93; black men incarcerated by, 193–94; black men with no rank in, 131; black veterans in, 191; crime prevention by, 193; employment, 130, 191; false banditry reports exposed by, 220; González Planas as officer in, 191; inadequacies of, 187; martial manhood and, 134; Monteagudo as chief of, 197; multiracial nature of, 132; personnel requirements for, 192; public law enforcement and, 188–89; salary increases for, 130–31; Santa Clara province pay schedules of, *130*; strict guidelines for, 190–91; US military controlling, 129–30; white officers refusing employment in, 130; white veterans in, 131; Wilson proposing elimination of, 189; Wilson reducing, 190–92
Rural Guardsmen, 10–11, 128, 254; anti-black violence and, 221; black veterans killed by, 222; white, 242, 242
rural law enforcement, 186–87

sacred ideal of Liberty, 39

salary increases, 130–31
Sánchez, Porfirio, 82
Sánchez, Serafín, 42, 77, 90, 97
Sánchez, Simeón, 92
Sanjenis, Avelino, 221, 302n36
San Juan Day riot, 141–42, 144, 147–50, 152–53
Santa Clara Province, 13, 196; age distribution in, *15*; agitation existing in, 218–19; anticolonial insurrection in, 27–29; banditry acts in, 220; black veterans in, 184; Constitutional Convention delegates from, 213–14, 299n103; Cuban army invading, 30; Cuban veterans in, 135; Gómez, M., and majasería in, 79–80; major cities of, *16*; military trenches near, *76*; mixed-race population of, 15; municipal elections in, 203–4; municipal police forces in, 128–29; political exclusion in, 127; postwar relief effort in, 111; prisoners by race in, *194*; racial agitation in, 240; reconcentration camps in, 54; reconcentration orders for, 47–49; Republican Party supporters in, 196; Rural Guard elimination proposed for, 189; Rural Guard pay schedules in, *130*; sugar plantations in, *76*; universal manhood suffrage in, 184–85; urban centers of, 14; veterans' reluctance to forfeit weapons in, 161; war and politics study of, 14; white mayors in, *207*
Santana, María H., 70, 99
Santiago, age distribution in, *15*
Santo Domingo, 202
Sardiñas y Villa, Juan, 169–70, 253
Sarría, Claudio, 27, 221–22, 250–51; confrontation with US employees, 142–44; court-martial of, 89; enlistment in Liberating Army of, 195; position of command for, 43
self-government, 110, 135, 223–24, 250
separatist rule, 132–33, 183
separatists, 19, 109
sexual activities, 61–62; on battlefield, 93–94; of black men, 94, 99–100; majasería and scrutiny of, 93–102
sexual assault, 64
sexual deviance, 64–65
sexual honor, 61–72
sexual immorality, 63, 80, 98, 99, 238
sexually transgressive women, 144
sexual morality, 94, 247
sexual promiscuity, 60
sexual transgressions, 79, 100, 101
sexual values, 102
sexual violence, 144
slavery, 5; abolition of, 62–63; end of, 9–10
social inequality, 254
social order, 253
social value, 115
soldierly conduct, 81–82
Sosa, Valentín, 27
sovereignty-limiting conditions, 215
Spain, 9–10, 24
Spanish-American War, 135
Spanish army: Bates' judgment of, 122–23; colonial masculinity deployed by, 245; country town pillaging by, 50; Cubans murdered by, 68; Cuban women abused by, 57, 143; Gomez's army driven back by, 76; insurgents suggesting incompetence of, 39; on insurrection as black rebellion, 28–29; noncombatants slaughtered by, 50–51; racial anxieties of officers in, 29; reconcentration enacted by, 56; violence against insurgents rationalized by, 32; women attacked by, 53

Spanish colonialism, 9
Spanish officers, 103, 107–8; Alemán on cowardice of, 53; on insurgents as bandits, 31; race war rumors from, 33–34
spiritual crisis, 77
state violence, 164–70, 253–54
stevedores, 139
Suárez, Manuel, 42
Suárez del Villar, Rita, 66
sugar industry, 14; banditry during harvest in, 220–21; Cuba's rise of, 8–9; plantations in, 76; prewar employment in, 118; racial labor hierarchy of, 42

Teller, Henry M., 103
Teller Amendment, 103, 135, 161, 206, 223
Ten Years' War, 9, 28, 83
Teresa, Luz Noriega, 69
Thevenet, F. N., 140
thief of its own gift, 124
tobacco farms, 14
Tomás, Antonio, 304n72
Treaty of Paris, 223
La Tribuna (newspaper), 227, 232
Trinidad, 203
Trujillo, Carlos, 40, 233

United States (US), 20; Cienfuegos property losses and, 277n46; civilian employees of, 284n11; Civil War of, 120; critiques of Gómez, M. complicity with, 159–60; Cuba choosing relations with, 226; Cuban annexation by, 109; Cuba ruled by, 159–60, 220, 224, 228; employees, 152; Figueroa as collaborator for rule by, 232–33; Frías opposition to rule by, 146; "Good Government vs. Revolution—An Easy Choice" and, 226; Lady Cuba and, *160*, 224–26; military intervention by, 103; Military Order 124, 201; Military Order 164, 185; New Men and neocolonialism of, 250–51; political fitness and rule of, 240–41; as thief of its own gift, 124; white employees from, 152; Wilson on efforts to prolong rule by, 220
universal manhood suffrage: Barker and restriction of, 182–83; black men and electoral results of, 214; Cuban delegates defending, 213–14; as Negro Rule, 216–17; opponents of separatist rule criticizing, 214–15; racial unrest reports and, 219–20; in Santa Clara Province, 184–85; US military response to, 215
unmanly behaviors, 78–79
urban centers, 14
US. *See* United States

vagrancy, 193
Valiant Army of Las Villas, 158
Valverde, Nicolás, 175, 177
Vega, Emilio, 176
Vega, Juana, 176
Venancio Schwiep, Juan, 123
veteran records, 281n114
veterans, 19, 127–28, 167; US military occupation and, 10
Veterans' Center of Baracoa, 199
vida holgada (easy life), 100
Vidal, José C., 199; Gómez, J. M., dispute with, 201–2; running mates of, 298n80; white elites supporting, 200
Vidal, Leoncio, 76, 199
Vieta, Gonzalo García, 204, *205*, 232; Campillo y D'Wolf removed by, 236; criticism of Campillo y D'Wolf by, 237; mayoral office assumed by, 236; police officers

Vieta, Gonzolo García (*continued*)
supporting, 306n95; political fitness of, 233–34; removal from office by US military, 237–38

Villuendas, Enrique, 39, 196, 226

violence: anti-black, 2, 11; black men and state, 253; against black rural laborers, 221; against black veterans, 221–22; masculinity, hegemony and, 252–53; against municipal police force, 145–46, 238; prisoners facing, 195; against protestors by US authorities, 140; sexual, 144; Spanish army rationalizing, 32; state, 164–70, 253–54

virtue, of Cuban women, 60–61

voluntary guard duty, 118

voting rights, 183–84

vulgar euphemism, 142–43, 285n33

Wade, Peter, 252

war, 49, 110–11

War of Independence, 17, 89, 245–46; Calunga entering, 83; of Cuba, 1–2, 7; military operations of, 15

wealthy property owners, 223–24, 236–37

weapons. *See* firearms

Weyler, Valeriano, 68, 75, 123; atrocities committed by, 53; reconcentration orders of, 47, 49–50

white (European ancestry), 19, 248; civil authorities, 160; Cuban-born men, 25; elites, 200; employees, 141–42; family, 73–74; male chivalric fallacy, 73; mambisas, 67–69; mayors, *207*; middle-class values, 252; municipal leadership, 151–52; patriots, 210; privilege, 8, 108; rebel women, 69; rule, 219; separatists, 117, 125; social prestige, 126

white insurgents: black officers targeted by, 11; black women and, 71; censure of black women by, 70; majasería allegations by, 78; mambisas reputation with, 69; manhood appeals of, 247–48; racial hierarchies perpetuated by, 247; racial inequalities revealed by, 74

white men, 32–33, 100, 126–27

whiteness: honorable womanhood and, 62; military officers linked to, 84; nonwhiteness and, 19; performance of, 110; police force and, 174; as a precondition of political power, 181–82; US military assumptions about, 191–92

white officers: anxiety over black officers' authority, 96; with concubines, 101; court-martial faced by, 101–2; criminal sanctions avoided by, 87; military rank and, 104, 108; as New Men, 108; parties honoring, 111–12; Rural Guard employment refused by, 130; sexual transgressions of, 101

white soldiers, 85–86, 109–10

white veterans: competing constituencies of, 249; criminalization of black veterans by, 254; Cuban cause betrayed by, 169–70; Gil, D., killed by, 164; local authority for, 136–37; in Rural Guard, 131; and visions of citizenship, 250

white women, 66, 70, 98

Wilson, James H., 113, *136*, 148, 150–51; on allowing veterans to keep weapons, 158–59; firearms allowed by, 187–88; on masculinity, 182; on nationalist electoral victories, 206; Rural Guard elimination proposed by, 189; Rural Guard reduced by, 190–92; on transition to Cuban self-government, 135; on US rule, 220; wealthy planters opposing, 189–90 women: Alemán on enemy, 59; on battlefield, 67; black, 62–65, 69–71; creole, 143; crimes against, 48; Cuban army detaining, 59; and domesticity ideals, 4, 66–67; enemy, 60–61; Gómez, M., criticizing, 67; Gómez, M., on sexually active, 61–62; male kin farewells from, 55; racial double standard and, 72–73; reconcentration as crime against, 48; sexual honor and morality of, 61–72; sexually transgressive, 144; sexual morality of, 247; Spanish attacks on, 53; subordination of, 4; US military transgressions against, 143; white, 66, 70, 98; whiteness and honorable, 62; white rebel, 69

Wood, Leonard, 208, 218–19, 234, 237

working-class scrutiny, 175–77

working-class veterans, 19

Yznaga, Carlos, 203

Zamora, Dimas, 99

Zayas, Alfredo, 16

Zayas, Juan Bruno, 16, 37, 40, 76, 84

Zerquera, Lino, 203

www.ingramcontent.com/pod-product-compliance
Lightning Source LLC
Chambersburg PA
CBHW030519230426
43665CB00010B/689